PRAISE FOR *THE ENVIRONMENTAL RIGHTS REVOLUTION*

"This book is indispensable for anyone interested in environmental rights. Boyd's astounding in-depth research spans more than 100 countries, and shows what a powerful tool constitutional rights can be for advancing sustainability – in courtrooms, legislatures, and broader society."

> – Dr. Stewart Elgie, Professor, University of Ottawa Faculty of Law, and Chair, Sustainable Prosperity

"This book is a must-read for scholars, jurists, and advocates of environmental law. Professor Boyd has single-handedly brought the field of environmental human rights into the twenty-first century."

> – Lynda M. Collins, Centre for Environmental Law & Global Sustainability, University of Ottawa

"David R. Boyd's thorough and carefully presented research provides a clear and detailed account of how environmental rights are being implemented throughout the world. After an initial orientation to the philosophical debates about human rights and the environment, Boyd moves on deftly to investigate which arguments are vindicated in practice. Identifying the evidence available about the practical effectiveness of environmental rights, he provides an invaluable assessment of developments to date as well as a guide to promising future directions of research. This extremely well-written book is an essential guide to environmental rights in theory and in practice."

> – Professor Tim Hayward, University of Edinburgh, author of *Constitutional Environmental Rights*

"A valuable study on the environmental rights revolution. The evidence presented in this book helps understand the powerful influence of the right to a healthy environment in promoting strong environmental legislation, public policies, and court decisions across the world. This is the most complete research available for professors, judges, practitioners, and students interested in the origins, consequences, and future of the most important legal revolution for the survival of humanity."

> – Dr. Rafael González Ballar, Faculty of Law, University of Costa Rica

"While the environmental rights theme is well-trodden scholarly ground, David Boyd eloquently frees this enquiry from the restrictive theoretical confines of the ivory tower by investigating the actual impact that rights have on environmental governance. This has not been done before in such a comprehensive, critical, and thorough manner. This work breaks new ground in terms of approach, content, scope, and methodology and is well worth a place on the bookshelves of anyone who takes environmental rights and governance seriously."

> – Louis J. Kotzé, Professor of Law, North West University, South Africa

The Environmental Rights Revolution ......

Law and Society Series
W. WESLEY PUE, GENERAL EDITOR

The Law and Society Series explores law as a socially embedded phenomenon. It is premised on the understanding that the conventional division of law from society creates false dichotomies in thinking, scholarship, educational practice, and social life. Books in the series treat law and society as mutually constitutive and seek to bridge scholarship emerging from interdisciplinary engagement of law with disciplines such as politics, social theory, history, political economy, and gender studies.

A list of titles in the series appears at the end of the book.

The Environmental Rights Revolution

A Global Study of Constitutions, Human Rights, and the Environment

...... David R. Boyd

UBCPress · Vancouver · Toronto

20 19 18 17 16 15 14 13   5 4 3

Printed in Canada on FSC-certified ancient-forest-free paper
(100% post-consumer recycled) that is processed chlorine- and acid-free.

Library and Archives Canada Cataloguing in Publication

Boyd, David R. (David Richard), 1964-
    The environmental rights revolution : a global study of constitutions, human rights, and the environment / David R. Boyd.

(Law and society series, ISSN 1496-4953)
Includes bibliographical references and index.
Also issued in electronic format.
ISBN 978-0-7748-2160-5 (bound); ISBN 978-0-7748-2161-2 (pbk.)

    1. Environmental law. 2. Constitutional law. 3. Human rights. 4. Environmental ethics. I. Title. II. Series: Law and society series (Vancouver, B.C.)

K3585.B69 2012   344.04′6   C2011-903715-7

Canadä

UBC Press gratefully acknowledges the financial support for our publishing program of the Government of Canada (through the Canada Book Fund), the Canada Council for the Arts, and the British Columbia Arts Council.

This book has been published with the help of a grant from the Canadian Federation for the Humanities and Social Sciences, through the Aid to Scholarly Publications Program, using funds provided by the Social Sciences and Humanities Research Council of Canada, and with the help of the K.D. Srivastava Fund.

Printed and bound in Canada by Friesens
Set in Giovanni and Scala Sans by Artegraphica Design Co. Ltd.
Copy editor: Audrey McClellan
Proofreader: Francis Chow
Indexer: Patricia Buchanan

UBC Press
The University of British Columbia
2029 West Mall
Vancouver, BC V6T 1Z2
www.ubcpress.ca

This book is dedicated to all of the citizens, lawyers, politicians, civil servants, judges, and organizations around the world who have contributed not only to fostering recognition of the right to a healthy environment in constitutions, laws, and court decisions, but also, more importantly, to ensuring that this vital human right is fulfilled through clean air, fresh water, fertile soil, and vibrant biodiversity.

Contents

Tables and Figures

FIGURES

Acknowledgments

I would like to thank Natasha Affolder, Will Amos, Carl Bruch, Anna Cederstav, Lynda Collins, Peter Dauvergne, Hadi Dowlatabadi, May du Monceau, Mark Haddock, Kathryn Harrison, Brad Hornick, Jim May, Karin Mickelson, Paul Richardson, Terre Satterfield, Dinah Shelton, John Swaigen, and Hugh Wilkins for generously sharing their time, knowledge, and wisdom at various stages of this project. I also would like to thank the Trudeau Foundation, the Social Sciences and Humanities Research Council, Tim and Ann O'Riordan, the Walter and Duncan Gordon Foundation, and the University of British Columbia for financial support. As usual, the staff at UBC Press, especially Randy Schmidt, Ann Macklem, and Peter Milroy, were a delight to work with.

I also owe an infinite debt to Margot and Meredith for their enthusiastic encouragement, love, and patience during the seemingly endless process of researching and writing this book.

Abbreviations

CNG	Compressed Natural Gas
COHRE	Centre on Housing Rights and Evictions
DNA	deoxyribonucleic acid
ENGO	Environmental Non-governmental Organization
EPIC	Environmental Provisions in Constitutions
ECHR	European Court of Human Rights
GDP	gross domestic product
GHG	greenhouse gas
GMO	genetically modified organism
IACHR	Inter-American Commission on Human Rights
ICCPR	*International Covenant on Civil and Political Rights*
ICESCR	*International Covenant on Economic, Social and Cultural Rights*
ICJ	International Court of Justice
ICSID	International Center for the Settlement of Investment Disputes
IUCN	International Union for Conservation of Nature
N/A	not available
NGO	Non-governmental Organization
NOx	nitrogen oxides
OAS	Organization of American States
OECD	Organisation for Economic Co-operation and Development
PCB	polychlorinated biphenyl
SFU	Simon Fraser University
SO_2	sulphur dioxide
UNEP	United Nations Environment Programme
USAID	United States Agency for International Development

PART 1

The Emergence and Evolution
of a New Human Right

1
Constitutions, Human Rights, and the Environment: The Context

> New wrongs, unimagined by our founding fathers, must generate new rights capable of preventing the recurrence of those wrongs.
>
> – Alan M. Dershowitz, *Rights from Wrongs*

In recent decades, three striking and related developments have taken place around the world – a wave of new and amended constitutions in both emerging and established democracies, the human rights revolution, and growth in the magnitude and awareness of the global environmental crisis. This book examines a concept that is situated at the convergence of these three developments – the constitutional right to live in a healthy environment.

Beginning in the 1970s, public recognition of worldwide environmental degradation and the inadequacy of state responses prompted constitutional changes and recourse to the powerful language of human rights. How widespread is the environmental rights revolution in today's world, and to what extent is it influencing laws, public policies, court decisions, environmental performance, and human well-being? While other books and articles have debated the philosophical pros and cons of the right to a healthy environment, this book breaks new ground in evaluating the extent and impacts of constitutional provisions requiring environmental protection. From Argentina to the Philippines, something remarkable is happening. In communities, legislatures, and courtrooms all around the world, a new human right is blossoming from seeds planted decades ago. The constitutional right to live in a healthy environment represents a tangible embodiment of hope, an aspiration that the destructive, polluting ways of the past can be replaced by cleaner, greener societies in the future. While no nation has yet achieved the holy grail of ecological sustainability, the evidence presented in this book indicates that constitutional protection of the environment can be a powerful and potentially transformative step toward that elusive goal.

Constitution Making

> Constitutions are where societies establish the values that are to
> guide political and social discourse for generations to come, and
> also where those values are protected by incorporating them as
> constitutional obligations or rights.
>
> – Richard P. Hiskes, *The Human Right to a Green Future*

The first of the three broad developments contributing to the emergence of
the constitutional right to a healthy environment is the remarkable shift
toward constitutional democracy across the globe in the countries of Eastern
Europe, Latin America, and Africa, and also in nations that have long traditions of parliamentary democracy.[1] The tragic legacies of fascism, colonialism,
and communism contributed to this unprecedented wave of constitution
making.[2] More than half of the world's national constitutions have been
written since the mid-1970s, and many more have been substantially
overhauled.[3]

A constitution represents the highest or supreme law in a nation, establishing the formal rules that direct and constrain government powers, defining
the relationships between government institutions, and protecting individual
rights.[4] In the words of a leading constitutional scholar: "A country's constitution is the set of fundamental principles that together describe the organiza-
tional framework of the state and the nature, the scope of, and the limitations
on the exercise of state authority."[5] In federal nations, such as Canada or the
United States, the constitution also allocates power and areas of legislative
jurisdiction between the national and subnational governments. Constitutions
trump other laws in the event of a conflict between a constitutional provision
and another law and are generally more difficult to amend than ordinary
laws.[6] The design of a nation's constitution can influence who gets to exercise
power and who does not, how laws and policies are created, and who wins
and loses in politics.[7] There is also a vital normative role for constitutions,
which express the deepest, most cherished values of a society. Thus one court
has described a constitution as a "mirror reflecting the national soul."[8]

Some scholars view the trend toward constitutionalism as a predominantly
positive evolution in governance. Constitutions, and particularly rights, provide guiding principles for all branches of government in the discharging of
their duties.[9] Constitutions implement the rule of law, creating predictability

and security in the relationship between government and people.[10] According to Tamanaha, "Everyone is better off, no matter where they live and who they are, if government officials operate within a legal framework ... in the sense of abiding by the legal framework and in the sense that there are limits on law-making power."[11]

The most common critique of constitutionalism is that the emphasis on rights and the empowerment of courts (through the process of judicial review) undermines democracy.[12] In order to ensure that governments act within the limits set forth in a constitution, the judicial branch is generally given the power to review legislation and other government actions and enforce individual rights. This results in a phenomenon labelled the judicialization of politics, which refers to "the infusion of judicial decision-making and of court-like procedures into political arenas where they did not previously reside."[13] Drivers of this phenomenon include constitutional recognition of rights, a dramatic rise in recourse to courts by interest groups, the public perception of courts as expert and principled while politicians are corrupt and incompetent, and increasing judicial activism (that is, a willingness on the part of judges to substitute their own policy solutions for those of democratically elected governments).[14]

More than eighty nations have enacted constitutional reforms that transfer some degree of power from democratically elected institutions to judiciaries.[15] Giving courts the power to strike down legislation and administrative acts has been described as one of the most significant political developments in democratic nations in recent decades.[16] As Stotzky observed: "The tidal wave of democratization that has spread across the globe in the past three decades is remarkable for its underlying dependence on the rule of law and the role of the courts."[17]

According to its supporters, judicial review is a fundamental aspect of constitutional democracy because it provides protection for vulnerable groups and individuals against the potential tyranny of majority rule. Courts are empowered to be guardians of both human rights and the constitution itself. In the words of Sunstein: "Without judicial review, constitutions tend to be worth little more than the paper on which they are written. They become mere words, or public relations documents, rather than instruments which confer genuine rights."[18]

On the other hand, it is a paradox of constitutional democracies that unelected "courts sit in judgment on the decisions made by the elected representatives of the people."[19] Critics of judicial review argue that reliance on judges tends to undermine democracy, diminish accountability, and distort public debate.[20] Tate and Vallinder warn that the global expansion of judicial power is a negative development because it is "likely to weaken majoritarian democratic institutions and sustain the rule of privileged and unrepresentative elites, shutting out those who should be represented in a democratic state from effective access to policy-making processes or to effective, responsive administration."[21] According to Waldron, open elections and decision making by majority rule are more likely to safeguard democracy, human rights, and the rule of law than judicial review.[22]

The persuasive rebuttal from defenders of constitutional democracy is that judicial power can be and is used creatively, not to block democracy but to energize it and make it more deliberative.[23] Experience in many nations demonstrates that this is the case. For example, Hogg and Bushell describe the back-and-forth process between governments and courts in Canada on issues of political and civil liberties and Aboriginal rights as a constructive dialogue.[24] As well, in the majority of nations, judicial power is used in a relatively cautious fashion because of conservative legal cultures, respect for the separation of powers, and particular national circumstances, such as institutional weakness (e.g., lack of tenure for judges).[25]

Critics of constitutionalism also point out the failure to acknowledge the role of private as opposed to public power, which is viewed as a serious flaw in an era dominated by multinational corporations; the lack of consideration accorded to other sites of constitutional law production in an era of globalization, when economic and trade considerations may outweigh constitutional commitments to public welfare; and the exaggeration of the instrumental capacities of rights-based constitutionalism (because law is subjective and litigation may produce unintended and counterproductive consequences).[26] Hirschl argues that constitutionalization of rights is motivated not by "politicians' genuine commitment to progressive notions of social justice or to an elevated vision of human rights" but rather by "attempts to maintain the social and political status quo and to block attempts to seriously challenge it through democratic politics."[27] Some researchers believe that constitutions are "legalistic window dressing," extraneous to what governments do, and serve largely as public relations exercises aimed at domestic or international audiences to improve a nation's image.[28]

Overall, the impacts of a particular constitution will depend on a suite of legal, social, cultural, economic, and political factors that vary from nation to nation. This book will demonstrate that in the environmental context, constitutional provisions requiring environmental protection appear to provide a range of benefits, including stronger laws, enhanced public participation, and improved environmental performance.

The Rights Revolution

> There is a human rights revolution, with the freedom explosion
> that is taking place all over the world.
>
> – Martin Luther King Jr., "Remaining Awake
> through a Great Revolution," Washington, DC,
> 31 March 1968

The second broad development that spurred the emergence of the right to a healthy environment is the rights revolution – at both the national and international levels. The "rights revolution" refers to the sustained, developmental process that has produced new rights or expanded existing rights, resulting in unprecedented recognition and protection of these rights and extension of rights to previously "right-less" groups.[29] Because of the prominent role of courts in this process, the rights revolution is closely tied to constitutionalism and the judicialization of politics. The rights revolution is attributed to a mixture of top-down and bottom-up factors. The top-down factors include constitutional guarantees of human rights, judicial independence, the leadership of individual judges, and government support for rights advocacy. The bottom-up factors that enable strategic rights advocacy include human rights organizations, rights advocacy lawyers, reliable funding sources, and rising rights consciousness and discourse in popular culture. These latter factors are described as the institutional support structure for advocacy and litigation.[30] Most of the initial rights revolution scholarship focused on the United States.[31] More recently, the concept has been applied in India, Canada, Great Britain, Costa Rica, and other nations.[32]

Human rights recognition and protection have grown immensely since the Second World War.[33] The proliferation of international human rights instruments began in 1945 with the UN Charter, which established the rules governing the structure and operations of the United Nations. The Charter explicitly sought "to reaffirm faith in fundamental human rights, in the dignity and worth of the human person."[34] The entrenchment of human rights advanced in 1948 with the *Universal Declaration of Human Rights* and in 1966 with the *International Covenant on Civil and Political Rights* and the *International Covenant on Economic, Social and Cultural Rights.*[35] Human rights have continued to expand in breadth and depth at the global, regional, national, and subnational levels.[36]

Scholars wax eloquent about the importance of human rights. McHugh wrote that "the most dynamic legal concept of the twentieth and twenty-first centuries has been the idea of rights."[37] Henkin praised human rights as "the idea of our time."[38] Former UN secretary-general Boutros Boutros-Ghali described rights as the "common language of humanity."[39] According to Mahoney, "The modern human rights movement has been, and continues to be, an astonishing moral phenomenon ... [reflecting a] remarkable development in human consciousness."[40]

Rights represent reasonable minimum demands upon society that are rooted in moral values and thus place compelling principles on the side of the person asserting a right.[41] As Ignatieff wrote, "Rights are not just instruments of the law, they are expressions of our moral identity as a people."[42] Because rights provide recognition for society's most cherished values, such as dignity, equality, and respect, the language of rights has considerable symbolic force and can be a source of political power. The power of rights discourse is demonstrated by the considerable progress achieved in some battles about justice, including those against racism and the oppression of women.[43] However, one of the key messages of the modern human rights movement is that moral rights are not adequate and must be supplemented with enforceable legal rights to make them meaningful. Legal rights are said to empower rights holders to control the behaviour of others, and are famously described as "trumps" by Dworkin.[44] Shapiro argues that "rights review almost always places courts on the side of the less politically powerful," protecting minority interests against majority tyranny and fecklessness.[45]

Not everyone has been seduced by the siren song of the rights revolution. It can be argued that rights are inherently undemocratic to the extent that they constrain governments from enforcing the preferences of the majority (as discussed earlier).[46] Human rights are criticized for being individualistic, disregarding duties to others and the interests of the broader community.[47] Despite their purported universality, the Western conception of human rights has been criticized as a form of cultural imperialism. Rights can be divisive when there are conflicts between deeply held values (as in the ongoing abortion debate that pits the rights of women against the rights of the fetus).[48] Glendon called for more thought to be given to "whether a particular issue is best conceptualized as a right; the relation a given right should have to other rights and interests; the responsibilities, if any, that should be correlative with a given right; the social cost of rights; and what effects a given right can be expected to have on the setting of conditions for the durable protection of freedom and human dignity."[49] Other criticisms take aim at the processes used to create rights, particularly when rights are established or enlarged through court decisions. For example, Bork argues that creating rights through judicial interpretation is "heresy" because the role of judges is to interpret law, not make law.[50]

Critics also argue that the focus on rights obscures underlying societal problems and their root causes. Capitalism and globalization, with their emphasis on free trade and market-based solutions, are accused of contributing to the erosion of human rights.[51] States are responsible for respecting, protecting, and fulfilling human rights, but critics argue the power of states is declining relative to international institutions (e.g., the World Trade Organization) and transnational corporations. For example, Baxi questions whether the right to food can be reconciled with a global agribusiness industry dominated by a handful of large corporations.[52]

Perhaps the most trenchant critique is that the unprecedented global diffusion of rights on paper is not matched by global respect for rights in practice. Violations of human rights remain commonplace, even in wealthy Western nations. As Falk observes, "The achievements in human rights over the course of the last fifty years are extraordinary, but the obstacles to full realization seem as insurmountable as ever."[53] The right to a healthy environment reflects these broader debates, as the evidence provided in this book will demonstrate that the right has contributed to environmental progress, yet ecological sustainability remains a distant goal.

The Global Environmental Crisis

> Now is our last chance to get the future right.
>
> – Ronald Wright, *A Short History of Progress*

The emergence of a global environmental crisis in the latter half of the twentieth century is the third factor spurring the development of the right to a healthy environment. Although concerns about human impacts on Nature date back centuries, widespread public awareness of global environmental problems emerged in the 1960s. The awakening was triggered by the publication of Rachel Carson's *Silent Spring* and by a series of high-profile ecological disasters, including the *Torrey Canyon* oil spill off the coast of England, the so-called death of Lake Erie, and the burning of the Cuyahoga River.[54] Humans' technological prowess, consumptive appetite, and global economy have made us a geological force, leading some scientists to conclude that the Holocene epoch has ended and we have entered the "Anthropocene."[55] There are close to 7 billion people living on the Earth today, with the population expected to reach 9 billion by the middle of this century.[56] Agriculture, transportation, housing, industry, consumer goods, and day-to-day human activities are placing an unprecedented level of pressure on the natural systems of the planet. The web of life, upon which our own future depends, is jeopardized by the interrelated problems of climate change, extinction, and toxic pollution.[57]

Climate change is among the most daunting environmental challenges ever confronted by humanity and may be the paramount threat to public health in the twenty-first century.[58] The burning of fossil fuels has pushed levels of carbon dioxide in the atmosphere to the highest levels in at least 650,000 years. Agriculture, deforestation, and livestock are also major contributors to climate change.[59] Human emissions of greenhouse gases are changing the climate in ways that are causing not only warmer temperatures, but also more frequent and intense heat waves, storms, and other extreme weather events; melting ice in the Arctic, Greenland, and the Antarctic; disappearing glaciers, melting permafrost, rising sea levels, disruptive floods, acidification of the oceans, droughts, and extinctions.[60] Forests are increasingly vulnerable to pests, disease, and wildfire, causing economic disruption and social dislocation in forest-dependent communities. Scientists are concerned that abrupt, unpredictable climate shifts could occur.[61] Climate change already causes an estimated 150,000 deaths and 5 million illnesses per year.[62] The World Health Organization projects a doubling of these figures by 2030.[63] Tens of millions of people may be displaced from their homes by flooding, spawning an unprecedented wave of environmental refugees. More than a billion people may face chronic water shortages as precipitation patterns change and water supplies stored in glaciers and snowpacks decline.

Biological diversity – the richness of life measured at the species, ecosystem, and genetic levels – is disappearing more rapidly than at any time since the extinction of the dinosaurs 65 million years ago.[64] Scientists estimate that species are going extinct at a rate that is one hundred to one thousand times faster than normal and fear that the pace of extinctions will accelerate in the decades ahead.[65] The Living Planet Index, created by several different institutions including the Zoological Society of London and the World Wildlife Fund, tracks populations of more than twenty-five hundred vertebrate species – mammals, birds, fish, amphibians, and reptiles – living in terrestrial, marine, and freshwater ecosystems. Between 1970 and 2007, the Living Planet Index fell 30 percent, suggesting that we are degrading natural ecosystems at a rate unprecedented in human history.[66] The United Nations' Millennium Ecosystem Assessment, a comprehensive analysis of the state of life on Earth prepared by more than thirteen hundred experts, concluded: "Human activity is putting such strain on the natural functions of the Earth that the ability of the planet's ecosystems to sustain future generations can no longer be taken for granted."[67] At least 60 percent of the world's natural resources and life-supporting ecosystems are in decline. Despite the fact that oceans cover close to three-quarters of the Earth's surface, marine ecosystems are among the most depleted on the planet. Populations of large predatory fishes – bluefin tuna, swordfish, and sharks – have declined by more than 90 percent.[68] Some scientists predict that if current fishing practices continue, all commercially targeted fish species will suffer population collapses by 2048.[69] As a result, the oceans will be unable to contribute to feeding a growing human population, and marine ecosystems will suffer a severe decrease in their ability to resist diseases, cope with invasive species, filter pollutants, and rebound from stresses.[70] Globally, biodiversity loss and damage to ecosystems is estimated to cost humanity trillions of dollars every year.[71]

Toxic industrial and agricultural chemicals now contaminate every ecosystem in the world. Humans are exposed to hundreds, if not thousands, of hazardous substances through air, food, water, and consumer products. Tests examining the blood and urine of Americans, Canadians, and Europeans find heavy metals, pesticides, flame retardants, stain repellants, and PCBs.[72] Even the umbilical cord blood of newborn infants in the United States contains over two hundred industrial chemicals.[73] These findings illustrate the fundamental connection between humans and the environment. Total releases of toxic chemicals into the environment by large industries in the United States and Canada alone are measured in the tens of billions of kilograms annually.[74] Agricultural runoff, urban runoff, small and medium-sized businesses, and motor vehicles release billions of additional kilograms of toxic substances. Exposure to these environmental hazards is a major cause of death and disease. According to the World Health Organization, approximately one-quarter of the burden of disease globally is attributable to environmental factors.[75] Exposure to environmental contaminants can cause cancer; increase the risk of birth defects; damage the respiratory, cardiovascular, reproductive, hormonal, immune, and nervous systems; and contribute to Parkinson's, Alzheimer's, and other neurodegenerative diseases.[76] Children are particularly vulnerable.[77]

Society has responded to the global environmental crisis with initiatives at every scale, from the global to the local. There has been an explosion of bilateral, regional, and global treaties on environmental subjects in the past three decades, with more than one thousand such agreements now in force around the world.[78] International environmental conventions cover all of the environmental issues facing humanity, including, *inter alia*, climate change, ozone depletion, destruction of marine ecosystems, loss of biodiversity, air and water pollution, trade in hazardous substances, trade in endangered species, and persistent organic pollutants. At the national and subnational levels, new institutions have been created and countless laws, regulations, standards, and policies enacted. Among these myriad responses are international instruments and national constitutions that recognize the right to live in a healthy environment.

The Right to a Healthy Environment

If, as many scholars assert, human rights trace their roots to specific historical wrongs, then it is understandable that the right to a healthy environment is not found in pioneering human rights instruments such as the *Universal Declaration of Human Rights* (1948), the *International Covenant on Civil and Political Rights* (1966), or the *International Covenant on Economic, Social, and Cultural Rights* (1966). Society's awareness of the magnitude, pace, and adverse consequences of environmental degradation was not sufficiently advanced during the era when these agreements were drafted and negotiated to warrant the inclusion of environmental concerns.[79]

The first written suggestion that there should be a specific human right to a healthy environment came from Rachel Carson in 1962:

> If the Bill of Rights contains no guarantees that a citizen shall be secure against lethal poisons distributed either by private individuals or by public officials, it is surely only because our forefathers, despite their considerable wisdom and foresight, could conceive of no such problem.[80]

Similarly, in her final public speech before dying of cancer, Carson testified before President Kennedy's Scientific Advisory Committee, urging it to consider

> a much neglected problem, that of the right of the citizen to be secure in his own home against the intrusion of poisons applied by other persons. I speak not as a lawyer but as a biologist and as a human being, but I strongly feel that this is or ought to be one of the basic human rights.[81]

In 1972, the first global eco-summit resulted in the pioneering *Stockholm Declaration*, which formally recognized the right to a healthy environment and the accompanying responsibility (although the agreement is not legally binding):

> *Principle 1*
> Man has the fundamental right to freedom, equality and adequate conditions of life, in an environment of a quality that permits a life of dignity and well-being, and he bears a solemn responsibility to protect and improve the environment for present and future generations.

> *Principle 2*
> The natural resources of the earth including the air, water, land, flora and fauna and especially representative samples of natural ecosystems must be safeguarded for the benefit of present and future generations through careful planning or management, as appropriate.[82]

While international law plays an important normative role, this book focuses on the right to a healthy environment at the national level, where human rights are largely implemented and enforced. As Hiskes observes, "Any human right, environmental or otherwise, is always operative mainly at the national level in the legal sense, even if morally or politically the language used to characterize it is more universal or at least global in scope."[83]

Almost forty years after the *Stockholm Declaration*, there is an ongoing debate about the right to a healthy environment – its philosophical underpinnings, moral and legal validity, parameters, and potential utility.[84] Supporters argue that the potential benefits of constitutionalizing the right to a healthy environment include the enactment and enforcement of stronger and more comprehensive environmental laws; a level playing field vis-à-vis other rights; greater government and corporate accountability; protection of vulnerable groups who currently shoulder a disproportionate burden of environmental harms; and increased citizen participation in decisions and actions to protect the environment.[85] Conversely, a vocal minority argues that any prospective advantages are outweighed by problems such as low likelihood of effectiveness; negative implications for democracy; the vague articulation of the right; the excessive focus on individuals; adverse effects on other rights; anthropocentrism; and the creation of false hopes.[86]

To date, however, there is a noteworthy absence of empirical evidence about whether and to what extent the constitutional right to a healthy environment is in fact realizing these anticipated effects, either positive or negative. Hayward, in one of the leading texts on this subject, discounts the possibility of conducting such an assessment because of methodological difficulties.[87] Shelton, another leading scholar in the field of environmental rights, writes that constitutional environmental rights "probably halted some environmental deterioration in some countries, although empirical studies are lacking and causality is difficult to demonstrate."[88] These evidentiary challenges are not new but are part of a broader discourse about the consequences – both theoretical and real – of law, constitutions, and public policy.

Do Constitutional Rights Matter?

There is a longstanding debate about whether, and to what extent, constitutional rights matter.[89] As Congleton asks, "Are constitutions simply symbols of the political time at which they were adopted, or do they systematically affect the course of public policy?"[90] Proponents of constitutional rights argue that laws will become stronger, institutions and norms will evolve, and courts will defend the rights of citizens.[91] There is an implicit faith that constitutions, in tandem with legal systems, will ensure the protection and fulfillment of rights.[92] This faith has come under attack from critics claiming that context is as important as, or more important than, the words on paper, and that on-the-ground results provide an indictment of the failure of constitutional rights to live up to their promises.[93]

Ignatieff argues that the acid test of the worth of constitutional and international human rights is whether they improve peoples' lives.[94] This is a compelling argument, for otherwise, rights may be mere paper tigers and their constitutional recognition nothing more than "cheap talk."[95] Paper tigers and cheap talk could result from the absence of the rule of law; competing social and economic priorities; a lack of resources for implementation and enforcement; or other social, legal, and cultural factors. For example, the constitutions of many communist nations and dictatorships often included extensive lists of human rights that were honoured in the breach, including the right to a healthy environment.[96] Article 67 of the Constitution of the Democratic People's Republic of Korea guarantees its citizens free speech; freedom of the press; freedom of assembly, demonstration, and association; and the right to form democratic political parties. None of these rights exist in any real sense in North Korea, underlining the fact that the impact of constitutional environmental provisions will depend on the specific culture and politics of an individual nation, institutional factors, the distribution of power between various polities, and the presence and resources of advocacy groups.[97]

The extent to which constitutions matter can be evaluated by either the instrumental or the constitutive approach.[98] The instrumental approach examines measurable or quantifiable effects and outcomes. For example, did the US Supreme Court decision in *Brown v. Board of Education*, striking down the practice of providing separate schools for black and white children, change the social, educational, and economic status of African Americans in concrete ways?[99] In contrast, the constitutive approach characterizes law as having a more pervasive (but more difficult to measure) impact on society through deeper channels, affecting fundamental beliefs, institutions, behaviour, and the legitimacy of authority. Did *Brown v. Board of Education* change American values regarding racism and equality? The constitutive approach suggests that law plays an influential role in shaping politics, economics, and culture. Another way of categorizing the effects of constitutions is by separating legal and extra-legal effects. Legal effects include influencing legislation, public policy, and court decisions, while extra-legal effects include the evolution of public opinion, attitudes, values, and behaviour. This book considers both the legal and extra-legal effects of constitutional provisions requiring environmental protection, but emphasizes the former.

The question of whether constitutions matter has been asked, and at least partially answered, in many different contexts, including Aboriginal rights,[100] economic effects,[101] civil and political rights,[102] the right to health,[103] and other social and economic rights.[104] Arthurs and Arnold assessed the impact of the *Canadian Charter of Rights and Freedoms* some two decades after that document revolutionized the Canadian legal landscape and found little evidence of positive effects on the status of women, the income gap between rich and poor, or the socio-economic status of Aboriginal people.[105] Hirschl examined the impact of constitutionalization of rights in Canada, Israel, New Zealand, and South Africa on the status of historically disenfranchised groups, finding little improvement in access to education, basic housing, health care, employment, and distribution of wealth.[106] In contrast, Carlson concluded that positive transformative changes have occurred in the recognition and protection of Aboriginal rights because of the recognition of those rights in Canada's 1982 constitution.[107] Montenegro identified a negative correlation between the length of a nation's constitution and per capita income.[108] De Vanssay and Spindler found that political rights have no significant effect on economic growth and economic wealth, whereas economic freedom (a concept that includes protection of property rights) and freedom of contract do have a significant positive effect.[109] Political scientists have examined the effects of constitutions and particular types of civil and political rights as they attempt to discern the influence of institutions on a wide range of outcomes, including environmental protection.[110] Several scholars have reported that protection for civil and political rights is positively correlated with environmental quality.[111] Kinney and Clark found no correlation between the strength of constitutional commitments to protect health and average per capita government expenditures on health care.[112]

Remarkably, none of this literature has been referred to in the ongoing debate about the right to a healthy environment, which continues to be characterized by theoretical rather than empirical observations. In this book, I will harness the approaches and insights of these scholars in an attempt to overcome the challenges inherent in assessing the effects of constitutionalizing the right to a healthy environment.

Overview

The question at the heart of this book is: Do environmental provisions in constitutions – in particular, the right to live in a healthy environment – matter? Do they have observable legal and extra-legal effects that contribute to improved environmental protection and reduced risks to human health? Part 1 examines the emergence and evolution of the right to a healthy environment at both the national and international levels. Chapter 2 reviews the debates about the nature and scope of the right to a healthy environment as well as the theoretical advantages and disadvantages of constitutional recognition of this right. Chapter 3 examines the extent to which the constitutions of the 193 member states of the United Nations address environmental issues by asking the following questions:

- How many national constitutions incorporate provisions related to environmental protection?
- How many constitutions explicitly recognize that individuals have a right to a healthy environment?
- What other types of environmental protection provisions are found?
- When were these constitutional provisions enacted?
- Are there limits imposed on the right to a healthy environment? Are these limits similar to, or different from, limits on other constitutional rights?
- Are the environmental protection provisions enshrined in national constitutions enforceable, at least on paper?

Chapter 4 offers an overview of the evolution of the right to a healthy environment at the international level. Increasing recognition of this right at the global and regional levels influences national constitutions, legislation, and jurisprudence.[113] For example, the *Stockholm Declaration* is often cited as an inspiration by nations that have included environmental rights and responsibilities in their constitutions.[114] Developments at the national level, in turn, influence the development of the right to a healthy environment internationally.

Part 2 explores the legal consequences of environmental provisions in constitutions, with an emphasis on the right to a healthy environment. Chapter 5 outlines an analytical framework for assessing the impacts of constitutional environmental provisions on legislation and court decisions. Chapters 6 to 10 assess the extent of the constitutional right's influence through a comprehensive examination of environmental laws and court decisions in one hundred nations in Latin America and the Caribbean, Africa, Asia, Eastern Europe, and Western Europe. These chapters also examine the factors responsible for variations in the extent of the rights revolution both within and among the five regions.

Part 3 evaluates the experiences of nations that have entrenched environmental protection in their constitutions. Chapter 11 assesses the extent to which the anticipated advantages and disadvantages of the constitutional right to a healthy environment are being borne out in practice. Chapter 12 presents an empirical comparison of the environmental performance of nations with and without constitutional provisions related to environmental protection. The data sets used in this comparison include the following:

- size of per capita ecological footprints for 150 nations
- rankings of environmental performance among the nations of the Organisation for Economic Co-operation and Development, published by researchers at Simon Fraser University
- rankings of environmental performance among seventeen wealthy industrialized nations, published by the Conference Board of Canada
- ratification of five major international environmental agreements
- progress in reducing greenhouse gas emissions
- trends in reducing sulphur dioxide emissions
- trends in reducing nitrogen oxide emissions.

Chapter 13 summarizes the results of the research, synthesizes the major conclusions, and offers suggestions for future research on constitutional environmental rights.

Conclusion

The right to live in a healthy environment continues to generate extensive interest at the national, regional, and international levels. Ecuador made headlines around the world in 2008 for adopting a new constitution that grants legal rights directly to Nature.[115] New constitutions incorporating extensive environmental provisions were enacted in Bhutan, Ecuador, the Maldives, and Turkmenistan in 2008; Bolivia in 2009; Kenya and the Dominican Republic in 2010; and Jamaica, Morocco, and South Sudan in 2011. Iceland's new constitution, pending parliamentary approval and possibly a public referendum, also includes strong environmental language. In the United Kingdom, a joint committee of the House of Commons and the House of Lords recently recommended that the right to a healthy environment be included in a proposed UK Bill of Rights.[116] In 2008, the president of the Parliamentary Assembly of the Council of Europe stated: "One of the objectives I have set myself during my term of office is the integration of the right to a healthy environment into the *European Convention on Human Rights*."[117] The president of the Maldives called for immediate negotiations on a comprehensive environmental rights agreement as a key element in addressing the threat to human rights posed by climate change.[118] In 2011, the UN General Assembly began debating a proposed Universal Declaration of the Rights of Mother Earth.

    In light of these ongoing developments, it is essential to move beyond philosophical debates about human rights and the environment. The time has come to begin the difficult process of evaluating the effectiveness of the right to a healthy environment, not through rose-coloured glasses but through an even-handed assessment of factual evidence. The conclusions will be relevant not only for nations that are engaged in implementing constitutional environmental provisions, but also for nations whose constitutions do not yet recognize the fundamental importance of protecting the environment. The results of this research will also contribute to the broader debates about whether law matters, whether constitutions matter, and whether rights are an effective tool in promoting social change.[119] As the world struggles to fulfill its aspirations to protect both human rights and the environment, efforts and resources must be re-directed toward the most effective, efficient, and equitable means of achieving these vital and intimately intertwined goals.

2

The Right to a Healthy Environment:
...... Framing the Issues

> As the Cold War ended two great secular religions have come to
> grip the world: environmentalism and human rights.
>
> – Martin Shapiro, "Judicial Review in Developed
> Democracies"

The concept of a human right to a healthy environment has been debated
extensively since human rights and environmental concerns converged in the
early 1970s. Does the right to a healthy environment possess the attributes of
a universal human right? How does it fit with established civil, political, economic, social, and cultural rights? What is the scope and nature of the right?
Is it an individual and/or a collective right? Is it a moral and/or a legal right?
Is it a negative (liberty) or a positive (welfare) right? Should the focus be on
a substantive environmental right or a set of procedural environmental rights?

This chapter will survey and engage in these ongoing debates because they
play a critical role in shaping the justification for, and potential content of,
the right to a healthy environment. However, the focus of this book is on the
practical consequences of *constitutional* recognition of the right to a healthy
environment, which raises additional questions. What kind of legal and extra-
legal benefits does a constitutional right to a healthy environment promise?
What are the potential disadvantages? These prospective pros and cons will
also be surveyed in this chapter, while subsequent chapters will provide insights
into whether and to what extent such predictions are borne out in practice.

Human Rights and the Environment: Ongoing Debates

Is the Right to a Healthy Environment a Human Right?

There are many definitions of human rights. Cranston wrote that a human
right is usually defined as "a universal moral right, something which all men

everywhere at all times ought to have, something of which no one may be deprived without a grave affront to justice, something which is owing to every human being simply because he is human."[1] A more recent definition is provided by Cullet, who states that "all human rights represent universal claims necessary to ensure that every person can enjoy a decent quality of life – part of the core moral codes common to all societies."[2] These definitions share three elements. First, human rights are universal, meaning that they are both widely agreed upon and held by everyone. Universal applicability is subject to the caveat that the precise interpretation or form of these rights can vary significantly according to local social, economic, cultural, political, and environmental conditions. Second, human rights have a moral basis, indicating that these rights exist whether or not a particular nation, government, or legal system recognizes them. Third, the basic intent of rights is to ensure the dignity of all human beings.

Does the right to a healthy environment meet these three requirements? The majority of scholars answer this question in the affirmative.[3] Hayward asserts that, "as a moral proposition, the claim that all human beings have the fundamental right to an environment adequate for their health and well-being is ... unimpeachable."[4] Shue writes that "unpolluted air, unpolluted water, [and] adequate food" are among the basic human rights.[5] According to Birnie and Boyle, constitutional recognition of the right to a healthy environment "would recognize the vital character of the environment as a basic condition of life, indispensable to the promotion of human dignity and welfare, and to the fulfillment of other rights."[6] Only a handful of experts have reservations on this point. Miller writes that "clean air, like other welfare aspirations, is best understood as a goal" rather than a right.[7] Similarly, Robertson and Merrills argue that "if one wishes to see some objective achieved – a clean and healthy environment, for example – it is tempting to say that this is a right to which we are all entitled. But it is not a good idea to take wishes for reality."[8] On balance, it seems inaccurate to describe a healthy environment as a mere goal or objective, given the vital importance of clean air, fresh water, fertile soil, and ecosystem services to human health, well-being, and dignity. The right to a healthy environment possesses the essential characteristics of all human rights.

THREE GENERATIONS OF HUMAN RIGHTS

Some scholars argue that there are three categories, or generations, of human rights. The first generation of rights is the basic civil and political rights, including the right to life, freedom of speech, the right to vote, etc. These rights are recognized in the *International Covenant on Civil and Political Rights* and are enshrined in almost all national constitutions.[9] The second generation of rights includes social, economic, and cultural rights, such as the right to health and the right to education. These rights are recognized in the *International Covenant on Economic, Social and Cultural Rights* but are not as widely entrenched in national constitutions as political and civil rights.[10] The third generation of rights – also called collective or solidarity rights – includes the rights to peace, development, and a healthy environment.[11] Third-generation rights are described as "one of the responses of the international community to changing circumstances and needs."[12] The suggestion that there are three generations of rights is controversial, and no global human rights treaty recognizes third-generation rights in the same way that the two *International Covenants* enshrine civil, political, economic, social, and cultural rights.

Ultimately, the distinction between different "generations" of human rights may not be helpful, or even valid. A more integrated approach, advocated by many scholars, views all human rights as indivisible, interrelated, interdependent, and not subject to a hierarchical classification.[13] The United Nations' *Vienna Declaration on Human Rights* of 1993 supports this perspective, stating that "the international community must treat human rights globally in a fair and equal manner, on the same footing, and with the same emphasis."[14]

Legal versus Moral Rights

In the field of human rights, there is a crucial difference between moral rights and legal rights. Moral rights are possessed by individuals simply by virtue of being human. These rights are universal, inalienable, and permanent, persisting even in emergencies and wars. While states ought to recognize and respect moral rights, they cannot grant them or take them away. Legal or positive law rights, in contrast, include only those rights that are formally recognized by the state or another level of government. Legal rights are granted by the state and, in theory, can be taken away by the state. Governments have four obligations that flow from legally recognized human rights:

- to avoid violating people's rights
- to prevent others from violating people's rights
- to assist people whose rights are being or have been violated

* to maintain effective institutions for ensuring rights are enjoyed and fulfilled.[15]

As noted earlier, most scholars agree that the right to a healthy environment meets the conditions to qualify as a moral right, providing a strong rationale for granting it constitutional protection.

POSITIVE AND NEGATIVE RIGHTS

Another distinction frequently encountered in human rights discourse involves negative (liberty) versus positive (welfare) rights. In theory, civil and political rights such as free speech, freedom of religion, and freedom of assembly are negative rights that prohibit state interference or coercion. Economic, social, and cultural rights, in contrast, are viewed as positive rights, which place a duty on the state to take action (and expend resources) in order to ensure that the right is fulfilled. Examples include government programs to provide health care, education, or housing.

A controversial aspect of this categorization involves the difference between immediate and progressive implementation of rights. Civil and political rights are to be recognized and protected immediately. As stated in the *International Covenant on Civil and Political Rights:*

> Article 2(2) Where not already provided for by existing legislative or other measures, each State Party to the present Covenant undertakes to take the necessary steps, in accordance with its constitutional processes and with the provisions of the present Covenant, to adopt such laws or other measures as may be necessary to give effect to the rights recognized in the present Covenant.

The overwhelming majority of nations in the world have recognized the fundamental nature of civil and political rights by enshrining them in their constitutions. In contrast, economic, social, and cultural rights were initially conceived as subject to progressive realization, meaning that states are not obligated to achieve them immediately but must strive to fulfill them over time as they acquire the necessary resources and expertise. Article 2(1) of the *International Covenant on Economic, Social and Cultural Rights* states:

> Each State Party to the present Covenant undertakes to take steps, individually and through international assistance and co-operation,

especially economic and technical, to the maximum of its available resources, with a view to achieving progressively the full realization of the rights recognized in the present Covenant by all appropriate means, including particularly the adoption of legislative measures.

Despite the clear reference to progressive implementation, the UN Committee on Economic, Social and Cultural Rights takes the position that many of the covenant's provisions can be immediately implemented.[16] However, as Hayward observes, "There are clearly limits to the usefulness of seeking to hold states to obligations which it is materially beyond their capacity to fulfill."[17]

One of the major implications of this distinction is that while civil and political rights became enforceable in courts of law, economic, social, and cultural rights were widely held to be unenforceable. Some experts have extended this line of thinking to suggest that the right to a healthy environment is not enforceable.[18] However, the notion that economic, social, and cultural rights are not justiciable has been eroded by court decisions in many countries.[19] A study of the right to food, conducted by the United Nations' Food and Agriculture Organization, concluded that "the distinction between the types of human rights is gradually dissolving."[20] According to Fredman, "Positive duties arising from human rights can no longer be ignored, or hidden behind artificial distinctions between different categories of rights."[21] It is now widely recognized that extensive and expensive state investments may be required in order to protect civil and political rights, as demonstrated by the costs of policing, prisons, and the judicial system.[22] There is a new *Optional Protocol* to the *International Covenant on Economic, Social and Cultural Rights* that establishes mechanisms for pursuing individual complaints and inquiries, further narrowing the gap.[23]

The right to a healthy environment appears to embody both negative and positive aspects. There is a negative right to be free from exposure to toxic substances produced by the state or by state-sanctioned activities. There is a positive right to clean air, safe water, and healthy ecosystems, which may require an extensive system of regulation, implementation, and enforcement as well as remediation efforts in polluted areas. Thus the right to a healthy environment illustrates that the distinction between positive and negative rights is increasingly outdated.

INDIVIDUAL VERSUS COLLECTIVE RIGHTS

As noted earlier, the rights to a healthy environment, peace, and development are sometimes described as collective rights. This categorization has created conceptual difficulties, because individuals, rather than groups, have traditionally been the focus of human rights.[24]

In national constitutions and international agreements, the right to a healthy environment is generally formulated and understood as an individual right. However, there are exceptions. Several national constitutions include the right to a healthy environment in chapters devoted to collective rights.[25] Most of the environmental cases brought to the Inter-American Court and the Inter-American Commission on Human Rights have dealt with the communal rights of indigenous people.[26] The *African Charter on Human and Peoples' Rights* expresses the right to a healthy environment in the following terms: "All peoples shall have the right to a general satisfactory environment favourable to their development."[27] Once again, the right to a healthy environment appears to transcend the conventional binary classification of human rights, as it has both individual and collective aspects.[28]

SUBSTANTIVE VERSUS PROCEDURAL RIGHTS

Another ongoing debate revolves around whether the right to a healthy environment should be substantive – entitling individuals to a certain level of environmental quality – or procedural, ensuring access to information, participation in decision making, and access to justice when one's right is violated.

Substantive environmental rights provide an assurance to all persons that they can enjoy environmental conditions that meet certain minimum requirements – clean air, safe water, and a level of environmental quality that does not jeopardize their health or well-being. Substantive rights create a corresponding obligation on the government to both refrain from taking or authorizing actions that impair citizens' right to a healthy environment and, where necessary, to take positive actions to ensure or safeguard citizens' right to environmental quality. What is not clear with respect to substantive environmental rights is precisely what level of environmental quality is to be protected or what constitutes a violation of the right. This will depend, in part, on the specific language of the right, as enacted in a constitution and/ or legislation. It will also depend on the economic, ecological, social, and political circumstances of a particular nation. The content of a substantive environmental right will evolve over time, and just as other human rights vary in content from nation to nation, so will environmental rights. For example, the right to life is perhaps the most basic and universally embraced of all human rights, yet it has very different meanings in different nations. Some nations whose constitutions recognize the right to life continue to allow capital punishment, while others prohibit this practice. A substantive environmental right could provide the right not to have one's health harmed or endangered by pollution; the right to a reasonable level of environmental quality (effectively protecting the environment as well as human health); the right to have one's private property protected from environmental damage caused by others; and the right of the environment to be protected for its own sake.[29] A substantive environmental right would likely have the corollary benefit of enhancing existing procedural rights or creating new ones.

Procedural rights related to the environment include access to information, the right to participate in decision making, and access to justice. These rights have deep roots in human rights instruments, although not specifically in the environmental context. The *Universal Declaration of Human Rights* and the *International Covenant on Civil and Political Rights* guarantee access to information, the right to participate in decision making, and the right to effective remedies.[30] In some nations, procedural rights already exist to some degree as a result of freedom of information legislation and policies and programs that promote citizen involvement in decision making, and through the gradual loosening of standing rules that had previously limited access to judicial and administrative appeal processes.[31]

In the environmental context, procedural rights are essential complements to substantive rights because they provide the tools to ensure that the latter are fulfilled. Procedural rights are practical and enforceable, enabling citizens and groups to contribute actively to the protection of their environment.[32] According to some scholars, "procedural rights promote the transparency, participation, and accountability that form the cornerstones of environmental governance."[33] Eckersley has suggested that procedural rights "facilitate the practice of ecological citizenship," which could help address the pervasive implementation deficit that plagues environmental law in Canada, the United States, and around the world.[34]

Douglas-Scott argues that because of the extensive challenges facing the implementation and enforcement of substantive environmental rights, a focus on procedural rights might be more effective, since these rights encourage participatory democracy.[35] Fitzmaurice and Marshall go one step further, suggesting that "a procedural environmental right is a more effective and flexible tool in achieving environmental justice than a substantive right, which ... is to a large extent only a policy statement."[36]

Despite their positive attributes, procedural environmental rights are necessary but not sufficient to address environmental problems. On their own, procedural rights are less stringent and less demanding, as they provide no guarantee of a specific substantive outcome. According to Hayward, "Procedural rights alone do too little to counterbalance the prevailing presumptions in favour of development and economic interests."[37] Similarly, Anderson concludes, "Procedures alone cannot guarantee environmental protection."[38]

The Promise of a Constitutional Right to a Healthy Environment

Beyond the debates about the place of the right to a healthy environment in the catalog of human rights, there are also ongoing arguments about the advisability of entrenching this right in national constitutions. To date, these arguments have taken place largely in the theoretical or philosophical realm. In his book *Constitutional Environmental Rights*, Hayward argues – based on moral and philosophical principles – that "any state which is constitutionally committed to the implementation and protection of human rights ought to constitutionalize a right to an adequate environment."[39] Hayward's logic has three parts. First, he suggests that all fundamental human rights should be protected by constitutions, which represent the highest form of law and provide the greatest assurance of adequate enforcement. Second, he makes the case that environmental rights meet all of the various tests for achieving the status of a fundamental human right (significant moral importance, universal, practicable, etc.). Third, it follows logically from his first two conclusions that the right to a healthy environment should be granted constitutional protection.

However, Hayward cautions "against supposing that the issue of effectiveness of a constitutional environmental right can be settled one way or the other by means of purely theoretical argument."[40] The purpose of this book is to take the next step, going beyond purely theoretical argument to begin garnering and evaluating empirical evidence to determine whether the asserted advantages and disadvantages of constitutional recognition for the right to a healthy environment are borne out in practice.

The paramount objectives of constitutional recognition of the right to a healthy environment are to reduce the level of harm being inflicted on humans and the Earth and to redistribute inequitable allocations of environmental harms. It is important to recognize that while much of the literature on the right to a healthy environment focuses on judicial enforcement of the right, litigation is merely a means to an end. The aim of a constitutional right to a healthy environment is to ensure the enjoyment and protection of the right, not to foster litigation.

The constitutional right to a healthy environment may result in or contribute to a broad range of legal and extra-legal outcomes that will advance environmental protection by

- providing an impetus for stronger environmental legislation
- bolstering the implementation and enforcement of existing environmental laws and policies
- offering a safety net by filling gaps in environmental legislation
- protecting environmental laws and regulations from rollbacks under future governments
- enabling a better balance with competing economic and social rights by ensuring a level playing field
- increasing accountability
- strengthening democracy by promoting greater citizen participation in decisions and actions to protect the environment, in part by enhancing rights of access to information, participation in decision making, and justice
- protecting vulnerable populations, including future generations, from environmentally destructive acts of the majority
- educating citizens, judges, politicians, and public servants about the urgent importance of environmental protection.

Each of these prospective advantages is described in detail below. The extent to which these positive outcomes are being realized in practice will be assessed in Chapters 6 to 12.

PROVIDE AN IMPETUS FOR STRONGER ENVIRONMENTAL LAWS
Constitutional protection of a right offers the strongest possible form of legal protection because a constitution is the "fundamental and paramount law of the nation."[41] A basic principle of constitutional law is that all legislation,

regulation, and government policy must be consistent with the constitution or risk being struck down by the judiciary. For example, the Canadian constitution states that "any law that is inconsistent with the provisions of the Constitution is, to the extent of the inconsistency, of no force or effect."[42] Lawmakers and government decision makers must always consider the implications of their actions on constitutionally protected rights.[43] Thus, constitutional recognition of the right to a healthy environment could have an integrating effect, putting environmental concerns on the agenda throughout government rather than in one or two isolated and often weak departments. In many nations, entrenchment of a constitutional right to a healthy environment would require the enactment of stronger environmental laws in order to protect and fulfill the right. Stevenson anticipates that constitutional recognition of the right to a healthy environment would cause environmental laws to improve "to a state in which they no longer flatter to deceive but justify the high hopes and claims of the draftsmen and legislators."[44]

IMPROVE ENFORCEMENT OF ENVIRONMENTAL LAWS

Constitutional rights are accompanied by an obligation upon the state to respect, protect, and, in some circumstances, take proactive steps to fulfill the right.[45] In theory, constitutional recognition of the right to a healthy environment should ensure that governments establish and adequately resource a system for implementing, monitoring compliance with, and enforcing environmental laws and regulations. In many nations, both South and North, there is a longstanding history of lackadaisical enforcement of environmental laws.[46] Constitutional recognition of the right to a healthy environment could "act as a powerful catalyst stimulating the more effective enforcement of existing environmental protection laws."[47] As de Sadeleer writes, a constitutional environmental provision "imposes on the law-maker and subordinate authorities an obligation that they may not evade. Equivocation is no longer an option."[48] The procedural rights available to citizens can provide both a stimulus for enhanced enforcement by the state and a supplementary means of enforcing environmental laws.

PROVIDE A SAFETY NET

Constitutionalizing the right to a healthy environment could help address gaps in legislation, regulations, policies, and implementation. Gaps in environmental law and policy may occur because of delays in addressing particular issues or because new threats arise. Delays may be caused by a lack of legal and/or technical resources, or by a lack of priority being assigned to particular environmental problems by the state. For example, few governments have developed new health or environmental regulations for products emerging from the burgeoning field of nanotechnology.[49] The existence of a constitutional right to a healthy environment gives concerned citizens or communities a set of tools that may be effective in addressing problems despite the absence of legislation.[50] Rights provide a flexibility and open-endedness that no rule could ever provide.[51]

Prevent Environmental Rollbacks

Constitutions are harder to amend than ordinary laws. As Hayward states, "The point of constitutionalizing rights is to set them above the vicissitudes of everyday politics, and this is also effectively to raise them above the possibility of routine democratic revision."[52] Constitutional entrenchment of the right to a healthy environment may prevent governments from weakening environmental laws and standards in the future. In effect, the constitutional right could establish a floor below which rules for environmental protection cannot descend.[53]

Level the Playing Field

As today's global environmental crisis demonstrates, when government and industry make decisions, economic and social considerations often trump environmental concerns. The purpose of a constitutional right to a healthy environment is to seek a better balancing of competing interests, not to unilaterally trump economic and social priorities. As Brandl and Bungert write, "Declaring an environmental right in a constitution challenges the privileged position accorded economic freedoms."[54] Every day, government policy makers, administrative agencies, and courts make countless decisions with environmental consequences. Constitutional protection of the right to a healthy environment could tip the balance in many different regulatory, administrative, corporate, and judicial decisions by acting as a guiding criterion in discretionary decision making and as a standard for interpretation.[55]

Foster Accountability

In the absence of a constitutional right to a healthy environment, it can be difficult to hold governments accountable for failing to protect human health and the environment. There may be a lack of publicly available information, an absence of opportunities to participate in decisions that have significant environmental consequences, and a lack of access to tribunals or courts when a person or community suffers harm because of environmental destruction or pollution. Both the substantive and procedural aspects of the constitutional right to a healthy environment can contribute to overcoming these problems, ensuring the availability of processes and forums that enable citizens and groups to hold governments accountable.

A constitutional right to a healthy environment could enhance the courts' role in ensuring accountability by facilitating citizen access to judicial remedies. The nature and scope of human rights are often defined and refined through litigation. Stephens argues that courts are ideally suited for this role:

> The institution of adjudication (in its independence), the process of argumentation (according to criteria of rationality), and the decision-making process (according to law) mean that courts, international and national, are uniquely placed to speak beyond the confines of the dispute at hand and confront the major environmental challenges of our time.[56]

Citizens could use the constitutional right to a healthy environment to seek remedies for violations of the right and also, in a preventive manner, to avoid prospective environmental damage. In theory, the impartiality of courts should enable them to balance the following: competing economic, social, and environmental interests; individual and collective interests; and public and private interests. As Du Bois observes, courts "can make a unique contribution by insulating environmental protection measures – typically accompanied by high short-term costs and resultant political disfavor – from political horse-trading."[57] Constitutional protection of the right to a healthy environment could result in the evolution of jurisprudence that currently undermines the efficacy of environmental law when it comes to issues regarding causation, the burden of proof, liability, and other problems.[58] Prerequisites for the achievement of these promises include adherence to the rule of law, the absence of corruption, and an independent judiciary.

STRENGTHEN DEMOCRACY

Recognition of a constitutional right to a healthy environment would empower citizens and civil society, especially if it resulted in the strengthening of procedural rights such as access to information, participation in decision making, standing in judicial review, and the ability to enforce environmental

laws. As Chiappinelli states, constitutional environmental rights would address the "institutional disenfranchisement" of individual citizens at the
hands of powerful corporations and faceless bureaucracies.[59] Eckersley asserts
that constitutional environmental rights have the potential to "challenge and
gradually transform not only the form, style, and content of democratic
deliberation but also society's relationship with nature."[60] Improved enforcement of environmental law, which demonstrates that the law applies to
everyone, could enhance respect for the rule of law, which is undermined by
weak or selective enforcement.

STRENGTHEN ENVIRONMENTAL JUSTICE

At the heart of constitutional law is "the idea of protecting minorities from
majoritarian actions," protecting the weak from the strong.[61] Both nationally
and internationally, there is a growing body of evidence that a disproportionate burden of harm from environmental degradation – toxic pollution,
overfishing, habitat destruction, etc. – is borne by people who are poor,
belong to ethnic minorities, or are otherwise disadvantaged.[62] In theory,
constitutional recognition of the right to a healthy environment could increase
the probability of effective protection; provide vulnerable individuals, affected
communities, and civil society with a powerful tool for holding governments
accountable; and offer remedies to people whose rights are being violated.
According to Fredman, "Human rights also constitute a focus for political
and grassroots campaigning, giving a specific and authoritative legitimacy to
demands for their fulfillment."[63] Similarly, lawsuits asserting the right to a
healthy environment "can be used as mobilizing tools to gather community
support and momentum on issues of environmental justice."[64]

EDUCATION AND PUBLIC VALUES

A country's constitution is intended to express, enshrine, and protect the
most cherished and fundamental values of its people. Scholars have long
recognized that constitutions both reflect and shape these values.[65] Brandl
and Bungert write that "constitutional provisions provide a model character
for the citizenry to follow, and they influence and guide public discourse
and behaviour."[66] As Kiss writes, "Every Constitution has an educational
value. Constitutionalization of fundamental rights and freedoms has undoubtedly contributed to securing for them general acceptance and observ-
ance."[67] The public tends to be more familiar with constitutional principles
than the dull details of laws and regulations.[68] Constitutional recognition of
the right to a healthy environment would both reflect and reinforce the

public's growing concerns about the severity of today's environmental problems, underscoring the fact that a healthy environment is a fundamental element of human well-being, and a prerequisite to the full enjoyment of other human rights.[69]

Critiques of the Constitutional Right to a Healthy Environment

Not everyone is convinced that granting constitutional protection to the right to a healthy environment is a good idea.[70] Opponents argue that the right is

- vague
- absolute
- redundant
- undemocratic
- neither enforceable nor justiciable
- going to open the floodgates to litigation
- problematic in that it may divert attention from other more important rights
- anthropocentric
- a form of cultural imperialism
- unduly focused on individuals
- likely to be ineffective
- capable of generating false hopes.

In many cases, the arguments made by opponents of constitutional environmental rights apply equally to all human rights. Each of these potential drawbacks will be examined in detail below, along with rebuttals from proponents of constitutional environmental rights.

VAGUE

A common criticism of constitutionalizing the right to a healthy environment is that there is too much uncertainty about what level of environmental quality will be protected.[71] Alston argues that for some new rights, such as the right to a healthy environment, "it is their chameleon-like quality that has facilitated the degree of consensus support they have received."[72] This concern is exacerbated by the fact that many different adjectives are used to describe the environmental right in national constitutions, including "healthy," "adequate," "clean," "safe," and "ecologically balanced." There is also uncertainty about the beneficiaries of the right and who bears the duties correlated with the right. Are future generations included among prospective beneficiaries?

Do the duties imposed by the right extend to private actors as well as government? As a result of these uncertainties, opponents speculate, the right will be meaningless, difficult to implement, and ineffective.[73]

The rebuttal to this critique is that constitutional provisions are by necessity brief and inherently vague. The right to a healthy environment is no more vague or uncertain than any other human right, from freedom of expression to protection from cruel and unusual punishment. The precise meaning of these words and phrases emerges over time, shaped by the legal, political, social, and cultural context of a particular nation. As well, it is the nature of human rights that they are dynamic rather than static, evolving with human values. Less than a century ago, women, Aboriginal people, African Americans, and other groups were denied basic human rights.

In the case of the right to a healthy environment, quantitative standards will change over time in response to the development of scientific knowledge and technological progress. As Kiss and Shelton write, "The variability of implementation demands imposed by the right to environment in response to different threats over time and place does not undermine the concept of the right, but merely takes into consideration its dynamic character."[74] For example, the so-called safe level of exposure to toxic substances such as benzene and lead has fallen repeatedly in recent decades.[75] Ambiguity can be an advantage because it provides flexibility in filling gaps in legislation, dealing with emerging issues, and responding to new knowledge in the fields of science, health, and ecology.[76]

Absolute (a Trump Card)

Critics warn that the constitutional right to a healthy environment will introduce an absolutist approach whereby environmental concerns always trump other societal interests. For example, they speculate, an absolutist interpretation of the right to a healthy environment could enable activists to halt most forms of economic development. In developing nations, there are concerns that the right to a healthy environment could trump the right to development. Lazarus fears that creating competing moral claims (e.g., right to a healthy environment vs. right to property) could create a polarized atmosphere where "compromise and deliberative discussion are difficult."[77]

These arguments appear to lack merit, in that rights are rarely absolute and are almost always balanced against other rights. The aim of environmental rights is not to eliminate the balancing of competing constitutional rights but, rather, to produce greater weight for environmental considerations vis-à-vis rights such as property and freedom of commerce. As Beatty observes with respect to constitutional rights, "Even when the language of the text is strong and categorical, it is never understood to provide an absolute, ironclad guarantee."[78] Just as the right to free speech is not a right to say anything at any time or place, the constitutional right to a healthy environment would not be the right to pollution-free air, pure water, and pristine ecosystems. Free speech is governed by laws prohibiting or restricting pornography, hate literature, false advertising, excessive noise, and other forms of communication. These laws achieve a balance by protecting other rights and interests. Rather than trumping development, the right to a healthy environment would compel, or at least increase the likelihood of, sustainable development.

REDUNDANT

The argument that the constitutional right to a healthy environment is redundant has two aspects. The first is based on the proposition that other human rights – the right to life, the right to health, and others – can be given a green interpretation in cases involving environmental harm. The second is based on the notion that existing environmental laws are adequate and that, at least in common-law nations, tort law already offers the same remedies for environmental harm that a right to a healthy environment could provide.[79] Among the established human rights that could potentially be used to address environmental degradation and adverse health effects are the rights to life, health, security of the person, privacy and the inviolability of home and family, property, and equality. Advantages of greening current human rights include widespread acceptance of the binding legal nature of these rights and the existence of established courts, commissions, and other bodies for seeking redress.[80]

On the other hand, the scope for pressing existing human rights into the service of environmental ends is circumscribed. Some situations, such as those calling for preventive or precautionary measures or where Nature rather than human health is threatened, cannot be shoehorned comfortably into existing human rights boxes. There are limits to judicial creativity, and legitimate concerns about relying on judicial activism. Extensive judicial activism (e.g., expanding other rights to address environmental harms in the absence of express recognition of the right to a healthy environment) could bolster a key argument against constitutional environmental rights – that shifting environmental decision making from legislatures to courts is undemocratic.

At the end of the day, greening other constitutional rights need not be considered mutually exclusive to recognizing the right to a healthy environment. Given the severity of the global environmental crisis, it would seem that both greening existing human rights and expanding the family of rights to include the right to a healthy environment are potentially useful approaches.[81]

As to the second part of the redundancy argument, it is true that there has been a proliferation of environmental laws and policies in the past four decades in many nations. While progress has been made on some issues, environmental laws and policies have failed to solve many of the problems they were intended to address, as demonstrated by the ongoing and pervasive problems of pollution, climate change, resource depletion, and declining biodiversity.[82] Hayward is correct in concluding that even in nations with strong laws governing both human rights and environmental protection, "a substantial environmental right with constitutional force would not be nugatory."[83]

Undermines Democracy by Transferring Power to Courts

Opponents of constitutional recognition of human rights argue that it is fundamentally undemocratic to transfer decision-making power from elected legislators to unelected judges.[84] This argument is based on the view that the legislature's role is determining *what* should be done and the courts' role is limited to reviewing *how* things are done.[85] In other words, courts ought to focus on process, not substance, and should avoid disturbing the decisions of elected governments about the distribution of risks, costs, and benefits within society. With specific reference to the environmental context, Sax warned that courts "should not be authorized to function as an environmental czar against the clear wishes of the public and its elected representatives."[86] Brandl and Bungert describe the potential for costly uncertainty due to the "destabilizing juridification of environmental politics."[87] Furthermore, these critics argue, courts lack the technical expertise and resources required to address complex environmental issues and are the wrong place for resolving polycentric issues involving conflicting values and diverse interests.[88] Eleftheriadis asserts that the ambiguity in the phrase "right to a healthy environment" could make it easy for judges to substitute their judgment regarding environmental policy for that of elected policy makers.[89] Some judges share these concerns. In dismissing a recent lawsuit against chemical giant E.I. du Pont, an American judge wrote: "The potential effects of these chemicals on human health are of great public concern. Issues of institutional competence, however, caution against judicial involvement in regulatory affairs. Courts are designed to remediate, not regulate."[90]

On the other hand, courts have a legitimate supervisory role in constitutional democracies, and elements of that role involve defending the rule of law; ensuring that government laws, policies, and actions are within their constitutionally defined jurisdiction; and adjudicating claims that constitutional rights have been violated. Courts have extensive experience and expertise in defining and refining the parameters of human rights.[91] The judicial role may constrain the legislature but does not disable it. As well, courts rarely have the final word in disputes about human rights because dialogues with legislatures are more likely.[92] Constitutional protection for human rights enhances, rather than undermines, democracy and accountability.[93] In the words of Dershowitz, "Rights serve as a check on democracy, and democracy serves as a check on rights."[94]

In response to concerns about technical expertise, it should be acknowledged that courts are adept at filtering complex facts in a broad range of contexts, from DNA evidence in criminal cases to Byzantine corporate structures in commercial litigation. Elected representatives are no more likely than judges to have the technical, medical, or scientific expertise required to resolve complicated environmental challenges.

UNENFORCEABLE/UNJUSTICIABLE

Some scholars argue that constitutional rights to a healthy environment are unenforceable because the provisions are not "self-executing."[95] A constitutional provision is not self-executing if it requires enabling legislation in order to define its parameters, be implemented, and be enforced. More broadly, the enforceability of a specific constitutional right to a healthy environment will depend on the wording of the right, other constitutional provisions, and the overall legal context of a particular nation.

Other scholars claim that issues raised by the right to a healthy environment are not justiciable, meaning not "appropriate or suitable for adjudication by a court."[96] For many years, the prevailing opinion was that social, economic, and cultural rights (and, by extension, the right to a healthy environment) ought not to be justiciable.[97] The main arguments were that such rights would subvert democracy by allowing judges to substitute their opinion for elected legislators; the judicial system lacked the capacity to resolve complex, polycentric disputes; and the concept of social, economic, and environmental rights was too vague.[98] According to critics, it is the exclusive purview of the legislature to determine how a government's budget is allocated, and courts have no jurisdiction or competence in this field. The concern is that these rights may represent open-ended claims on societal resources and that judicial decisions allocating those resources could be made without consideration of other societal priorities.[99] Leading constitutional scholar Cass Sunstein once claimed that courts are incapable of properly enforcing social, economic, and environmental rights because they cannot create government programs and lack the resources to oversee implementation of their orders. He argued that it would be a "large mistake, possibly a disaster," to include positive rights, including the right to a healthy environment, in the new constitutions of Eastern European nations.[100] Similarly, writing about South Africa's new constitution, Davis warned that justiciable social and economic rights would act as a Trojan horse for politics to enter the courtroom, placing an undue amount of power in the hands of unelected judges.[101]

Today, however, a growing number of scholars – including Sunstein and Davis – believe that economic, social, and environmental rights ought to be considered justiciable.[102] Courts apply the principles of proportionality and reasonableness in cases that call for a careful balance between the economic and social rights of individuals and the public interest (recognizing societal priorities and limited government resources).[103] The acclaimed decision of South Africa's Constitutional Court in *Grootboom*, a case about the right to housing, demonstrated that "the legal enforcement of social and economic rights isn't so different from the protection that is provided by the more traditional political and civil guarantees."[104] The *Grootboom* case involved a group of homeless people asserting their constitutional right to housing. South Africa's Constitutional Court did not require the government to address the needs of the specific individuals who brought the lawsuit, but ruled the government's existing efforts to address homelessness were inadequate. The court ordered the government to develop and implement a comprehensive and effective strategy to fulfill the right of access to housing.[105] Innovative and successful judicial interpretation and application of social and economic rights in a number of different countries appear to be answering many, if not all, of the objections that were raised against their implementation and enforcement. In light of these judicial developments, Sunstein and Davis reversed their opposition and now endorse the justiciability of social and economic rights.[106] Ramcharan concludes that "there is no doubt that the era of justiciability of economic, social, and cultural rights has arrived."[107]

In addition, Schwartz points out that constitutions are not merely legal documents but are also political, social, and moral instruments that reflect a nation's hopes and aspirations for its future.[108] From this perspective, even if concerns about enforceability and justiciability are legitimate, there may be other compelling reasons for including the right to a healthy environment in constitutions.

OPENS THE FLOODGATES TO LITIGATION

An argument at the opposite end of the spectrum from unenforceability and/ or lack of justiciability of the right to a healthy environment is the fear that constitutionalizing this right would open the floodgates to litigation, imped-ing economic development and exacerbating the backlogs already facing many courts.[109] Hayward responds that "professed worries about opening the floodgates to litigious busybodies who threaten to undermine the legitim-ate activities of hard-pressed businesspersons or to overload the courts ring very hollow in view of the prodigious expense involved in engaging in such a pastime."[110] Other significant constraints on litigation include restrictions on access to courts (standing), long delays, and the risk of losing.

THE PROLIFERATION OF NEW RIGHTS WATERS DOWN EXISTING RIGHTS

Another argument against the recognition of the right to a healthy environ-ment is that doing so would diminish, devalue, or water down the importance of other, more basic human rights.[111] As Miller states, "A plethora of rights might lead to a depreciation of those which we value most."[112] Etzioni criti-cizes "rights inflation," claiming it devalues the fundamental rights of liberty and equality.[113] While acknowledging the necessity of a dynamic approach to human rights, Alston warns of "the haphazard, almost anarchic manner in which this expansion is being achieved. Indeed, some such rights seem to have been literally conjured up, in the dictionary sense of being brought into existence as if by magic."[114]

Conversely, there are scholars who believe that recognizing new rights, such as the right to a healthy environment, will complement, enrich, and enhance pre-existing rights.[115] Proponents of the right to a healthy environ-ment point out that human rights evolve over time, as demonstrated by the abolition of slavery, the evolution of Aboriginal rights, the recognition of women as persons, the demise of state-sanctioned racial segregation, and the growing recognition of same-sex marriage. The UN General Assembly has articulated guidelines for new human rights, concluding that such rights should be consistent with existing international human rights law; be funda-mental and based on the inherent dignity of the human person; be sufficiently precise to create clear rights and obligations; provide effective implementation machinery; and attract broad international support.[116] Given that the right to a healthy environment meets all of these criteria, it seems odd to think that it ought not be constitutionally recognized because there is an unwritten limit on the number of human rights that can be protected effectively.

ANTHROPOCENTRIC

Both procedural and substantive versions of environmental rights are some-times criticized because of their anthropocentric approach, allegedly focusing on the environment solely as an instrument for providing human health and well-being.[117] Scholars, philosophers, and activists argue that because the environment has intrinsic value, ecosystems should be protected, rather than just one species *(Homo sapiens)* within an ecosystem. In other words, Nature itself ought to be protected, and human rights approaches, by their very nature, miss the mark.[118]

The notion that Nature itself ought to have legal rights dates back many centuries.[119] The idea gained widespread notoriety in 1972 when Stone wrote a seminal article called "Should Trees Have Standing?" in which he argued that there was no legal barrier to granting rights to Nature given that other non-human entities such as ships and corporations had legal rights conferred upon them.[120] The idea attracted additional attention when endorsed by Justice Douglas of the US Supreme Court in his dissenting opinion in a pi-oneering environmental lawsuit.[121] Nash asserts that the extension of legal rights to Nature represents the logical evolution of rights.[122] Sunstein argues that animals already enjoy some legal rights, at least in some nations.[123]

Scholars have discussed and debated, at length, various means of ascrib-ing rights to Nature, but profound questions remain.[124] Should rights be limited to sentient creatures or held by all living organisms, including bacteria and viruses? Should rights be extended to non-living elements of Nature, such as stones, rivers, or mountains? How would these rights be exercised – by specially appointed guardians or by ordinary citizens acting on behalf of Nature? Is extending rights to Nature merely an extension of the anthropo-centric approach, since humans determine who or what should enjoy rights, and what those rights will entail?[125] Eckersley concludes that "rights discourse becomes considerably strained (in all its dimensions) when we come to consider ecological entities."[126]

Until recently, these debates could be considered largely philosophical. The new constitutions of Ecuador and Bolivia, with their pioneering provisions recognizing the rights of Nature, mark a turning point in the debate by trans-forming abstract concepts into legally binding rights. Shelton asserts that "by developing a holistic, rights-based approach to environmental quality, long-term soundness of environmental conditions and concern for biological diversity can be brought into relationship with human rights ... reflecting the reality of human connectedness with all natural systems."[127] Chapters 6 to 12 will explore whether the constitutional protection of a human right to a healthy environment has a "fortuitous spill-over effect to non-humans."[128]

CULTURAL IMPERIALISM

Human rights are occasionally accused of being a form of cultural imperial-ism in which Western values are imposed on other societies and cultures.[129] It can be argued that the constitutional right to a healthy environment "may suffer from cultural relativism, particularly from a North-South perspective, and lack the universal value normally thought to be inherent in human rights."[130] Mushkat suggests that the right to a healthy environment lacks legitimacy in some Asian nations, including China.[131]

Is this critique well-grounded with regard to protection of the environ-ment? International environmental instruments such as the 1992 *Rio Dec-laration on Environment and Development* have been endorsed by virtually every nation in the world. Environmental protection is supported as a fundamental value by all of the world's religions.[132] As Subedi writes, to claim that human rights are a Western concept "is to ignore the history and contributions of other nations."[133] Chapter 3 assesses the extent to which environmental protection provisions, including the right to a healthy environment, have been incorporated into the constitutions of nations South and North, East and West, Muslim and Christian, thus addressing the question of whether the right to a healthy environment is a strictly or predominantly Western concept.

EXCESSIVE FOCUS ON THE INDIVIDUAL

A general critique of human rights is that they focus excessively on individuals at the expense of the broader public interest.[134] The focus on rights is accom-panied by a lack of attention to responsibility, leading to erosion of com-munity.[135] In the environmental context, Handl suggests that a focus on individual rights is inappropriate because the environment is a public good.[136] Weiss argues that the obligation to protect the planet deserves equal billing with the right to a healthy environment.[137] Similarly, Swaigen, Woods, and others argue that environmental duties and responsibilities (e.g., the duty to conserve natural resources) would be more effective than rights.[138]

The rebuttal to these criticisms is that environmental damage and degradation harm both individuals and the public interest. According to Raz, "At least some constitutional rights are primarily means of formal or informal institutional protection of collective goods."[139] As well, in law, there can be no right without a corresponding responsibility. As Cranston states, "Unless certain interests give rise to clear corresponding duties, they do not qualify as rights."[140]

LIKELY TO BE INEFFECTIVE

Critics claim that constitutional environmental rights would be ineffective.[141] Scholars have long recognized that there can be major gaps between laws on paper and laws in action, even constitutional laws.[142] Ruhl writes that, "in itself, a constitutional amendment would not save a single wetland or forest; it would remove no cement plants or automobile exhausts; and it would clean no streams."[143] A strong argument can be made that problems related to political economy – capitalism's focus on limitless growth, the relentless and sometimes reckless pursuit of new technologies, harmful forms of production, and pervasive wealth inequity – are the root cause of society's environmental crisis and are not addressed by a constitutional right.[144] The legal system tends to favour those with education, money, and power, rather than the poor and marginalized communities that suffer the disproportionate burden of environmental harm.[145] The opponents of stronger environmental regulation are powerful and organized, while the prospective beneficiaries are weak and diffuse. Scheingold argues that misperceptions about the power of rights have led social movements to focus on legal tactics instead of potentially more effective political strategies.[146] Another argument used to suggest the ineffectiveness of a constitutional right to a healthy environment is that the most pressing environmental problems facing humanity today are global in scope. Therefore, critics suggest, individual rights are of limited utility in addressing issues like climate change or the loss of biodiversity. Finally, constitutional rights focus on constraining or compelling government actions, when it is arguably the activities of private parties, both individual and corporate, that cause the lion's share of environmental harm.

In response to these arguments, it must be acknowledged that constitutional rights are not a silver bullet for today's environmental problems. As Epp concludes, "Rights are not magical solutions to any or all problems."[147]

Despite constitutional rights to equality, the pernicious effects of racism, sexism, and other forms of discrimination continue to adversely affect many individuals in contemporary society. Yet surely rights have contributed to some amelioration of the wrongs they are intended to address.[148] As well, there are experts who believe that a rights-based approach to environmental protection is the only effective alternative to today's market-based approach, which is failing to adequately protect the environment.[149] Cullet argues that economic globalization needs to be counterbalanced by the globalization of the right to a healthy environment.[150] Ultimately, the effectiveness of constitutional environmental rights should not be judged on theoretical arguments but on practical experience and empirical evidence.

FALSE HOPES

An argument related to ineffectiveness is that constitutional environmental rights could create false expectations in nations where little environmental progress is likely in the short term.[151] East Germany and other communist nations had constitutions that recognized the right to a healthy environment and mandated both the state and citizens to protect Nature. These constitutional provisions had little or no positive effect.[152] Brandl and Bungert suggest that empty promises "may be pernicious to the reputation of the constitution and detract from the credibility of the legal system."[153]

For many human rights there is a wide gulf between what has been promised and what is being delivered, both globally and locally. However, this argument cannot be used to obviate the need to recognize and protect the right to a healthy environment. The fact that the right to life or the right to food is not universally respected does not mean that the rights themselves ought to be rescinded or ignored. All human rights face implementation challenges, and the right to a healthy environment is no exception. In some nations, the right to a healthy environment and other social and economic rights may represent emerging values and aspirations rather than a concrete reality, at least in the short term.

Conclusion

At the confluence of human rights and the environment are many contentious issues. This chapter briefly highlighted some of these ongoing controversies, which have important consequences for the normative basis of environmental rights. In summary, the right to a healthy environment clearly meets the criteria for recognition as a human right. This right is both individual and collective and includes aspects of both positive (welfare) and negative (liberty) rights, bringing the usefulness of these distinctions into question. On paper, at least, constitutional recognition of the right to a healthy environment appears to offer a host of potential benefits for human and ecological well-being as well as democracy. Many of the arguments marshalled against the right to a healthy environment have been levelled at other human rights and found wanting. All human rights are phrased in brief, general terms whose meaning evolves over time. Rights are almost always balanced against competing rights, so absolutism is a non-issue. Whether and to what extent the potential benefits and drawbacks of constitutionalizing the right to a healthy environment will be borne out are questions that are best answered with empirical evidence. On-the-ground experience with the right to a healthy environment will shine new light on the longstanding theoretical arguments discussed in this chapter.

3
The Prevalence and Enforceability of Environmental Provisions in National Constitutions

While Chapter 2 addressed many of the philosophical and theoretical questions about the right to a healthy environment, this chapter explores the extent to which the right has gained legal recognition in national constitutions since the early 1970s. There have been previous surveys of environmental provisions in national constitutions. Edith Brown Weiss's groundbreaking book *In Fairness to Future Generations*, published in 1989, listed environmental provisions from fifty-three constitutions.[1] In 1994, Fatma Zohra Ksentini, the UN's Special Rapporteur on Human Rights and the Environment, listed sixty-one constitutions with environmental provisions in her final report.[2] In 1998, Don Anton, of Australia's Environmental Defenders Office, inventoried constitutional provisions related to the environment or natural resources from 127 nations.[3] In recent years, similar surveys have been published.[4] These efforts suffer from several critical problems in that they are out of date, are not comprehensive, or do not address the fundamental issues of enforceability or limits imposed by other constitutional provisions.

To build a solid foundation for analyzing the effects of environmental provisions in constitutions, it is necessary to answer the following questions:

- How many national constitutions incorporate provisions related to environmental protection?
- How many constitutions specifically recognize that individuals have a right to a healthy environment?
- What other types of environmental protection provisions are found in constitutions?
- When were these constitutional provisions enacted?
- Are there limits imposed on the right to a healthy environment? Are these limits similar to, or different from, limits on other human rights protected by constitutions?

● Are the environmental protection provisions enshrined in national constitutions enforceable, at least on paper?

Professor Tim Hayward, author of *Constitutional Environmental Rights*,
acknowledges that "the exact number [of nations with constitutions recognizing environmental rights] is somewhat difficult to determine" because of
uncertainties created by the "language, positioning, and framing of constitutional provisions."[5] And as Brandl and Bungert point out, "the efficacy of
a particular environmental constitutional provision is directly related to the
overall character and conception of the constitution."[6]

Another significant challenge involved in carrying out this kind of assessment is that constitutions in some nations are often amended. Frequent revisions can make it challenging to locate current versions of constitutions, a
problem exacerbated by the many different languages in which constitutions
are written. In recent years, new constitutions or substantial constitutional
amendments were passed in Bangladesh, Belgium, Bhutan, Bolivia, the Dominican Republic, Ecuador, Egypt, Jamaica, Kenya, Luxembourg, the Maldives,
Mexico, Montenegro, Morocco, Myanmar, Nepal, South Sudan, Thailand,
and Turkmenistan. Constitutional amendments or new constitutions have
been proposed or are in the process of being enacted in many nations, including Iceland, Tonga, Turkey, the United Kingdom, Uzbekistan, Zambia, and
Zimbabwe. In some nations – e.g., Cyprus, Nepal, Somalia, and Sudan –
interim constitutions are in place. To ensure a consistent approach, the analysis is based on constitutions that were legally in force as of 1 August 2011.

In addition, this chapter is limited to the explicit language of national
constitutions in the 193 countries that are members of the United Nations.[7]
It does not analyze environmental provisions in supranational agreements
(e.g., the *African Charter on Human and Peoples' Rights*) or subnational constitutions (e.g., provincial or state constitutions in federal nations, including
Argentina, Canada, and the United States). Also excluded from this chapter
is judicial interpretation of constitutional provisions that relate, directly or
indirectly, to environmental protection. As will be discussed in Chapters 6
to 11, courts in some nations (e.g., India, Italy) have liberally interpreted
other constitutional provisions, such as the right to life, as encompassing
environmental protection. As a result, this chapter's descriptions of the extent
of constitutional protection for the environment are inherently conservative.
For additional details of the methodology employed, see Appendix 1.

The Prevalence of Environmental Provisions in National Constitutions

Over the past four decades, there has been a remarkable and ongoing shift toward constitutional recognition of the importance of protecting the environment. At the time of the *Stockholm Declaration* in 1972, there were no constitutions that incorporated environmental rights and only a handful of constitutions that imposed modest environmental responsibilities. Today, three-quarters of the world's constitutions (147 out of 193) include explicit references to environmental rights and/or environmental responsibilities (see Figure 3.1). This majority holds for nations belonging to the Organisation for Economic Co-operation and Development, the Commonwealth, La Francophonie, and even the Organization of Petroleum Exporting Countries. The majority applies in all regions, including Africa, the Americas (except North America), Asia-Pacific, Europe, and the Middle East/Central Asia. Appendix 2 provides the current constitutional provisions related to environmental protection from the 147 nations examined in this study. It is posted on the Internet on the following site: http://hdl.handle.net/2429/36469.

A handful of nations included rudimentary constitutional provisions related to protecting natural beauty or conserving natural resources prior to the rise in global environmental consciousness in the late 1960s and early 1970s. For example, the constitutions of Italy (1948), Malta (1964), Guatemala (1965), and San Marino (1974) share similar provisions requiring that the state "safeguard natural beauty and the historical and artistic heritage of the nation."[8] In a similar vein, the constitutions of four Middle Eastern nations – Kuwait (1962), the United Arab Emirates (1971), Bahrain (1973), and the Syrian Arab Republic (1973) – contain provisions requiring the protection, preservation, and proper use of natural resources.[9] Finally, it should be noted that for the purposes of this study, the purely symbolic constitutions of the Soviet-bloc communist nations were not included, although many contained environmental provisions.[10]

The first substantial provisions focusing on the protection of the environment appear in the constitutions of Switzerland (1971), Panama (1972), Greece (1975), Papua New Guinea (1975), India (1976), and Portugal (1976). Every year since the 1972 *Stockholm Declaration*, at least one nation has written or amended its constitution to include or strengthen provisions related to environmental protection. During the 1980s, the leaders in greening constitutions were nations in Latin America and Western Europe. The

FIGURE 3.1

Map of nations with environmental protection provisions in their constitutions

Nations with environmental protection
provisions in their constitutions as of 2011

Nations without environmental protection
provisions in their constitutions as of 2011

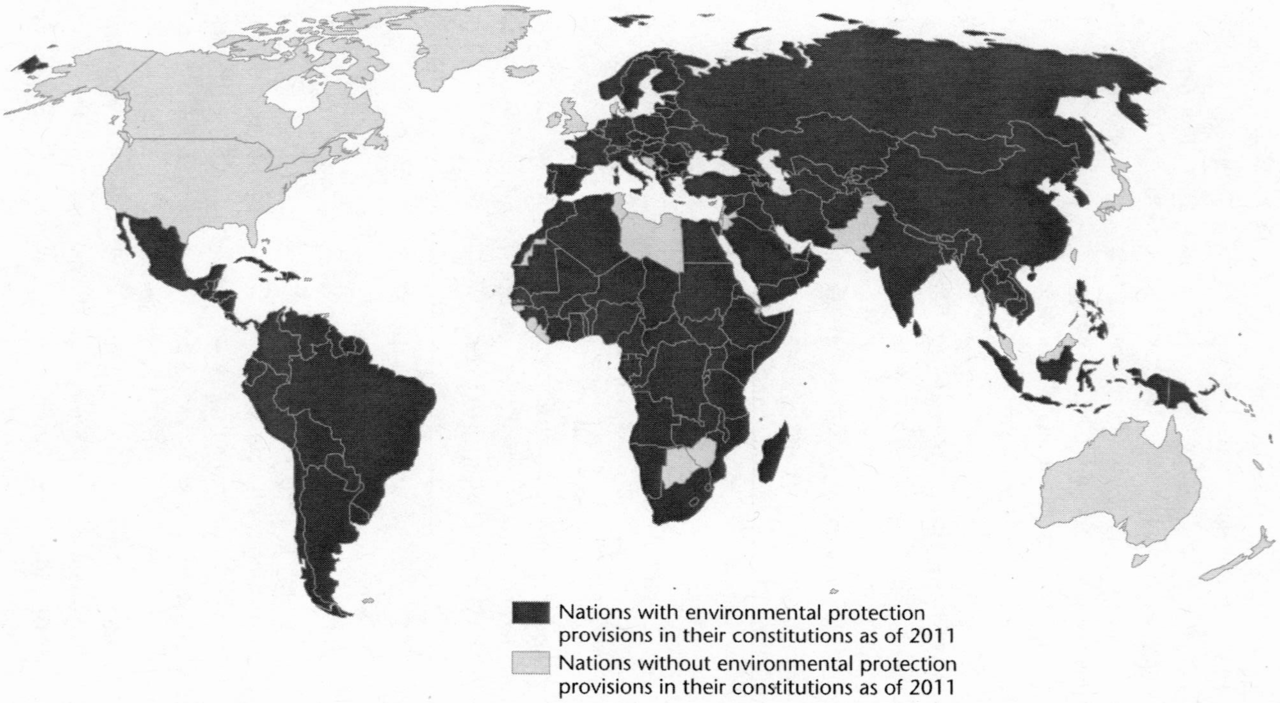

trend accelerated in the early 1990s, led by African and Eastern European nations. This pattern is consistent with other observations about patterns of constitutionalization. Hirschl described five scenarios involving broader political events that led to constitutional changes – post–Second World War reconstruction; former colonies achieving independence; the transition from authoritarian or quasi-democratic regimes to democracy; the dual transition to both democracy and a market economy; the incorporation of international law into domestic law – and a "no apparent transition" scenario, in which constitutional reform is not accompanied by any fundamental changes in political or economic regimes.[11]

The peak year for the incorporation of environmental rights and responsibilities into national constitutions was 1992, with new environmental provisions included in eighteen constitutions that year alone. Not coincidentally, 1992 was a peak year in terms of global attention to environmental issues, marked by the Earth Summit in Rio, which attracted an unprecedented number of heads of state to an international environmental meeting.[12] Broken down by decade, the incorporation of environmental protection provisions in national constitutions is as follows:

Pre-1970	5	1980-89	22	2000-09	27
1971-79	19	1990-99	68	2010-11	6

A year-by-year breakdown is provided in Table 3.1.

There are forty-six UN members whose constitutions are silent on the matter of environmental protection.[13] Among these nations one can discern several political, geographic, and legal patterns. The United Kingdom is one of the forty-six, as are twenty-nine nations that are former British colonies.[14] Almost all (eleven out of thirteen) of the English-speaking nations of the Americas are among the nations without environmental provisions in their constitutions.[15] Belize and Jamaica are the sole exceptions. In contrast, all of the twenty-two non-English-speaking nations in the Americas have incorporated environmental protection provisions into their constitutions.[16] It is also noteworthy that twenty-four of the forty-six nations without constitutional environmental provisions are small island states.[17]

National legal systems provide another pattern that partially explains the variation in the presence of constitutional environmental provisions. The UN's 193 member states can be divided into fifteen categories according to the type of legal system.[18] There is a striking difference between common and

Table 3.1

Year that environmental provisions were first included in national constitutions

Year	Countries
1948	Italy
1959	Madagascar
1962	Kuwait
1964	Malta
1965	Guatemala
1971	Switzerland, United Arab Emirates
1972	Panama
1973	Bahrain, Syrian Arab Republic
1974	San Marino
1975	Greece, Papua New Guinea
1976	Cuba, India, Portugal
1977	Tanzania
1978	Micronesia, Spain, Sri Lanka, Thailand, Yemen
1979	Iran, Peru
1980	Chile, Guyana, Vanuatu, Vietnam
1981	Belize, Palau
1982	China, Equatorial Guinea, Honduras, Turkey
1983	El Salvador, Netherlands
1984	Austria, Ecuador
1986	Nicaragua
1987	Haiti, Philippines, South Korea, Suriname, Sweden
1988	Brazil
1989	Hungary
1990	Benin, Croatia, Guinea, Mozambique, Namibia, São Tomé and Príncipe
1991	Bulgaria, Burkina Faso, Colombia, Gabon, Laos, Macedonia, Mauritania, Slovenia, Zambia
1992	Angola, Cape Verde, Czech Republic, Estonia, Ghana, Lithuania, Mali, Mexico, Mongolia, Norway, Paraguay, Saudi Arabia, Slovak Republic, Togo, Turkmenistan, Uzbekistan
1993	Andorra, Cambodia, Kyrgyzstan, Lesotho, Russia, Seychelles
1994	Argentina, Belarus, Belgium, Costa Rica, Germany, Malawi, Moldova, Tajikistan
1995	Armenia, Azerbaijan, Ethiopia, Finland, Georgia, Kazakhstan, Uganda
1996	Algeria, Cameroon, Chad, Gambia, Niger, Oman, South Africa, Ukraine, Uruguay
1997	Eritrea, Poland
1998	Albania, Latvia, North Korea
1999	Nigeria, Venezuela
2000	Cote d'Ivoire (Ivory Coast), Indonesia
2001	Comoros, Senegal
2002	Bolivia, Congo-Brazzaville, East Timor
2003	Qatar, Romania, Rwanda
2004	Afghanistan, Central African Republic, Somalia
2005	Burundi, Congo (Democratic Republic of the), France, Iraq, Sudan, Swaziland
2006	Nepal, Serbia
2007	Egypt, Luxembourg, Montenegro
2008	Bhutan, Maldives, Myanmar
2010	Dominican Republic, Kenya
2011	Bangladesh, Jamaica, Morocco, South Sudan

civil law nations in the extent to which they do or do not incorporate environmental provisions into their constitutions. Of the twenty-three nations employing exclusively common-law systems, only three have environmental provisions in their constitutions.[19] This reflects the Anglo-American caution regarding constitutional recognition of social and economic rights.[20] While the constitutions of most former British colonies contain bills of rights, these bills adopt the classic liberal approach to human rights – i.e., they focus on civil and political rights while economic, social, and cultural rights are not protected (except for property). In contrast, among the seventy-seven nations with exclusively civil law systems, seventy-two have environmental provisions in their constitutions.[21] Among the twenty-five nations with mixed legal systems that combine civil law and customary law, twenty-three have environmental provisions in their constitutions.[22] The remaining types of legal mono-systems and mixed systems fall in between the civil and common-law extremes.[23]

The distribution of constitutional environmental provisions across the world provides a convincing rebuttal to the charge of cultural imperialism levelled by critics who assert that environmentalism is a Western conception. The 147 nations whose constitutions contain provisions related to environmental protection include a majority of nations in Central and South America, Africa, Asia, the Middle East, and Eastern Europe. In fact, it is in the Western nations – the United States, Canada, the United Kingdom, Australia, and others – where constitutional recognition of the value of environmental protection lags.

It is often mistakenly observed that virtually every constitution enacted or amended since 1970 has included either environmental rights or environmental responsibilities.[24] In fact, eleven nations that wrote or amended their constitutions in the 1970s and 1980s failed to include environmental provisions.[25] For example, Canada, despite pleas from environmentalists, did not include any environmental provisions in its 1982 constitution. An additional twenty-nine nations whose constitutions remain silent on the matter of environmental protection have written or amended their constitutions since 1990 without including environmental provisions.[26] In 1996, an expert committee tasked with reviewing Ireland's constitution rejected the inclusion of a right to a healthy environment but recommended inclusion of a government duty to protect the environment.[27] The Irish constitution has been amended nine times since the report but still lacks any environmental protection provisions.[28] In other nations, such as the United States and Denmark, it is extremely difficult to amend the constitution. In summary, while 147 nations added environmental rights and/or responsibilities to their constitutions since the early 1970s, forty of the remaining forty-six nations bypassed the opportunity to do so despite carrying out other constitutional reforms.

Types of Environmental Protection Provisions in Constitutions

Constitutional provisions related to environmental protection can be grouped into five categories: government's responsibility to protect the environment; substantive rights to environmental quality; procedural environmental rights; individual responsibility to protect the environment; and a miscellaneous "catch-all" category of less common provisions. Each of these five categories is discussed in greater detail below, while Table 3.2 indicates the types of environmental provisions found in each of the 193 national constitutions.

GOVERNMENT'S ENVIRONMENTAL DUTIES

The most common form of constitutional provision related to environmental protection is the imposition of a duty on the government, found in 140 constitutions (see Table 3.2). In the majority of cases, the governmental duty is explicitly articulated, as in, for example, the *Instruments of Government Act*, which is part of Sweden's constitution:

> Article 2. ...
> The public institutions shall promote sustainable development leading to a good environment for present and future generations.

Portugal's constitution sets out the state's duty in more detail:

> Article 66(2) In order to ensure enjoyment of the right to the environment within an overall framework of sustainable development, acting via appropriate bodies and with the involvement and participation of citizens, the state shall be charged with:
>
> a) Preventing and controlling pollution and its effects and the harmful forms of erosion;
> b) Conducting and promoting town and country planning with a view to a correct location of activities, balanced social and economic development and the enhancement of the landscape;
> c) Creating and developing natural and recreational reserves and parks and classifying and protecting landscapes and places, in

TABLE 3.2

Types of environmental protection provisions in national constitutions

	Environmental protection provisions			
Country	Substantive right	Procedural right	Individual responsibility	Government duty
Afghanistan	N	N	N	Y
Albania	Y	Y	N	Y
Algeria	N	N	Y	N
Andorra	Y	N	N	Y
Angola	Y	N	N	Y
Antigua and Barbuda	N	N	N	N
Argentina	Y	Y	Y	Y
Armenia	Y	N	Y	Y
Australia	N	N	N	N
Austria	N	Y	N	Y
Azerbaijan	Y	Y	Y	Y
Bahamas	N	N	N	N
Bahrain	N	N	N	Y
Bangladesh	N	N	N	Y
Barbados	N	N	N	N
Belarus	Y	Y	Y	Y
Belgium	Y	N	N	Y
Belize	N	N	N	Y
Benin	Y	N	Y	Y
Bhutan	N	N	Y	Y
Bolivia	Y	Y	Y	Y
Bosnia and Herzegovina	N	N	N	N
Botswana	N	N	N	N
Brazil	Y	Y	Y	Y
Brunei Darussalam	N	N	N	N
Bulgaria	Y	N	Y	Y
Burkina Faso	Y	Y	Y	Y
Burundi	Y	N	N	Y
Cambodia	N	N	N	Y
Cameroon	Y	N	Y	Y
Canada	N	N	N	N
Cape Verde	Y	N	Y	Y
Central African Republic	Y	N	N	Y
Chad	Y	N	Y	Y
Chile	Y	Y	N	Y
China	N	N	N	Y
Colombia	Y	Y	Y	Y
Comoros	Y	N	Y	Y
Congo-Brazzaville	Y	N	Y	Y

▶

◀ Table 3.2

	Environmental protection provisions			
Country	Substantive right	Procedural right	Individual responsibility	Government duty
Congo, Democratic Republic of the	Y	N	Y	Y
Costa Rica	Y	Y	N	Y
Cote d'Ivoire	Y	N	Y	Y
Croatia	Y	N	Y	Y
Cuba	N	N	Y	Y
Cyprus	N	N	N	N
Czech Republic	Y	Y	Y	Y
Denmark	N	N	N	N
Djibouti	N	N	N	N
Dominica	N	N	N	N
Dominican Republic	Y	Y	Y	Y
East Timor	Y	N	Y	Y
Ecuador	Y	Y	Y	Y
Egypt	Y	N	Y	Y
El Salvador	Y	N	N	Y
Equatorial Guinea	N	N	N	Y
Eritrea	N	N	N	Y
Estonia	N	N	Y	N
Ethiopia	Y	Y	Y	Y
Fiji	N	N	N	N
Finland	Y	N	Y	Y
France	Y	Y	Y	Y
Gabon	Y	N	N	Y
Gambia	N	N	Y	Y
Georgia	Y	Y	Y	Y
Germany	N	N	N	Y
Ghana	N	N	Y	Y
Greece	Y	N	N	Y
Grenada	N	N	N	N
Guatemala	N	N	N	Y
Guinea	Y	N	N	Y
Guinea-Bissau	N	N	N	N
Guyana	Y	N	Y	Y
Haiti	N	N	Y	Y
Honduras	Y	N	N	Y
Hungary	Y	N	N	Y
Iceland	N	N	N	N
India	N	N	Y	Y
Indonesia	Y	N	N	Y
Iran	Y	N	N	Y

▶

◄ TABLE 3.2

Country	Environmental protection provisions			
	Substantive right	Procedural right	Individual responsibility	Government duty
Iraq	Y	N	N	Y
Ireland	N	N	N	N
Israel	N	N	N	N
Italy	N	N	N	Y
Jamaica	Y	N	Y	Y
Japan	N	N	N	N
Jordan	N	N	N	N
Kazakhstan	N	N	Y	Y
Kenya	Y	Y	Y	Y
Kiribati	N	N	N	N
Korea, North	N	N	N	Y
Korea, South	Y	N	Y	Y
Kuwait	N	N	N	Y
Kyrgyzstan	Y	N	N	Y
Laos	N	N	Y	N
Latvia	Y	Y	N	Y
Lebanon	N	N	N	N
Lesotho	N	N	N	Y
Liberia	N	N	N	N
Libya	N	N	N	N
Liechtenstein	N	N	N	N
Lithuania	N	N	Y	Y
Luxembourg	N	N	N	Y
Macedonia	Y	N	Y	Y
Madagascar	N	N	Y	Y
Malawi	Y	N	N	Y
Malaysia	N	N	N	N
Maldives	Y	N	Y	Y
Mali	Y	N	Y	Y
Malta	N	N	N	Y
Marshall Islands	N	N	N	N
Mauritania	Y	N	N	Y
Mauritius	N	N	N	N
Mexico	Y	N	N	Y
Micronesia	N	N	N	N
Moldova	Y	Y	Y	Y
Monaco	N	N	N	N
Mongolia	Y	N	Y	Y
Montenegro	Y	Y	Y	Y
Morocco	Y	N	N	Y
Mozambique	Y	N	Y	Y

►

◄ TABLE 3.2

Country	Environmental protection provisions			
	Substantive right	Procedural right	Individual responsibility	Government duty
Myanmar	N	N	Y	Y
Namibia	N	N	N	Y
Nauru	N	N	N	N
Nepal	Y	N	N	Y
Netherlands	Y	N	N	Y
New Zealand	N	N	N	N
Nicaragua	Y	N	N	Y
Niger	Y	N	Y	Y
Nigeria	N	N	N	Y
Norway	Y	Y	N	Y
Oman	N	N	N	Y
Pakistan	N	N	N	N
Palau	N	N	N	Y
Panama	Y	N	Y	Y
Papua New Guinea	N	N	Y	N
Paraguay	Y	N	N	Y
Peru	Y	N	N	Y
Philippines	Y	N	N	Y
Poland	Y	Y	Y	Y
Portugal	Y	Y	Y	Y
Qatar	N	N	N	Y
Romania	Y	N	Y	Y
Russia	Y	Y	Y	Y
Rwanda	Y	N	Y	Y
Saint Kitts and Nevis	N	N	N	N
Saint Lucia	N	N	N	N
Saint Vincent and the Grenadines	N	N	N	N
Samoa	N	N	N	N
San Marino	N	N	N	Y
São Tomé and Príncipe	Y	N	Y	Y
Saudi Arabia	N	N	N	Y
Senegal	Y	N	N	Y
Serbia	Y	Y	Y	Y
Seychelles	Y	N	Y	Y
Sierra Leone	N	N	N	N
Singapore	N	N	N	N
Slovakia	Y	Y	Y	Y
Slovenia	Y	N	Y	Y
Solomon Islands	N	N	N	N
Somalia	N	N	Y	Y

►

◄   TABLE 3.2

	Environmental protection provisions			
Country	Substantive right	Procedural right	Individual responsibility	Government duty
South Africa	Y	N	N	Y
South Sudan	Y	N	Y	Y
Spain	Y	N	Y	Y
Sri Lanka	N	N	Y	Y
Sudan	Y	N	Y	Y
Suriname	N	N	N	Y
Swaziland	N	N	Y	Y
Sweden	N	N	N	Y
Switzerland	N	N	N	Y
Syrian Arab Republic	N	N	Y	N
Tajikistan	N	N	Y	Y
Tanzania	N	N	Y	Y
Thailand	Y	Y	Y	Y
Togo	Y	N	N	Y
Tonga	N	N	N	N
Trinidad and Tobago	N	N	N	N
Tunisia	N	N	N	N
Turkey	Y	N	Y	Y
Turkmenistan	Y	N	N	Y
Tuvalu	N	N	N	N
Uganda	Y	N	Y	Y
Ukraine	Y	Y	Y	Y
United Arab Emirates	N	N	N	Y
United Kingdom	N	N	N	N
United States	N	N	N	N
Uruguay	N	N	Y	Y
Uzbekistan	N	N	Y	Y
Vanuatu	N	N	Y	N
Venezuela	Y	Y	Y	Y
Vietnam	N	N	Y	Y
Yemen	N	N	Y	Y
Zambia	N	N	N	Y
Zimbabwe	N	N	N	N
Total environmental provisions in constitutions	92	30	83	140

Note: Y = Yes, N = No.

such a way as to guarantee the conservation of nature and the preservation of cultural values and assets that are of historic or artistic interest;

d) Promoting the rational use of natural resources, while safe-guarding their ability to renew themselves and maintain ecological stability, with respect for the principle of inter-generational solidarity;

e) Acting in cooperation with local authorities, promoting the environmental quality of rural settlements and urban life, particularly on the architectural level and as regards the protection of historic zones;

f) Promoting the integration of environmental objectives into the various policies of a sectoral nature;

g) Promoting environmental education and respect for environmental values;

h) Ensuring that tax policy renders development compatible with the protection of the environment and the quality of life.

In a handful of constitutions there is no provision directly articulating the government's obligation to protect the environment, but there is recognition of the right to live in a healthy environment.[29] In these cases, the basic human rights concept that there can be no right in the absence of a corresponding duty can be used to infer that the government has an obligation to protect the environment.[30]

The likelihood that a governmental duty to protect the environment will be effective depends on its wording, its location in a constitution, whether it is enforceable by individuals and groups, and a host of factors external to the constitution. For example, it is unlikely that the environmental duty articulated in the preamble to the constitution of Belize will be effective because preambles generally are not legally binding.

Preamble
Whereas the people of Belize ...
    (e) require policies of state ... which protect the environment.

In contrast, legally binding and specific provisions, such as this excerpt from the constitution of Bhutan, are more likely to be effective in ensuring governments are held accountable:

Article 5. Environment

2. The Royal Government shall:

    (a) Protect, conserve and improve the pristine environment and safeguard the biodiversity of the country;

    (b) Prevent pollution and ecological degradation;

    (c) Secure ecologically balanced sustainable development while promoting justifiable economic and social development; and

    (d) Ensure a safe and healthy environment.

3. The Government shall ensure that, in order to conserve the country's natural resources and to prevent degradation of the ecosystem, a minimum of sixty percent of Bhutan's total land shall be maintained under forest cover for all time.[31]

SUBSTANTIVE ENVIRONMENTAL RIGHTS

Ninety-two national constitutions recognize that citizens have a substantive right to live in a healthy environment (see Table 3.2 and Figure 3.2), illustrated by this example in Norway's constitution (1992):

Article 110(b) Every person has a right to an environment that is conducive to health and to natural surroundings whose productivity and diversity are preserved. Natural resources should be made use of on the basis of comprehensive long-term considerations whereby this right will be safeguarded for future generations as well.

The environmental rights entrenched in constitutions are universal (i.e., held by all individuals in a nation), except in the case of El Salvador, where the right to a healthy environment appears to be limited to children, and the Maldives, where the right appears to be limited to Muslims (a limitation discussed below).[32] The constitutions of Burundi and Mauritania are unusual because they do not explicitly mention the right to a healthy environment but, rather, incorporate by reference all the rights recognized in the *African (Banjul) Charter on Human and Peoples' Rights*, which includes "the right to a general satisfactory environment."[33] The constitution of Bosnia and Herzegovina refers to international human rights obligations, but because it does not specify any particular agreement that includes an explicit right to a healthy environment, it is not counted in this analysis.[34]

There are ambiguous environmental rights provisions found in the constitutions of Albania, Andorra, Honduras, Malawi, the Netherlands, and Poland. For example, in Albania, the constitution provides for the following right:

> *Part Two: Fundamental Human Rights and Freedoms, Chapter IV, Economic, Social, and Cultural Rights and Freedoms*
> Article 56. Everyone has the right to be informed about the status of the environment and its protection.

Narrowly interpreted, this article could be read as limited to a right to information about both the status of the environment and the protection of the environment. Broadly interpreted, it could be read as a right to information about the status of the environment and a right to the protection of the environment. In some cases, it is possible that the ambiguity is caused by translation difficulties. The status of the constitutional right to a healthy environment in these six nations will be discussed in Chapters 6 to 10, as resolution of the ambiguities depends on the interpretations of national legislatures and courts.

There is a major division between common-law and civil law systems when it comes to the extent of constitutional recognition of the right to a healthy environment. Of the twenty-three exclusively common-law systems, only Jamaica, in 2011, has incorporated the right to a healthy environment in its constitution. In contrast, fifty-two out of seventy-seven nations with civil law mono-systems have constitutions that include the right to a healthy environment. Among mixed legal systems that are partially based on common law, only nine out of forty-four nations have recognized the right in their constitutions.[35] These statistics indicate that there is ongoing resistance among common-law nations to the constitutional recognition of the right to a healthy environment. This resistance extends to social and economic rights, which may be a consequence of the historical and/or continuing influence of the British and American legal systems.

Some scholars argue that constitutions imposing a duty on governments to protect the environment contain an implicit right to a healthy environment. The constitutions of forty-eight nations fall into this category, potentially raising the number of constitutions that recognize the right to a healthy environment, explicitly and implicitly, to 140 out of 193. As we will see in Chapters 6 to 11, courts in a number of nations have been sympathetic to this interpretation, and some governments appear to share this perspective. For example, although Kazakhstan's constitution does not include an explicit

Figure 3.2

Map of nations recognizing the constitutional right to a healthy environment

Nations recognizing constitutional right to a healthy environment as of 2011

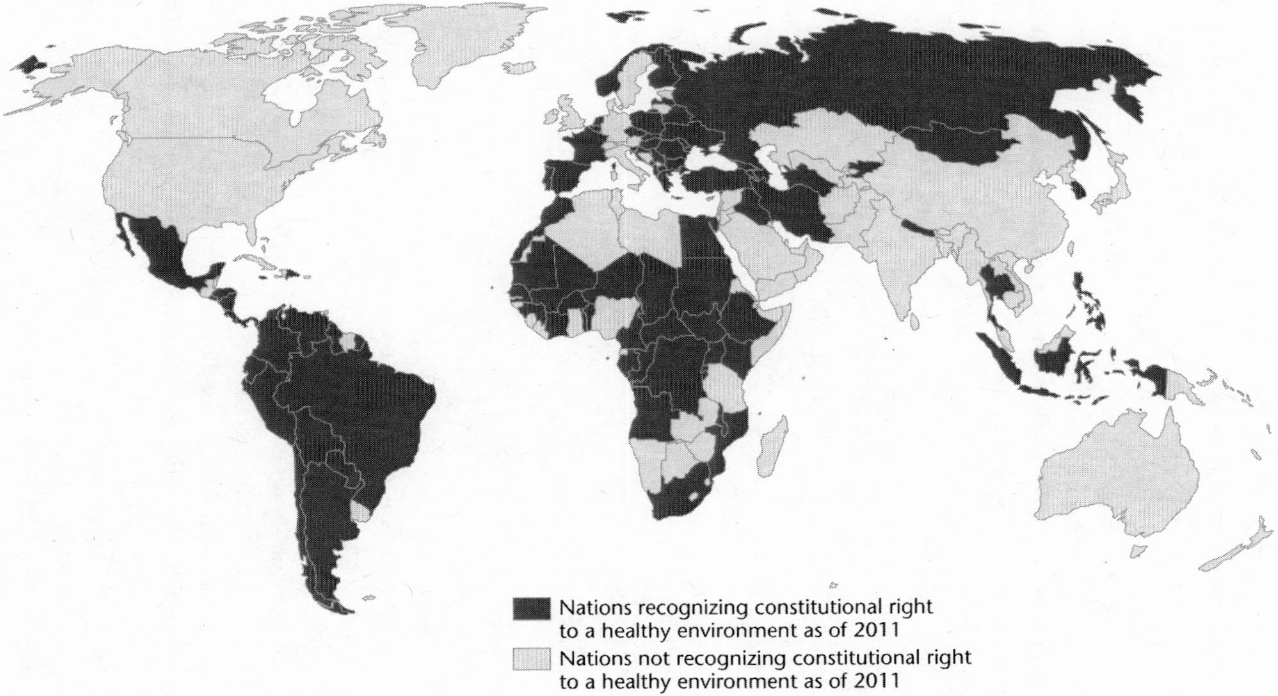

Nations not recognizing constitutional right to a healthy environment as of 2011

right to a healthy environment, the new Kazakh *Environmental Code* contains an expansive articulation of the substantive and procedural aspects of the right, and the government's report to the Compliance Committee of the Aarhus Convention acknowledges citizens' environmental rights.[36] As well, a leading Kazakh ENGO, Green Salvation, is asserting the right to a healthy environment in numerous court cases.[37]

Portugal (1976) and Spain (1978) were the first nations to recognize the right to live in a healthy environment. As was the case for environmental provisions generally, the peak year for constitutionalization of the right to a healthy environment was 1992. Table 3.3 provides a timeline of the incorporation of this right in national constitutions.

Broken down by decade, the incorporation of provisions recognizing the right to a healthy environment in national constitutions is as follows:

1976-79	4	2000-09	23
1980-89	13	2010-11	5
1990-99	47		

Broken down by region, the incorporation of provisions recognizing the right to a healthy environment in national constitutions is as follows:[38]

Africa	32[39]	North America	0
Asia	14[40]	Caribbean	2[43]
Europe	28[41]	Oceania	0
Latin America	16[42]		

Sixty-three of the ninety-two constitutions that include substantive environmental rights use the language of a healthy environment. Twenty-two of the ninety-two constitutions also describe the right in terms of an ecologically balanced environment, language that could, to some extent, assuage concerns about the anthropocentric focus of human rights. A wide variety of other words and phrases are used to describe the right to a healthy environment, including the following (with their frequency in parentheses): fit or adequate for human development or well-being (10), preserved/protected (7), clean (7), safe (6), favourable (5), satisfying (5), natural (3), unpolluted (2), sound (2), free from contamination (2), sustainable (2), good (2), diverse (2), harmonious (2), wholesome (1), lasting (1), human (1), productive (1), pleasant (1), and benevolent (1).[44] Some of this variability may be a result of inconsistent translation.

TABLE 3.3

Year that the right to a healthy environment was first included in national constitutions

Year	Countries
1976	Portugal
1978	Spain
1979	Iran, Peru
1980	Chile, Guyana
1982	Honduras, Turkey
1983	El Salvador, Netherlands, Panama
1984	Ecuador
1986	Nicaragua
1987	Philippines, South Korea
1988	Brazil
1989	Hungary
1990	Benin, Croatia, Guinea, Mozambique, São Tomé and Príncipe
1991	Bulgaria, Burkina Faso, Colombia, Gabon, Macedonia, Mauritania, Slovenia
1992	Angola, Cape Verde, Czech Republic, Mali, Mongolia, Norway, Paraguay, Slovak Republic, Togo
1993	Andorra, Kyrgyzstan, Russia, Seychelles
1994	Argentina, Belarus, Belgium, Costa Rica, Malawi, Moldova
1995	Armenia, Azerbaijan, Ethiopia, Finland, Georgia, Uganda
1996	Cameroon, Chad, Niger, South Africa, Ukraine
1997	Poland
1998	Albania, Latvia
1999	Mexico, Venezuela
2000	Cote d'Ivoire, Indonesia
2001	Comoros, Senegal
2002	Bolivia, Congo-Brazzaville, East Timor, Greece
2003	Romania, Rwanda
2004	Central African Republic
2005	Burundi, Congo (Democratic Republic of the), France, Iraq, Sudan
2006	Nepal, Serbia
2007	Egypt, Montenegro, Thailand
2008	Maldives, Turkmenistan
2010	Dominican Republic, Kenya
2011	Jamaica, Morocco, South Sudan

LIMITS ON CONSTITUTIONAL RIGHTS, INCLUDING THE RIGHT TO A HEALTHY ENVIRONMENT

There are four types of constitutional provisions that can limit all or a subset of the rights recognized in a given constitution: generic limits; restrictions during emergencies; acknowledgment that rights will be fulfilled on the basis of progressive implementation; and limits on who is eligible to enjoy constitutional rights. More than one of these limitations is often found in the same constitution.

First, constitutions may include provisions that authorize restrictions on all human rights in order to meet the public interest in security, order, health, and/or the exercise of other rights. These generic limits are found in the constitutions of forty-one of the ninety-two nations that recognize the right to live in a healthy environment.[45] For example, the constitution of South Africa includes the following provision:

Chapter 2: Bill of Rights
36. Limitation of rights
    (1) The rights in the Bill of Rights may be limited only in terms of law of general application to the extent that the limit is reasonable and justifiable in an open and democratic society based on human dignity, equality and freedom, taking into account all relevant factors, including
        a. the nature of the right;
        b. the importance of the purpose of the limitation;
        c. the nature and extent of the limitation;
        d. the relation between the limitation and the purpose; and
        e. less restrictive means to achieve the purpose.
    (2) Except as provided in subsection (1) or in any other provision of the Constitution, no law may limit any right entrenched in the Bill of Rights.

These kinds of provisions make it clear that no rights are intended to be absolute, contrary to the concern raised by critics of constitutionalizing rights.

Second, forty-six out of ninety-two constitutions expressly authorize restrictions on the exercise of rights during emergencies such as wars, invasions, and natural disasters.[46] These emergency provisions either enumerate specific rights that can be suspended or identify specific rights that cannot be restricted even during these times of crisis. There are four nations where environmental rights are not listed among those that may be suspended.[47] No constitutions identify the right to a healthy environment as one of the rights that is immune from restriction during emergencies.

Third, in the constitutions of six nations, the right to a healthy environment and other social and economic rights are explicitly limited by the concept of progressive implementation, which recognizes that individual nations have different capacities and resources for respecting, protecting, and fulfilling social and economic rights.[48] In this sense, social and economic rights have traditionally been distinguished from civil and political rights, which are subject to immediate implementation. An example of a provision requiring progressive implementation is found in the constitution of Turkey, which classifies the right to a healthy environment among the social and economic rights:

> Part Two: Fundamental Rights and Duties
> Chapter Three: Social and Economic Rights and Duties
> XIII. The Extent of Social and Economic Duties of the State
> Article 65. The State shall fulfill its duties as laid down in the Constitution in the social and economic fields within the capacity of its financial resources, taking into consideration the priorities appropriate with the aims of these duties.

Fourth, the Maldives provides an example of a constitution in which provisions seemingly unrelated to the right to a healthy environment appear to narrow or restrict the application of that right. The constitution of the Maldives recognizes that every citizen has the right to a healthy and ecologically balanced environment, but also states that "a non-Muslim may not become a citizen of the Maldives."[49] Article 9(d) of the constitution of the Maldives has been criticized as inconsistent with international human rights law by constitutional experts because it appears to indicate that non-Muslims in the Maldives do not have equal constitutional rights.[50]

Finally, there do not appear to be any explicit limitations placed on the right to a healthy environment in the constitutions of twenty-three nations.[51] This ought not to be interpreted as suggesting that the right to a healthy environment is absolute in these nations. The right will still have to be balanced against other rights in cases where conflicts arise.

The location and classification of the right to a healthy environment within a constitution can also influence its implementation, enforceability, and judicial interpretation. In fifty-six out of ninety-two constitutions, the right to a healthy environment is articulated in the same section or chapter as other fundamental human rights.[52] Theoretically, this will result in similar treatment for all of the human rights identified as fundamental, although, in practice, legal developments may not always reflect words on paper or the intent of the constitution's framers. In seventeen constitutions, the right to a healthy environment is grouped together with economic, social, and cultural rights, a classification that is sometimes viewed as of secondary importance compared to civil and political rights.[53] Eleven nations describe the right to a healthy environment in a section of their constitutions that sets out general provisions or guiding objectives and principles of state policy.[54] This may diminish the legal strength of the environmental right. In three constitutions (Cameroon, Comoros, and Mauritania), the right to a healthy environment is found in the preamble, where it would generally be of limited practical value. However, while the constitutions of these nations place rights only in the preamble, they also explicitly state that the preamble is an integral part of the constitution. In two constitutions (Colombia and Democratic Republic of the Congo), the right to a healthy environment is included in a chapter called "Collective Rights" that follows a chapter enumerating social, economic, and cultural rights. Three other nations have unique constitutional arrangements for the right to a healthy environment: Argentina includes it in a section called "New Rights and Guarantees"; Egypt in a section called "Public Rights"; and France in the "Charter for the Environment." The unusual location of the right to a healthy environment within these constitutions could possibly affect its interpretation.

Procedural Environmental Rights

Thirty national constitutions provide procedural rights specifically related to environmental protection, including the right to information, the right to participate in decision making, and the right of access to the judicial system to challenge particular decisions, unconstitutional laws, or alleged violations of individual rights (see Table 3.2). The Czech Republic's constitution provides an example:

> Article 35. (2) Everybody is entitled to timely and complete information about the state of the environment and natural resources.

Many constitutions incorporate generic procedural rights that apply to a broad spectrum of issues including the environment. As well, in many industrialized nations these procedural rights are already available because of existing laws and policies, although constitutional affirmation will generally strengthen the individual's position. In every case except Austria, procedural environmental rights are included in constitutions that also contain a substantive right to live in a healthy environment. This suggests that procedural environmental rights are viewed as a complement to, rather than a substitute for, substantive environmental rights.

Procedural environmental rights are most commonly found in constitutions from Eastern Europe and Latin America. In some countries, this may be due to the historical suppression of environmental information by autocratic regimes. For example, in the Ukraine, a compelling motivation for the inclusion of guaranteed access to environmental information in the constitution was the Chernobyl nuclear disaster, where vital information about high radiation levels was withheld from the public.[55]

Some constitutions also create an independent office with responsibility for monitoring human rights violations. This can take the form of a human rights commission, an ombudsman, or a defender of human rights. For example, El Salvador has a Procurator for the Defense of Human Rights.[56] The powers available to these human rights bodies and officers vary widely, ranging from merely preparing reports to initiating litigation intended to protect citizens' rights and ordering reparation for rights that have been violated. In general, these officials can act on complaints received by citizens or initiate their own investigations. Namibia's constitution is noteworthy, as it specifically empowers the ombudsman to investigate problems related to environmental damage.[57]

INDIVIDUAL ENVIRONMENTAL DUTIES

A Declaration of Rights is, by reciprocity, a Declaration of Duties also. Whatever is my right as a man, is also the right of another; and it becomes my duty to guarantee, as well as to possess.

– Thomas Paine, *The Rights of Man*

Individual responsibility for protecting the environment is provided in eighty-three constitutions, a total slightly lower than the number of constitutions recognizing the right to live in a healthy environment (see Table 3.2). For example, France's *Charter for the Environment* (2005) states:

Article 2. Every person has the duty to take part in the preservation and the improvement of the environment.
Article 3. Every person must, in the conditions defined by law, prevent or, at a minimum, limit the harm that it is susceptible to bring on the environment.

There are six nations whose constitutions establish an individual duty to protect the environment but neither establish an individual right to a healthy environment nor impose environmental obligations upon the state.[58] This seems to run counter to the fundamental idea that constitutions are intended to provide constraints upon government power.[59] Constitutions are generally enforceable against the state, not individuals. It is unclear what legal purpose is served by the constitutionalization of individual environmental duties. These provisions appear to be symbolic, hortatory, and educational, confirming that everyone has a part to play in protecting the environment from human-imposed damage and degradation. The Gambian constitution explicitly states that the individual's duty to protect the environment is unenforceable.[60]

OTHER ENVIRONMENTAL PROTECTION PROVISIONS

Not surprisingly, given the diverse legal systems of the world, there is a broad variety of constitutional environmental provisions, ranging from generic to highly detailed. Among the most common provisions in this miscellaneous category are authorization of restrictions on the use of private property in order to protect the environment: prohibitions on importing toxic, hazardous, or nuclear waste; recognition of the right to clean water; and value statements regarding the importance placed on protecting the environment. In a handful of constitutions, provisions related to environmental protection are extremely comprehensive, with a level of detail that in most nations would be found in environmental legislation.

Many constitutions authorize limits on the exercise of private property rights as justified by the public interest, which is not defined but generally refers to a suite of considerations including environmental concerns. For example, Article 27(2) of the constitution of Andorra states: "No one shall be deprived of his or her goods or rights, unless upon justified consideration of the public interest, with just compensation by or pursuant to a law."[61] At least fifteen constitutions specifically restrict the use of private property when that use could cause environmental damage.[62] For example, the constitution of Romania states: "The right to own property implies an obligation to comply with duties relating to environmental protection."[63] Jamaica's 2011 *Charter of Fundamental Rights and Freedoms* clarifies that property rights shall not affect the making or operation of any law "reasonably required for the protection of the environment."[64] Another fifteen nations (all former British colonies) share a weak constitutional provision that could authorize environmental limits on property rights.[65] The inclusion of both property rights and the right to a healthy environment in a constitution will create conflicts that require careful balancing by legislatures, bureaucracies, and courts. However, constitutions that explicitly authorize environmental constraints on the use of private property provide helpful guidance to lawmakers, civil servants, and judges.

A handful of nations, employing a very different constitutional model, spell out environmental policies in extensive detail, closer to what ordinarily, in a nation like Canada or the United States, would be found in environmental legislation. For example, Switzerland's constitution includes specific provisions about zoning, water, forests, nature reserves, fishing, hunting, protecting alpine ecosystems, energy policy, and biotechnology. Colombia's constitution incorporates thirty-four provisions related to environmental protection. Brazil's constitution requires "a prior environmental impact study, which shall be made public, for the installation of works or activities which may cause significant degradation of the environment."[66] In Argentina, the constitution requires the federal government to "dictate laws containing a minimum budget necessary for protecting the environment."[67] Portugal's constitution compels the government to ensure "that tax policy renders development compatible with the protection of the environment and the quality of life."[68]

Many African nations have provisions in their constitutions dealing with environmental issues of particular concern to their citizens or unique to their history. For example, Benin, Chad, the Democratic Republic of the Congo, and Niger each have provisions prohibiting the importation of toxic or hazardous waste. Uganda and Malawi have specific references to the protection of biological diversity. Several Oceanic nations (e.g., Micronesia and Palau) have specific sections prohibiting nuclear testing or the deployment of nuclear weapons within their territories.[69]

Latin America has been a leader in constitutional innovation, with numerous novel provisions related to environmental protection. In Brazil, Colombia, and several other nations, the constitution empowers an independent agency, known as the Ministerio Publico, to protect collective interests, including the environment. In effect, these agencies function as public prosecutors, at arm's length from the state, to whom the public can turn to enforce environmental laws and prevent actions that could cause ecological damage and violate the right to a healthy environment. Constitutions throughout Latin America also provide for expedited forms of legal action, known variously as the *amparo,* writ of protection, and *tutela.* While the precise procedure varies from nation to nation, they have in common a relaxation or simplification of the legal process that lowers costs, reduces delays, and dramatically increases access to the judicial system in constitutional cases.[70] The right of *amparo* dates back to the Mexican constitution of 1857 and has been adopted in almost every Spanish-speaking nation in Latin America.[71]

In 2008, Ecuador became the first nation in the world to provide explicit constitutional recognition of rights of Nature, followed by Bolivia in 2009.[72] Ecuador's constitution states:

> Article 71. Nature or Pachamama, where life is reproduced and exists, has the right to exist, persist, maintain and regenerate its vital cycles, structure, functions and its processes in evolution. Every person, people, community or nationality, will be able to demand the recognitions of rights for Nature before the public organisms. The application and interpretation of these rights will follow the related principles established in the Constitution.

As noted in Chapter 2, there has been an intense debate among scholars regarding the viability of extending human rights to Nature. Now there is an opportunity to observe whether the results predicted by legal experts and philosophers will be borne out. Ecuador has experience in the environmental law vanguard – as a pioneer in extending its territorial waters to two hundred miles in the early 1970s, the country seized American fishing boats and imposed heavy fines. The two-hundred-mile exclusive economic zone was incorporated in the United Nations' *Convention on the Law of the Sea* in 1982. Ecuador and Bolivia also have among the most detailed constitutions in the world in terms of provisions related to environmental protection. For example, Ecuador's new constitution prohibits genetically modified organisms; reverses the legal burden of proof so that those accused of causing environmental harm must prove that their actions caused no such harm; mandates that uncertainties regarding the interpretation of environmental laws be resolved in favour of Nature; and requires the promotion of non-motorized forms of transport in urban areas, particularly through the creation of cycling routes.[73]

More than forty nations include constitutional references to the rights, health, or well-being of future generations.[74] Almost all of these references appear in the context of provisions dealing with environmental concerns.[75] For example, the Brazilian constitution states that "the Government and the community have a duty to defend and preserve the environment for present and future generations."[76] The constitutions of Bhutan and Portugal refer to the closely related concept of intergenerational equity.[77]

Finally, a growing number of constitutions address the right to an adequate supply of clean water. South Africa is perhaps best known for incorporating this right into its constitution, as follows:

27. Health care, food, water, and social security

   (1) Everyone has the right to have access to –

   ...

       (b) sufficient food and water

   ...

   (2) The state must take reasonable legislative and other measures, within its available resources, to achieve the progressive
   realization of each of these rights.[78]

Constitutional provisions requiring the protection and/or provision of clean
water are found in at least seventeen other nations.[79]

The Enforceability of Environmental Provisions in National Constitutions

Enforceability is an essential aspect of constitutional provisions, for it ensures
accountability when rights are violated or responsibilities go unfulfilled. For
the purposes of this analysis, a simple working definition of enforceability
was adopted: the ability of an individual, group, or other organization to
access the legal system to resolve a constitutional complaint.[80] In some cases,
the authorization or prohibition of legal action is specific to a constitution's
environmental provisions. In other cases, the authorization or prohibition
relates to broader aspects of the constitution, but applies equally to the environmental provisions. An example of an explicit confirmation of enforceability is found in Portugal's constitution:

Article 52 (Right to petition and right to popular action)

3. Everyone shall be granted the right of actio popularis, to include
   the right to apply for the appropriate compensation for an ag-
   grieved party or parties, in such cases and under such terms as
   the law may determine, either personally or via associations that
   purport to defend the interests in question. The said right shall
   particularly be exercised in order to:

   a) Promote the prevention, cessation or judicial prosecution
      of offences against public health, consumer rights, the qual-
      ity of life or the preservation of the environment and the
      cultural heritage.

Conversely, an example of an explicit limit on enforceability is found in Nepal's constitution, which imposes extensive duties on the government to protect the environment in Article 35. However, Article 36 makes it clear that these duties are not enforceable:

> 36. Questions not to be Raised in Courts: (1) No questions shall be raised in any court as to whether provisions contained in this Part are implemented or not.

In the absence of enforceability, governments may evade their responsibility to protect the environment, and affected individuals may be deprived of a remedy for violations of their right to a healthy environment. Although unenforceable provisions are toothless tigers, they may still influence interpretation and decision making, and they offer moral, symbolic, and educational value.

There are both internal and external factors that affect the enforceability of constitutional provisions. Internal factors refer to explicit guarantees or limits within the text of a constitution. External factors encompass a broad range of legal, social, political, economic, and cultural considerations. For example, the lack of financial resources may act as a *de facto* bar to enforceability for poor communities, which are likely to suffer a disproportionate share of the pollution burden.[81] A nation's judiciary may be extremely conservative or even unfamiliar with the idea of judicial review of government action, thus imposing an external limit. For example, judicial review was introduced into Japan's legal system by the post–Second World War rewriting of the Japanese constitution, but it continues to have limited utility due to societal and judicial conservatism.[82] This chapter focuses on internal factors that affect the enforceability of environmental provisions in constitutions, while external factors are examined in Chapters 6 to 11.

ENFORCEABILITY OF THE RIGHT TO A HEALTHY ENVIRONMENT

Of the ninety-two national constitutions that include recognition of a right to live in a healthy environment, sixty-seven include provisions that clearly support enforceability.[83] An example of a *prima facie* guarantee of enforceability is found in the Chilean constitution:

> Article 20. ...
> The action for the protection of fundamental rights (*recurso de protec-
> cion*) shall always lie in the case of numeral 8 of Article 19, when

the right to live in an environment free from contamination has been affected by an illegal act or omission imputable to an authority or specific person.

In thirteen nations, constitutional provisions specify that certain rights, including the right to a healthy environment, may be invoked only according to specific conditions determined by law.[84] This is described as a constitutional provision that is not "self-executing." For example, in Spain, the right to a healthy environment is subject to the following restriction:

Article 53 (3) Recognition, respect and protection of the principles recognized in Chapter III shall guide legislation, judicial practice and actions by the public authorities. They may only be invoked before the ordinary courts in accordance with the legal provisions implementing them.

Article 53(3) limits the ability of citizens and NGOs to file lawsuits based directly on their constitutional right to a healthy environment, requiring them to rely on other legal provisions. A similar provision in South Korea's constitution led Grote to conclude that while most rights in the Korean Bill of Rights are guaranteed in unconditional terms, "the practical significance of this right [to a healthy environment] is limited since its substance has to be defined by parliamentary legislation."[85]

Nine national constitutions contain no provisions that directly address the issue of enforceability (i.e., they are silent about citizens' access to court and the availability of remedies for breaches of constitutional rights).[86] In these countries, standing to address alleged violations of constitutional rights will be determined on the basis of legislation, jurisprudence, and custom.

Analyzing the enforceability of constitutional provisions related to environmental protection in Malawi, Hungary, and the Netherlands entails greater complexity. In Malawi, the right to a healthy environment does not appear to be enforceable because the right is expressed as a directive principle, although "courts shall be entitled to have regard" to these principles when interpreting the constitution, laws, and government actions (see Chapter 7). Because of the complex provisions related to the right to a healthy environment in Hungary's constitution, the enforceability of this right will be determined by Hungarian courts (see Chapter 9). In the Netherlands, where the constitutional provision related to the right to a healthy environment is ambiguous, the constitution provides broad access to the courts for citizens but prohibits courts from reviewing the constitutionality of Acts of Parliament and treaties (see Chapter 10).[87]

Enforceability of Procedural Environmental Rights

The enforceability of procedural environmental rights is effectively identical to that of substantive environmental rights in twenty-nine out of thirty nations because the procedural provisions overlap with substantive rights. In Austria, the only nation with procedural environmental rights but no substantive right, the constitutional rights related to environmental impact assessment do appear to be *prima facie* enforceable, although some disagreement exists.[88]

Enforceability of Governmental Responsibilities to Protect the Environment

While much of the enforceability debate focuses on individual rights, it is also possible to hold governments accountable through legal actions intended to ensure that they fulfill their constitutional obligations. Of the 140 constitutions that incorporate environmental responsibilities for government, 82 include explicit provisions that support enforceability.[89] For example, the constitution of Colombia states:

> Article 86. Every person has the right to file a writ of protection before a judge, at any time or place, through a preferential and summary proceeding, for himself/herself or by whomever acts in his/her name for the immediate protection of his/her fundamental constitutional rights when that person fears the latter may be violated by the action or omission of any public authority.

> Article 87. Any person may appear before the legal authority to demand the application of a law or fulfillment of an administrative act. In case of a successful action, the sentence will order the delinquent authority to perform its mandated duty.

> Article 88. The law will regulate popular actions for the protection of collective rights and interests related to the homeland, space, public safety and health, administrative morality, the environment, free economic competition, and others of a similar nature.

Twenty-two constitutions contain no provisions that directly address the issue of the enforceability of government's duty to protect the environment (i.e., they are silent about citizens' access to court).[90] In these countries, standing to challenge government's failure to fulfill its constitutional obligation to protect the environment will be determined on the basis of legislation, jurisprudence, and custom.

Fifteen nations have constitutions in which the enforceability of government duties to protect the environment appears to be explicitly precluded.[91] Each of these fifteen nations has constitutional environmental provisions that are expressed in terms of "Directive Principles of State Policy." For example, in Gambia the directive principles include protecting the environment for posterity and cooperating in preserving the global environment. However, "these principles shall not confer legal rights or be enforceable in any court."[92] Olowu describes such guiding principles as "worthless platitudes because of their inherently emasculated constitutional status."[93]

In six nations, progressive implementation is another factor that could restrain the enforceability of government's duty to protect the environment.[94] Where a constitution includes this government duty but specifically states that the duty is subject to the availability of financial resources and other national priorities, it is less likely that a court will enforce the duty by substituting its policy judgment for that of the government. For example, Gabon's constitution provides that "the State, according to its possibilities, shall guarantee to all, notably to the child, the mother, the handicapped, to aged workers and to the elderly ... a preserved natural environment."[95]

There are fifteen nations where the enforceability of government duties to protect the environment is unclear.[96] For example, Germany's constitution makes it clear that constitutional rights are enforceable.[97] However, there is no right to a healthy environment, and the government duty to protect the environment is found in a different part of the German constitution ("The Federation and the Lander").

The enforceability of environmental provisions cannot be determined with certainty by examining constitutional texts in isolation. There can be significant differences between enforceability on paper and enforceability in practice. For example, the constitution of India makes rights enforceable.[98] However there is no explicit right to a healthy environment in India's constitution, and the government's duties to protect the environment (Article 48A) are among the explicitly unenforceable "Directive Principles of State Policy."[99] However, as described in Chapter 8, courts in India have consistently, and in some cases dramatically, circumvented the plain words of the constitution, building a body of jurisprudence that interprets the directive principle regarding environmental protection as legally binding. Indian jurisprudence serves as a compelling example of the unpredictability of constitutional law and a powerful reminder not to rely upon abstract conclusions regarding the enforceability of particular constitutional provisions. As Beatty observed, "Even though most constitutions now contain provisions guaranteeing some set of social and economic rights, it is rare that the particular way they are written in the text is the critical or determining factor in how cases are resolved."[100]

Conclusion

As of 1 August 2011, 147 out of 193 national constitutions incorporate some form of environmental protection provisions, including government's duty to protect the environment, the individual right to a healthy environment, procedural environmental rights, the individual responsibility to protect the environment, and a diverse array of other provisions (see Figure 3.3). The right to live in a healthy environment enjoys explicit recognition in ninety-two constitutions. No other human right has achieved such a broad level of constitutional recognition in such a short period of time.[101] For purposes of comparison, the right to health is recognized in seventy-four constitutions, while the right to food is recognized in at least twenty-one constitutions.[102] Constitutional environmental provisions are now the norm throughout Europe, Asia, Latin America, and Africa. The forty-six nations whose constitutions remain silent on environmental protection are mainly former British

Figure 3.3

Prevalence of environmental protection provisions in national constitutions

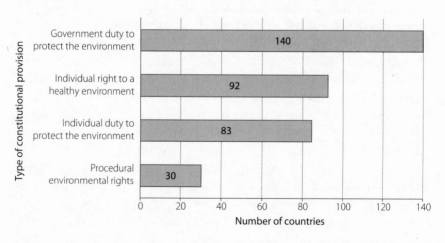

colonies, nations with common-law legal systems, and small island states (with some overlap in these three categories).

The constitutionalization of environmental protection began in earnest in the 1970s and peaked in the early 1990s, but the trend continues. New constitutions enacted in 2010 in Kenya and the Dominican Republic include the right to a healthy environment and extensive provisions related to environmental protection.[103] Jamaica's 2011 *Charter of Fundamental Rights and Freedoms* includes the right to a healthy environment, as do the new constitutions in Morocco and South Sudan.[104] Iceland's draft constitution contains the right to a healthy environment and other strong environmental provisions in a chapter titled Human Rights and Nature.[105] A broad coalition of Zimbabwean civil society organizations has called for the drafting of a new constitution with a "justiciable Bill of Rights that recognises civil, political, social, economic, cultural and environmental rights."[106]

A review of the enforceability of constitutional environmental provisions indicates that the majority appear to be *prima facie* enforceable. This conclusion applies to government's duty to protect the environment, the individual right to live in a healthy environment, and procedural environmental rights. In most constitutions, the right to a healthy environment is treated in much the same way as any other fundamental human right. In a minority of cases, the right to a healthy environment and other social, economic, and cultural rights appear to have less legal strength than civil and political rights. Only in a small number of nations are these constitutional provisions described as unenforceable guiding principles or subject to requirements that enabling legislation be introduced to facilitate their enforcement.

Overall, these constitutional developments appear to reflect a rapid evolution of human values, with environmental protection gaining the requisite moral importance to merit inclusion in written documents that express a society's most cherished and deeply held values.

4
The Influence of International Law

The focus of this book is on the right to a healthy environment at the national level. This chapter shifts gears to examine the significant influence of international law upon national recognition of the right. International law in the fields of human rights and environmental protection affects national constitutions, legislation, and court decisions. As well, there are international courts, commissions, and other institutions that can respond to human rights complaints from individuals or NGOs.[1] In essence, these international bodies can offer a court of last resort for those whose complaints about violations of their right to a healthy environment fall upon deaf ears in national judicial arenas. This chapter also describes the transnational processes that are stimulating the globalization of this right. These transnational processes involve interactions between judges, lawyers, ENGOs, constitutions, legislation, and court decisions. Legal developments (constitutional, legislative, or judicial) at any level or in any region contribute to further recognition of the right to a healthy environment at all levels and in all regions. National environmental law is "uploaded" into international law, while international principles and precedents are "downloaded" into national and regional systems.[2] The result is what Yang and Percival describe as "global environmental law" – a field of law that is international, national, and transnational in character all at once.[3] While an entire book could be devoted to this subject, this chapter provides a brief but necessary overview.

Whether international law recognizes the right to live in a healthy environment as a substantive human right is "a hotly debated issue."[4] Scholars come down on both sides and also straddle the fence, arguing that the right is unsubstantiated, *lex lata* (the law as it exists), *lex ferenda* (the law as it ought to be), or somewhere in between, in the process of emerging as a legally enforceable right. Assessing the status of any given right at international law is a subjective, rather than objective, exercise. Despite complexities and ambiguities, determining the status of the right to a healthy environment at international law is vitally important. A growing number of regional human rights institutions can enforce this right, and the dynamic dialogue between international law and national law contributes to its evolution.[5]

The Sources of International Law

To determine whether the right to a healthy environment has acquired binding status under international law, one must apply the principles responsible for the contentious process of establishing international law. The *Statute of the International Court of Justice* sets out the basic framework:

> Article 38(1). The Court, whose function is to decide in accordance with international law such disputes as are submitted to it, shall apply:
>
> a. international conventions, whether general or particular, establishing rules expressly recognized by the contesting states;
> b. international custom, as evidence of a general practice accepted as law;
> c. the general principles of law recognized by civilized nations;
> d. subject to the provisions of Article 59,[6] judicial decisions and the teachings of the most highly qualified publicists of the various nations, as subsidiary means for the determination of rules of law.[7]

Article 38 sets out three primary sources of hard law (a-c) and two subsidiary means of determining rules of law (d). However, these traditional categories of international law are supplemented by a wide range of instruments known as "soft law," which are defined as "principles with potentially great political, practical, humanitarian, moral, or other persuasive authority, but which do not strictly speaking correspond to extant legal obligations or rights."[8] Soft law covers a grey zone, where instruments may affect the international behaviour of states but are not regarded as legally binding and therefore are not directly enforceable in courts or tribunals.[9] Soft law includes non-binding state declarations, resolutions of the UN General Assembly and other international institutions, statements of principles, and other so-called aspirational authorities.

Where there are perceived gaps in legal rules, soft law can fill the void. Soft law can be more responsive than hard law and more attractive to states because reaching agreement on such instruments can be easier, and statements or declarations can thus be more detailed and precise; for some states, soft law may enable them to avoid political difficulties associated with the domestic treaty-ratification process; and soft law instruments may be more flexible than formal treaties – easier to amend, supplement, or replace.[10] Because of these attributes, soft law is particularly important in international law related to human rights and the environment.[11] The 1992 *Rio Declaration on Environment and Development* is a good example of soft law, as it is fairly detailed, was negotiated quickly, and was endorsed by 175 nations. A treaty covering similar ground would likely have taken longer to negotiate, included fewer commitments, and attracted fewer parties.[12]

Some scholars argue that soft law is an increasingly important source of international environmental law, while others maintain that it is of no probative value. This debate is important to the status of the right to a healthy environment because many international declarations and resolutions articulating and recognizing environmental rights are soft law instruments. Guzman and Boyle endorse a less formal approach to international human rights law, arguing that there is really little practical difference between the traditional sources of international law and "soft" law.[13] On the other hand, traditionalist legal scholars maintain that only hard law can create legally binding rights and obligations. As Weil wrote about soft law instruments, "neither is there any warrant for considering that, by dint of repetition, non-normative resolutions can be transmuted into positive law through a sort of incantatory effect: the accumulation of non-law or pre-law is no more sufficient to create law than is thrice of nothing to make something."[14] Szekely believes that states have made a deliberate effort in the field of international environmental law to avoid establishing enforceable commitments.[15]

On balance, it appears that soft law has the potential to evolve into, or influence the creation of, more formal and binding international law norms.[16] Cassese describes soft law instruments as the building blocks of treaties and customary rules.[17] Boyle notes that "widespread acceptance of soft law instruments will tend to legitimize conduct, and make the legality of opposing positions harder to sustain."[18] Soft law also can be used as evidence of existing law, state practice, and *opinio juris*. A prominent example of this in the environmental context is the *Stockholm Declaration*, which sets forth non-binding principles of international environmental law, some of which, arguably, have evolved into binding rules of customary international law.

CONVENTIONAL INTERNATIONAL LAW

Conventional international law consists of treaties, conventions, and other forms of legally binding agreements among nations at the global, regional, or bilateral level.

Conventions are often described as analogous to contracts between nations. The advantages of conventional international law are its relative clarity, its binding nature, and the existence of mechanisms for enforcement in the event of violations.[19] Because of these advantages, treaties, such as the *Vienna Convention for the Protection of the Ozone Layer*, form an integral part of international environmental law.[20] However, treaties are subject to troubling weaknesses, including the slow and cumbersome negotiation process, the tendency to end up with lowest-common-denominator provisions, the failure of some states to participate, and delays or weaknesses in implementation.[21] Another shortcoming is that, unlike customary international law, treaties are binding only on participants. These weaknesses are demonstrated by the ongoing ineffectiveness of the *United Nations Framework Convention on Climate Change* and the *Kyoto Protocol*.[22]

Global Treaties and Agreements

The main human rights agreements were negotiated at a time when the pace and magnitude of human-induced environmental degradation were not widely recognized. The *Universal Declaration of Human Rights, International Covenant on Civil and Political Rights*, and *International Covenant on Economic, Social and Cultural Rights* make no mention of an explicit right to live in a healthy environment. The drafters of these documents could not be expected to "foresee the enormity of ecological degradation and the consequent necessity for human rights norms to encompass environmental considerations."[23]

Three international human rights treaties – the *Convention on the Rights of the Child*, the *Convention on the Elimination of All Forms of Discrimination against Women*, and the *Geneva Conventions* governing state conduct in times of war – indirectly suggest that a minimum level of environmental quality is a basic human right. The *Convention on the Rights of the Child* guarantees, as part of children's right to health, "the provision of adequate nutritious foods and clean drinking water, taking into consideration the dangers and risks of environmental pollution."[24] The *Convention on the Rights of the Child* also requires that children's education include "the development of respect for the natural environment."[25] The *Convention on the Elimination of All Forms of Discrimination against Women* requires that governments ensure women "enjoy adequate living conditions, particularly in relation to ... sanitation, electricity, and water supply."[26] The *Geneva Conventions* and related protocols governing humanitarian standards during war explicitly set forth an obligation to provide prisoners of war and internees with potable drinking water.[27] It would be contradictory and illogical if prisoners of war somehow enjoyed greater rights than ordinary civilians, or if greater rights were applicable in times of war than peace. An *Additional Protocol to the Geneva Conventions*, finalized in 1977, imposes a duty on governments to protect the environment from "widespread, long-term and severe damage" even during war.[28]

While the *Convention on the Rights of the Child, Convention on the Elimination of All Forms of Discrimination against Women,* and *Geneva Conventions* include provisions linking human rights and the environment, the language of these treaties cannot be characterized as recognizing the right to a healthy environment. Given the lack of explicit treaty references, it is often argued that the right to a healthy environment is a prerequisite to, or implicit in, other more widely recognized rights such as the right to life, the right to health, the right to decent living conditions, and the right to respect for private and family life and the home.[29] These basic rights are entrenched in the *Universal Declaration of Human Rights,* which is the backbone of international human rights law, even though it was not originally drafted as a legally binding agreement.[30] The two detailed treaties negotiated to supplement it – the *International Covenant on Civil and Political Rights (ICCPR)* and the *International Covenant on Economic, Social and Cultural Rights (ICESCR)* – are legally binding on state parties. Both the *Universal Declaration of Human Rights* and the *ICCPR* articulate the right to life:

> Article 6. (1) Every human being has the inherent right to life. The right shall be protected by law. No one shall be arbitrarily deprived of his life.[31]

It is often argued that the right to a healthy environment is an essential component of the right to life.[32] As reported in Chapters 6 to 10, this approach has been adopted by at least twelve national courts in countries whose constitutions do not explicitly include the right to a healthy environment. In another eight nations (Argentina, Costa Rica, El Salvador, Greece, Kenya, Nepal, Peru, and Romania), judicial recognition of an implicit constitutional right to a healthy environment was followed by constitutional amendments that explicitly included this right.[33]

The most authoritative expression of the right to health is found in the *ICESCR* and includes an explicit reference to the environment:

Article 12. (1) The States Parties to the present Covenant recognize the right to the enjoyment of the highest attainable standard of physical and mental health. (2) The steps to be taken by the State Parties in the present Covenant to achieve the full realization of this right shall include those necessary for:

...

(b) The improvement of all aspects of environmental and industrial hygiene.[34]

The UN Committee on Economic, Social and Cultural Rights has stated that Article 12(2)(b) includes

the requirement to secure an adequate supply of safe and potable water and basic sanitation; to prevent and reduce the population's exposure to harmful substances such as radiation and harmful chemicals or other detrimental environmental conditions that directly or indirectly impact upon human health.[35]

The same UN committee noted that states violate their duty to protect the right to health if they fail to "enact or enforce laws to prevent the pollution of water, air and soil by extractive and manufacturing industries."[36] Governments must also observe the following examples of environment-related obligations stemming from the right to health in the *ICESCR*:

* abstain from environmental and industrial policies detrimental to health
* not withhold environmental information
* adopt legislation to protect people against environmental activities that could harm their health
* ensure dissemination of adequate information on environmental risks
* take measures to ensure, safeguard, and promote a healthy environment
* provide basic water and sanitation services.[37]

There is clearly some degree of overlap between the rights to life, health, and a healthy environment. While the rights to life and health are well established in global treaties and can be used in cases of environmental degradation that directly harm humans, there is not yet a global treaty that explicitly recognizes the right to a healthy environment.[38]

Regional Treaties and Agreements

At the regional level, the right to a healthy environment is recognized in legally binding agreements covering Africa, the Americas, Europe, and the Middle East. These treaties provide formal processes for addressing claims that human rights have been violated. At least 115 UN member nations are parties to these regional agreements.[39] To date there are no comparable agreements in Asia or Oceania, although the draft *Asian Human Rights Charter* incorporates the right to a healthy environment, and the Association of Southeast Asian Nations has ratified a charter that includes references to human rights and the environment.[40]

Africa

The 1981 *African (Banjul) Charter on Human and Peoples' Rights* is the earliest regional human rights treaty to explicitly recognize the right to live in a healthy environment:

> Article 24. All peoples shall have the right to a general satisfactory environment favorable to their development.[41]

Fifty-three nations are parties to the *African Charter*.[42] The reference to "All peoples" in Article 24 led Birnie and Boyle to suggest that the *African Charter* protects only a collective right rather than an individual right.[43] However, the African Commission on Human and Peoples' Rights has interpreted it as encompassing both collective and individual rights.[44] The recent *Protocol to the African Charter on Human and Peoples' Rights on the Rights of Women in Africa* confirms this reading, as it states that "Women shall have the right to live in a healthy and sustainable environment."[45]

The African Commission on Human and Peoples' Rights has limited powers. Although it can receive complaints (formally known as "communications") from individuals and NGOs, it can only produce reports and nonbinding recommendations. As Nwobike points out, "The greatest institutional weakness of the African Commission is its inability to enforce its decisions against State parties."[46] A study of forty-four cases in which the commission found human rights violations and issued recommendations revealed only six cases in which state parties complied fully with the recommendations.[47]

Because of the commission's weakness, an African Court on Human and Peoples' Rights was created in 2004, with enhanced powers.[48] However, access to the court is limited to states unless a state makes a declaration accepting the competence of the court to hear cases from individuals and NGOs. The African Court is now operational but has not yet ruled on any environmental cases.[49]

Americas

The inter-American human rights system was born with the adoption of the *American Declaration of the Rights and Duties of Man* in 1948. In 1969, the *American Convention on Human Rights* was adopted, entering into force in 1978. The convention has been ratified by twenty-four countries (not including the United States or Canada).[50] The jurisdiction of the Inter-American Court of Human Rights is limited to nations that have ratified the *American Convention* and accepted the court's optional jurisdiction. However, the Inter-American Commission on Human Rights issues reports and hears cases regarding all thirty-five member nations of the Organization of American States.

In 1988, parties to the *American Convention* agreed to the *Additional Protocol to the American Convention on Human Rights* (known as the *San Salvador Protocol*), which provides:

> Article 11.1 Everyone shall have the right to live in a healthy environment and to have access to basic public services.
> 11.2 The States Parties shall promote the protection, preservation, and improvement of the environment.[51]

The *San Salvador Protocol* entered into force in 1999. However, only fifteen out of the twenty-four parties to the *American Convention* have ratified the agreement.[52] Although Article 11 seems to be a strong articulation of the right to live in a healthy environment, several other articles weaken it. Article 1 provides for the progressive, rather than immediate, implementation of the *Protocol's* rights. Article 19(6) does not include the right to a healthy environment among the rights whose violation can give rise to individual petitions. This precludes citizens who believe their right to a healthy environment has been infringed from bringing a case before the Inter-American Commission unless other rights are also violated.[53] Because of these provisions, some experts criticize the *San Salvador Protocol* as being weak.[54]

Europe

Despite its reputation for environmental leadership, Europe lagged behind Africa and the Americas in crafting a regional agreement that explicitly acknowledges the right to live in a healthy environment. The *European Convention for the Protection of Human Rights and Fundamental Freedoms* (1950) and the *European Social Charter* (1961) both predate the modern environmental era and are silent on the matter of environmental rights. The European Union's *Charter of Fundamental Rights*, proclaimed in 2000, states that "a high level of environmental protection and the improvement of the quality of the environment must be integrated into the policies of the Union and ensured in accordance with the principles of sustainable development."[55] However, the *European Charter* did not explicitly recognize the right to live in a healthy environment, an omission criticized by NGOs and legal experts. Neither the 1999 *Treaty of Amsterdam* (revising the *Maastricht Treaty* of the European Union) nor the as yet unratified *European Constitution* recognize the right to live in a healthy environment.[56]

Proposals to amend European human rights agreements to recognize the right to a healthy environment date back four decades.[57] In 1970, the Council of Europe proposed adding a new protocol to the *European Convention on Human Rights* "guaranteeing the right of every individual to enjoy a healthy and unspoiled environment."[58] In 1990, the Parliamentary Assembly of the Council of Europe proposed that the draft *European Charter of Fundamental Rights* include a provision stating that "Every person has the fundamental right to an environment and living conditions conducive to his good health, well-being, and development of the human personality."[59] In 2010, the Committee of Ministers of the Council of Europe rejected a proposal from their own Parliamentary Assembly to add a protocol recognizing the right to a healthy environment to the *European Convention on Human Rights*.[60]

Although there is no European human rights agreement that explicitly recognizes the right to a healthy environment, the 1998 *Aarhus Convention on Access to Information, Public Participation in Decision-making and Access to Justice in Environmental Matters* includes the following provisions:

Preamble

...

Recognizing that adequate protection of the environment is essential to human well-being and the enjoyment of basic human rights, including the right to life itself,

Recognizing also that every person has the right to live in an environment adequate to his or her health and well-being, and the duty, both individually and in association with others, to protect and improve the environment for the benefit of present and future generations,

Article 1. Objective
In order to contribute to the protection of the right of every person of present and future generations to live in an environment adequate to his or her health and well-being, each Party shall guarantee the rights of access to information, public participation in decision-making, and access to justice in environmental matters in accordance with the provisions of this Convention.

The *Aarhus Convention* is regarded as globally significant in its recognition of environmental rights.[61] As Pallemaerts observes, "The Aarhus Convention is the first multilateral environmental agreement whose main purpose is to impose on its contracting parties obligations toward their own citizens."[62] In this sense, *Aarhus* represents a hybrid of environmental law and human rights law. The *Aarhus Convention* has been ratified by forty-three nations and the European Community. However, the United Kingdom made the following reservation when ratifying the agreement:

The United Kingdom understands the references in article 1 and the seventh preambular paragraph of this Convention to the "right" of every person "to live in an environment adequate to his or her health and well-being" to express an aspiration which motivated the negotiation of this Convention and which is shared fully by the United Kingdom. The legal rights which each Party undertakes to guarantee under article 1 are limited to the rights of access to information, public participation in decision-making and access to justice in environmental matters in accordance with the provisions of this Convention.[63]

In other words, the United Kingdom rejected recognition of a legally enforceable right to live in a healthy environment. Other commentators have denied that *Aarhus* introduces a substantive right to environmental protection, arguing that it only safeguards procedural rights.[64] For example, Pedersen suggests that "the Convention refers to a right on an aspirational level."[65] This interpretation appears to be at odds with the plain wording of the agreement and the decision of the United Kingdom to make a reservation on this point.

Middle East

Article 38 of the *Arab Charter on Human Rights* explicitly acknowledges the right to a healthy environment:

> Every person has the right to an adequate standard of living for himself and his family, which ensures their well-being and a decent life, including food, clothing, housing, services and the right to a healthy environment. The States Parties shall take the necessary measures commensurate with their resources to guarantee these rights.[66]

The *Arab Charter on Human Rights* entered into force in 2008 and provides for the creation of an Arab Human Rights Committee to review reports from states parties. The committee does not have the authority to receive petitions or complaints from individuals or NGOs. An Arab Court on Human Rights is being discussed but is not yet established.

CUSTOMARY INTERNATIONAL LAW

Customary international law, described by the *Statute of the International Court of Justice* as "evidence of a general practice accepted as law," has two key elements. The first is objective evidence of state practice, which must be consistent over time and across the majority of nations, although not necessarily uniform. The second element is subjective evidence that states perceive their conduct as responding to legal obligations, a concept known as *opinio juris*. This is comparable to the way that proving guilt for some crimes requires evidence of both *actus reus* (the criminal act) and *mens rea* (the intention to commit the crime). Customary law also includes peremptory norms (i.e., *jus cogens*), which are considered to be binding rules by the international community. Peremptory norms in the realm of human rights include prohibitions on slavery; genocide; piracy; war crimes; the murder or intentional disappearance of individuals; torture or other cruel, inhuman, or degrading treatment or punishment; prolonged arbitrary detention; systematic racial discrimination; and crimes against humanity.[67]

Evidence of customary international law is provided by constitutions, legislation, regulations, government policy documents and statements, opinions of official legal advisors, diplomatic correspondence, treaty ratifications, the practice of international institutions, and UN General Assembly resolutions relating to legal questions.[68] Judicial decisions (from national and international courts and tribunals) and teachings of publicists can also influence customary international law.[69]

An important advantage of customary international law over conventional international law is that it can bind all states, even without their consent. As Birnie and Boyle describe it, "the inactive are carried along with the active."[70] Only persistent objectors, meaning nations that actively and consistently deny the applicability or existence of a rule of customary international law, may not be bound by it.[71] In the environmental context, one of the most frequently cited principles of customary international law is "the existence of the general obligation of States to ensure that activities within their jurisdiction and control respect the environment of other states or of areas beyond national control."[72]

On the other hand, customary international law is complex and controversial because it is unwritten and open to conflicting interpretation.[73] Janis writes: "The determination of customary international law is more an art than a scientific method."[74] The distinction between what a state does and what it believes is inherently problematic, as it can be difficult to discern the latter. The problem has been addressed by assuming that state practice reflects an underlying intent, and by relying on statements of belief and other positive evidence as a substitute for actual beliefs.[75] There is an ongoing dispute among legal scholars as to whether state practice or *opinio juris* should be given greater weight in assessing the status of customary international law.[76] Other weaknesses of customary international law include the practical difficulty of demonstrating widespread or consistent practice in a world with approximately two hundred nations, the lengthy amount of time required to establish evidence of consistent practice, and the lack of institutions to adjudicate disputes or enforce the law. Because of these weaknesses, Guzman argues that customary international law may have less influence on the behaviour of states than soft law.[77]

Resolutions and Declarations

The first time the UN General Assembly explicitly linked environmental degradation and human rights was in 1968, in a resolution calling for an international conference on the environment.[78] The ensuing Stockholm Conference in 1972 marked a seminal point in the evolution of the right to a healthy environment, with the resultant *Stockholm Declaration on the Human Environment* containing the following principle:

Principle 1
Man has the fundamental right to freedom, equality and adequate conditions of life, in an environment of a quality that permits a life of dignity and well-being, and he bears a solemn responsibility to protect and improve the environment for present and future generations.[79]

Some scholars argue that Principle 1 of the *Stockholm Declaration* "stops short of proclaiming a right to environment, but it clearly links human rights and environmental protection."[80] In fact, the intention of the drafters of the *Stockholm Declaration* was to recognize the right of individuals to an adequate environment.[81] Although not generally considered to be legally binding, the *Stockholm Declaration* has had an enduring impact at both the national and international levels. Gormley claimed that the *Stockholm Declaration*, like the *Universal Declaration of Human Rights*, represents customary international law.[82] Pallemaerts asserted that the "*Stockholm Declaration* inspired many national constitutional provisions, adopted since the early 1970s, which recognize the right to the environment as a fundamental right under domestic law."[83]

Since 1972, many non-binding declarations have incorporated the right to a healthy environment, including the following:

- the 1989 *Hague Declaration on the Environment*
- resolutions from the UN General Assembly in 1990 and 2000
- the Council of Europe's 1990 *Dublin Declaration*
- the 1990 *Cairo Declaration on Human Rights in Islam*[84]
- repeated resolutions from the UN Commission on Human Rights[85]
- the Earth Charter, a unique international agreement that was drafted by civil society rather than states[86]
- the 2007 *Male' Declaration on the Human Dimension of Climate Change*[87]
- the 2010 *Universal Declaration of the Rights of Mother Earth.*

On the other hand, the right to a healthy environment was not explicitly included in the *Rio Declaration on Environment and Development* produced at the 1992 Earth Summit, nor was it endorsed at the 2002 World Summit on Sustainable Development.[88] The *Rio Declaration* was viewed by some scholars as a step toward the codification of environmental rights in international law, while others worried that the "failure to give greater explicit emphasis to human rights is indicative of continuing uncertainty and debate."[89]

According to Shelton, it was surprising that, "in light of two decades of con-vergence and growing acceptance of a right to environment in various legal instruments, consensus was absent."[90] The *Rio Declaration* was endorsed by more than 175 nations and has been repeatedly affirmed (e.g., at the 1994 UN Conference on Population and Development – 179 nations; the 1995 World Summit for Social Development – 186 nations; and Habitat II: the 1996 Second Conference on Human Settlements – 175 nations).[91] Lee views this pattern of endorsements as "evidence of a widespread and consistent state practice that can contribute to the creation of a right to a healthy en-vironment as a principle of customary international law."[92]

Critics observe that a proliferation of declarations cannot be equated with a legally binding right to a healthy environment.[93] Pevato writes that most of the international declarations articulating environmental rights "set forth aspirational goals within non-legally binding soft law documents."[94] On the other hand, declarations and resolutions can influence both state behaviour and the evolution of binding law.[95]

The United States appears to be the only nation that expressly denies the existence of the right to a healthy environment in both domestic and inter-national law. The US argues that if the right is in fact part of customary international law, it does not apply to Americans because the US government has persistently objected to its recognition.[96]

GENERAL PRINCIPLES

National laws and the decisions of national courts serve as evidence of "the general principles of law recognized by civilized nations," the third source of international law articulated in the *Statute of the International Court of Justice*. This category of international law comprises legal principles so basic and fundamental that they are reflected in the majority of national legal systems, such as *res judicata* ("a matter already judged" is not subject to being litigated again by the same parties). Determining general principles of law is a matter of comparative analysis of national laws.[97] Again, although this source of international law may sound relatively straightforward and objective, in reality it is complex and subjective. How many nations must adhere to a principle in order for it to qualify as a general principle? Malone and Pas-ternack state that "when a sufficient number of domestic constitutions rec-ognize the same right, then the right can be considered a general principle of law."[98] However, there is no golden rule or even rule of thumb as to what constitutes "a sufficient number" of nations.

An argument can be made that the right to live in a healthy environment constitutes a general principle of international law, based on a comparative assessment of domestic laws from around the world. Of the 193 UN members, there are ninety-two nations whose constitutions recognize the right to a healthy environment. An additional twelve nations have recognized an implicit right to a healthy environment through decisions of their Constitutional or Supreme Court. On the basis of regional treaties, 115 UN member nations recognize the right to a healthy environment. To this total may be added seven nations belonging to the Council of Europe, whose members are subject to the jurisprudence of the European Court of Human Rights (ECHR).[99] The ECHR recognizes the right to a healthy environment is implicit in the *European Convention on Human Rights* (discussed below). On the basis of recognizing the right to a healthy environment either in a constitution or through ratification of a legally binding regional treaty, the total is 150 out of 193 nations.[100] If one includes the small island states that signed the *Male' Declaration* recognizing the right to a healthy environment, then 175 UN nations recognize the right to a healthy environment.[101] If national legislation recognizing the right to a healthy environment is included, the total would be 178 nations out of 193, or 92 percent of the nations of the world (see Figure 4.1).[102] This is a very strong majority and suggests that the right to a healthy environment is very close to becoming, if it is not already, a general principle of international law.

The fifteen nations that do not yet recognize that their citizens possess a legal right to live in a healthy environment are Afghanistan, Australia, Brunei Darussalam, Cambodia, Canada, China, Japan, Kuwait, Laos, Lebanon, Myanmar, New Zealand, North Korea, Oman, and the United States. Even among these nations there are subnational jurisdictions that recognize the right to a healthy environment, including five provinces and territories in Canada and six American states.[103]

In terms of regional recognition of the right to a healthy environment, there is unanimity in Africa and Latin America and near unanimity in Europe. Within these three regions, a strong case can be made that the right to a healthy environment has evolved from a normative concept to a legally enforceable human right. In Asia, the majority of nations recognize the right to a healthy environment, including India and Indonesia, two of the largest and most populous nations in the region. China, with its large population and massive economy, is a significant exception. In the three remaining regions – North America, Oceania, and the Caribbean – the picture is starkly different. Apart from the Dominican Republic and Jamaica, there are no other nations within these regions whose constitutions recognize the right to a

FIGURE 4.1

Map of nations recognizing the right to a healthy environment

■ Nations recognizing the right to a healthy environment in constitutions, legislation, or international agreements

▨ Nations not recognizing the right to a healthy environment at the national or international level

healthy environment, nor have any national courts ruled that this right is implicit in other constitutionally protected rights. There is no regional human rights agreement in Oceania, and while nations in North America and the Caribbean are potentially part of the inter-American human rights system, none of them has ratified the *San Salvador Protocol.*

JUDICIAL DECISIONS AND LEGAL EXPERTS

Judicial decisions and the teachings of the most highly qualified experts are described in the *Statute of the International Court of Justice* as subsidiary means of determining international law. Brownlie suggests that the label "subsidiary means" ought not to be exaggerated in import and that judicial decisions should be regarded as authoritative evidence of the state of the law.[104] As noted earlier, decisions of global and regional courts and similar bodies also serve as evidence of customary international law.

Almost all global and regional human rights institutions, including the UN Human Rights Committee, the Inter-American Court of Human Rights, the Inter-American Commission on Human Rights, the European Court of Human Rights, and the African Commission on Human and Peoples' Rights, have developed jurisprudence that links environmental degradation to human rights violations. Air pollution, water pollution, toxic waste, deforestation, and excessive noise have been implicated in violations of the rights to life, health, property, information, and respect for private life, family life, and the home. According to Kiss and Shelton, "International courts and other treaty bodies have expanded or reinterpreted these guarantees in light of environmental concerns, despite the lack of explicit reference to environmental rights in most human rights instruments."[105] In light of the foregoing, it is vital to distinguish between the many cases that link environmental harm and human rights, and the small but growing number of cases that specifically endorse the right to a healthy environment. The following discussion briefly reviews the key environment/human rights decisions from both global and regional courts and commissions. Taken as a whole, these decisions indicate that the right to a healthy environment is gradually gaining broader recognition.

Decisions of Global Courts and Tribunals

International Court of Justice
The International Court of Justice (ICJ) settles disputes between UN members and issues advisory opinions on legal questions submitted by authorized international institutions.[106] Although the ICJ established a special chamber

CHAPTER 4: THE INFLUENCE OF INTERNATIONAL LAW

to deal with environmental questions in 1993, there have been no decisions directly addressing the question of a right to a healthy environment.[107] However, in an oft-cited portion of *Gabčíkovo-Nagymaros*, a case involving a controversial dam project in Eastern Europe, Judge Weeramantry wrote, in a separate opinion:

> The people of both Hungary and Slovakia are ... entitled to the preservation of their human right to the protection of their environ- ment ... The protection of the environment is ... a vital part of contemporary human rights doctrine, for it is a *sine qua non* for numerous human rights such as the right to health and the right to life itself ... damage to the environment can impair and under- mine all the rights spoken of in the *Universal Declaration* and other human rights instruments.[108]

United Nations Human Rights Committee

The UN Human Rights Committee was established to monitor the imple- mentation of the *International Covenant on Civil and Political Rights (ICCPR)*. Individuals can file communications with the committee asserting violations of their rights, but only if their nation has ratified the *Optional Protocol* to the *ICCPR*.[109] There will also be a process for adjudicating complaints alleging violations of the human rights identified in the *International Covenant on Economic, Social and Cultural Rights (ICESCR)*, but not until the *Optional Protocol* to the *ICESCR* comes into force.[110]

Only a handful of the more than one thousand communications submit- ted to the UN Human Rights Committee since 1976 have involved allegations of environmental degradation.[111] For example, a group of Sri Lankan citizens filed a communication asserting that their right to life, including a healthy environment, had been violated by the construction of a major expressway. The committee found their claim to be inadmissible on technical grounds.[112] The most prominent environmental case addressed to the Human Rights Committee was also ruled inadmissible, yet it is frequently cited by propon- ents of the right to a healthy environment.[113] In the Port Hope case, residents of a Canadian town alleged that dumping nuclear waste near their residences constituted pollution that threatened their right to life. The committee decided against the residents based on the residents' failure to exhaust domestic remedies; however, the committee noted that the case raised serious issues about the state's obligation to protect the right to life.[114]

Regional Court Decisions

Inter-American Commission on Human Rights
The Inter-American Commission on Human Rights (IACHR) has issued recommendations in a number of situations where environmental degradation
has affected human rights, including several cases where petitioners alleged
a violation of their right to a healthy environment. Most of the cases have
involved adverse effects on indigenous people. The IACHR first established a
link between environmental quality and the right to life in 1985, determining
that a highway and authorizations for natural resource exploitation in Brazil
violated the rights of the Yanomani Indians to health, life, liberty, personal
security, and free movement.[115] The contested highway was built prior to the
IACHR's ruling.[116] In a similar situation involving the effects of oil and gas
development in Ecuador on the Yanomani people, the IACHR concluded that
toxic chemicals were contaminating the Yanomani's water, air, and soil,
jeopardizing their health and their lives.[117] The IACHR observed:

> The realization of the right to life, and to physical security and in-
> tegrity is necessarily related to, and in some ways dependent upon
> one's physical environment. Accordingly, where physical contamina-
> tion and degradation pose a persistent threat to human life and
> health, the foregoing rights are implicated ... Conditions of severe
> environmental pollution, which may cause serious physical illness,
> impairment and suffering on the part of the local populace, are in-
> consistent with the right to be respected as a human being.[118]

The recommendations of the IACHR are non-binding but are expected
to influence government policies and actions. As well, if a state fails to follow
the IACHR's recommendations, the commission can ask the Inter-American
Court to issue an enforcement order. Scott argues that because of a lack of
implementation, the commission's recommendations regarding Ecuador and
Brazil "have not effectively improved conditions for native people and their
lands."[119] The Yanomani cases from Brazil and Ecuador predate the *San Salvador
Protocol*, which explicitly recognizes the right to a healthy environment.

Several cases brought after the *San Salvador Protocol* came into force raised
the right to a healthy environment but were decided on the basis that environmental degradation violated other human rights. In 2000, the
Association of Lhaka Honhat Aboriginal Communities alleged that a highway
being built in Argentina would violate members' rights to life and to a healthy

environment. The IACHR requested that Argentina conduct meaningful consultation.[120] In 2003, the Maya Indigenous Communities of the Toledo District in Belize alleged that logging and oil concessions violated their right to a healthy environment as part of their rights to life and health. The Maya also alleged violations of their rights to property, religious freedom, family protection, and cultural life, and their right to participate in government decision making. The IACHR held that environmental damage from logging was part of a broad suite of actions that violated the Maya's right to property and determined it was unnecessary to address the other alleged human rights violations.[121] In a second 2003 case, a mine contaminated a small indigenous community in Peru with toxic sludge containing arsenic, lead, mercury, and cadmium. The IACHR requested that Peru implement provisional measures to protect human health, including conducting an environmental assessment and removing the toxic waste.[122] In 2005, a petition filed by Inuit people from Canada and the United States alleged that climate change violated their human rights, including the right to live in a healthy environment, but the petition was declared inadmissible.[123]

Currently pending before the IACHR are three additional petitions linking environmental degradation to human rights. The Cacataibo people, residents of a remote region in the Peruvian Amazon, filed a petition seeking to block oil and gas exploration in their territory.[124] In 2006, the residents of La Oroya, a Peruvian town contaminated by the operation of a lead smelter, won a case in Peru's Constitutional Court on the basis that a number of their rights were being violated, including the right to a healthy environment (this case is discussed in Chapter 6). The government did not comply with the court's order, so the residents filed a petition with the IACHR. The commission requested that the Peruvian government immediately provide specialized medical treatment to residents of La Oroya who were suffering poor health linked to air, water, and soil pollution.[125] In 2009, the IACHR agreed to adjudicate the case.[126] In 2010, the IACHR asked Guatemala to suspend a mining project and prevent environmental contamination threatening the water supply of eighteen Maya communities.[127]

The Inter-American Court of Human Rights

Like the IACHR, the Inter-American Court of Human Rights has decided a number of cases involving the effect of environmental degradation on human rights.[128] Again, most of the cases have involved indigenous communities. None of the court's decisions has directly addressed the right to a healthy environment. For example, in 2001, the Inter-American Court held that Nicaragua's decision to grant timber licences to a foreign company without considering indigenous people's dependence on the land in question violated their human rights.[129] The *Awas Tingni* case represented the first time that the Inter-American Court, relying on the *San Salvador Protocol*, made the connection between environmental degradation and human rights. The court ordered Nicaragua to abstain from permitting any resource extraction activities within the area occupied and used by the Awas Tingni. In 2008, the government of Nicaragua awarded the Awas Tingni Community title to 73,000 hectares of its land, marking a major step forward in the resolution of the case.

In 2003, the Kichwa Peoples of the Sarayaku Indigenous Community accused Ecuador of allowing foreign oil companies to carry out activities on ancestral lands without consent or due process.[130] The IACHR requested that Ecuador take provisional steps to protect protestors, secure the indigenous people's special relationship with their land, and investigate criminal acts against the indigenous people. Ecuador refused to cooperate, so the IACHR went to the Inter-American Court to seek assistance in enforcing the provisional measures. The Inter-American Court ordered Ecuador to comply with the IACHR's recommendations.[131] The case is now awaiting the court's decision on the merits.[132]

The Yakye Axa are an indigenous people who were resettled and are seeking a return to their ancestral lands in Paraguay. Their traditional lands have been sold to multinational corporations. In 2005, the Inter-American Court found that Paraguay had violated the Yakye Axa's right to life, interpreting right to life broadly as encompassing other rights including the right to a healthy environment.[133] A similar case involving the Sawhoyamaxa Indigenous Community produced the same outcome.[134]

The most recent environmental decision of the Inter-American Court came in 2007, in the *Twelve Saramaka Clans* case, which involves the government of Suriname's actions in granting mining and logging concessions in the traditional territory of the Saramaka people. The Inter-American Court found that serious environmental damage had occurred, violating the Saramaka's right to property (in the collective sense) and their right to judicial protection (since the domestic legal system of Suriname failed to recognize the legitimate legal interest represented by collective title).[135]

European Court of Human Rights

Despite the absence of an explicit right to a healthy environment in the *European Convention on Human Rights*, the European Court of Human Rights

(ECHR) has adjudicated numerous cases where victims of environmental degradation or hazards relied on other human rights in their search for re- dress.[136] In environmental cases, the ECHR has relied on the following rights:

- right to life (Article 2)
- right to a fair trial (Article 6)
- right to respect for private and family life, and home (Article 8)
- freedom of expression (Article 10)
- right to peaceful assembly (Article 11)
- right to an effective remedy (Article 13)
- right to peaceful enjoyment of property (Article 1 of the First Protocol).

Because of the extensive ECHR jurisprudence related to environmental issues and human rights, not all cases will be described in this chapter. Instead, the analysis will draw out the key legal principles articulated by the ECHR in linking human rights and the environment, discuss crucial judgments, and trace the evolution of the right to a healthy environment.

Article 8: Respect for Private and Family Life, and Home
Of the *European Convention*'s provisions, Article 8 has been the most frequently cited in an environmental context:

> Article 8.1 Everyone has the right to respect for his private and family life, his home and correspondence.
> 8.2 There shall be no interference by a public authority with the exercise of this right except such as is in accordance with the law and is necessary in a democratic society in the interests of national secur- ity, public safety or the economic well-being of the country, for the prevention of disorder or crime, for the protection of health or morals, or for the protection of the rights and freedoms of others.

The ECHR's breakthrough in protecting human rights from environmental harm came in 1994 in the *Lopez Ostra* case, in which the court determined that "severe environmental pollution may affect individuals' well-being and prevent them from enjoying their homes in such a way as to affect their private and family life adversely without, however, seriously endangering their health."[137] The court found that the Spanish authorities had failed to strike a fair balance between economic interests and the applicant's right to respect for her home, resulting in a violation of Article 8. Sands wrote that the *Lopez*

Ostra decision "implies a general right to a clean environment" in Europe.[138] However, the ECHR itself has made conflicting statements on this point, as the following discussion demonstrates.

Since the *Lopez Ostra* decision, many cases have found violations of Article 8 on the basis of environmental hazards, including toxic emissions from a fertilizer factory,[139] air pollution from a steel plant,[140] excessive noise,[141] the operation of a hazardous-waste treatment facility,[142] air pollution and vibration from the rerouting of a highway,[143] and the use of sodium cyanide in gold mining.[144] In contrast, in several cases involving allegations of excessive noise from airports, the ECHR did not find that Article 8 was violated. The court held that the measures taken by states in relation to noise abatement were within the margin of appreciation (deference accorded to government decision makers), and in these circumstances it was not for the court to substitute its assessment of what might constitute the best policy.[145]

Article 2: Right to Life

In *Oneryildiz*, at least twenty-six people died because of an explosion at a municipal dump/landfill site, with evidence that Turkish governments knew for years about the serious danger of such an event.[146] Although the right to a healthy environment was mentioned, the case was decided on the basis of violations of the rights to life, effective remedies, and peaceful possession of property. From an environmental perspective, *Oneryildiz* established a positive obligation upon states to protect life from "industrial activities, which by their very nature are dangerous, such as the operation of waste-collection sites."[147] In the words of the ECHR, "The positive obligation to take all appropriate steps to safeguard life for the purposes of Article 2 entails above all a primary duty on the State to put in place a legislative and administrative framework designed to provide effective deterrence against threats to the right to life."[148]

Article 6: Right to a Fair Hearing

Article 6 of the *European Convention* guarantees that everyone is entitled to a fair hearing, and has been used to provide procedural safeguards in environmental cases. In *Zander*, the lack of a judicial review process available to a Swedish citizen wishing to challenge a permit for a neighbouring waste treatment facility was found to violate Article 6.[149] In *Okyay*, the ECHR found a violation of Article 6 because the Turkish government failed to enforce court orders, based on environmental damage, to halt pollution from three thermal power plants.[150] The court orders had been upheld on appeal by Turkey's

Supreme Administrative Court. The case turned on whether the applicants could establish that they had a civil right relevant to the operation of the power plants despite their acknowledgment that they had suffered no physical or economic harm. Because their right to live in a healthy environment was protected by the Turkish constitution, the ECHR held that they had a civil right for purposes of Article 6. The ECHR also referred to "relevant international texts on the right to a healthy environment."[151] In the *Taskin* case, the court also found a violation of Article 6, because Turkish authorities circumvented court orders, again based on the constitutional right to a healthy environment, that quashed operating permits for a gold mine.[152]

Other ECHR Jurisprudence Related to the Environment
The ECHR has defended the ability of states to infringe human rights in the legitimate pursuit of environmental protection objectives. For example, permission to carry out construction in a green belt has been revoked, restrictions on fishing rights justified, and revocation of a licence to extract gravel upheld.[153] Most recently, the ECHR rejected a complaint about excessive noise allegedly caused by wind turbines.[154] In these cases, the broader societal interest in environmental protection has outweighed property rights and rights under Article 8. In several Article 10 cases involving freedom of expression, the court emphasized the importance of publicizing environmental information and the watchdog role played by civil society organizations.[155] The court has also addressed the rights to peaceful assembly and freedom of association (Article 11) in cases involving a proposed rally by an ENGO and the state-ordered dissolution of an ENGO.[156]

The preceding discussion focuses on the extent to which the ECHR has found that environmental hazards or harm violated various human rights explicitly recognized in the *European Convention*. The ECHR has also made a number of observations regarding the right to a healthy environment. In *Hatton*, the Grand Chamber split 12-5 on whether Article 8 was violated by excessive noise from Heathrow Airport. The majority wrote: "There is no explicit right in the *Convention* to a clean and quiet environment, but where an individual is directly and seriously affected by noise or other pollution, an issue may arise under Article 8."[157] The dissenting judges wrote: "Article 8 of the *Convention* guarantees the right to a healthy environment," including "protection against nuisance caused by harmful chemicals, offensive smells, agents which precipitate respiratory ailments, noise, and so on," and the majority judgment "seems to us to deviate from the above developments in the case-law and even to take a step backwards."[158]

In *Kyrtatos*, the court ruled that urban development that harmed a swamp, damaging birds and other protected species, did not constitute interference with Article 8.[159] The court reiterated its position that the crucial element in determining whether environmental damage interferes with Article 8(1) is

> the existence of a harmful effect on a person's private or family sphere and not simply the general deterioration of the environment. Neither Article 8 nor any of the other Articles of the *Convention* are specifically designed to provide general protection of the environment as such; to that effect, other international instruments and domestic legislation are more pertinent in dealing with this particular aspect.[160]

In a perplexing statement, however, the court added that "it might have been otherwise if, for instance, the environmental deterioration complained of had consisted in the destruction of a forest area in the vicinity of the applicants' house, a situation which could have affected more directly the applicants' own well-being."[161] One might ask why the destruction of a forest would cause a different legal outcome than the destruction of a swamp. In *Fadeyeva*, a Russian air pollution case, the court reiterated that "Article 8 has been relied on in various cases involving environmental concern, yet it is not violated every time that environmental deterioration occurs: no right to nature preservation is as such included among the rights and freedoms guaranteed by the *Convention*."[162]

Recent decisions in *Tatar*, *Atanasov*, and *Grimkovskaya* confirm the scope of the ECHR's interpretation of the right to a healthy environment. *Tatar* contains a clear endorsement of the right to a healthy environment.[163] In *Tatar*, a Romanian case dealing with the dangers of using sodium cyanide for mining, the court observed that the right to a healthy environment is protected in both the Romanian constitution and Romanian environmental legislation.[164] The court concluded that the state's failure to take positive actions to prevent an environmental disaster violated "the rights to life, private and family life and, more generally, to the enjoyment of a healthy and protected environment."[165] In *Atanasov*, dealing with the reclamation of a tailings pond from a copper mine, the ECHR found evidence of pollution but no proof of direct impact on the applicant or his family and reiterated that there is no right to nature preservation.[166] In *Grimkovskaya*, the court found that the cumulative effect of noise, vibrations, and air and soil pollution from a rerouted motorway directly harmed the applicant, and violated Article 8.[167]

As Shelton concludes, "Environmental rights have found a place in the European system, despite the lack of reference to them in the Convention."[168] Boyle also concludes that the ECHR's case law entrenches environmental rights, although only for individuals directly affected by environmental degradation.[169] However, there are limits on what the court considers as falling within the ambit of the right. The human rights guarantees in the *European Convention* have been useful primarily when the environmental harm consists of pollution (air, water, or noise) that threatens human health. At the present time, nature conservation and protecting biodiversity are excluded, although the court's musings about damage to a forest in *Kyrtatos* and the recent *Tatar* decision suggest that it may be open to expanding the scope of this right in future cases.

European Committee of Social Rights

The European Committee of Social Rights, established in 1998 to address violations of the *European Social Charter*, recently entered the debate about the right to a healthy environment.[170] In a case asserting that the Greek government was failing to adequately address air pollution from coal mining, the committee determined that the right to a healthy environment is an integral aspect of the right to health.[171] Trilsch described the *Marangopoulos* case as one of the most important decisions of the European Committee of Social Rights to date, as it "places the right to a healthy environment in the mainstream of human rights."[172]

African Commission on Human Rights

The African Commission on Human Rights has issued one major decision that focuses specifically on the impact of environmental degradation on human rights, while a more recent decision involves indigenous people and the protection of the environment.[173] In *SERAC et al. v. Nigeria*, the commission *concluded* that the failure of Nigeria's government to prevent toxic pollution from oil development activities violated two rights in the *African Charter*: the right to health and the right to a general satisfactory environment. The Nigerian government argued that the economic, social, and cultural rights in the *African Charter* are vague and incapable of legal enforcement. The *SERAC* decision is significant because the African Commission rejected this claim, instead offering a comprehensive interpretation of the right to a healthy environment. The commission concluded that Article 24 "imposes clear obligations upon a government ... to take reasonable measures to prevent pollution and ecological degradation, to promote conservation, and to secure an ecologically sustainable development and use of natural resources."[174]

Kiss and Shelton note that "the Commission gives the right to environment meaningful content by requiring the state to adopt various techniques of environmental protection, such as environmental impact assessment, public information and participation, access to justice for environmental harm, and monitoring of potentially harmful activities."[175] Shelton describes this decision as "landmark, like the decisions of the Inter-American Commission on Human Rights in its investigations of Ecuador and Brazil," in that it offers "a blueprint for merging environmental protection, economic development, and guarantees of human rights."[176] Despite the seemingly powerful decision, there apparently has been little change on the ground in Nigeria.[177] As noted earlier, the African Commission's decisions are neither legally binding nor enforceable.

Opinions of Legal Experts

The second subsidiary source of international law is "the teachings of the most highly qualified publicists," referring to the published work of academics, lawyers, and judges. Over the years, the academic and legal communities have been divided on both the legal status and desirability of the right to a healthy environment. However, a clear trend has emerged in recent years as international law organizations, the majority of scholarly books and articles, and the majority of experts agree that there is an emerging human right to a healthy environment. However, a vocal minority continues to raise important objections, and their perspective should not be overlooked.

International recognition of the right to a healthy environment has been endorsed by:

- the World Commission on Environment and Development (also known as the Brundtland Commission)[178]
- the UN Special Rapporteur on Human Rights and the Environment, whose final report included a *Draft Declaration of Principles on Human Rights and the Environment*[179]
- the World Health Organization[180]
- a Global Judges Symposium[181]
- the International Law Association[182]
- the International Union for Conservation of Nature's (IUCN) Commission on Environmental Law and the International Council of Environmental Law[183]

- an international group of experts brought together in 1999 by the UN Educational, Scientific and Cultural Organization and the UN High Commissioner for Human Rights[184]
- the Institute of International Law[185]
- groups of experts assembled in 2002 and 2009 by the UN High Commissioner for Human Rights and the UN Environment Programme.[186]

Experts in international law have also produced a series of declarations endorsing the right to a healthy environment, including the following:

- the 1991 *Draft Charter on Environmental Rights and Obligations*[187]
- the 1999 *Bizkaia Declaration on the Right to the Environment*[188]
- the *Limoges Declarations* (1990, 2001)[189]
- the *Draft International Declaration on Human Rights and Environment.*[190]

Individual scholars can be characterized, according to their viewpoints about the right to a healthy environment, as evangelicals, frustrated idealists, hopeful realists, or hardened cynics. At one end of the spectrum are the evangelicals, a small minority of scholars who look at the legal evidence through rose-coloured glasses, going so far as to suggest that the right to a healthy environment is *jus cogens*, meaning a principle of law that is so deeply entrenched as to be beyond debate.[191] Frustrated idealists believe that the right to a healthy environment should be an established principle of international environmental law but lament its current lack of legal recognition. For example, Atapattu writes: "It seems unjust to deny the right to environment, which by far is more fundamental than any of the protected rights in existence today."[192]

Hopeful realists perceive the right to a healthy environment as a promising development in solving environmental problems but take a more measured view of the state of the law. Many international environmental and human rights experts fall into this category.[193] These scholars believe that while the right to a healthy environment lacks recognition in a binding global human rights agreement, it is firmly entrenched in some regions, as evidenced by regional human rights agreements, decisions of national and regional courts, trends in state practice, and numerous international declarations. For example, the former president of the ICJ argues that environmental rights "deserve to be promoted with all possible vigour" but are not well established in international law.[194]

The hardened cynics deny the existence of the right to a healthy environment under international law, deem it unnecessary (given existing human rights and environmental laws), reject its bona fides as a human right, or contend that there are fundamental practical weaknesses that make recognizing it undesirable.[195] For example, Handl argued that the right to a healthy environment has an "exceedingly slim evidentiary basis in international law."[196] The hardened cynics, like their evangelical counterparts, ignore evidence that contradicts their perspective. Yet it is difficult to maintain that there are no signs of the emergence of a right to a healthy environment when faced with regional human rights agreements, constitutions, laws, regulations, and court decisions that recognize, implement, and enforce it.

An examination of twenty leading books in the fields of international environmental law, international human rights law, and international law yielded four books that did not mention the right to a healthy environment;[197] five that discussed the right to a healthy environment but expressed no opinion regarding its status at international law;[198] one that acknowledged the existence of the right regionally but not globally;[199] and ten that considered the right to a healthy environment to be emerging or gaining broader acceptance both regionally and globally.[200]

Overall, it appears that the majority of organizations and experts specializing in international law, human rights law, and environmental law agree that there is an emerging human right to a healthy environment.

Downloading International Law into National Law

It is well established that international environmental law influences national environmental law.[201] Recognition of the right to a healthy environment at the global and regional levels has influenced the development of the law within nations, affecting constitutions, legislation, and jurisprudence. The 1972 *Stockholm Declaration* is commonly cited as the inspiration for including the right to a healthy environment and other environmental provisions in constitutions.[202] For example, international environmental law was a factor in the decisions of Argentina, Brazil, and Georgia to provide constitutional recognition of the right to a healthy environment.[203] The *Aarhus Convention* influenced the amendment of Finland's constitution to include environmental provisions.[204]

There are many examples of international law influencing decisions about the right to a healthy environment in national court systems. The *Stockholm Declaration* had a major influence on the Supreme Court of India's decisions protecting the constitutional right to a healthy environment.[205] The right to a healthy environment in the *African Charter* led Kenyan and Nigerian courts to make important rulings based on this right, finding it to be an essential part of the constitutional right to life, although not explicitly articulated as such in either the Kenyan or Nigerian constitutions.[206] Costa Rican courts have cited the *San Salvador Protocol* in cases involving the constitutional right to a healthy environment.[207] From Colombia to the Philippines, national courts interpreting the right to a healthy environment often turn to international law for guidance.

In Europe, because the regional law created by European courts is effectively superior to national law, the jurisprudence of the ECHR has a powerful effect, which grows larger in reach as the EU adds nations from Eastern Europe. Lasser observed that in Europe an "inter-institutional dynamic has prompted a frantic race to the 'top,'" with the result that the "rights revolution is transforming the judicial landscape at breakneck speed."[208] In essence, Europe's regional and national courts are competing with each other to push the envelope of human rights jurisprudence, with no court wanting to be left behind. In addition to its growing legal influence, the ECHR is also experiencing a dramatic increase in its caseload, from 3,500 in 1995 to 10,500 in 2000 to over 40,000 cases in 2007.[209] As discussed earlier, the ECHR now recognizes the right to a healthy environment, which may create a ripple effect throughout Europe.[210] While many European nations and courts already recognize the right at the domestic level, others do not. Hottelier and Martenet suggest that the emerging case law of the ECHR may hold the key to recognition of the right to a healthy environment in Switzerland, because of the ECHR's influence on Swiss courts.[211]

In environmental cases, the ECHR consistently refers to the constitutional right to a healthy environment in nations from which cases originate (e.g., Romania, Russia, Turkey).[212] The ECHR has ruled that the failure of national authorities to implement domestic court orders based on violations of the right to a healthy environment is a breach of Article 6 of the *European Convention*. In effect, the European Court has become the final appellate court for violations of the right to a healthy environment that are either not recognized by domestic courts or not enforced by national authorities.[213]

Transnational Cross-Pollination and the Right to a Healthy Environment

Four processes are contributing to the globalization of environmental law: transplantation, harmonization, convergence, and integration.[214] Transplantation is the "deliberate copying and adaptation of significant portions of statutes or particular doctrines of law by one country from another."[215] It is clear that this has occurred in the context of the constitutional right to a healthy environment, given that similar language is used around the world. For example, the phrase "right to a healthy and ecologically balanced environment" was first used in the Portuguese constitution in 1976 and is now found in twenty-one other constitutions. National courts frequently cite decisions from other national courts. The Supreme Court of India's decisions on the right to a healthy environment have influenced courts in Bangladesh, Pakistan, Sri Lanka, Uganda, and Kenya.[216] An Indonesian court relied on the right to a healthy environment as well as precedents from Spain, Portugal, and the Netherlands to grant standing to an ENGO.[217] The Internet facilitates transplantation by making constitutions, legislation, and case law increasingly accessible. As Slaughter observed, "Courts are talking to one another all over the world," especially about human rights because of their universal nature.[218] These developments are not without their critics. McCrudden raises concerns about cherry-picking and fears that important cultural differences could be glossed over.[219]

Harmonization refers to the process of adjusting and conforming national standards to meet the requirements of an international system. Integration is the process of linking national legal systems. Both harmonization and integration are occurring, most prominently in the European Union, where new members must upgrade environmental laws and all members must comply with EU-wide environmental directives. Convergence describes how distinct legal systems, like biological species, can evolve to become more similar, not as a result of deliberate acts of copying but rather as a response to similar external pressures, especially environmental pressures.[220] Again, this phenomenon can be observed in the similarities between constitutions, national environmental laws, and court decisions related to the right to a healthy environment. For example, the court decisions in the leading cases involving the Matanza-Riachuelo River in Argentina and Manila Bay in the Philippines share many common elements (see Chapters 6 and 8, respectively).[221] In both cases, the courts imposed extensive duties upon multiple government agencies, employed independent scientific experts to inform their judgments, and established innovative measures to ensure compliance with their orders. The judgments occurred independently in response to similar environmental pressures and ongoing failures to respond.

Liefferink and Jordan describe elite networking (i.e., sharing of ideas among individuals who interact internationally) as another process contributing to the cross-pollination of environmental law.[222] Elite networking has played a vital role in the globalization of the right to a healthy environment through the activities of judges, prosecutors, legislators, academics, lawyers, and ENGOs.[223]

JUDGES

Judges have formed organizations and issued resolutions to promote the importance of ecologically informed judicial decision making. For example, the EU Forum of Judges for the Environment was established in 2004 to promote the enforcement of national, European, and international environmental law.[224] The organization hosts regular forums for judges interested in environmental law. The Philippine Supreme Court has hosted meetings to share its innovative policies, practices, and precedents with judges from other Asian nations.[225] Prior to the World Summit on Sustainable Development in 2002, there was a Global Judges Symposium held in South Africa. More than one hundred judges from fifty nations produced the *Johannesburg Principles on the Role of Law and Sustainable Development*, which state:

> We emphasize that the fragile state of the global environment requires the judiciary, as the guardian of the Rule of Law, to boldly and fearlessly implement and enforce applicable international and national laws, which in the field of environment and sustainable development will assist in alleviating poverty and sustaining an enduring civilization, and ensuring that the present generation will enjoy and improve the quality of life of all peoples, while also ensuring that the rights and interests of succeeding generations are not compromised
>
> ...
>
> We recognize that the people most affected by environmental degradation are the poor, and that, therefore, there is an urgent need to strengthen the capacity of the poor and their representatives to defend environmental rights, so as to ensure that the weakest sections of society are not prejudiced by environmental degradation and are enabled to enjoy their right to live in a social and physical environment that respects and promotes their dignity.[226]

The past decade has witnessed an explosion in efforts to train judges in environmental law. The UN Environment Programme has an extensive program dedicated to providing environmental education for judges, which offers capacity building, handbooks, casebooks, and information on international treaties.[227] UNEP hosted at least eight regional symposia for judges between 1995 and 2003.[228] Along with several partner organizations, UNEP provided judicial training for all Kenyan High Court and Court of Appeal judges in 2005-07.[229]

Governments and ENGOs also offer environmental education programs for judges.[230] These programs often include materials related to the right to a healthy environment, including cases from different jurisdictions. In Mozambique, for example, international organizations provide training courses, reference materials, and bi-national exchanges for judges, lawyers, and civil servants.[231] A leading Ugandan ENGO, Greenwatch, has organized an ongoing series of educational workshops on environmental law for environmental officers, police, magistrates, and judges of the High Court, Court of Appeal, and the Supreme Court.[232] The United States–based Environmental Law Institute runs education programs for judges from all over the world, striving to familiarize them with environmental law and also cross-pollinating jurisprudence between nations.[233] An Australian program has produced over eight hundred judges with environmental specialization in Indonesia.[234] Taken together, these efforts are instilling an unprecedented level of environmental awareness in judges, with positive implications for decisions involving the right to a healthy environment.

Lawyers and Environmental Law NGOs

Lawyers participate in international networks that share cases, precedents, and litigation strategies. There are networks of public interest environmental law organizations – both global and regional – at the forefront of litigation seeking to enforce the right to a healthy environment. The Environmental Law Alliance Worldwide (ELAW) works with partners on every continent to share legal and scientific information.[235] The Inter-American Association for Environmental Defense (AIDA) includes environmental law NGOs in the United States, Canada, Argentina, Chile, Ecuador, Costa Rica, Peru, and Mexico. The GUTA Association includes lawyers from Central and Eastern Europe and the Newly Independent States,[236] while Justice and Environment is a European network of environmental law organizations from twelve nations.[237]

In addition to litigation, lawyers from around the world are involved in drafting new constitutions and constitutional amendments. Epp describes "constitutional engineering" as "the process of creating new constitutions for other countries – on the assumption that new or revised constitutional structures or guarantees will re-form societies."[238] In the recent development of

Ecuador's groundbreaking constitutional provisions recognizing the rights of Nature, the government of Ecuador consulted groups ranging from the UN Food and Agriculture Organization to the Community Environmental Legal Defense Fund, a small NGO based in Pennsylvania.[239]

International organizations that specialize in environmental law, including the IUCN Commission on Environmental Law,[240] the IUCN Academy of Environmental Law,[241] the International Network for Environmental Compliance and Enforcement,[242] and the UN Environment Programme, do extensive work related to constitutions and environmental rights.[243] For example, the IUCN operates a project whose goal is to "mainstream" the right to a healthy environment in Nepal.[244]

A recent court case involving the right to water under South Africa's constitution illustrates the globalization of constitutional law. The case was brought on behalf of impoverished residents in Soweto, a suburb of Johannesburg. The Centre on Housing Rights and Evictions (COHRE), an NGO based in Switzerland that runs a program on the right to water, intervened in the case.[245] COHRE is funded by the governments of Sweden, Finland, and the Netherlands as well as the Ford Foundation. Peter Gleick, a renowned water policy expert from California's Pacific Institute for Studies in Development, Environment, and Security, provided affidavit evidence in the case on behalf of COHRE.[246]

Conclusion

It is clear that environmental degradation violates human rights, including the rights to life, health, respect for private and family life and the home, and peaceful enjoyment of property.[247] But what about the more contentious question of the status of the right to a healthy environment in international law? It has been suggested that the answer to this question depends on one's perspective.[248] Those who favour a liberal, progressive interpretation of international law are more likely to affirm the establishment of the right to a healthy environment, while those who adhere to a more traditional, positivist approach will deny the existence of this right.[249] Some legal experts continue to deny the emergence of the right to a healthy environment, although they are in the minority.[250]

On balance, however, the evidence assembled in this book indicates that the traditionalists need to rethink their conclusion. The academic debate has been overtaken by legal developments, including new regional treaties, constitutions, laws, and court decisions at the regional and national level. Out of 193 UN nations, 153 are legally obligated to respect, protect, and fulfill the right to a healthy environment, through constitutions, constitutional case law, legislation, regional treaties, and regional court decisions. Another 25 UN member states signed the non-binding *Male' Declaration*, bringing the total to 178 nations, or 92 percent of UN members. The right to a healthy environment is recognized in the jurisprudence of the African Commission on Human and Peoples' Rights, the Inter-American Commission on Human Rights and Inter-American Court of Human Rights, the European Court of Human Rights, and the European Committee of Social Rights. The trend toward constitutional and legal recognition of the right continues, demonstrated by new constitutional provisions in the Dominican Republic, Kenya, Jamaica, Morocco, and South Sudan.

There are many global declarations and resolutions – dating back to the 1972 *Stockholm Declaration* – that support the recognition of the right to a healthy environment. The UN General Assembly and various UN organs have repeatedly endorsed the right. Admittedly, these are soft law instruments, but soft law can have a significant influence on the behaviour of states in the fields of international environmental law and international human rights law. Many experts and environmental law organizations – from lawyers who assisted the Brundtland Commission to the International Law Association – have endorsed the right to a healthy environment. Finally, the majority of scholars in the fields of international environmental law and international human rights law agree that the right is entrenched in certain regions and emerging globally.

This rapid legal evolution of the right to a healthy environment was facilitated by a back-and-forth dialogue between international environmental and human rights law and national environmental and constitutional law. The diffusion or migration of the idea of incorporating environmental protection into constitutions can be attributed to the processes of transplantation, convergence, harmonization, integration, and elite networking, and to the dedicated efforts of legislators, judges, lawyers, academics, non-governmental organizations, and international organizations. Since the seminal *Stockholm Declaration*, international law has had a profound effect on the constitutionalization of environmental protection and on national case law regarding the right to a healthy environment. As Yang and Percival conclude, "No longer can one see the national environmental law systems as distinct or separate from international environmental law or from each other. Instead, global environmental law is emerging as an amalgam of national and international environmental law and their interactions."[251]

Overall, legal developments are heading in the same direction – regional treaties, decisions of regional courts and commissions, international resolutions, national constitutions, and national court decisions. The right to live in a healthy environment is now a firmly established legal principle in Africa, Latin America, and Europe. It is emerging in Asia and the Middle East. While there is not yet global unanimity regarding the right to a healthy environment, the threshold for becoming customary international law or a general principle of law is very close to being met, if it has not already been surpassed.

PART 2

The Constitutional Right to a Healthy Environment in Practice

5
A Framework for Assessing the Legal Influence of the Right to a Healthy Environment

As discussed in Chapter 1, it can be challenging to determine whether and to what extent constitutional rights matter. There are difficulties in establishing a cause-and-effect relationship between a constitutional provision, such as the right to a healthy environment, and an environmental outcome (e.g., improved air quality). Among the key challenges is the lengthy chain of events between the establishment of constitutional provisions and the environmental outcomes, with each step characterized by myriad causal influences and pervasive uncertainty.[1]

In response to these challenges, this chapter outlines two approaches that can be used to demonstrate that constitutional provisions related to environmental protection can influence public policy. Instead of trying to follow the long and complicated chain of events from constitutional enactment to environmental outcomes, the focus is on two shorter, more direct sequences of events (see Figures 5.1 and 5.2).

The first approach involves reviewing national environmental legislation to determine whether the right to a healthy environment is subsequently incorporated in laws (the initial step in Figure 5.1). In order for the promise of a constitutional right to be realized, an essential step is the drafting or strengthening of relevant legislation. The research focuses on the framework environmental law of a nation because such laws are "indispensable for the implementation of constitutional environmental provisions."[2] However, other environmental laws are also examined in an effort to gauge the full extent of constitutional influence on relevant legislation. If environmental laws have been amended to explicitly incorporate the right to a healthy environment and other direct references to the constitution, this provides a *prima facie* indication that the right does have tangible, practical impacts. Chapters 6 to 10 will examine the extent to which the constitutional right to a healthy environment has had a discernible influence on environmental

Figure 5.1

From constitution to environmental outcome via legislation: A simplified sequence

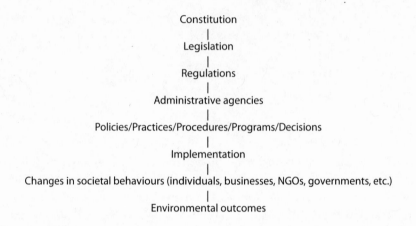

Constitution
|
Legislation
|
Regulations
|
Administrative agencies
|
Policies/Practices/Procedures/Programs/Decisions
|
Implementation
|
Changes in societal behaviours (individuals, businesses, NGOs, governments, etc.)
|
Environmental outcomes

legislation in ninety-two nations spanning five regions – Latin America and the Caribbean, Africa, Asia, Eastern Europe, and Western Europe.

The second approach investigates whether lawsuits have been filed, and judicial decisions made, based on the constitutional right to a healthy environment (the first two steps in Figure 5.2). The analysis includes cases where the constitutional right to a healthy environment was not necessarily the primary basis of the lawsuit but was relied upon by the court in reaching its decision. For example, there are cases based on alleged violations of property rights in which courts rejected legal challenges to environmental laws, regulations, or taxes while justifying their decisions (in whole or in part) using the constitutional provisions for environmental protection.

There is a direct relationship between a constitutional right to a healthy environment and court decisions specifically based on that right, minimizing concerns about other causal influences. Like other human rights, the right to a healthy environment must be enforceable in order to be effective. As documented in Chapter 3, the majority of constitutional environmental rights appear to be directly enforceable, at least on paper. However, a number of scholars have asserted that "only a handful" or a "vast minority" of constitutional provisions recognizing the right to a healthy environment are enforceable.[3] Chapters 6 to 10 will examine the empirical evidence in order

FIGURE 5.2

From constitution to environmental outcome via litigation: A simplified sequence

Constitution
|
Lawsuit alleging violations of the right to healthy environment
|
Court decision
|
Possible appeals of lower court decision
|
Final determination of case
|
Implementation of court order
|
Changes in societal behaviours (individuals, businesses, NGOs, governments, etc.)
|
Environmental outcomes

to determine the extent to which constitutional environmental rights are being enforced through the courts. Included in this assessment are nations whose high courts have recognized the constitutional right to a healthy environment despite the absence of an explicit right in the national constitution. The rationale used by these courts is that the right to live in a healthy environment is an essential element of the constitutional right to life or right to health.

Analytical Framework
In Chapters 6 to 11, the influence of the right to a healthy environment is viewed through two distinct lenses. First, the analytical frameworks established by Epp (in his analysis of the civil and political rights revolution) and Gloppen (in her analysis of the role of courts in supporting social and economic rights) are adapted to focus on the right to a healthy environment.[4] Second, the anticipated benefits and drawbacks of constitutionalizing the right to a healthy environment (discussed in Chapter 2) are reviewed in order to evaluate the extent to which the predicted consequences are occurring.

According to Epp and Gloppen, the following elements are key factors in determining the extent to which legally recognized rights will be effective in promoting social change:

- the strength of constitutional provisions
- the rule of law (e.g., an independent judiciary, effective legal institutions)
- the pool of prospective litigants (i.e., individuals, communities, civil society, and state enforcement institutions)
- access to justice
- resources available for legal mobilization (including lawyers, rights advocacy networks, and sources of funding)
- the responsiveness of the judiciary
- social, economic, and political conditions.

In theory, the potential influence of the constitutional right to a healthy environment should be higher where: the wording of the provision is clear and it is treated as a fundamental right within the structure of a specific constitution; the rule of law is firmly entrenched; there is a robust ENGO community; lawyers are available who specialize in public interest environmental law; funding is available to support the ENGOs and public interest lawyers; the public is aware of its constitutional rights and connects them to environmental degradation; the legal system offers simplified processes for the resolution of cases involving alleged violations of constitutional rights; there are activist judges; and there is a reasonable degree of political stability and economic prosperity. Conversely, factors likely to diminish the potential influence of the constitutional right to a healthy environment include ambiguous constitutional wording; lack of adherence to the rule of law; the absence of the litigation support structure; a conservative judiciary; long-term political crises; and extreme poverty and other adverse socio-economic conditions. The particular balance of positive and negative factors in a given nation will likely determine whether the constitutional right to a healthy environment has an extensive, limited, or negligible influence.

Each of these seven factors is the product of multiple considerations and will vary in significance from nation to nation. The strength of the constitutional provisions related to the right to a healthy environment will depend on wording, other provisions related to the enforceability of rights, placement in the constitution, and the constitution's role in a specific political and legal culture. The rule of law requires laws that are clear, consistent, reasonably stable, generally applicable, enforced, and accepted by most people, as well as the existence of accessible, independent courts to interpret and enforce the law and review legislative and executive actions for legal conformity.[5] As Chavez notes, under the rule of law, "powerful state and private actors are subject to legality and are bound by formal rules of the game."[6] The rule of law is thus fundamentally important in determining the influence of constitutional environmental rights. In nations governed by the rule of law, there is a higher likelihood that the constitutional right to a healthy environment will achieve its anticipated influence. Legislation, regulations, policies, and programs will be developed and implemented through the machinery of government, subject to availability of resources, political will, and the public's priorities. As Beatty observes, for a right to be legally enforceable "implies, at a minimum, a functioning legal order, which can ensure the words on the page match the events in real life."[7]

The pool of prospective litigants can be influenced by awareness and knowledge of rights, associative capacity (the ability to join forces and mobilize around environmental issues), and attitudes toward the judicial system.[8] Access to justice is affected by rules governing standing, procedural requirements, language or cultural barriers, geography (proximity to courts), and both the risks and costs of legal action. The level of resources available for legal mobilization depends on whether there are trained environmental lawyers, rights advocacy networks, applicable legal aid programs, and alternative sources of funding.[9]

The judiciary's responsiveness to cases asserting violations of the right to a healthy environment is influenced by the composition of the bench (judges' professional and social backgrounds), resources (access to legal material, specialized education related to environmental law, caseloads, infrastructure, and budgets), attitudes regarding the role of courts, and judicial independence (tenure, appointment process, and freedom from government and corporate influence). Dickson suggests that judges have "considerable discretion to decide disputes in accordance with personal predilections" but "are adept at clothing their conclusions in legal language which disguises their personal preferences."[10]

Social, economic, and political conditions such as widespread poverty, civil wars, and authoritarian or unstable governments can play a decisive role in determining the influence of constitutional provisions. Collectively, these factors will be used to explore and explain interregional differences in the extent of influence the constitutional right to a healthy environment appears to have on legislation and litigation, as well as the considerable variability within regions.

The practical experiences with the constitutional right to a healthy environment in ninety-two nations could settle some of the theoretical debates regarding perceived strengths and weaknesses of the right. To reiterate, constitutionalizing the right to a healthy environment could offer some or all of the following benefits:

- provide a stimulus for stronger environmental legislation
- enhance implementation and enforcement of environmental laws and policies
- create a level playing field with competing economic and social rights
- offer a safety net, filling gaps in environmental legislation
- compel progress in alleviating the unjust distribution of environmental harms
- play an educational role, articulating the urgent need for environmental protection
- increase accountability
- protect environmental laws from rollbacks under future governments
- encourage greater citizen participation in decisions and actions to protect the environment, in part through enhancing rights of access to information, participation in decision making, and access to justice.

Opponents argue that the right is

- vague
- absolute
- redundant
- undemocratic
- anthropocentric
- a form of cultural imperialism
- unenforceable
- a diversion from other more important rights
- likely to open the floodgates of litigation
- unduly focused on individuals
- likely to be ineffective
- capable of generating false hopes.

Examining environmental laws and court decisions related to the constitutional right to a healthy environment will begin to provide some evidence as to whether these theoretical pros and cons have in fact been realized. For example, evidence that the current generation of environmental laws in nations with constitutional environmental protection makes no reference to the right to a healthy environment would undermine the claim that such a right would strengthen legislation. Similarly, arguments that the right to a healthy environment is too vague to be effective would lose much of their weight if the right consistently affects laws and court decisions across a broad spectrum of nations.

Conclusion

Chapters 6 to 10 offer a comprehensive assessment of the effects of the constitutional right to a healthy environment on environmental laws and jurisprudence. The results are presented region by region because of similarities and patterns in Latin America and the Caribbean, Africa, Asia, Eastern Europe, and Western Europe. Each regional chapter includes a country-by-country assessment of environmental legislation and court decisions as well as a discussion of the key factors that have affected the influence of the constitutional right to a healthy environment, based on the analytical framework identified in this chapter. Chapter 11 then summarizes the lessons learned from national experiences with the constitutional right to a healthy environment over the past three decades. It is essential to recognize that national legal systems and the cultures in which they are embedded are complex, reflecting diverse economic, social, political, and historical attributes. A broad comparative approach raises the danger of overgeneralization. Therefore, the findings presented in Chapters 6 to 11 should be corroborated by future research focusing on in-depth national studies.

6

Latin America and the Caribbean

In many Latin American nations, the 1980s and 1990s were a period of transition from authoritarian regimes to democracy. Constitutional reforms during this period incorporated a broad suite of social and economic rights, including the right to a healthy environment, and empowered stronger, more independent judiciaries.[1] The right to a healthy environment is now entrenched in sixteen Latin American constitutions, and there is evidence that it has influenced both legislation and litigation in the majority of these nations. As early as 1994, Aguilar asserted that "no other region in the world has witnessed the promotion and protection of environmental rights with the enthusiasm and progressiveness as in Latin America."[2] In 2003, Repetto reiterated that Latin America is in "the vanguard of modern constitutionalism as regards environmental issues."[3] The ecologically innovative constitutions enacted by Ecuador (2008) and Bolivia (2009) reinforce this leadership. The following analysis confirms these assertions, particularly in a handful of leading nations. In 2010 and 2011, the Dominican Republic and Jamaica became the first Caribbean nations to incorporate the right to a healthy environment into their constitutions. Because these provisions are so recent, they have not yet had time to influence legislation or litigation.

Legislation

In sixteen of eighteen Latin American and Caribbean nations, framework environmental laws refer directly to the right to live in a healthy environment (see Figure 6.1, and see Table 6.A at the end of this chapter). Typically, the right to a healthy environment is set forth as one of the fundamental principles governing the framework environmental law. In many Latin American nations, procedural rights related to freedom of information, participation in decision making, and access to justice are also spelled out in environmental legislation. Ankersen describes the constitutionalization of environmental law in Latin America as a revolutionary development.[4]

FIGURE 6.1

Constitutional influence on environmental legislation and litigation in Latin America and the Caribbean

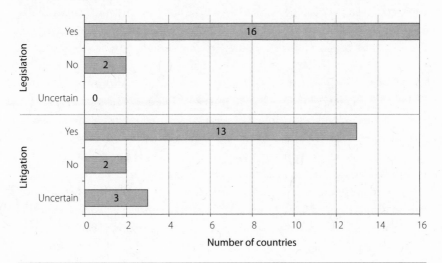

Several examples will illustrate the extent to which constitutional recognition of the right to a healthy environment has acted as an impetus to enact stronger, more comprehensive environmental laws. According to Walsh, the reform of Argentina's constitution in 1994 to include the right to a healthy environment "triggered the need for a new generation of environmental legislation."[5] After 1994, Argentina passed a new comprehensive environmental law, a law governing access to environmental information, and minimum standard laws governing industrial waste, PCBs, and water.[6] Sabsay writes that the *General Law on the Environment* (2002) "sought to make the Constitution a reality."[7] The national constitution also led to a cascade effect, with provincial constitutions incorporating the right to a healthy environment (e.g., Rio Negro, Córdoba, and Tierra del Fuego) and new provincial environmental laws incorporating the right as a guiding principle.[8] In Brazil, laws and institutions for protecting the environment were strengthened significantly following the constitutional reforms of 1988.[9] The Organisation for Economic Co-operation and Development identified the Chilean constitution of 1980 as "the paramount mandate for government action" to protect the environment, including safeguarding both human health and biodiversity from harm.[10]

In Colombia, dozens of new laws, regulations, and decrees have been passed since the incorporation of detailed environmental provisions in the 1991 constitution.[11] The power of the constitution's effect on environmental decision making was demonstrated in 2011 when Colombia's Ministry of the Environment relied on the right to a healthy environment to reject an open-pit gold mine proposed by a Canadian mining company (Greystar Resources Ltd.).[12] In Venezuela, "the recognition of environmental rights as constitutional rights in the year 2000 has led to the creation and development of a contemporary environmental legal framework."[13] Venezuela's *Organic Law on the Environment*, passed in 2006, is a detailed law that refers repeatedly to the right to a safe, healthy, and ecologically balanced environment, and includes extensive procedural environmental rights.[14] Article 4 states that "environmental rights take precedence over economic and social rights, limiting them in the terms established in the Constitution of the Bolivarian Republic of Venezuela and special laws." Since 2000, Venezuela has enacted new environmental laws, resolutions, and decrees governing water, solid waste, hazardous waste, forests, biological diversity, parks, coastal zones, and agriculture.[15]

In 2010, Bolivia introduced one of the most radical and potentially far-reaching environmental laws ever drafted. The *Law of the Rights of Mother Earth* sets out a series of ecological principles; describes the rights held by Mother Earth; imposes a responsibility on the state, individuals, and organizations to respect those rights; and authorizes a new ombudsperson to ensure the implementation of Mother Earth's rights.[16] The enforceability and effectiveness of this groundbreaking law are difficult to predict.

Peru and Paraguay are two countries where there are conflicting views about whether the environmental provisions in the constitution have strengthened the development of environmental laws. Constitutional principles are further defined in Peru's framework natural resource and environmental laws.[17] For example, Article 4 of Peru's *General Law on the Environment* grants standing to any person or NGO to bring a "fast, simple, and efficient" proceeding for actual or imminent violation of the constitutional right to a healthy environment, regardless of personal harm.[18] Turner, however, argues that Peru's constitutional provisions have not prevented the government from weakening environmental laws to encourage foreign investment.[19] For example, Peru's *Code for Environment and Natural Resources* (1990) was undermined by the *Framework Law for the Creation of Private Investment* (1991). Turner concludes that "the environmental provisions within the constitution have not necessarily influenced key legislation."[20] However, it would be more accurate to say that although the constitution has influenced the development of environmental legislation, economic priorities continue to dominate decision making and limit the enforcement of environmental laws in Peru.[21]

In Paraguay, the 1992 constitution and the transition to democracy triggered the enactment of several new environmental laws.[22] However, Paraguay lacks a national framework environmental law, although one is reportedly under development.[23] An anomalous feature of the Paraguayan legal system is its heavy reliance on criminal law (as opposed to environmental, administrative, and civil law) to safeguard the environment.[24] These factors combine to result in a minimal role for the public and an ineffective, reactive system for environmental protection.

The sole clear exception to the rule that constitutions influence environmental legislation in this region is Guyana. Despite constitutional recognition of the right to a healthy environment, environmental law in Guyana lags behind other Latin American nations.[25] One explanation is that Guyana is a former British colony and relies on a common-law legal system rather than the civil law system prevalent throughout most of Latin America. As noted in Chapter 3, common-law nations trail civil law nations in recognizing social, economic, and environmental rights. Another factor is that Guyana is one of the poorest nations in Central and South America.[26]

In the few Latin American nations lacking constitutional recognition of the right to a healthy environment, the modernization of environmental legislation has lagged behind. For example, Uruguay, where there is no explicit constitutional right to a healthy environment, trails other Latin American nations in updating and strengthening its environmental legislation.[27]

Litigation

According to the United Nations Economic Commission for Latin America and the Caribbean, new constitutional provisions and stronger framework laws are "opening up new spaces for citizen participation in defence of the environment."[28] In at least thirteen of eighteen Latin American nations, there has been litigation based on the right to a healthy environment (see Figure 6.1, and see Table 6.A at the end of this chapter).[29] Aguilar observed in 1994 that, throughout the region, courts treat the right to a healthy environment as a fundamental right and have defined the nature and content of the right.[30] A review of the jurisprudence available through the websites of supreme courts and constitutional courts in Latin America yields more than six hundred reported decisions based on the right to a healthy environment.

Courts in Argentina, Brazil, Colombia, and Costa Rica are particularly active in enforcing the right, with more than one hundred reported decisions in each of these nations. Cases based on the right to a healthy environment appear to be brought less frequently in Bolivia, Chile, Ecuador, El Salvador, Panama, Peru, and Venezuela.[31] In Mexico, constitutional amendments were made in 2011 to make the right to a healthy environment (and other human rights) enforceable and effective in a broad range of circumstances. In Paraguay, the ability to enforce the constitutional right to a healthy environment through litigation is contested and does not appear to be possible at this time. Information on environmental jurisprudence for Guyana, Honduras, and Nicaragua is not yet publicly available on the Internet. It is also essential to recognize that this research captures only the tip of the iceberg of litigation involving the constitutional right to a healthy environment in Latin America because unreported decisions, lower-court decisions, and determinations made by administrative and quasi-judicial tribunals are generally not included.[32]

One of the major factors contributing to the extensive use of litigation to enforce the constitutional right to a healthy environment in Latin American nations is the availability of several distinctive legal procedures.[33] The *amparo*, which has roots in Mexico dating back to the middle of the nineteenth century, allows citizens to apply directly to courts when their constitutional rights have been violated.[34] The *actio popular*, or popular action, allows citizens in many Latin American nations to use the courts to defend collective, as opposed to personal, interests. Although the precise name of the procedures for enforcing constitutional rights varies from nation to nation (e.g., *tutela* in Colombia, *amparo* in Costa Rica, and *recurso de proteccion* in Chile), these special judicial procedures tend to be expedited, informal, and inexpensive compared to regular forms of litigation. The *amparo* or a similar procedure is used in Argentina, Bolivia, Brazil, Chile, Colombia, Costa Rica, Dominican Republic, Ecuador, El Salvador, Guatemala, Honduras, Nicaragua, Panama, and Peru. Another unique Latin American legal process, *habeas data*, enables citizens or NGOs to access information related to constitutional rights. For example, Peru's Supreme Court has granted a *habeas data* motion brought by an ENGO to obtain government documents related to a mine disaster that caused eight deaths and serious environmental damage.[35]

It is important to recognize that the nations where courts are actively enforcing the right to a healthy environment are generally more active in enforcing social and economic rights. Thus the right to a healthy environment is part of a broader rights revolution underway in Latin America.[36]

ARGENTINA

In Argentina, the constitutional right to a healthy environment "constitutes the main principle around which environmental law and governance revolves."[37] Prior to the 1994 constitutional reforms, "there was a considerable vacuum in national legislation on the judicial protection of so-called diffuse and collective interests," including the environment.[38] Today, Argentina is a Latin American leader in judicial recognition and enforcement of the constitutional right to live in a healthy environment. This has occurred in the context of a broader expansion of the judiciary's role in Argentine society.[39] According to Argentina's Defensor del Pueblo (Ombudsperson), there were 151 cases involving the right to a healthy environment in 2007.[40] Cases have dealt with PCB contamination, the environmental impacts of the oil and gas industry (including spills), wildlife, water pollution, noise pollution, high-voltage power lines, construction of a building in an ecological reserve, and ecosystem restoration.[41] According to one oft-cited Argentine court judgment, "The right to live in a healthy environment is a fundamental attribute of people. Any aggression to the environment ends up becoming a threat to life itself and to the psychological and physical integrity of the person, which is based on ecological balance."[42] The right to clean drinking water is regarded as an integral element of the constitutional right to a healthy environment. Courts have repeatedly ordered governments to provide potable water, construct drinking-water treatment facilities, treat individuals harmed by contaminated drinking water, and carry out environmental remediation.[43]

Argentina's *General Law on the Environment* explicitly authorizes judges to take a preventive approach.[44] Dug and Faggi conclude that "preventive action by judges has become a key factor in the effective protection of the environment."[45] For example, the constitutional duty to protect the environment led an Argentine court to order a suite of actions to minimize the risk of contamination from PCBs.[46] The court noted that while there remained some scientific uncertainty as to the links between PCBs and cancer, the constitutional and legislative provisions regarding environmental protection warranted a precautionary approach.

The leading Argentine case based on the constitutional right to live in a healthy environment is globally important. In 2004, a group of concerned citizens sued the national government, the provincial government, and the City of Buenos Aires, along with forty-four industrial facilities, for polluting the Matanza-Riachuelo River, asserting a violation of their right to a healthy environment.[47] Millions of people, many of them poor, live near the Matanza-Riachuelo River, one of the most polluted rivers in South America. In 2006, the Supreme Court issued an order requiring the government to conduct an environmental assessment of the state of the river and initiate an environmental education program. The court also required all of the polluting facilities to provide information about their wastewater treatment equipment, programs, and practices.[48] In 2007, the Supreme Court ordered the government defendants to establish a comprehensive cleanup and restoration plan for the river. Recognizing the limits of its own expertise in evaluating this plan, the court commissioned an independent evaluation by scientists at the University of Buenos Aires. The expert review and comments from both the plaintiffs and NGOs identified extensive weaknesses in the draft plan. The court also convened five public hearings to ensure that broad-based community participation informed its judgment. In 2008, the Supreme Court issued a comprehensive final ruling in which it identified three objectives:

1   improved quality of life for the inhabitants of the basin
2   reconstruction of the environment in the basin in all of its components
3   prevention of injury with sufficient degree of predictability.

Accordingly, the court ordered the following actions:

- inspections of all polluting enterprises, creation and implementation of plans for industrial wastewater treatment, all on a strict schedule
- closure of all illegal dumps, redevelopment of legal landfills, and cleanup of the riverbanks
- improvement of drinking-water, sewage treatment, and stormwater discharge systems
- development of a regional environmental health plan, including contingencies for emergencies
- supervision, by the federal Auditor General, of the budget allocation for implementation of the restoration plan
- formation of a committee of NGOs involved in the litigation to monitor compliance with the court's decision
- ongoing judicial oversight of the implementation of the plan, with a federal court judge empowered to resolve any disputes
- notice that any violations of the timelines established by the court would result in daily fines against the president of the Matanza-Riachuelo Watershed Authority (the new intergovernmental body responsible for implementing the restoration plan).

The court's decisions were grounded in Articles 41 and 43 of the constitution, which recognize the right to a healthy environment and citizens' power to defend their rights through recourse to the judicial system. The decision reflects the growing use of creative approaches to ensure compliance with court orders, including daily fines, reports to the judge, and entrusting compliance to a third party.[49] Argentina's Supreme Court "made it clear that extraordinary measures may be required on the side of judges where environmental issues and interests are at stake."[50]

The World Bank has approved US$2 billion in financing for the Matanza-Riachuelo Basin Sustainable Development Project, which the bank acknowledges was triggered by the Supreme Court's decision and is intended to contribute to compliance with that court's order.[51] Argentina will increase the number of environmental inspectors in the region from 3 to 250.[52] A federal law created a new river basin authority that must (i) implement a comprehensive action plan, (ii) coordinate and harmonize activities, and (iii) control and monitor environmental compliance.[53] Progress made by mid-2011 included provision of clean drinking water to one million people, a new sewage system serving half a million people, 167 polluting companies closed, 134 garbage dumps closed, and the creation of 139 sampling points for monitoring water, air, and soil quality.[54] As the World Bank observes, there have been previous pledges to restore the Matanza-Riachuelo watershed, but the Supreme Court ruling ensures political and legal accountability.[55]

BRAZIL

The amendment of the Brazilian constitution in 1988 is widely heralded as a turning point in both environmental consciousness and the legal system in Brazil.[56] The constitutional reforms incorporated the right to a healthy environment and other legal changes that facilitated improved environmental enforcement.[57] The Ministerio Publico, whose previous mandate had been limited to criminal matters, was given the responsibility to conduct investigations and enforce environmental laws. Federal environmental agencies were consolidated in the more powerful Brazilian Institute of the Environment and Renewable Resources.[58] Another change was the creation of a new form of legal action (the public civil action) and the extension of the *acao popular* (popular action) to cover environmental issues. The public civil action authorizes citizens' access to courts to protect diffuse and collective interests, such as urban air quality.[59] The *acao popular* enables anyone eligible to vote to file a legal action, free of costs, challenging any government act or omission that could harm the environment. A direct action of unconstitutionality can be brought against any government action, including legislation, which is alleged to violate the constitution. In 1998, another important federal law, the *Environmental Crimes Act*, was passed.[60]

The result of these legal changes has been a dramatic increase in the enforcement of environmental laws in some regions of Brazil by both citizens and the Ministerio Publico.[61] These constitutional reforms have contributed to "the development of a veritable juridical subsystem, whereby new laws are guided by the idea of collective protection of rights and by the reinforcement of the guardianship role of the MP."[62] The Ministerio Publico frequently uses the threat of prosecution to compel the negotiation of "conduct adjustment agreements," which are akin to contractual obligations to cease actions causing environmental harm and to carry out restoration or remediation.[63] The main advantage of conduct adjustment agreements is that they avoid the delays, expenses, and uncertainty associated with the judicial process.

Brazilian courts are somewhat unusual in several aspects: they do not defer to the technical expertise of government agencies but rely on their own experts to reach factual conclusions; parties are not constrained by the administrative record and can present new evidence to the court; and courts can consider new issues that were not raised in the administrative proceedings under appeal.[64] In one particularly important innovation, based on the constitutional right to a healthy environment, Brazilian courts have reversed the burden of proof so that defendants must prove that their actions were not harmful to the environment.[65] This eliminates one of the major hurdles to environmental prosecutions.

A Brazilian judge quoted by Passos de Freitas writes that "hundreds of pages would be needed to mention all the precedents" dealing with constitutional protection for the environment that have been set by Brazilian courts in recent years.[66] In the state of Sao Paolo alone, between 1984 and 2004, the Ministerio Publico filed over four thousand public civil actions in environmental cases addressing issues ranging from deforestation to air pollution.[67] Federal prosecutors successfully relied on the constitution's environmental provisions to delay construction of the proposed Belo Monte dam on the Xingu River (an Amazon tributary), which would be the world's third-largest hydroelectric project.[68] A series of important cases have established that "a positive duty rests on the executive to preserve, protect, and secure a core of environmental services," and budget constraints are not a valid defence for failing to meet minimum standards for environmental quality.[69] Core environmental services include water, sanitation, and waste management.[70] In

2007, a lawsuit brought by Sao Paolo's Ministerio Publico and an ENGO forced the government to enact stronger standards for diesel fuel.[71] It is estimated that 67.5 percent of environmental public civil actions are successful, and 63 percent of injunction requests are granted.[72] Daibert concludes that Brazil's constitutional right to a healthy environment has made "a fundamental difference."[73] The constitutionalization of environmental protection "brought a degree of legal fidelity and sanctioning power that environmental regulatory agencies lacked, and prosecution of environmental cases worked to dispel the longstanding notion of impunity for environmental harm."[74]

Despite the legal reforms, there continues to be concern about inadequate enforcement of environmental laws in some Brazilian regions.[75] Roberts and Thanos quote Brazilian prosecutor Jose Carlos Meloni Sicoli, who stated: "The legislative arsenal in Brazil is infinitely superior to those in countries like the USA, for example, but the implementation of the law there is still light-years more efficient than here. As a result, betting on impunity is still frequent."[76] As well, the explosion of litigation to protect constitutional rights has reportedly contributed to a backlog of cases, long delays, and growing public distrust.[77] In some quarters there are concerns about prosecutorial accountability because of the independence of the Ministerio Publico.[78]

COLOMBIA

In 1991, the new Colombian constitution set forth a comprehensive suite of social, economic, and environmental rights, as well as enhanced powers for the Constitutional Court. The inclusion of 34 distinct environmental provisions led the Constitutional Court to describe it as an "ecological constitution."[79] According to Cepeda Espinosa, "Through the production of an extraordinary amount of case law in regards to practically every phase of Colombian affairs ... the Constitutional Court has become a vital actor."[80] The Colombian constitution provides for several innovative legal actions including *acciones populares, acciones de tutela,* and *acciones de cumplimiento.*[81] *Acciones populares* are lawsuits based on the defence of collective interests (under traditional legal rules, plaintiffs would have been denied standing based on a lack of direct economic or personal interest). *Acciones de tutela* enable citizens to apply for immediate protection when violations of constitutional rights pose a danger of imminent harm to life or health. Remarkably, judges must rule on *tutela* cases within ten days of the action's being filed.[82] *Acciones de cumplimiento* are enforcement actions to require full compliance with laws, including environmental laws. Colombia's constitution, like Brazil's, empowers the Ministerio Publico to protect collective interests, including the environment.[83] Although the right to a healthy environment is described as a collective right in the constitution, it is enforceable by individuals.

Colombia's Defensoria del Pueblo has published detailed studies of the use of constitutional lawsuits to protect the right to water. There were 7,961 *tutela* cases in Colombia between 1991 and 2008 related to the provision of potable drinking water and basic sanitation.[84] Of these cases, 239 were brought primarily on the basis of violations of the constitutional right to a healthy environment.[85] During the same period, there were 1,041 *acciones populares* related to the provision of potable drinking water and basic sanitation, of which 137 cases were brought based on violations of the right to healthy environment.[86] In 53 percent of the *acciones populares*, the plaintiffs were successful.[87] Among the *tutelas* that were brought between 2003 and 2005, 1,089 invoked collective constitutional rights, which include the right to a healthy environment (as well as consumer protection).[88] In 2008 alone, court decisions protected the right to a healthy environment in at least 45 *acciones populares.*[89] These statistics demonstrate that the constitutional right to a healthy environment is being directly and regularly enforced in Colombian courts.

Cases based on the constitutional right to a healthy environment have involved dumping of untreated sewage, location of landfills, mining, industrial pollution, noise, burning coal, hog farms, quality of drinking water, ozone depletion, protection of health from toxic substances, and urban planning.[90] The Constitutional Court has stated that, "side by side with fundamental rights such as liberty, equality, and necessary conditions for people's life, there is the right to the environment ... The right to a healthy environment cannot be separated from the right to life and health of human beings. In fact, factors that are deleterious to the environment cause irreparable harm to human beings. If this is so we can state that the right to environment is a right fundamental to the existence of humanity."[91] The Constitutional Court also stated that because Colombia is so rich in biological diversity, it has a special responsibility to protect the environment for the common well-being of humanity.[92]

The NGO Fundepublico (Fundación para la Defensa del Interés Público) was a pioneer in using litigation to enforce the constitutional right to a healthy environment in cases involving air pollution from an asphalt plant, a chemical company's obligation to disclose information, a ban on imports of toxic waste, and legal obligations to restore lands damaged by clearcut logging.[93]

According to some experts, the Constitutional Court has altered the balance of political power in Colombia, strengthening the position of previously marginalized or weak groups, including poor communities harmed by pollution.[94] As Aguilar concluded, "The Colombian courts have not only written remarkable decisions in defence of the right to a healthy environment, but have also ordered concrete enforcement measures to this end."[95]

COSTA RICA

Costa Rica is acknowledged as a leader in environmental protection in Latin America, with a constitution and court decisions contributing to stronger laws and better enforcement.[96] The creation of a new Constitutional Chamber of the Supreme Court in 1989 "sparked a judicial revolution that shook the country's judicial system out of a 200-year slumber and has touched virtually every aspect of the country's social, economic, and political life."[97] The new court's caseload quickly grew from two thousand cases to more than ten thousand cases annually, necessitating reliance on expedited and simplified processes.[98] To put this caseload in perspective, a total of approximately 150 cases of unconstitutionality were filed with the Supreme Court between 1938 and 1989.[99] Procedural rules have been relaxed so that anyone can file a *recurso de amparo* for protection of a constitutional right, with or without a lawyer, with no filing fees, and the court is open twenty-four hours a day, 365 days a year, with at least one magistrate always available. The court employs dozens of lawyers whose mandate is to transform public submissions into cases that can be properly adjudicated.[100]

The rights revolution in Costa Rica has included a surge in judicial attention to environmental issues. The Constitutional Court first affirmed the right to a healthy environment in a 1993 case concerning a municipality's practice of dumping waste in a stream close to a poor neighbourhood.[101] The court stated that life "is only possible when it exists in solidarity with nature, which nourishes and sustains us – not only with regard to food, but also with physical well-being. It constitutes a right that all citizens possess to live in an environment free from contamination. This is the basis of a just and productive society." Remarkably, this precedent-setting case was initiated by a letter to the court from a minor, demonstrating the relaxation of procedural requirements. In a 1994 decision, the court stated that the rights to health and to a healthy environment emanate from the right to life and from the state's obligation to protect Nature. The court added that if the rights to health and to the environment were not recognized, the right to life would be severely limited.[102] In 1995, the court stated that in order to avoid degradation and deterioration of the environment, precaution and prevention must be the dominant legal principles, and the concept of *"in dubio, pro natura"* must be applied, which means that if there is any doubt regarding legal interpretation, the ambiguity should be resolved in favour of Nature.[103]

More than one hundred cases involving the constitutional right to a healthy environment are now reported on the website of the Constitutional Court. In approximately two-thirds of leading cases, the party asserting a violation of its constitutional right was successful.[104] In cases involving solid waste, sewage treatment, air pollution, and illegal construction the court has ruled that the right to a healthy environment includes a number of key principles including the precautionary principle, the concept of polluter pays, and the idea of intergenerational equity.[105] According to the Constitutional Court, the right to a healthy environment imposes two duties on governments: to refrain from directly violating the right through their own actions, and to prevent the activities of others from violating the right.[106] Another key decision by the court is that the right to water is a vital element of the right to a healthy environment.[107]

A series of controversial decisions in which the Constitutional Court struck down approvals for offshore oil and gas exploration led to a dispute between the government of Costa Rica and Harken Energy.[108] Costa Rica eventually rescinded Harken's contract, prompting Harken to attempt to sue for $57 billion in damages through the World Bank's International Center for the Settlement of Investment Disputes (ICSID).[109] Costa Rica rejected ICSID's jurisdiction and refused to pay compensation, citing Harken's failure to comply with environmental laws as a breach of the contract. Carminati described the outcome as a "resounding victory" in Costa Rica's efforts to protect the environment, even when threatened with a multi-billion dollar lawsuit by a foreign investor.[110]

The Constitutional Court has also made a number of rulings protecting endangered species and their habitat. In 1999, the court ruled that a law permitting the hunting of green turtles violated both the constitutional right to a healthy and ecologically balanced environment and international law (specifically the *Convention on International Trade in Endangered Species*).[111] In 2002, the court struck down government authorization of timber harvesting in habitat for the endangered green macaw.[112] In 2004, the court ruled that the Costa Rican government was violating the right to a healthy and ecologically balanced environment by failing to stop the wasteful practice of shark finning. In 2008, the Constitutional Court nullified a municipal zoning regulation that authorized construction in Las Baulas National Park. The court also ordered the government to expropriate private lands within the national park that were slated for tourist development but provided critical habitat for endangered sea turtles.[113]

An important precedent was established in 2004 by the *Linda Vista* case, which involved a proposed high-density urban development in an area important for groundwater.[114] When the development was approved, local citizens filed a lawsuit. The Constitutional Court scrutinized the technical evidence closely and ruled that the government had failed to exercise the precautionary principle, failed to comply with the law, and violated the right to a healthy environment. The court set forth a range of detailed measures to be taken by the government to protect groundwater and made it clear that a lack of resources was not an adequate excuse for failing to protect a natural asset vital to human health and the environment.[115]

In 2009, the Constitutional Court issued a ruling that illustrates the dialogic relationship between the court and the executive branch.[116] Citizens and NGOs brought a lawsuit based on the government's failure to enact regulations required for the implementation of the *Fisheries and Aquaculture Act*. The court agreed that the failure to enact regulations violated the constitutional right to a healthy and ecologically balanced environment, and gave the government ninety days to enact the regulations.

PERU

Peru's constitution, like that of many Latin nations, authorizes the use of *amparo* proceedings to enforce constitutional rights.[117] Peru's Constitutional Court has ruled repeatedly that the constitutional right to a healthy environment imposes a twofold duty upon the government: to not impair the right through its own actions; and to undertake positive actions to prevent the violation of the right by others (such as businesses).[118]

Cases based on the constitutional right to a healthy environment have challenged the toxic contamination of a town, suspended shrimp farming in coastal mangroves, ordered restoration of shrimp farms to their natural state, and struck down a municipal ordinance that rezoned parkland for intensive commercial use.[119] An ongoing case involves the town of La Oroya, where an American multinational (Doe Run) operated a lead smelter that is alleged to have poisoned an entire town. Ninety-nine percent of children tested had blood lead levels exceeding the World Health Organization's recommended maximum, and many children were hospitalized. The Constitutional Court ordered the implementation of a variety of measures to protect peoples' health and the environment, including declaring a state of emergency, taking immediate steps to protect vulnerable populations (children and pregnant women), and creating monitoring programs.[120] The Peruvian government's failure to adequately follow the court's orders was the subject of a complaint to the Inter-American Commission on Human Rights. In accepting the complaint, the IACHR concluded that Peru had unjustifiably delayed compliance with the decision of the Constitutional Court. The IACHR also ordered Peru to take a number of interim measures, which included providing comprehensive medical exams and medical treatment.[121]

A controversial Peruvian case sheds light on the judicial approach to balancing the constitutional right to a healthy environment with other protected rights.[122] The Camisea project involved a network of pipelines and a natural gas plant, with the latter to be sited in the buffer zone of Paracas National Park, an area listed under the *Convention on International Trade in Endangered Species* and designated as a wetland of international importance under the *Ramsar Convention*. The Constitutional Court held that the certainty of substantial social and economic benefits outweighed potential but uncertain environmental harms. To rule in favour of the plaintiffs, in the court's opinion, would have violated the proportionality principle. Turner criticized the court for failing to give adequate weight to environmental considerations, arguing that the outcome illustrates the ineffectiveness of Peru's constitutional environmental provisions.[123]

Chile

Since 1980, the Chilean constitution has specified that the right to live in a healthy environment is subject to judicial enforcement through a special procedure called the *recurso de proteccion*. Chilean courts have made it clear that the constitutional recognition of the right to a healthy environment authorizes restrictions and limitations on the exercise and enjoyment of other rights, including the right to property.[124] One of the most important early court decisions anywhere in the world enforcing the constitutional right to a healthy environment occurred in Chile. Residents of Chanaral and local farmers won a legal action against CODELCO (the National Copper Company of Chile), one of the world's leading copper-producing companies.[125] The Supreme Court ordered CODELCO to stop discharging tailing wastes onto Chilean beaches and into adjoining waters.[126] Although there did not appear to be any violation of Chilean environmental legislation, the court ruled that the severe impact on marine life violated people's constitutional right to live in an environment free from contamination. The Supreme Court explained that these problems "affect not only the well being of man but also his own

life, and actually not only the [the livelihood] of a single community of persons at present: future generations would claim the lack of foresight of their
predecessors if the environment would be polluted and nature destroyed."[127]
The mining company was ordered to build facilities for waste disposal and
treatment. The case demonstrated that citizens empowered by constitutional
environmental rights could successfully fight large corporations and un-
responsive governments.[128]

The Chilean Supreme Court also voided a timber licence in a case where
the government approved an environmental impact assessment despite a
lack of evidence.[129] According to Bruch, Coker, and VanArsdale, "The Court
held that by acting in such an arbitrary and illegal way, the government
violated the rights of all Chileans, not just those who would be affected
locally."[130] In 2007, hundreds of Chilean citizens received compensation for
the violation of their right to live in a healthy environment after they suffered
the adverse effects of living near a site where a foreign company, with government approval, dumped toxic waste (including lead, arsenic, cadmium,
and mercury).[131] Also in 2007, the Supreme Court ordered a wastewater
treatment plant to cease its toxic emissions because they violated the rights
to life and an environment free of pollution.[132] Most recently, an American
company's plan to build a coal-burning power plant in an environmentally
protected area was blocked by Chile's Supreme Court on several grounds,
including violation of the constitutional right to live in an environment free
of pollution.[133]

Despite constitutional protection of the environment, economic interests
outweighed environmental concerns in cases brought to stop the construction
of a pulp mill and to prevent a mining company from constructing a tailings
dam near the headwaters of a river.[134] In the latter case, residents reached an
out-of-court settlement, with the mining company agreeing to pay them
compensation.[135] The OECD reports that many environmental cases are
brought to Chilean courts, but "the judicial system lacks the capacity to deal
adequately with many environmental matters, for instance when it comes to
obtaining evidence or estimating environmental damage and compensation
values."[136] Despite the presence of growing numbers of NGOs and the strong
provisions of the Chilean constitution, judicial conservatism has constrained
the rights revolution in Chile.[137]

ECUADOR AND BOLIVIA

As described in Chapter 3, Ecuador and Bolivia recently passed new constitutions that reiterate the recognition of the right to a healthy environment

found in earlier constitutions. They also include extensive new provisions related to environmental protection, including rights for Nature. In 2010, Ecuador's Constitutional Court rejected a legal challenge to the new *Mining Law* that was based in part on the rights of Nature and the right to a healthy environment.[138] However in 2011, in a case involving damage to a river from road construction, a provincial court in Ecuador made a powerful decision affirming the importance and enforceability of the constitutional rights of Nature.[139] Citizens and NGOs also brought litigation under the previous constitutional regimes. Ecuador's Constitutional Court ruled that the sale of leaded gasoline violated the right to a healthy environment.[140] In a case involving proposed mining activities in a national park, the court said that "environmental degradation in Podocarpus National Park is a threat to the environmental human right of the inhabitants of the provinces of Loja and Zamora Chinchipe to have an area which ensures the natural and continuous provision of water, air, oxygenation, and recreation."[141] In 2008, the Constitutional Court ruled that the proposed construction of a water diversion and dam project (the Baba Multi-purpose Project) could not proceed because the anticipated impacts on human health and ecology would violate the constitutional right to a healthy and ecologically balanced environment.[142] Although the extent of the anticipated effects was uncertain, the court applied the precautionary principle in determining that the project was unconstitutional. An Ecuadorean law passed in 2009 authorizes the establishment of specialized courts to adjudicate claims asserting violations of the constitutional rights of Nature.[143] Efforts are underway to establish such a court for the Galapagos Islands. The controversial decision of an Ecuadorian court to award billions of dollars in damages to indigenous plaintiffs in litigation resulting from extensive contamination of the rainforest caused by oil and gas exploitation was based in part on the constitutional right to a healthy environment.[144] In two cases decided in 2010, Bolivia's Constitutional Court referred to the right to a healthy environment, determining that it includes the right to potable drinking water.[145]

EL SALVADOR, PANAMA, AND VENEZUELA

In El Salvador, Panama, and Venezuela, litigation based on the right to a healthy environment appears to be relatively uncommon compared to the preceding Latin American nations. However, in Panama, courts recently nullified a permit authorizing construction of a commercial cable-car operation in a nature reserve and suspended the construction of a cellular telephone tower.[146] Although El Salvador's constitutional right to a healthy environment appears limited to children, the Constitutional Chamber of El Salvador's Supreme Court of Justice has ruled that this constitutional right is held by everyone by virtue of the state's obligation to protect the environment and the importance of a healthy environment for fulfilling the rights to life and dignity.[147] Venezuela's 1999 constitution replaced the Supreme Court with a Supreme Tribunal consisting of six *salas* or chambers. However, the Supreme Tribunal has been the subject of political interference, and thus its efforts have been compromised by a perceived lack of impartiality. Judges are appointed by Congress (led by the president) and have consistently ruled in the government's favour.[148]

DOMINICAN REPUBLIC AND JAMAICA

The right to a healthy environment was included in the new constitution of the Dominican Republic in 2010, but the concept had previously influenced the Supreme Court of Justice in one decision overturning an unduly light sentence handed down in an environmental prosecution, and another case blocking construction of a cement plant.[149] In a leading Jamaican environmental law case, the Supreme Court held that although environmental protection is an issue with far-reaching consequences, it is not on par, from a legal perspective, with human rights.[150]

PARAGUAY

In Paraguay, courts have relied on the constitutional right to a healthy environment to reject lawsuits claiming that environmental regulations violated the constitutional rights to property and economic development.[151] The Supreme Court of Paraguay referred to the profound importance of environmental protection to the well-being of citizens and held that the public interest can outweigh private interests.[152] As well, a Paraguayan court ruled that "environmental crimes are in open breach of Article 7 of the Constitution, which enshrines the right of everyone to live in a healthy environment."[153]

Paraguayan courts previously had ruled that citizens have the right to bring constitutional cases to protect their right to live in a healthy environment.[154] However, in 2008, the Supreme Court issued a ruling in a case brought by indigenous people whose land was flooded by a new hydroelectric facility.[155] The indigenous people won at lower court, based in part on their constitutional right to live in a healthy and balanced environment. The Supreme Court overturned that decision, ruling that because the government of Paraguay had negotiated an international treaty and passed domestic legislation related to the dam, the judiciary could not second-guess those decisions, although it did state that people ought to be compensated if adversely affected for the greater good of society. The court contradicted some of its earlier decisions by concluding that collective rights, such as the right to a healthy environment, are not directly enforceable in courts but must be regulated through legislation. According to the Supreme Court, the complexity involved in environmental problems makes them ill-suited for judicial resolution; instead, they should be addressed "through sustainable policies planned in a coordinated manner by the national government, through compliance with laws passed by Congress, and through bodies such as the Ministry of Environment."[156] This decision, and the focus on using criminal law to protect the environment, led Abed to conclude that "the juridical configuration of the Paraguayan environmental judicial system is dysfunctional with regard to the objective of guaranteeing the right to live in a healthy and ecologically equilibrated environment."[157]

MEXICO
Article 4 of the Mexican constitution was amended in 1999 to recognize the right to a healthy environment, but no cases have been brought successfully to a Mexican court on the basis of a violation of this constitutional clause.[158] Although the Mexican Supreme Court has become increasingly activist on other social and economic issues, it has ruled repeatedly that citizens do not have the right to bring *amparo* cases involving environmental protection despite their constitutional rights.[159] The OECD concluded that Mexican citizens have very limited access to courts for resolving environmental problems.[160] In response to these decisions, Ojeda-Mestre asserted that "the ignorance of judges, magistrates, and ministers about environmental laws is shocking."[161] The courts' jurisprudence led to a vigorous effort by civil society to have the constitutional right to a healthy environment strengthened to enable citizens to enforce their rights.[162] In 2011, these efforts were rewarded by amendments that dramatically strengthened the *amparo* provisions in the constitution to enable the enforcement of the right to a healthy environment, the right to water, and other human rights.

GUATEMALA AND URUGUAY
In at least two other Latin American nations, Guatemala and Uruguay, courts have recognized an implicit constitutional right to live in a healthy environment, despite the absence of explicit language. Guatemala's Constitutional Court explained that the objective of environmental measures is to guarantee

the right to health and the achievement of a standard of living that guarantees the survival of future generations.[163] As a result, Guatemalan courts have allowed NGOs to bring lawsuits based on the implicit constitutional right to a healthy environment.[164]

Uruguayan legal experts argue that the right to a healthy environment is implicit in that country's constitution.[16] The right is recognized explicitly in Uruguay's framework environmental law.[166]

Factors Affecting the Influence of the Constitutional Right to a Healthy Environment in Latin America and the Caribbean

Latin America is a global leader in recognizing the constitutional right to a healthy environment, while Caribbean countries are just beginning to recognize this right. The following are some of the key factors in Latin America's environmental rights revolution (see also Table 6.1):

- constitutional reform, including recognition of the right to a healthy environment, stronger provisions for judicial review, increased scope of judicial powers, and creation of institutions such as the Ministerio Publico and Defensor del Pueblo with mandates to protect collective interests
- shifting legal culture, with greater emphasis on public law, precedents, and public interest litigation
- increased legal mobilization as non-governmental organizations and networks of activist lawyers are advancing rights cases
- improved access to justice, achieved though procedural innovations
- influence of international norms, networks, and institutions.[167]

Latin American nations are characterized by strong civil society movements, including environmental NGOs, some of whom specialize in environmental law. Examples include El Centro de Derecho Ambiental y de los Recursos Naturales (CEDARENA) in Costa Rica, Centro de Derechos Humanos y Ambiente (CEDHA) and Fundación Ambiente y Recursos Naturales (FARN) in Argentina, Fiscalía del Medio Ambiente (FIMA) in Chile, Fundación para la Defensa del Interés Público (Fundepublico) in Colombia, and Sociedad Peruana de Derecho Ambiental (SPDA) in Peru.[168] These NGOs advocate for stronger environmental legislation and provide legal representation to concerned citizens, communities, and environmental groups.

Environmental law NGOs benefit from their participation in international networks that provide strategic advice and financial assistance, including the

TABLE 6.1

Factors influencing the extent of the environmental rights revolution in Latin America

Factor	Generally positive	Generally negative	Mixed	Examples of positive influence	Examples of negative influence
Constitutional provisions	×			Argentina, Brazil, Colombia, Costa Rica	Honduras, Mexico
Prospective litigants	×			Argentina, Brazil, Chile, Colombia, Costa Rica	Guyana, Honduras, Nicaragua
Access to justice	×			Argentina, Brazil, Colombia, Costa Rica	Bolivia, Mexico, Paraguay
Resources for legal mobilization			×	Argentina, Brazil, Chile, Colombia, Costa Rica, Ecuador, Peru	Guyana, Honduras, Nicaragua, Paraguay
Rule of law			×	Argentina, Costa Rica	Bolivia, Venezuela
Responsive judiciary	×			Argentina, Brazil, Colombia, Costa Rica	Chile, Mexico, Paraguay
Social, economic, and political conditions			×	Costa Rica	Guyana

Asociacion Interamericana para la Defensa del Ambiente (AIDA) and the Environmental Law Alliance Worldwide (ELAW).[169] Many Latin American environmental law NGOs rely on American and European foundations and governments for funding.[170] Additional dissemination of laws, policies, and precedents occurs through the Organization of American States (OAS), United Nations Environment Programme (UNEP), and the International Union for Conservation of Nature (IUCN). Several Latin American courts have cited the right to a healthy environment included in the *San Salvador Protocol* (discussed in Chapter 4) in cases involving the constitutional right to a healthy environment.[171] International networking facilitates the diffusion of ideas, particularly with respect to successful litigation strategies and precedents from foreign courts. Sikkink points out the interaction between domestic and international systems, as key actors employ venue shopping, transfer precedents between systems, and strategically use multiple options to maximize impacts.[172]

As noted earlier, judicial systems in Latin America have pioneered the use of simplified and expedited legal procedures that have dramatically increased access to justice. These processes have provided citizens and ENGOs with an unprecedented opportunity to employ the judicial system in pursuit of the right to a healthy environment. The simplified procedures and elimination of barriers have reduced the need for what Epp described as the "litigation support structure" to facilitate the rights revolution.[173] Individuals in countries such as Costa Rica and Colombia can easily go to court to enforce their right to a healthy environment, without lawyers or high costs. On the other hand, the OECD has warned that the excessive use of *amparo* procedures can undermine the effectiveness of laws and policies enacted by democratically elected legislative branches of government.[174] Another downside of increasing access to the courts is that high numbers of cases can contribute to backlogs and delays.[175]

One key factor that appears to explain the variability among Latin American nations in the volume of litigation based on the right to a healthy environment is the degree of judicial activism.[176] The creation of a new Constitutional Court in Costa Rica triggered an era of unprecedented judicial activism in that nation, which has encouraged citizens and NGOs to defend their rights in court.[177] Constitutional changes in Colombia in 1991 created a strong and independent Constitutional Court, paving the way for greater activism.[178] Responding to media interest in its landmark case involving the restoration of the Matanza-Riachuelo River, the chief justice of Argentina's Supreme Court noted that "one of a court's functions is to make noise."[179] In contrast, Chile's Constitutional Court continues to be far more conservative, a tendency attributed to the legal culture, legal education, and socialization of Chilean judges.[180]

According to Rojas and Iza, "In order to prevent the existence of the right to a healthy and ecologically balanced environment being restricted to the semantic level, environmental law has integrated a number of guiding principles that guarantee the effective protection of the right."[181] These principles, including the precautionary principle, the concept of polluter pays, and the principle of intergenerational equity, are widely accepted in Latin American environmental law, partially in response to the constitutionalization of environmental protection.

On the other hand, Latin American environmental laws are notorious for being strong on paper but weak in reality. The main reasons for this are a lack of enforcement resources and a reluctance to enforce laws when doing so could adversely affect economic interests.[182] In some nations, the challenge of adequate enforcement is exacerbated by ineffective, complicated, and incomplete laws; officials who lack skills, training, and resources; high costs; and the need for extensive technical and scientific expertise.[183] Implementation and enforcement of environmental laws in Latin America have also been constrained by high inflation, regional financial crises, and international agendas related to deregulation and privatization.[184] Some Latin American nations face ongoing political turmoil (demonstrated by the recent coup d'état in Honduras), extensive poverty, and dependence on a small number of export commodities, mainly agricultural products, minerals, and energy resources.[185] Latin America is a major supplier of natural resources to the global economy, at a significant cost to the regional environment.[186] Another problem is that some Latin American nations are plagued by "ultra-presidentialism," in which the president has extraordinary powers that undermine both the operation of, and respect for, the rule of law.[187]

Conclusion

Despite these ongoing challenges, the overall conclusion, based on an assessment of legislation and litigation, is that constitutional recognition of the right to a healthy environment has had a major positive effect on the development of environmental law and policy in most Latin American nations (with exceptions such as Mexico and Paraguay).[188] Both the legislative and judicial branches of government have relied extensively on the right to a healthy environment as they attempt to move toward ecologically sustainable development. Argentina, Brazil, Colombia, and Costa Rica are at the forefront with strong legal frameworks and a growing body of jurisprudence. The ongoing efforts to clean up and restore Argentina's Matanza-Riachuelo River represent a compelling example of tangible action flowing from a court decision based on the right to a healthy environment. Even among the Latin American leaders, however, a note of caution is warranted because of continuing difficulties with implementation and enforcement. Salazar's warning, though specific to Costa Rica, can be applied more broadly: "Although Costa Rica's environmental law frameworks are innovative and far-reaching in intent and have had an important presence in the country, there are many shortcomings that hinder their effectiveness."[189]

TABLE 6.A

Constitutional influence on environmental legislation and litigation in Latin America and the Caribbean

Nation	Year*	Legislation	Litigation
Argentina	1994	Yes[1]	Yes[2]
Bolivia	2002	Yes[3]	Yes[4]
Brazil	1988	Yes[5]	Yes[6]
Chile	1980	Yes[7]	Yes[8]
Colombia	1991	Yes[9]	Yes[10]
Costa Rica	1994	Yes[11]	Yes[12]
Dominican Republic	2010	Yes[13]	Yes[14]
Ecuador	1984	Yes[15]	Yes[16]
El Salvador	1983	Yes[17]	Yes[18]
Guyana	1980	No[19]	N/A[20]
Honduras	1982	Yes[21]	N/A[22]
Jamaica	2011	No[23]	No[24]
Mexico	1999	Yes[25]	No[26]
Nicaragua	1986	Yes[27]	N/A[28]
Panama	1983	Yes[29]	Yes[30]
Paraguay	1992	Yes[31]	Yes[32]
Peru	1993	Yes[33]	Yes[34]
Venezuela	1999	Yes[35]	Yes[36]

*   Year when right to healthy environment was constitutionalized.

1 *General Law on the Environment* (2002).

2 Supreme Court of Justice, http://www.csjn.gov.ar/. Nineteen hits for the phrase "derecho a un medio ambiente sano" (right to a healthy environment).

3 *Law on the Environment* (1992), Articles 17, 92, 93.

4 Supreme Court of Justice, http://suprema.poderjudicial.gov.bo/. Eighty-eight hits for the phrase "medio ambiente" (healthy environment). The Constitutional Court has cited the right to a healthy environment in five cases, http://www.tribunalconstitucional.gob.bo/.

5 *National Environmental Policy Law*, Law 6,938/1991.

6 Supreme Court of Justice, http://www.stj.jus.br/SCON/. A search for Article 225 of the constitution and "environment" in Portuguese) produced twenty-seven hits. See also Federal Supreme Court, http://www.stf.gov.br. A search for Article 225 of the constitution and "environment" (in Portuguese) produced twenty hits.

7 *General Environment Framework Law* (1994), Articles 1, 33. Amended by Law No. 20.173.

8 Constitutional Court, http://www.tribunalconstitucional.cl. Seven hits for the phrase "medio ambiente libre de contaminacion" (healthy environment free of contamination").

9 *Law No. 99 of 1993*, Articles 1, 65, 69, 74, 97.

10 Constitutional Court, http://www.corteconstitucional.gov.co/. A search of the court's jurisprudence database for the phrase "derecho a un ambiente sano" (right to a healthy environment) yielded 107 decisions.

11 *Organic Law on the Environment* (1995), Articles 1, 2.

12 Constitutional Chamber of the Supreme Court (Sala IV), http://www.poder-judicial.go.cr/salaconstitucional/. A search of the court's jurisprudence database for the phrase "derecho a un ambiente sano" (right to a healthy environment) yielded 449 decisions.

13 *General Law on Environment and Natural Resources* (2000), No. 64-00. Preamble, Articles 6, 11.

14 Appeal by Deputy Attorney for the Defense of the Environment and Natural Resources(2009), Supreme Court of Justice. See also Judgment No. 024-2009 (Tax and Administrative Law Court).

15 *Law on Environmental Management* (1999), Preamble, Articles 28, 29, 41-44. See also Decree 1040 of 22 April 2008, outlining participation mechanisms of the *Law on Environmental Management*.

16 Constitutional Court, http://www.corteconstitucional.gov.ec/. Cases decided before 2008 (when new court was established) are not searchable online. Six cases for "medio ambiente" in 2008-09, but details of cases not available online.

17 *Environmental Law 1988*, Articles 1, 2, 9.

18 Supreme Court of Justice, Constitutional Chamber, http://www.jurisprudencia.gob.sv. Nine cases for "derecho a un medio ambiente sano" (right to a healthy environment).

19 *Environmental Protection Act* (1996).

20 Supreme Court of Judicature consisting of a Court of Appeal (the highest court) and a High Court. No website available.

21 *General Environmental Law* (1993), Preamble, Article 103.

22 Centro Electrónico de Documentación e Información Judicial, http://www.poderjudicial. gob.hn/ejes/institucional/organizacion/dependencias/cedij. Jurisprudence available to subscribers only.

23 Jamaican environmental legislation reviewed at http://faolex.fao.org/. No mention of right to a healthy environment.

24 *Northern Jamaica Conservation Association et al. v. Natural Resources Conservation Authority et al.* (2006) Judgment HCV 3002 of 2005, Supreme Court of Jamaica. http:// www.sc.gov.jm/Judgments/judgments.htm.

25 *General Law on Ecological Equilibrium and Environmental Protection* (1988), Articles 1, 15.

26 Supreme Court of Justice, http://www.scjn.gob.mx/default.asp. See Ojeda-Mestre (2007).

27 *General Law of Environment and Natural Resources* (1996), Article 109.

28 Jurisprudence not available on courts' website, http://www.web.poderjudicial.gob.ni/ buscador/.

29 *General Law on Environment* (1998), Articles 117-19.

30 Supreme Court of Justice, http://www.organojudicial.gob.pa. Two reported decisions in 2009 on the right to a healthy environment.

31 *Sanctioning Crimes against the Environment* (1996).

32 Supreme Court of Justice, Constitutional Chamber, http://www.pj.gov.py/. Three cases dealing with the right to a healthy environment.

33 *General Law on the Environment* (2005), Law No. 28611, Articles I-V (Preliminary Title), Articles 1, 41, 46, 114, 127.

34 Constitutional Court, http://www.tc.gob.pe/search/search.pl. Twenty-two cases found when searching for "derecho a un medio ambiente sano" (right to a healthy environment).

35 *Organic Law on the Environment* (2006), Articles 1, 4, 39, 43.

36 Supreme Court of Justice, http://www.tsj.gov.ve. Sixty-three hits for "healthy environment."

7
Africa

In a short period of time, constitutional recognition of the right to a healthy environment has become widespread in Africa. Since 1990, when Benin, Guinea, Mozambique, and São Tomé and Príncipe all incorporated this right into their constitutions, a total of thirty-two African nations have taken this step, including Morocco and South Sudan in 2011. For a host of social, economic, political, and cultural reasons, fulfilling the right to a healthy environment represents a stiff challenge in Africa. Most of the thirty-two nations have taken an initial step toward implementing the right to a healthy environment by strengthening national environmental legislation and incorporating the right therein. However, judicial enforcement of the right appears to be rare, occurring in reported cases in only a handful of nations. While the proliferation of constitutional provisions recognizing the right to a healthy environment offers a beacon of hope, the current capacity of African states to fulfill this aspiration is limited.

Legislation
Of the thirty-two African nations whose constitutions recognize the right to live in a healthy environment, at least twenty-three have enacted environmental laws incorporating this right (see Figure 7.1, and see Table 7.A at the end of this chapter). In part, this reflects ongoing national efforts, supported by international agencies, to modernize environmental laws throughout Africa. South Africa offers a leading example of the influence of constitutional provisions on environmental legislation.[1] The new South African constitution (1996) triggered a complete overhaul of the country's environmental laws. The *National Environmental Management Act, 1998*, repeatedly refers to the right to a healthy environment, articulates the right of access to information, and guarantees legal standing for citizens and groups to challenge and enforce environmental laws.[2] The right to a healthy environment is also included in

other major South African environmental laws dealing with water, air quality, and biodiversity, as well as legislation outlining the responsibilities of local governments.[3] In 2000, South Africa also passed legislation implementing the procedural rights entrenched in the constitution, which are essential for the full enjoyment of all substantive rights, including the right to a healthy environment.[4]

Benin amended its constitution in 1990 to recognize the right to a healthy, satisfying, and sustainable environment. The framework environmental law that came into effect in 1999 explicitly acknowledges that it is a response to the new constitutional mandate and echoes the wording of the constitution in referring to "the right to an environment that is healthy, satisfactory, and sustainable." Benin's framework environmental law guided the establishment of air quality standards, drinking-water standards, environmental assessment regulations, and other important legal rules.[5] Similarly, after Uganda recognized the right to a healthy environment in its 1995 constitution, the country passed a suite of environmental laws, including a *National Environment Act* that also guarantees the right to a healthy environment.[6]

The transformation of environmental laws subsequent to constitutional recognition of the right to a healthy environment is not always as comprehensive as it has been in South Africa, Benin, or Uganda. In Ethiopia, for example, national environmental laws passed subsequent to the inclusion of the right to a healthy environment and other environmental protection provisions in the 1995 constitution simply require that the environmental rights and objectives set forth in the constitution be achieved or fostered.[7] In some cases, the national framework environmental law included the right to a healthy environment before the constitution recognized this right. In Comoros, for example, the right is included in *Framework Law No. 94-018 relating to the environment* (1994), while constitutional recognition did not occur until 2001. Kenya's 2010 constitution offers an innovative new wrinkle intended to overcome legislative lethargy. It mandates that new environmental laws to implement constitutional commitments must be enacted within four years of the constitution's coming into force.[8] An extension is available in extenuating circumstances if approved by Kenya's Parliament, but the extension is only for one year and is nonrenewable.

Litigation

An extensive search of legal databases and secondary sources revealed only five African nations – South Africa, Uganda, Seychelles, Malawi, and Kenya – out of thirty-two where the constitutional right to a healthy environment

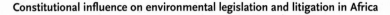

FIGURE 7.1

Constitutional influence on environmental legislation and litigation in Africa

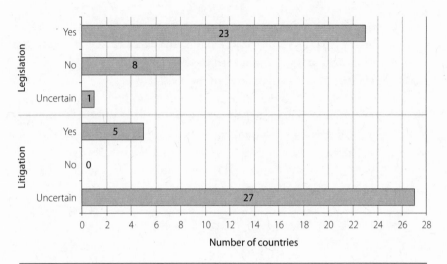

has been enforced or mentioned in court decisions (see Figure 7.1, and see Table 7.A at the end of this chapter). Leading cases are discussed below. The inability to identify court decisions based on the right to a healthy environment does not provide conclusive evidence that no such decisions have been issued, but it does suggest that the constitutional provisions are having a minimal effect on litigation to date. The right to a healthy environment has also played a major role in environmental litigation in two African nations where the right is not explicitly included in national constitutions. In Nigeria and Tanzania, courts have enforced the right to a healthy environment as part of the constitutional right to life.

SOUTH AFRICA

Even before the new South African constitution took effect, there was a vigorous debate about the extent to which courts should be empowered to enforce its extensive social, economic, and environmental rights. In *Grootboom*, a landmark case involving the right to housing, the Constitutional Court wrote that "socio-economic rights are expressly included in the Bill of Rights; they cannot be said to exist on paper only ... The question is therefore not whether socio-economic rights are justiciable under our Constitution, but how to enforce them in a given case."[9] According to Corder, "The formulation of socio-economic rights clearly anticipates a relatively extensive but nuanced judicial role for their appropriate realization, and the judges have generally not disappointed."[10]

The combination of the constitutional right to a healthy environment, constitutionally guaranteed procedural rights, and provisions in the *National Environmental Management Act* have led to very open rules governing standing.[11] South African courts have applied the right to a healthy environment in cases involving commercial land development, mining, nuclear energy, air pollution, waste incineration, and toxic substances.[12] Among the remedies available to plaintiffs are rulings that declare laws or regulations invalid, set aside administrative actions, grant injunctions, and award damages.[13]

In a 1999 case involving open-pit mining, the Supreme Court of Appeal of South Africa held that the constitution,

> by including environmental rights as fundamental, justiciable human rights, by necessary implication requires that environmental considerations be accorded appropriate recognition and respect in the administrative processes in our country. Together with the change in the ideological climate must also come a change in our legal and administrative approach to environmental concerns.[14]

In 2007, the court warned that if a real estate project went ahead in an area with high biodiversity values and several endangered species, "the resultant damage and harm to the environment would have farreaching and irreversible consequences for the broader society which would nullify the lofty ideals encapsulated in the Constitution of a healthy environment for everyone."[15] In another case, the High Court wrote: "By elevating the environment to a fundamental justiciable human right, South Africa has irreversibly embarked on a road which will lead to the goal of attaining a protected environment by an integrated approach, which takes into consideration, inter alia, socio-economic concerns and principles."[16] Furthermore, the court added, the "balancing of environmental interests with justifiable economic and social development is to be conceptualized well beyond the interests of the present living generation."[17]

The Constitutional Court's leading decision to date on the right to a healthy environment arose under unexpected circumstances, with a national association of gasoline stations using the right in an attempt to prevent the approval of a competing business, ostensibly on environmental grounds.[18]

In the words of Justice Sachs, "It is ironic that the first appeal in this court to invoke the majestic protection provided for the environment in the Bill of Rights comes not from concerned ecologists but from an organized section of an industry frequently lambasted both for establishing worldwide reliance on nonrenewable energy sources and for spawning pollution. So be it. The doors of the Court are open to all."[19] The court overturned the authorization of the proposed gas station, concluding that "the present generation holds the Earth in trust for the next generation. This trusteeship position carries with it the responsibility to look after the environment. It is the duty of the court to ensure that this responsibility is carried out."[20]

In a 2009 decision involving the right to information in an environmental context, the Constitutional Court observed that the protection of the right to a healthy environment will depend not only on the diligence of public officials but also on the active participation of civil society and, in some cases, on public interest litigation.[21] The court held that litigants acting in the public interest (e.g., seeking to enforce or defend constitutionally protected rights) should be exempt from the usual cost rules requiring unsuccessful plaintiffs to reimburse the legal costs of their opponents. Most recently, the Constitutional Court issued a controversial decision overturning lower-court decisions that had found that water meters limiting the volume of free water to twenty-five litres per person per day and requiring advance payment for additional water violated the constitutional right to water.[22]

South Africa ranks near the top of the Ibrahim Index of African Governance, with particularly high scores on indicators related to "Rule of law, transparency, and corruption" and "Participation and human rights."[23] Among the factors that set South Africa apart from other African nations is the presence of a relatively strong civil society. South Africa also enjoys advantages related to specific provisions in its constitution, including the right of access to information (s. 32), the right to enforce individual rights (s. 38), and safeguards regarding administrative justice (s. 33). The latter section is vital because so many environmental conflicts involve administrative decisions, such as the approval of a landfill or the issuance of a licence for an industrial activity. Glazewski observes that

> while it is difficult to give a precise legal definition to the abstract notion of environmental justice, the inclusion of an environmental clause in the Bill of Rights has added considerable momentum to its legal development. In South Africa this has been done both judicially

and legislatively by the new government's clear commitment to give effect to the imperative of the environmental clauses to enact legislative and other measures for environmental protection.[24]

Kotze concludes that the judiciary has, at least in most instances, reinforced the protective value and objectives of the environmental right to the benefit of South Africans.[25]

UGANDA

The right to a healthy environment was incorporated into the Ugandan constitution in 1995. Based on the constitutional right, courts have taken a liberal approach to standing.[26] Cases based on the right to a healthy environment have been brought to challenge the issuance of a permit for a sugar cane farm in a forest reserve (a type of legally protected natural conservation area), the development of a power project without a completed environmental impact assessment, excessive dust from a factory, and the export of chimpanzees.[27] In 2009, the Constitutional Court denied a claim brought by a property owner who sought to build a home on land he owned that included a wetland. The court held that the constitutional right to property was not absolute, that building on a wetland was a misuse of the right, and that there was a government obligation to protect natural assets like wetlands.[28] In 2008, the Environmental Action Network sought a declaration that smoking in public places violated the right to a healthy environment.[29] Before the court issued a final ruling, the National Environmental Management Agency issued a new regulation that limited smoking in public places.[30] Another example of litigation influencing legislation involved a court case that sought regulation of the manufacture, distribution, and use of plastic bags.[31] Although the court did not issue the requested order, legislation limiting the use of plastic bags was subsequently enacted.

Since 2000, a leading Ugandan ENGO, Greenwatch, has organized an ongoing series of educational workshops on the enforcement of environmental laws for environmental officers, police, magistrates, and judges of the High Court, Court of Appeal, and Supreme Court.[32] Ugandan courts have relied on jurisprudence from other nations in shaping their decisions about the right to a healthy environment. For example, the High Court of Uganda cited case law from India when it struck down a sugar cane licence issued in a forest conservation area and granted the plaintiffs all of the remedies they sought.[33] The Indian precedents had been presented to Ugandan High Court judges as part of the judicial education programs on environmental law.[34]

Generally, however, Ugandan courts are conservative and reluctant to grant effective remedies in environmental cases. Several lawsuits in which citizens asserted violations of their constitutional right to a healthy environment have been dismissed on the basis of legal technicalities.[35] As well, the costs of litigation are high, environmental and human rights knowledge is low, and widespread poverty makes litigation uncommon.[36] Another major concern is that the Ugandan Parliament does not always respect judicial decisions. In the case of the sugar cane licence referred to above, Parliament effectively overruled the court and allowed the company to proceed with its activities in the forest conservation area.[37]

Despite these challenges, Okidi notes that Uganda's civil society has been relatively active in using litigation to protect the right to a healthy environment and has been reasonably successful in the courts.[38] Twinomugisha concludes that, "through a creative application of the right, the judiciary has to some extent held the state, its agencies, and private actors accountable for violations of the right."[39]

KENYA

In Kenya, access to courts has broadened in recent years, contrary to a 1989 environmental case that denied standing to Wangari Maathai (who later won the Nobel Peace Prize).[40] The new constitution of 2010 recognizes the right to a healthy environment. However, Kenyan courts had already decided several cases based on the right, which was included previously in the *Environmental Management and Co-ordination Act*.[41] Kenyan High Court and Court of Appeal judges were trained in environmental law principles between 2005 and 2007.[42] Kenya also has a National Environmental Tribunal that decides cases, including cases that raise the right to a healthy environment. Kameri-Mbote suggests that the previous lack of constitutional provisions requiring environmental protection is an important reason for the Kenyan government's weak environmental record.[43]

SEYCHELLES AND MALAWI

The Seychelles and Malawi each offer one reported case in which reference to the constitutional right to a healthy environment plays a significant role. In a case involving the prosecution of eight individuals for unlawful possession of meat from protected species, including sea turtles and boobies, the Supreme Court of Seychelles referred to the constitutional right in interpreting the *Wild Animals and Birds Protection Act*.[44] The court wrote: "The right to a healthy environment has become a fundamental right. In Seychelles that right extends to the Management of Marine Resources as well as protected Land or Sea Birds." The court also referred to jurisprudence from the Supreme Court of India on the right to a healthy environment.[45]

The only reported decision from Malawi involving the right to a healthy environment involved an effort to remove protection from an area of land owned by a former Malawian president.[46] Malawi's High Court cited the constitution and the *Environment Management Act* as the basis for standing to enforce the right to a healthy environment. The court took a strong stand on environmental protection, ruling that the government's proposed action would result in "environmental degradation and unsustainable utilization of the resources," thereby violating the constitution.[47] Generally, however, Malawi's constitutional provisions, including the ambiguous right to a healthy environment, are undermined by their relative weakness compared to other rights (e.g., property, economic activity, and development), which are directly enforceable instead of mere guiding principles.[48] Gloppen and Kanyongolo add that poverty and lack of legal literacy are important *de facto* limits on access to courts for most Malawians.[49]

NIGERIA AND TANZANIA

Courts in Nigeria and Tanzania have held that the right to a healthy environment is implicitly incorporated in the right to life even where no explicit constitutional provisions exist.[50] For example, Nigeria's High Court ruled that Shell's practice of flaring gas from its oil operations in the Niger Delta was "a gross violation of the fundamental right to life (including healthy environment) and dignity of human person as enshrined in the Constitution."[51] This decision is under appeal and has not yet been implemented, and severe environmental and health problems in the region are ongoing.[52] The Nigerian Court of Appeal overturned a High Court decision that refused to grant standing to an individual who argued that the construction of a hazardous liquefied natural gas plant without the requisite environmental assessment violated his right to a healthy environment under Article 24 of the *African Charter*.[53] However, prospects for asserting constitutional environmental rights in Nigeria are limited because courts are subject to political interference and adhere to strict rules on standing, procedure, and costs.[54]

In Tanzania, there have been several high-profile cases involving the operation of garbage dumps near residential communities. The High Court ruled that the right to a healthy environment was an integral part of the right to life and was violated by these dumps.[55] Tanzania's framework environmental law recognizes the right to a healthy environment.[56] However,

Pallangyo has expressed concern that Tanzania's constitution "does not directly spell out the environmental rights which could prompt the development of environmental laws."[57]

Factors Affecting the Influence of the Constitutional Right to a Healthy Environment in Africa

When dealing with a huge and diverse continent such as Africa, one must be cautious in making generalizations, for there are bound to be exceptions, distinctions, and nuances lost in the process. Africa faces massive environmental challenges, including deforestation, desertification, loss of biodiversity, air and water pollution, and improper waste disposal. In many cases, Africa bears the burden of environmental damage inflicted by foreign corporations and governments that exploit natural resources for export to other continents. Exacerbating these problems are poverty, armed conflicts, a growing population, stagnant economies, migration, corruption, political instability, illiteracy, and foreign debt.[58]

There has been a rapid proliferation of environmental laws, regulations, and policies in Africa since the early 1990s. While the development of framework laws and other environmental policies is a step in the right direction, there continues to be a huge gap between the aspirations expressed on paper and the actions that take place on the ground. Implementation and enforcement of environmental law, including the right to a healthy environment, are limited in the majority of African nations (see Table 7.1).[59] An anonymous African official quoted by Keeley and Scoones commented: "There are too many conferences and workshops. What are they actually doing to improve things?"[60]

The short-term prospects for recognition and fulfillment of the right to live in a healthy environment in Africa are limited. Some of the problems hindering enforcement of environmental laws on the continent are government institutions that lack the financial and human resources to monitor and control activities; government officials entrusted with enforcing laws or protecting rights under those laws who often have more to gain by condoning violations or engaging in violations themselves; court systems that are backlogged, bankrupt, or otherwise not functioning; and the imperatives of daily life for the poor, which overwhelm any likely risks associated with violating the law.[61] African constitutions have failed to constrain the use and abuse of executive power, which is at the heart of what constitutions must achieve, leading people to perceive them as mere rhetoric.[62] Ihonvbere writes that governance in Africa has often been interpreted as "an opportunity to get rich

TABLE 7.1

Factors influencing the extent of the environmental rights revolution in Africa

Factor	Generally positive	Generally negative	Mixed	Examples of positive influence	Examples of negative influence
Constitutional provisions			×	South Africa, Uganda	Burundi, Central African Republic, Gabon, Malawi, Maldives
Prospective litigants		×		South Africa, Uganda	Most African nations
Access to justice		×		South Africa, Uganda	Most African nations
Resources for legal mobilization		×		South Africa, Uganda	Most African nations
Rule of law		×		South Africa	Chad, Cote d'Ivoire, Congo (Democratic Republic of the), Sudan
Responsive judiciary	×			Kenya, South Africa, Tanzania, Uganda	
Social, economic, and political conditions		×			All African nations

and use public instruments of violence to protect class interests [while] power is used arbitrarily and irresponsibly."[63]

National governments seek foreign investment, but this often comes at the expense of local people, communities, and the environment.[64] Foreign governments and multinational corporations are racing to exploit Africa's rich natural resources, inflicting environmental damage that is rarely monitored or remedied because of a lack of enforcement. Although most African nations have in place framework laws and regulations requiring environmental impact assessments, environmental abuses persist, with Nigeria providing a notorious example.[65] Billions of dollars worth of oil has been extracted from the Niger Delta, yet the region continues to suffer from crumbling social infrastructure and services, high unemployment, chronic poverty, terrible environmental conditions, and endemic conflict.[66] Because of extreme poverty and the compelling need for economic development, environmental protection is often not a priority.[67] Moseley quotes a Malian official: "The priority is development. One cannot stop development, even to save the country's heritage."[68]

Effective legal and political institutions are prerequisites for enforcing the rule of law but are lacking in many African nations, such as Sudan and the Democratic Republic of the Congo.[69] In some countries, military governments or one-party governments ignore judicial decisions.[70] Some judicial systems suffer from inadequate budgets, a shortage of trained professionals, and extensive political interference.[71] Other problems that constrain efforts to protect the environment include jurisdictional battles between levels of government and ministries within government; institutional instability, caused by shuffling of ministers and responsibilities; lack of institutional capabilities and resources (e.g., financial, human, and technological); and lack of public concern/understanding.[72] In some nations, such as Burkina Faso, customary rules are still more important to the majority of the population than formal national laws. Environmental laws are poorly known, rarely applied, and generally ineffective.[73]

Many nations have limited ENGO communities, while existing organizations often lack resources, information, and expertise.[74] Few African ENGOs, apart from Greenwatch in Uganda, specialize in environmental law. International agencies, including UNEP and the IUCN, have worked hard to improve environmental legislation in African nations. International law is having a positive, albeit limited, influence. For example, the right to a healthy environment in the *African Charter* led Kenyan and Nigerian courts to make important rulings based on this right, finding it to be an essential part of the constitutional right to life, even though it was not explicitly articulated as such in either the Nigerian or Kenyan constitutions (although the right was included in Kenya's new constitution in 2010).[75] In contrast to Latin America, African nations have made little progress in establishing simplified and expedited procedures to enforce constitutionally protected rights. As a result, the challenges facing fulfillment of the right to a healthy environment are common to many human rights in Africa.

Conclusion

Optimists suggest that environmental law is rapidly evolving in Africa and that the continent is on the brink of an environmental renaissance.[76] Ihonvbere writes that although previous constitutions lacked legitimacy, new democratically formulated constitutions are a step forward and, as a result, "Africans are beginning to see the constitution as an instrument for addressing pressing socio-economic, cultural, and economic questions."[77] The process of democratization should provide an impetus to the implementation and enforcement of environmental law, including the right to a healthy environment.[78] South Africa represents a beacon of hope with its strong constitution and comprehensive environmental laws. Amechi concludes that "there must be a shift in the attitude of African governments towards the protection or conservation of the environment if African citizenry are ever to enjoy the right to a general satisfactory environment."[79] Indeed, despite constitutional environmental provisions and strengthened environmental laws, the other prerequisites for respecting and protecting the human right to a healthy environment – that is, the rule of law, an independent judiciary, a strong civil society, and litigation-support infrastructure – are largely not yet present in most African nations.[80] It is an open question, worthy of future research, whether the presence of constitutional environmental provisions in African nations results in measurable improvements in environmental performance despite the extensive obstacles to implementation.

TABLE 7.A

Constitutional influence on environmental legislation and litigation in Africa

Nation	Year*	Legislation	Litigation
Angola	1992	Yes[1]	N/A[2]
Benin	1990	Yes[3]	N/A[4]
Burkina Faso	1991	Yes[5]	N/A[6]
Burundi	2005	Yes[7]	N/A[8]
Cameroon	1996	Yes[9]	N/A[10]
Cape Verde	1992	Yes[11]	N/A[12]
Central African Republic	2004	No[13]	N/A[14]
Chad	1996	No[15]	N/A[16]
Comoros	2001	Yes[17]	N/A[18]
Congo-Brazzaville	2002	No[19]	N/A[20]
Congo, Dem. Republic of the	2005	No[21]	N/A[22]
Cote d'Ivoire	2000	Yes[23]	N/A[24]
Egypt	2007	No[25]	N/A[26]
Ethiopia	1995	Yes[27]	N/A[28]
Gabon	1991	Yes[29]	N/A[30]
Guinea	1990	No[31]	N/A[32]
Kenya	2010	Yes[33]	Yes[34]
Malawi	1994	Yes[35]	Yes[36]
Mali	1992	Yes[37]	N/A[38]
Mauritania	1991	Yes[39]	N/A[40]
Morocco	2011	Yes[41]	No[42]
Mozambique	1990	Yes[43]	N/A[44]
Niger	1996	Yes[45]	N/A[46]
Rwanda	2003	Yes[47]	N/A[48]
São Tomé & Príncipe	1990	Yes[49]	N/A[50]
Senegal	2001	Yes[51]	N/A[52]
Seychelles	1993	No[53]	Yes[54]
South Africa	1996	Yes[55]	Yes[56]
South Sudan	2011	No[57]	No[58]
Sudan	2005	N/A[59]	N/A[60]
Togo	1992	Yes[61]	N/A[62]
Uganda	1995	Yes[63]	Yes[64]

* Year when right to healthy environment was constitutionalized.
1 *General Environmental Law* (1998), Articles 1, 3, 4, 8, 21, and 22.
2 Angola Constitutional Court, http://www.tribunalconstitucional.ao/. Available only in Portuguese, no search function.
3 Law No. 98-030 *Framework Law on the Environment* (1999).
4 Benin Constitutional Court, http://www.cour-constitutionnelle-benin.org/. No search function available.
5 *Environmental Code for Burkina Faso* (1997).
6 Constitutional Council of Burkina Faso, http://www.conseil-constitutionnel.gov.bf. No search function.
7 *Code on the Environment* (2000).

8   Constitutional Court of Burundi. No website available as of 25 July 2009.

9   *Law No. 96-12 concerning law on environmental management* (1996).

10 Supreme Court of Cameroon, http://www.coursupreme.cm. No hits for environment ("environnement" in French).

11 *Act No. 86/IV/93 defining environmental policy* (1993), Articles 1, 2, 41, 43, 45.

12 Cape Verde Supreme Court of Justice, http://www.stj.cv/. No hits for environment ("ambiente" in Portuguese).

13 Reviewed fifty-five statutory instruments related to environmental protection.

14 Constitutional Court of Central African Republic. No website available as of 3 May 2011.

15 *Law No. 014/PR/98 Act defining the general principles of environmental protection* (1998).

16 Supreme Court, http://www.primature-tchad.org/. No jurisprudence available on judicial website.

17 *Framework law relating to the environment* (1994), Article 4.

18 Constitutional Court of Comoros. No website available as of 3 May 2011.

19 *Law on the protection of the environment,* Law No. 003/91 (1991).

20 Supreme Court. No website available as of 3 May 2011.

21 *Ordinance No. 75-231 of 22 July 1975 determining the functions of the department of environment, nature conservation and tourism* and supplementing *Ordinance No. 69-147 of 1 August 1969.*

22 Constitutional Court. No website available as of 3 May 2011.

23 *Framework Law No. 96-766 on the Environmental Code* (1996), Articles 2, 35, 36.

24 Constitutional Court of Cote d'Ivoire. No access to decisions.

25 *Law No. 4 of 1994 on environment.*

26 Supreme Constitutional Court of Egypt. No website available in English.

27 *Environmental Protection Organs Establishment Proclamation* (2002), Article 6.

28 Ethiopia's Federal Supreme Court. No case database to search.

29 *Loi n° 16/93 relative à la protection de l'environnement* (1993), Article 3.

30 Constitutional Court of Gabon. No jurisprudence available.

31 *Ordonnance n° 045\\PRG\\87 portant Code sur la protection et la mise en valeur de l'environnement* (1987).

32 Supreme Court of Guinea. No website available as of 3 May 2011.

33 *Environmental Management and Co-ordination Act* (1999), Article 3 (Part II).

34 *P.K. Waweru v. Republic of Kenya* (2006).

35 *Environment Management Act* (1996), Article 5.

36 *Kamuzu v. Attorney General* [2004]

37 *Law No. 01-020 relating to pollution and nuisance* (2001).

38 Constitutional Court of Mali. No website available as of 3 May 2011.

39 *Law No. 2000-045 concerning the Framework Environmental Law* (2000), Articles 5, 6.

40 Constitutional Council of Mauritania, http://www.mauritania.mr.

41 *Morocco Charter for the Environment and Sustainable Development.* See Idllalene (2010).

42 As the right to a healthy environment only gained constitutional recognition in 2011, it is too early to discern an influence on litigation.

43 *Environment Act* (1997), Articles 4, 19-24.

44 Mozambique Constitutional Council. No website available as of 3 May 2011.

45 *Framework Law on Environmental Management* (1998).

46 Constitutional Court of Niger. No website available as of 3 May 2011.

47 *Organic Law No. 04/2005 laying down rules to protect, preserve and promote the environment in Rwanda*, Articles 1, 3, 6.

48 Supreme Court of Rwanda, http://www.supremecourt.gov.rw. No reported cases about the environment.

49 *Basic Law of the Environment* (1999), Articles 1, 2, 8, 9, 54-56.

50 Constitutional Court of São Tomé and Príncipe (established 2005). No website available as of 3 May 2011.

51 *Code on the Environment* (2001), Articles 1, 7, 107.

52 Senegal Constitutional Council, http://www.gouv.sn/. No case law on website.

53 *Environmental Protection Act* (1994).

54 *R. v. Marengo, Azemia, Antat et al.* (2004).

55 *National Environmental Management Act* (1998), Preamble, Articles 2, 31; *National Environmental Management: Air Quality Act* (2004), Articles 2, 3; *National Environmental Management of Biodiversity Act* (2004), Article 3; *National Water Act* (1998), Preamble, Article 4.

56 *Fuel Retailers Association of South Africa v. Director-General* (2007).

57 As a new nation, South Sudan is in the very early stages of enacting legislation.

58 As the right to a healthy environment only gained constitutional recognition in 2011, it is too early to discern an influence on litigation.

59 *Environmental Protection Act of 2001*. Unable to locate English translation (document available only in Arabic).

60 Constitutional Court of Sudan. No website available as of 3 May 2011.

61 *Framework Law on the Environment* (2008), Articles 1, 3, 5.

62 Constitutional Court of Togo. No website available as of 3 May 2011.

63 *National Environment Act* (1995), Articles 2, 3, 4.

64 *Advocates Coalition for Development and Environment v. Attorney General* (2004).

8

...... Asia

Asia is a vast continent with an incredible diversity of cultures, languages, political institutions, history, and legal systems. Fourteen nations in Asia explicitly recognize the right to a healthy environment in their constitutions. In most of these countries, the constitutional provision has influenced national environmental laws. Litigation appears to be confined to a minority of countries, although this underestimates the extent of the right's legal influence in the region. A handful of South Asian nations, led by India, are in the global vanguard in judicial recognition of an implicit constitutional right to a healthy environment as an essential element of the right to life. On the other hand, China, home to one in five humans and a rapidly expanding economy, does not recognize the right to a healthy environment. While this reflects a broader pattern of reluctance to recognize human rights, the enormity of environmental challenges posed by China makes this particular omission an important gap from a global perspective.

Legislation

At least twelve of the fourteen Asian nations whose constitutions include the right to live in a healthy environment have also incorporated this right into national environmental legislation (see Figure 8.1, and see Table 8.A at the end of this chapter). The exceptions are the Maldives (where the right was only granted constitutional protection in 2008) and Iran, as no English translation of Iran's environmental legislation is currently available.[1]

Environmental laws in the Philippines are considered to be at the forefront among Asian nations.[2] Since the greening of its constitution in 1987, the country has incorporated the right to a healthy environment throughout its domestic environmental legislation, including the *Clean Air Act of 1999*,[3] *Clean Water Act*,[4] *Ecological Solid Waste Management Act*,[5] *National Environmental Awareness and Education Act of 2008*,[6] *Climate Change Act of 2009*,[7] and the regulations associated with implementing these statutes.[8] The *Clean Air Act of 1999* provides a comprehensive articulation of substantive and procedural environmental rights:

> S. 4. *Recognition of Rights.* Pursuant to the above-declared principles, the following rights of citizens are hereby sought to be recognized and the State shall seek to guarantee their enjoyment:
>
> (a) The right to breathe clean air;
> (b) The right to utilize and enjoy all natural resources according to the principles of sustainable development;
> (c) The right to participate in the formulation, planning, implementation, and monitoring of environmental policies and programs and in the decision-making process;
> (d) The right to participate in the decision-making process concerning development policies, plans, programs, projects, or activities that may have adverse impact on the environment and public health;
> (e) The right to be informed of the nature and extent of the potential hazard of any activity, undertaking, or project and to be served timely notice of any significant rise in the level of pollution and the accidental or deliberate release into the atmosphere of harmful or hazardous substances;
> (f) The right of access to public records that a citizen may need to exercise his or her rights effectively under this Act;
> (g) The right to bring action in court or quasi-judicial bodies to enjoin all activities in violation of environmental laws and regulations, to compel the rehabilitation and cleanup of affected areas, and to seek the imposition of penal sanctions against violators of environmental laws; and
> (h) The right to bring action in court for compensation of personal damages resulting from the adverse environmental and public health impact of a project or activity.

As well, the *Local Government Code* of the Philippines imposes a duty on local governments to promote citizens' constitutional right to a healthful and balanced ecology.[9]

According to the UN Economic Commission for Europe, Azerbaijan's 1995 constitution laid "the foundation for the development of national environmental policy."[10] The constitutional right to a healthy environment

FIGURE 8.1

Constitutional influence on environmental legislation and litigation in Asia

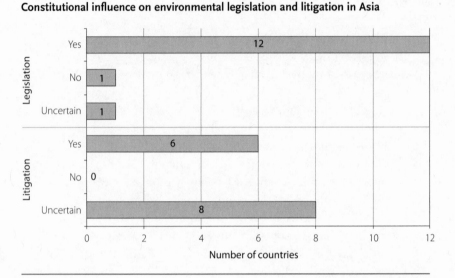

has been incorporated into Azerbaijan's *Law on Environmental Protection, Law on Air Protection, Law on Environmental Safety,* and the *Law on Sanitary-Epidemiological Services.* In South Korea, the incorporation of the right to a healthy environment in the constitution triggered the establishment of the country's first major environmental agency and the passage of new legislation, including the *Framework Act on Environmental Policy,* the *Air Quality Conservation Act,* the *Water Quality Conservation Act,* and the *Toxic Chemicals Control Act.*[11] Turkey has strengthened its environmental laws significantly in recent years, motivated in part by its constitutional mandate but also by a series of high-profile environmental scandals and the European Union harmonization process.[12]

Litigation

At least six of the fourteen Asian nations – the Philippines, Nepal, Turkey, South Korea, Thailand, and Indonesia – have experienced litigation based on the right to a healthy environment (see Table 8.A). Jurisprudence related to this right could not be identified for eight nations – Azerbaijan, East Timor, Iran, Iraq, Kyrgyzstan, the Maldives, Mongolia, and Turkmenistan – because of lack of access to court decisions. However, the failure to identify court decisions related to the right should not be interpreted as conclusive evidence of the absence of such decisions.

There is also an extensive body of case law from India, Pakistan, Bangladesh, Sri Lanka, Malaysia, and Israel on the constitutional right to live in a healthy environment, despite the absence of an explicit mention of this right in the constitutions of these countries. Public interest litigants have successfully persuaded courts in these nations that the right to life includes an implicit, and enforceable, right to a healthy environment. India is among the world leaders in terms of the volume of cases brought based on the implicit right to a healthy environment, while courts in Bangladesh, Pakistan, and Sri Lanka have followed Indian precedents. Hassan and Azfar go so far as to assert that "the South Asian judiciary leads the world in its role as the guarantor of the legal protection of sustainable development," in particular the right to a clean or healthy environment.[13] Courts in Malaysia and Israel have issued constitutional judgments regarding the right to a healthy environment, but the case law in these nations is characterized by contradictory statements.

PHILIPPINES

Following the enactment of the constitutional right to a healthful and balanced ecology in 1987, the first precedent-setting case on the constitutional right to a healthy environment in the Philippines was decided in 1993. The *Minors Oposa* case involved a lawsuit, filed on behalf of children and future generations, that sought cancellation of all the timber-harvesting licences in the Philippines.[14] When the government challenged the standing of the plaintiffs, the Supreme Court issued a forceful ruling on the urgent need to protect the environment on behalf of both present and future generations. Although the right to a "balanced and healthful ecology" is found in the constitution's "Declaration of Principles and State Policies" and is not part of the "Bill of Rights," the court held that the right was legally enforceable without need for further legislation – i.e., it is a self-executing provision. The *Minors Oposa* case has been criticized for not directly contributing to improved environmental conditions.[15] However, when the case was filed, there were ninety-two timber-harvesting licences in the Philippines; by 2006, there were only three, and the rate of deforestation had fallen.[16] In a lawsuit brought by a timber company, the Supreme Court upheld the government's ability to cancel licences, based in part on the *Minors Oposa* precedent.[17] A retired Philippine judge, A.D. Agcaoili, observed in 2009 that *Minors Oposa* "enunciated seminal principles likely to influence profoundly the direction and course of the protection, management and preservation of the environment."[18]

Other leading court decisions in the Philippines based on the right to a balanced and healthful ecology have ordered an end to waste dumping, urged a concerted government effort to stop illegal logging, and refused to recognize private title to land in public forests.[19] Local government regulations restricting destructive fishing practices have also been upheld on the basis of the constitutional right to a healthy environment.[20]

In 2008, the Supreme Court of the Philippines released a globally significant judgment based on the right to a healthy environment in the *Manila Bay* case.[21] According to the court:

> The importance of the Manila Bay as a sea resource, playground, and as a historical landmark cannot be overemphasized. It is not yet too late in the day to restore the Manila Bay to its former splendor and bring back the plants and sea life that once thrived in its blue waters. But the tasks ahead, daunting as they may be, could only be accomplished if those mandated, with the help and cooperation of all civic-minded individuals, would put their minds to these tasks and take responsibility. This means that the State, through petitioners, has to take the lead in the preservation and protection of the Manila Bay.
>
> The era of delays, procrastination, and *ad hoc* measures is over. Petitioners must transcend their limitations, real or imaginary, and buckle down to work before the problem at hand becomes unmanageable. Thus, we must reiterate that different government agencies and instrumentalities cannot shirk from their mandates; they must perform their basic functions in cleaning up and rehabilitating the Manila Bay.

In a judgment reminiscent of the Argentine Supreme Court's ruling in the *Matanza-Riachuelo River* case, the Philippine Supreme Court ordered twelve government agencies to develop a comprehensive plan, within six months, to rehabilitate and restore Manila Bay. More specifically, the court ordered the responsible agencies to take the following actions:

- install and operate sewage treatment facilities
- clean up hazardous and toxic wastes
- prevent pollution and wastes from ships
- develop adequate facilities and programs for the proper disposal of solid waste

- remove structures that obstruct the free flow of waters to Manila Bay
- revitalize the marine life by reintroducing indigenous aquatic species
- require septic and sludge companies to use adequate treatment facilities
- prevent all forms of illegal fishing
- establish a comprehensive environmental education program
- allocate a budget sufficient to carry out the restoration plan.

Borrowing from the jurisprudence of the Supreme Court of India, the court adopted the extraordinary remedy of continuing mandamus (see the section on India below), giving itself the power to supervise implementation of the restoration plan, with the goal "of ensuring that its decision would not be set to naught by administrative inaction or indifference."[22] The government agencies are required, by court order, to submit quarterly progress reports, and the Supreme Court established an expert advisory committee to review these reports. In its conclusion, the court stated that the responsible government agencies "cannot escape their obligation to future generations of Filipinos to keep the waters of the Manila Bay as clean and clear as humanly possible. Anything less would be a betrayal of the trust reposed in them."[23] The government has established a task force and budgeted roughly US$100 million to begin the cleanup project.[24] In 2011, the Supreme Court issued an additional order requiring government agencies to complete specific tasks by fixed deadlines, based on detailed recommendations made by the Manila Bay Advisory Committee (comprised of two judges and three technical experts).[25]

In 2008, the Supreme Court announced plans to create a national network of more than a hundred environmental courts, using its unique powers under the constitution.[26] These "green courts" were to be staffed by judges with specialized training in environmental matters. In 2010, the court issued special procedural rules for environmental cases, with four objectives: protecting and advancing the constitutional right to a balanced and healthful ecology; providing a simplified, speedy, and inexpensive procedure for enforcing environmental rights; adopting innovations and best practices for enforcing environmental laws; and enabling courts to monitor and ensure compliance with orders in environmental cases.[27] The court also created a new type of civil action, called the writ of *kalikasan* (nature), which authorized any person (natural or legal) to bring a legal action asking the court to order a respondent to cease an environmentally harmful activity; protect the environment; or carry out restoration or rehabilitation activities. Collectively, these procedural changes could contribute to the successful use of constitutional environmental rights, as has been the case in Latin American nations.

Another potentially groundbreaking case is currently working its way through the Filipino judicial system. Two lawyers are seeking to stop offshore oil and gas exploration by acting as legal guardians for whales, dolphins, and other species whose habitat would be disturbed by underwater blasting and drilling. Finally, it is worth noting that the Supreme Court of the Philippines recognizes the boundary between its adjudicative role and the lawmaking role of the legislature. In a 2006 case, citizens sought an order of mandamus requiring that government vehicles be converted to run on CNG (compressed natural gas) rather than diesel. The court acknowledged the adverse health and environmental consequences of motor vehicle pollution and the constitutional right to clean air but concluded that "the legislature should provide first the specific statutory remedy to the complex environmental problems bared by herein petitioners before any judicial recourse by mandamus is taken."[28]

Nepal

While Nepal's interim constitution (2006) explicitly recognizes the right to a healthy environment, previous Nepalese constitutions did not. Nevertheless, the Supreme Court of Nepal has repeatedly ruled that the right to a healthy environment is a prerequisite for the enjoyment of other constitutional rights. As the court stated, "Since a clean and healthy environment is an essential element for our survival, the right to life encompasses the right to a clean and healthy environment."[29]

Public interest environmental lawyers have won cases involving issues ranging from motor vehicle pollution (including the prohibition of leaded gasoline) to industrial pollution.[30] In the *Godavari Marble* case, the Supreme Court instructed the government to "frame an environmental piece of legislation as soon as possible so that it can end the confusion on this matter and fulfill its national and international obligations."[31] The government responded by passing the *Environmental Protection Act 1997* and *Environmental Protection Regulations 1997*.[32] The court also used the constitutional right to a healthy environment as a basis for rejecting a challenge to a government ban on certain highly polluting vehicles, stating that the right to clean air outweighed the freedom to carry out business.[33] In 2001, the court ordered the government to immediately stop the import of Indian vehicles that did not meet Euro-I emission standards.[34] Other cases have addressed water pollution, noise, waste management, and the right to clean water.[35] Experts anticipate that the stronger provisions in the 2006 constitution will increase access to justice and the likelihood of successful environmental litigation in the future.[36]

However, the right to a healthy environment appears to have greater utility for urban residents than for rural Nepalese, for whom costs, distance from courts, lack of familiarity with the judicial system, and reliance on customary law (instead of statutory law) constitute significant barriers.[37] As well, the impact of the Supreme Court's strong environmental decisions is limited by the judiciary's relatively weak role in Nepalese governance. Finally, the promising developments in constitutional environmental law that took place in the 1990s have been slowed by the rapid turnover of governments, the Maoist insurgency, and the institution of royal rule.[38]

TURKEY

In Turkey, a strong body of environmental laws has been enacted since environmental protection was incorporated into the constitution in 1982. However, citizens have been forced to seek protection of their right to a healthy environment in the courts because Turkish "governments have consistently resisted, delayed, or willfully misinterpreted environmental legislation," and the Ministry of Environment has been chronically underfunded and excluded from important economic policy decisions.[39] A major weakness in Turkish environmental law is the relative lack of provision for public participation, although now that Turkey has signed the *Aarhus Convention on Access to Information, Public Participation in Decision-making and Access to Justice in Environmental Matters,* the situation is improving.[40] Turkish jurisprudence is generally inaccessible, but several leading cases have been translated and published because lack of enforcement of court orders in Turkey has led to complaints heard (and upheld) by the European Court of Human Rights.

The best-known Turkish case involving the right to a healthy environment involved a mining company, Eurogold, which used cyanide leaching in its gold mines.[41] Three lawsuits, filed on behalf of more than 650 plaintiffs, sought cancellation of the mine's operating permits. The First Administrative Court ruled against the plaintiffs in 1996, but on appeal the Council of State (Turkey's highest administrative court) ruled in favour of the plaintiffs based on their constitutional rights to life and to a healthy, balanced environment.[42] The government ordered a new study of the environmental risks of mining using cyanide leaching and then reissued Eurogold's permits in 2002. The Council of State issued a new ruling in 2004 that temporarily shut down the mine. When the mine was again reopened, citizens took their case to the

European Court of Human Rights (ECHR).[43] The ECHR ruled in favour of ten citizens in 2004 because of the Turkish government's failure to close the mine. The European Court referred to the violation of the constitutional right to a healthy environment and decided that compensation was required on the basis of a violation of the rights to a fair hearing and to respect for private life, family life, and the home.

The other leading Turkish case involved a longstanding effort on the part of citizens to reduce pollution from three coal-fired power plants. After public petitions failed, lawsuits were filed in 1993 and 1994 based on alleged violations of the constitutional right to a healthy environment. Turkey's Aydin Administrative Court appointed a panel of scientific experts to investigate the power plants. The experts concluded that the plants generated excessive sulphur dioxide and nitrogen oxide pollution and threatened human health and the environment. The court found that the air pollution violated the right to a healthy environment and ordered the government to either install pollution-abatement equipment (which would reduce emissions by approximately 95 percent) or close the plants. In 1998, the Turkish government's appeal to the Supreme Administrative Court was dismissed. However, the Turkish government refused to comply with the court's order, forcing the citizens to pursue their complaint at the European Court of Human Rights. The ECHR ordered compensation paid to the citizens after it found that the government had violated the right to a healthy environment and the right to a fair hearing.[44]

South Korea

South Korea's Constitutional Court has been praised because "since its establishment in 1988, the court has systematically sought to expand its jurisdiction to make itself accessible to the public, has created new unwritten constitutional rights (e.g., right to information), and has actively promoted freedom of expression."[45] Experts speculated that the right to a healthy environment in Article 35 of the South Korean constitution was a promising trigger for public interest litigation.[46] However, environmental cases have been relatively rare, and the Constitutional Court has taken a conservative approach to environmental jurisprudence.[47] The court has determined that while the right to a healthy environment may be used to buttress arguments in favour of upholding environmental legislation, it does not give citizens standing to bring public interest environmental lawsuits. The wording of the right indicates that it is not self-executing but requires enabling legislation.

On the one hand, the Constitutional Court upheld the legality of multiple pollution audits of a business based on the constitutional right to a healthy environment and the related public interest in environmental protection.[48] On the other hand, the court ruled in favour of property developers who challenged regulatory limits on the use of land in a protected zone.[49] The government argued that the limitations had a constitutional basis in the right to a healthy environment. However, the majority of the court struck down the impugned provisions of the *Urban Planning Act*. A dissenting judge warned:

> Today is the day that the Constitutional Court's decision extinguished our constitutional provision on the environment (Article 35), the basis for realization of human dignity and worth and pursuit of happiness. The phrase carefully calligraphed on the rice paper, "all people have right to live in a healthy and enjoyable environment, and the state and people must work toward environmental preservation ..." was pushed out by the guarantee of private property into the role of an antiquarian decoration.[50]

South Korea's Supreme Court has also taken a very narrow approach to the constitutional right to a healthy environment, construing the provision as not self-executing unless an environmental lawsuit is based on a specific statute.[51] In a case where concerned citizens challenged the disposition of farmland and water rights, the court held that citizens living outside the directly affected area lacked standing.[52] The court also ruled against two Buddhist temples and an ENGO in a case where the plaintiffs sought an injunction to prevent construction of a tunnel through a mountain for a bullet train network that would damage the habitat of about thirty different endangered species. In this case, the court stated that salamanders do not enjoy legal rights.[53]

One of the most prominent South Korean cases involved citizen efforts to stop the construction of the world's largest seawall and the conversion of over forty thousand hectares of ecologically important tidal flats into farmland.[54] In rejecting the legal challenge, the Supreme Court held that Article 35 of the constitution could not be seen as establishing the specific content and means of exercise of the environmental right. It also held that Article 6 of the *Framework Act on Environmental Policy* did not provide citizens with the specific right.[55] Because both the environment and development enjoy constitutional protection, the court engaged in a balancing test and ruled that the economic interests of the national community as a whole prevailed over the environmental interests of some individuals. Two dissenting judges held that because the value of Nature is not quantifiable in monetary terms, it cannot be weighed against competing economic interests and therefore the government should have applied the precautionary principle.

Despite the unfavourable case law from the Constitutional and Supreme Courts, lower courts have recognized that the right to a healthy environment represents a sufficient interest on which to base a lawsuit. For example, residents living downstream from a proposed resort successfully brought a lawsuit blocking construction based on concerns that waste water would contaminate their drinking supply.[56]

Historically, South Korean courts have been reluctant to make decisions with adverse economic consequences.[57] This may be due, in part, to the fact that the executive branch of government maintains strong control over the judiciary (e.g., the president appoints judges to both the Constitutional and Supreme Courts).[58] However, several elements of the litigation support structure identified as prerequisites for a rights revolution are emerging in South Korea, including a growing NGO community and an "expanding legal profession, particularly an active civil rights bar."[59] Overall, judicial oversight is increasing but still falls short of public expectations.[60] In terms of environmental protection, Cho concludes that "while the bureaucracy neither behaves as expected by the public nor performs as mandated by legislation, the courts just look on with folded arms."[61]

INDONESIA

The Indonesian constitution was amended in 2000 to include the right to a healthy environment. Although it is difficult to gain access to Indonesian jurisprudence, there is some evidence that citizens and NGOs are invoking the constitutional right to a healthy environment in court cases.[62] Indonesia's *Environmental Management Act* explicitly grants ENGOs standing to sue.[63] In the wake of a deadly landslide linked to poor forestry practices, citizens brought a class action lawsuit based in part on their right to a healthy environment.[64] The District Court ordered restoration of the affected area and compensation to affected individuals.[65] The Indonesian Forum on Environment (WALHI) and the Indonesian Center for Environmental Law have both brought court cases based on the right to a healthy environment.[66] In a challenge to the constitutionality of Indonesia's *Water Resources Law*, the Constitutional Court held that the right to water is part and parcel of the constitutionally guaranteed right to a healthy environment.[67]

Despite these promising precedents, recourse to courts to address environmental degradation appears to be infrequent in Indonesia. Bedner conducted an extensive search for civil and administrative environmental cases in Indonesia and found few examples.[68] Among the main obstacles to greater reliance on the judicial system are the complex legal and regulatory framework, with jurisdictional overlaps fostering buck-passing; the lack of institutional capacity; cumbersome enforcement and prosecution processes; corruption; a lack of technical and legal skills; lack of public knowledge; and opposition from powerful business interests.[69] The majority of the lawsuits brought by ENGOs are unsuccessful.[70] In a telling case, ENGOs challenged open-pit mines whose operations in protected forests were grandfathered. The Constitutional Court ruled in favour of the mining companies based on their vested economic interests and the sanctity of contracts.[71] Bedner asserts that the Indonesian judiciary suffers from an "extremely negative image," and "there is a widespread belief that in environmental disputes companies control the judiciary and the government."[72] Ratnawati adds that there are also constraints on the availability of environmental information.[73] Despite these barriers, Heringa concludes that the incorporation of the right to a healthy environment in the Indonesian constitution will provide a "beacon about where to go and what to do."[74]

THAILAND

In a decision concerning complaints against the construction of a new airport, Thailand's Supreme Court ruled that the 1997 constitution recognized rights and duties in the preservation and exploitation of natural resources and the environment.[75] According to Thailand's National Human Rights Commission, the court ruled that "a person shall have the right to clean air for good health and quality of life, the right to enjoy nature, and the right to be free from the effects of environmental damages such as flood, traffic congestion, [and] air pollution."[76] Thailand's 1997 constitution was abrogated by the 2006 coup d'etat and replaced by a new constitution in 2007. In the first environmental cases under the new constitution, the Supreme Administrative Court halted dozens of major projects at a petrochemicals hub due to violations of constitutional provisions related to health and environmental protection.[77]

INDIA

Among the nations whose constitutions do not recognize explicitly the right to a healthy environment, no judiciary has gone further than the Supreme Court of India. Article 48A of the Indian constitution mandates that the state "shall endeavour to protect and improve the environment and to safeguard the forests and wildlife of the country." This provision is framed (by Article 37) as a "Directive Principle of State Policy," which "shall not be enforceable by any court." While the directive principles are explicitly unenforceable, Article 32 guarantees all citizens the right to petition the Supreme Court when their fundamental rights are violated or threatened. There is a long line of cases in which the Indian Supreme Court and High Courts have sought the "harmonious construction" of the directive principles (which include many social, economic, and cultural rights) and the fundamental rights (the traditional civil and political rights).[78]

India was traumatized in 1984 by the Bhopal disaster, in which toxic fumes from a Union Carbide factory killed thousands of Indians and harmed many more. In 1987, two court decisions suggested that there could be an implicit right to a healthy environment among the fundamental rights in the Indian constitution. In a case dealing with limestone quarries causing deforestation, soil erosion, and river siltation, the Supreme Court mentioned "the right of the people to live in a healthy environment with minimal disturbance of the ecological balance."[79] The High Court of Andhra Pradesh wrote that "slow poisoning caused by environmental pollution and spoliation should be treated as amounting to a violation of Article 21 of the Constitution [right to life]."[80] In a 1988 case, the High Court of Rajasthan indicated that the state's constitutional duty to protect the environment gave rise to a corresponding right to a healthy environment.[81] In 1991, the Supreme Court clarified the state of the law, ruling:

> The right to live is a fundamental right under Article 21 of the Constitution and it includes the right to enjoyment of pollution-free water and air for full enjoyment of life. If anything endangers or impairs that quality of life in derogation of laws, a citizen has the right to have recourse to Article 32 of the Constitution for removing the pollution of water or air which may be detrimental to the quality of life.[82]

In 1995, the Supreme Court expanded upon its earlier articulation of the right, stating that the right to life

> encompasses within its ambit the protection and preservation of the environment, ecological balance, freedom from pollution of air and

water, and sanitation, without which life cannot be enjoyed. Any contract or action which would cause environmental pollution ... should be regarded as amounting to violation of Article 21 ... Therefore, there is a constitutional imperative on the state government and the municipalities, not only to ensure and safeguard proper environment but also an imperative duty to take adequate measures to promote, protect, and improve both the manmade and the natural environment.[83]

Since that time there have been hundreds of cases decided by the Supreme Court and High Courts on the basis of, or influenced by, the right to a healthy environment.[84] The following are some of the environmental issues addressed by these cases:

- air pollution in Delhi caused by motor vehicles[85]
- water pollution of the Ganges River by tanneries[86]
- protection of the Taj Mahal (292 industrial plants ordered to either switch from coke/coal to natural gas or relocate)[87]
- industrial air pollution[88]
- groundwater management[89]
- the right to water[90]
- location of a plant for liquefied petroleum gas[91]
- mining and quarrying activities[92]
- forest conservation[93]
- disasters caused by hazardous activities[94]
- large dam projects[95]
- sentencing for environmental crimes[96]
- genetically modified organisms[97]
- smoking in public places[98]
- protection of wildlife[99]
- noise pollution.[100]

Jariwala examined decisions of the Supreme Court up to 1999 and found that nearly 80 percent of cases were resolved in favour of the environment.[101] Cullet, however, observed that the court is less likely to rule against the government in cases involving major development projects, such as the controversial Sardar Sarovar dam.[102] A series of recent cases prompted concerns that the court's commitment to the environment may be weakening.[103]

India's environmental enforcement agencies have a poor track record, except where compelled to act by the judiciary.[104] In response, the Supreme Court has emphasized the importance of strict enforcement of India's *Environmental Protection Act*, writing:

> It is the duty of the State to make sure the fulfilment of conditions or direction under the Act. Without strict compliance, right to environment under Article 21 could not be guaranteed and the purpose of the Act will also be defeated.[105]

Many of the environmental rights cases brought to the Indian courts fall under the rubric of public interest or social action litigation: cases brought by concerned citizens or NGOs to advance collective interests. Public interest litigation in India incorporates five key innovations, including broad standing (similar to *actio popularis*); an independent investigative role for the court that may be achieved by appointing experts or committees; enhanced collaboration between parties in finding solutions; creative remedies; and post-litigation monitoring by the court.[106]

In addition to recognizing the right to a healthy environment, the Supreme Court has relied upon constitutional protection for the environment to justify the application of principles derived from international environmental law, including intergenerational equity,[107] the public trust doctrine,[108] absolute liability for harm caused by hazardous industries,[109] the polluter pays principle,[110] reversal of the burden of proof onto the party that is allegedly causing environmental harm,[111] and the precautionary principle.[112]

One of the more innovative approaches taken by the Supreme Court is known as continuing mandamus, a remedy that is intended to overcome problems with the non-implementation of court orders. Rather than issuing a judgment and closing a case as is customary, a court using continuing mandamus will issue directives to be implemented by specific deadlines and will require the government to report back to the court on its progress. Complex cases involving motor vehicle pollution in Delhi, pollution of the Ganges River, and forest conservation have been before the court for more than a decade, with petitioners returning repeatedly to seek additional orders.[113]

The lawsuit seeking the cleanup of motor vehicle pollution in Delhi, which also addressed industrial pollution, was originally filed in 1985.[114] The Supreme Court's first order in the case required the municipal government to provide information on its pollution initiatives and prosecutions against dirty vehicles. Then the court established an expert committee to identify technological options for improving air quality.[115] In the 1990s, the court ordered the phase-out of leaded gasoline in Delhi and other major cities; mandatory installation of catalytic converters on new vehicles; and conversion of all public transportation (buses, taxis, and autorickshaws or three-wheeled taxis) to compressed natural gas (CNG).[116] In 1998, the court ordered the city to begin removing all public and private vehicles older than ten years and begin regular emissions testing of vehicles.[117] Court orders in the 1990s also led to the closure or relocation of thousands of polluting facilities.[118] Additional court decisions were issued in 2002 and 2003 (the latter ordering the national government and nine cities to develop air quality action plans).[119] The transition to CNG was supposed to be completed by 2001. As a result of delays, the Supreme Court issued an order in 2002 mandating the immediate introduction of fifteen hundred CNG buses, the monthly replacement of eight hundred diesel buses, and fines for further delays. By the end of 2002, all public transport in Delhi was converted to CNG.[120] According to the Energy and Resources Institute, "The role of the judiciary in prodding the government to act against rising air pollution has been significant."[121] Studies about the effects on air quality offer mixed results.[122] However, a World Bank study estimated that 3,629 lives are being saved annually due to improvements in Delhi's air quality.[123]

In the Ganges River pollution case, the Supreme Court published notices in newspapers inviting industries and municipalities to enter an appearance in the litigation.[124] The court then prohibited the discharge of untreated effluent and ordered the closure of hundreds of polluting facilities (many through *ex parte* orders, meaning the facilities did not participate in the legal proceedings).[125]

In the forest conservation case, the original writ petition focused on illegal logging in one forest region, but the Supreme Court expanded the case to cover the entire country's forests and forest policies.[126] On the basis of a single lawsuit, the court addressed deforestation, illegal logging, timber pricing, licensing, transport of timber, mining, and planning.[127] The court also created its own committee to investigate and report on illegal mining in state forests.[128] More than two thousand interlocutory applications related to forestry have been adjudicated pursuant to this single writ petition.[129]

The Supreme Court has opened the door wide to judicial remedies by treating the right to a healthy environment as a fundamental right capable of being protected by citizens and NGOs by means of writ petitions. The procedures are relatively informal, but the caseload of the court creates lengthy delays in the resolution of disputes. Jariwala determined that 12 percent of environmental cases had taken at least a decade to reach a resolution.[130] The constitutional right to a healthy environment has also contributed to improvements in the recognition of procedural rights, including access to information and participation in decision making. Additional procedural innovations pioneered by the court include making spot visits to do on-the-ground assessments of environmental problems; appointing *amicus curiae* (friends of the court) to speak on behalf of the environment; and using cash rewards to encourage petitioners and lawyers to draw the court's attention to environmental problems.[131] An innovative (and somewhat controversial) remedy pioneered by the court requires the government to implement environmental education programs in schools and through the media.[132] In a tannery pollution case, the court directed the national government to require all educational institutions in India to provide at least an hour of weekly instruction on protecting the natural environment, with a specific direction that the government should have textbooks written for this particular purpose and distributed to educational institutions for free.[133] A later case included directions to have cinemas and media outlets provide environmental education.[134]

The Supreme Court has attempted to balance competing interests, including environment and development,[135] and nature conservation and the rights of tribal people.[136] For example, the court denied approval for a bauxite mine on the grounds that the proposed mine did not meet the constitutional requirement of sustainable development due to major environmental impacts, impacts on tribal people, and lack of local economic benefits. The court outlined a list of potential improvements to the proposal and invited the company to reapply.[137] India's Minister of Environment accurately observed that "it is not an 'environment versus development' question, but simply one of whether laws enacted by Parliament will be respected or not."[138] In another case, petitioners challenged, on the basis of violation of the constitutional right to a healthy environment, the issuance of a large number of fishing permits to members of tribes that previously lived in what is now Pench National Park Tiger Reserve.[139] The court balanced the right to a healthy environment with the right to livelihood of tribal villagers by upholding the fishing permits but attaching conservation requirements.

On the basis of its considerable environmental jurisprudence, India's Supreme Court has been both complimented and condemned. Supporters argue that the court has filled a vacuum left by the environmental negligence of the legislative and executive branches of government; provided remedies to marginalized communities that were disproportionately harmed by environmental degradation; and levelled the playing field between development and environmental protection.[140] Traditional barriers to environmental litigation – restrictions on standing, complex legal procedures, high costs, and challenges associated with the burden of proof – have been removed. Judicial activism is described as "the impetus for new legislation encouraging more effective and quicker executive resolution of environmental issues."[141] For example, three years after a Supreme Court decision that banned smoking in public places, India passed the *Anti-Smoking Act* (2004).[142] A World Bank report concluded that a vocal civil society and the judiciary "have successfully directed the executive branch to act far more aggressively in tackling air pollution than would have been otherwise possible."[143] The Law Commission of India concluded that "the Supreme Court of India has made [an] immense contribution to [the] environmental jurisprudence of our country."[144] Narain and Bell write that the Supreme Court played a constructive and defensible judicial role by pushing the government in two main ways: to implement existing policies, and to develop new policies to address air pollution. In their view, the court prodded the government to overcome bureaucratic logjams and partisan politics and "provided a form of protective cover that allowed the government to avoid taking direct responsibility for implementing controversial policies."[145] According to Sharma, the "extension of constitutional umbrella over environmental issues through dynamic judicial activism has augured well for environmental governance in India."[146]

Critics of the Supreme Court raise a number of points. A major complaint is that the court has trespassed on the jurisdiction of the legislative and executive branches of government, thus upsetting the separation of powers and undermining democracy. Dam and Tewary suggest that "the Court's over-enthusiasm in environmental matters has severely dented India's institutional balance and has contributed to a polity that is becoming consistently reliant on the judiciary for remedying all its problems, of both life and law."[147] Cassels identifies a series of weaknesses in litigation about constitutional rights in India, including non-adversarial proceedings and the spectre of judge shopping.[148] Iyer acknowledges that there have been some significant improvements in environmental quality, protection of human rights, and respect for the rule of law but expresses concerns about violations of the principles of natural justice (e.g., court-appointed experts provide evidence but are not subject to cross-examination, firms are ordered to cease operations without an opportunity to make arguments in court), disregard for the costs of judgments, and articulation of detailed requirements without necessarily having proper technical qualifications.[149]

On the other hand, the Supreme Court has also been criticized for failing to do enough to protect the environment, favouring the trivial environmental concerns of the wealthy rather than the pressing problems of the poor, and failing to punish polluters such as Union Carbide, the company responsible for the Bhopal disaster.[150] Galanter and Krishnan claim that the middle class has effectively used public interest litigation to improve the environment in the cities, in many cases leaving the poor worse off.[151]

The long-term cases involving motor vehicle pollution, the Ganges River, and forest conservation most inflame the critics. The Supreme Court's detailed involvement in forest policy decisions in the forest conservation case has prompted charges of inappropriate micromanagement.[152] The court's "vast assumption of powers" in the forest conservation case is blamed for paralyzing India's timber industry.[153] Sahu suggests that the constitutional rights of tribal people have been overlooked in the forest conservation case and that public support for the court is declining.[154] The court's actions in the Delhi motor vehicle case are accused of threatening the institutional and constitutional structure of the nation by undermining the authority of the Pollution Control Boards and the legislature.[155]

The Indian courts are plagued by major backlogs and long delays. Back in 1987, the Supreme Court warned that it could take up to fifteen years to address the backlog of public interest petitions.[156] In 2007, there were 28 million pending court cases in India (forty thousand in the Supreme Court, 3 million in the High Courts, and 25 million in the lower courts).[157] One-sixth of all High Court cases have been pending for more than ten years.[158] A new national environmental tribunal created in 2010 is intended to accelerate the judicial process in green cases.[159]

It is difficult to reach a conclusion regarding the role of Indian courts in protecting the right to a healthy environment. Expert opinion is widely divergent. Epp concludes that "the Indian Supreme Court clearly tried to spark a rights revolution – but nothing happened."[160] Anderson writes that the Indian Supreme Court is responsible for "nothing short of a revolution in constitutional jurisprudence."[161] The situation in India is a paradox, with the Supreme Court issuing many bold court orders based on the constitutional right to a healthy environment while overall environmental quality remains poor. Ultimately, this paradox "points to the importance of making rights effective with well-designed enforcement strategies, as well as the limits of a rights-based approach to environmental protection without an underlying transformation in social and economic conditions."[162]

PAKISTAN

Pakistan's constitution is silent on environmental protection but, as in India, the Supreme Court has been active. The leading case in Pakistan on the constitutional right to live in a healthy environment involved the potential hazard of electromagnetic radiation from an electrical grid station and associated high-voltage power lines. Local residents in a suburb of Islamabad, led by the widow of Pakistan's former ruler, filed a petition with the Supreme Court alleging violation of their constitutional right to life. The court held that the constitutional rights to life and dignity included a "clean atmosphere and unpolluted environment,"[163] and it stayed construction of the project pending the report of a court-appointed expert commission and a court-ordered public consultation process. Another case focused on the right to clean water, threatened by effluent from coal-mining operations. The Supreme Court held that "the right to have water free from pollution and contamination is a right to life itself ... the right to have unpolluted water is the right of every person wherever he lives."[164] In a procedural innovation, the court appointed an expert commission to inspect the Khewra region's water supply to ensure that water was not being polluted by mining effluents and to recommend methods of preventing further damage.[165] These Supreme Court decisions invoked international environmental law and case law from the Supreme Court of India.[166] Other cases involved illegal urban development, dumping of waste in coastal areas, sewage treatment in Karachi, and plastic bags (on the grounds that they were not biodegradable and that burning them contributes to harmful air pollution).[167]

Lower courts also have applied the constitutional right to a healthy environment.[168] For example, in a lawsuit about health problems caused by municipal waste, the Lahore High Court stated:

Lives of tens of thousands of citizens of this country ... are sinking in the ocean of dirt, solid waste, garbage and pollution and that too, at the hands of City District Government. It is high time that the public functionaries should realize their duties and perform their functions, keeping in view the import of word "life" as defined by the apex Court of this country in the *Shehla Zia* case.[169]

An expert commission – including government officials, scientists, and members of civil society – was appointed by the court to formulate recommendations for solid waste management in Lahore.[170] Among the recommendations implemented was a composting facility that now handles roughly 20 percent of the city's solid waste, producing 250 tonnes of organic fertilizer daily. In a case involving vehicle emissions, the Lahore High Court established a Clean Air Commission that recommended phasing out two-stroke rickshaws, introducing CNG buses, and establishing standards for vehicle emissions and air quality.[171]

The courts in Pakistan have been praised for their progressive articulation of the right to a healthy environment.[172] According to Hassan, the Pakistani judiciary is "boldly and proactively applying international and national laws to meet local needs and in granting the widest latitude in procedural matters that may affect the vindication of environmental rights."[173] The use of expert commissions has the potential to resolve complex environmental issues in a collaborative and open manner. The judiciary in Pakistan is cognizant of its own limited powers. In a case that challenged the lack of air and noise pollution standards for motor vehicles and industry, the court declined to formulate such rules but ordered the responsible government authorities to take action.[174]

There is relatively little public interest environmental litigation in Pakistan, despite the magnitude and urgency of the environmental problems facing large swaths of the population. As Hassan and Hassan observe, Pakistan's Supreme Court has "accorded environmental rights constitutional legitimacy and status," yet the "activism of the courts is not a substitute for proper policy-making and implementation."[175] One of the major challenges to fulfillment of the right to a healthy environment is the lack of respect for the rule of law. The judiciary is not independent and has approved military coups that violated Pakistan's constitution. As Lau remarks, "A climate of military dictatorship is not conducive to the enforcement of fundamental rights."[176] The chief justice of the Supreme Court, who had issued a number of decisions that could be described as environmentally friendly (and contrary to government and business interests), was deposed by General Musharraf and then, following extensive public protests, reinstated.[177]

BANGLADESH
Bangladesh's constitution contained no environmental provisions until 2011 when the government's duty to protect was added, but courts previously

recognized an implicit right to a healthy environment. The leading case involved a petition against various authorities for not fulfilling their statutory duties to mitigate air and noise pollution caused by motor vehicles in Dhaka, the capital. The court stated, in a ruling similar to many decisions of India's Supreme Court: "Articles 31 and 32 of our constitution protect right to life as a fundamental right. It encompasses within its ambit, the protection and preservation of environment, ecological balance free from pollution of air and water, and sanitation without which life can hardly be enjoyed. Any act or omission contrary thereto will be violative of the said right to life."[178] The court ordered the elimination of taxis using highly polluting two-stroke diesel engines and the conversion of government vehicles to CNG; it also required that all imported vehicles be equipped with catalytic converters. The Bangladesh Environmental Lawyers Association has brought additional cases based on the constitutional right to a healthy environment – including attempts to address industrial air pollution, illegal shrimp cultivation, lack of compliance with environmental permit requirements, dumping waste in a flood zone, decommissioning of contaminated ships, and commercial development in municipal green space – with mixed results.[179]

Sri Lanka

Sri Lanka's constitution imposes a duty on the government and the people to protect the environment. In several cases the Supreme Court has implicitly recognized the right to a healthy environment as an essential part of other constitutional rights, including the right to life.[180] For example, in 1998 a lawyer filed a lawsuit claiming that his constitutional right to life, including a healthy environment, was violated by the government's failure to enact standards to protect air quality from vehicle emissions.[181] The Minister of Forestry and Environment provided the court with an undertaking to enact regulations to control vehicle emissions, making it unnecessary to decide the legal issues related to the rights to life and a healthy environment. The promised regulations were enacted.[182] In another case, the Supreme Court determined that a proposal to develop a phosphate mine without conducting an environmental impact assessment violated the fundamental constitutional rights of a group of concerned local citizens. The court referred to the collective fundamental rights of the petitioners and enjoined the government from entering into a contract to develop the phosphate mine until a comprehensive environmental assessment had been completed and all relevant environmental permits approved. In the words of the court:

Decisions with regard to the nature and scale of activity require the most anxious consideration from the point of view of safeguarding the health and safety of the people, naturally, including the petitioners, ensuring the viability of their occupations, and protecting the rights of future generations of Sri Lankans.[183]

Atapattu suggested that while these are encouraging decisions, they are limited to a few judges rather than the Supreme Court as a whole.[184]

Israel

Israel does not have a conventional constitution but rather a series of Basic Laws with constitutional status. An Israeli ENGO brought a constitutional (or Basic Law) challenge to the *Law on Planning and Construction*, which was amended in 2002 to accelerate approvals for major national infrastructure projects.[185] The Supreme Court wrote that there is an implicit constitutional right to a minimum environmental quality (which it did not define), based on the constitutional right to "honor of his being and his freedom."[186] However, in the absence of legislative action, the right does not extend to a level of "appropriate environmental quality" (also undefined). According to Levinson and Page, the decision "implicitly clarifies that property rights – also enshrined in quasi-constitutional fashion – will invariably trump a claim to an 'appropriate' level of environmental protection as a constitutional matter where a conflict between property rights and 'appropriate' environmental quality exists."[187]

Malaysia

A government committee recommended adding the right to a healthy environment to Malaysia's constitution in 1993, but the recommendation has not been implemented.[188] The Malaysian Court of Appeal has a mixed record in referring to the right to a healthy environment as part of the constitutional right to life. In several cases, the court followed the lead of the Supreme Court of India by interpreting the right to life broadly as including "the right to live in a reasonably healthy and pollution free environment."[189] However, in the Bakun Dam case, involving a proposed hydroelectric project with major environmental consequences and impacts on indigenous people, the Malaysian Court of Appeal reverted to a narrower interpretation of the constitutional right to life.[190] Sharom described the Bakun Dam case as the "final nail" for public interest litigation in Malaysia and concluded that "as long as economic growth is the driving force of Malaysian policy, environmental matters will always be the neglected stepchildren in official action and decision-making."[191] Many human rights are suppressed in Malaysia, and environmental activism is discouraged by the government.[192] On balance, it cannot be concluded that Malaysia recognizes the constitutional right to a healthy environment.

Factors Affecting the Influence of the Constitutional Right to a Healthy Environment in Asia

As noted earlier, there is a wide variety of legal cultures in Asia, as well as major differences in history, political institutions, and economic development, all of which militate against making broad generalizations. The so-called Asian tigers or dragons – South Korea, Thailand, and Malaysia – experienced rapid industrialization in recent decades, with the attendant environmental consequences. Azerbaijan, Kyrgyzstan, and Turkmenistan are experiencing the turbulent changes associated with the transition from communism to capitalism, and from authoritarian government to democracy. East Timor is newly independent, while the Maldives is newly democratic. Turkey is in the process of joining the European Union. Iran and Iraq face daunting political and social challenges.

Despite these differences, there are some features common to many Asian nations. Prevalent environmental problems include rapid urbanization, acute industrial pollution, and overexploitation of natural resources.[193] The prioritization of economic growth is widely viewed as a systemic problem that undermines the implementation and enforcement of environmental laws.[194] The regional economic crises that struck during the 1990s caused cuts to environmental budgets and increased reluctance to enact and enforce strong environmental laws and policies. A summary of the factors influencing the extent of the environmental rights revolution in Asia is provided in Table 8.1.

In some Asian nations, the rule of law is fragile or in early stages of development. Richardson offers a useful conception of the minimum elements necessary for achieving the rule of law in Asia: laws that are clear, consistent, reasonably stable, generally applicable, enforced, and accepted by most people; and the existence of independent courts to interpret and enforce the law.[195] Political turmoil is prominent in Iran, Iraq, Nepal, and Pakistan. Rapid constitutional turnover undermines legal stability. In Thailand, for example, there have been more than nineteen constitutions since 1932.[196] Governments in some nations continue to be plagued by corruption, collusion, and

TABLE 8.1

Factors influencing the extent of the environmental rights revolution in Asia

Factor	Generally positive	Generally negative	Mixed	Examples of positive influence	Examples of negative influence
Constitutional provisions	×			Philippines, Turkey	Thailand
Prospective litigants			×	India, Philippines, South Korea	Azerbaijan, Kyrgyzstan, Mongolia
Access to justice			×	India, Philippines	Iran, Iraq, Turkmenistan
Resources for legal mobilization		×		India	East Timor, Iran, Iraq
Rule of law		×			East Timor, Iran, Iraq
Responsive judiciary			×	India, Nepal, Philippines	Indonesia, South Korea
Social, economic, and political conditions		×			East Timor, Iran Iraq, Nepal, Pakistan

nepotism.[197] Noted environmental lawyer M.C. Mehta has identified rampant corruption as the single most important factor inhibiting the enforcement of environmental law in India.[198]

Some scholars argue that "environmental issues are primarily a 'Western' ethic being unduly imposed on developing countries."[199] A compelling rebuttal is that environmental values are actually an integral part of many Asian cultures, from Islam to Buddhism. Tookey's observation that, "like much of Thailand's flora and fauna, traditional Thai values are heading for extinction" is applicable to many Asian nations.[200]

Despite constitutional recognition of the right to a healthy environment, environmental laws in some nations are weak, plagued by poor drafting, vague language, undefined terms, gaps, and inconsistencies.[201] In Indonesia, laws are strong on paper, but "when one grasps at the practical operation of the rules, their substance has a tendency to disappear between the fingers."[202] Inadequate implementation and enforcement are the Achilles heel of environmental law in much of Asia.[203] Another major problem in the region is the failure to coordinate laws, policies, and enforcement between national and subnational levels of government.[204] The following are some of the other problems that undermine environmental protection:

- diffuse and sectoral, rather than coordinated and comprehensive, legislation
- lack of systematic planning or policy coordination
- lack of detailed regulations
- gaps in terms of more recent challenges such as greenhouse gas emissions
- lenient standards
- inadequate use of economic instruments
- lack of political will
- lack of capacity for implementation and enforcement
- lack of training for judges, prosecutors, and enforcement officials.[205]

Robinson suggests that increased reliance on the constitutional right to live in a healthy environment reflects recognition of the inadequacy of traditional legal approaches to environmental protection.[206] International organizations – UNEP, UNDP, and the IUCN – are working to strengthen laws, policies, and institutions.[207]

Asian judicial systems also pose problems in terms of enforcing the constitutional right to a healthy environment. While some judiciaries are relatively powerful (e.g., India, Philippines), others are weak (e.g., Nepal). In some nations, such as Indonesia, courts continue to be perceived as a relic of colonialism.[208] Judges are criticized for their deferential attitude toward legislative and executive branches of government (e.g., South Korea) and their lack of environmental awareness and knowledge. In general, there is a pressing need for additional capacity, training, and institutional development.[209] There are signs of improvement, including extensive environmental education programs for judges in countries ranging from Indonesia to the Philippines. The Indian Supreme Court, with its progressive jurisprudence interpreting the right to life as incorporating the right to a healthy environment, has influenced courts throughout Asia (and beyond). International environmental law related to the right to a healthy environment is a major influence in some nations, including India, Pakistan, and the Philippines.[210]

The extent of the litigation support structure varies dramatically from nation to nation. There is increasing ENGO activity throughout the region, consistent with the overall rise in the importance of civil society.[211] The

Philippines and India have particularly vibrant ENGO cultures. There are legal NGOs in some nations, such as the Bangladesh Environmental Lawyers Association and the Center for Indonesian Environmental Law. In contrast to the situation in Latin America, many environmental lawyers work independently rather than in organizations.[212] Environmental laws in some nations – e.g., Indonesia, Thailand, and the Philippines – recognize the important role that ENGOs can play in environmental governance. On the other hand, Turkmenistan passed a *Law on Public Associations* in 2003 that imposes harsh restrictions on NGOs and led to the dissolution of many ENGOs by the Ministry of Justice.[213] A complaint against the law was lodged with the Compliance Committee of the Aarhus Convention, which determined that Turkmenistan was violating the Convention.[214] A similar situation in Azerbaijan led to a ruling from the European Court of Human Rights, which held that the government violated citizens' right to freedom of association by forcing an ENGO to dissolve.[215] In most Asian nations, even those with adequate legal provisions, there are still practical barriers to access to information, participation in decision making, and access to justice.[216] These barriers include lack of awareness and knowledge, high costs, and limited institutional capacity. The Philippines and India are regional leaders in creating simplified legal procedures that dramatically increase access to justice in environmental cases.

Conclusion

A decade ago, Boer concluded that "the great revolution of environmental law has only just begun, particularly in the countries of the Asia region."[217] Today, the extent of the revolution varies, but it is still primarily in its early stages. Overall, the legal influence of the constitutional right to a healthy environment in Asia ranges from extensive in nations such as the Philippines and India to negligible in nations such as Azerbaijan and East Timor. As more constitutions, laws, and courts recognize this fundamental right, its influence – both legal and extra-legal – is likely to continue to grow.

TABLE 8.A

Constitutional influence on environmental legislation and litigation in Asia

Nation	Year*	Legislation	Litigation
Azerbaijan	1995	Yes[1]	N/A[2]
East Timor	2002	Yes[3]	N/A[4]
Indonesia	2000	Yes[5]	Yes[6]
Iran	1979	N/A[7]	N/A[8]
Iraq	2005	Yes[9]	N/A[10]
Kyrgyzstan	1993	Yes[11]	N/A[12]
Maldives	2008	No[13]	N/A[14]
Mongolia	1992	Yes[15]	N/A[16]
Nepal	2006	Yes[17]	Yes[18]
Philippines	1987	Yes[19]	Yes[20]
South Korea	1987	Yes[21]	Yes[22]
Thailand	2007	Yes[23]	Yes[24]
Turkey	1982	Yes[25]	Yes[26]
Turkmenistan	2008	Yes[27]	N/A[28]

*   Year when right to healthy environment was constitutionalized.

1   *Law on Environmental Protection* (1999), Article 2, 6, 7. See also *Law on Protection of Air* (2001); *Law on Access to Environmental Information* (2002).

2   Supreme Court and Constitutional Court, http://www.supremecourt.gov.az/ and http://www.constcourt.gov.az/. Judicial decisions are not searchable.

3   Indonesian laws remain in force in East Timor unless inconsistent with the constitution or specifically repealed. Therefore, see Indonesia's *Environmental Management Act* (1997) (No. 23 of 1997), Articles 5, 6, 37-39.

4   Supreme Court of Justice, http://www.timor-leste.gov.tl/. No jurisprudence for East Timor is available.

5   *Environmental Management Act* (1997), Articles 5, 6, 37-39.

6   Constitutional Court, http://www.mahkamahkonstitusi.go.id/. No hits for "environment."

7   *Environmental Protection Law* (1974). Available only in Farsi.

8   No jurisprudence available online for the Supreme Court of Iran.

9   *Law No. 3 of 1997 on protection and improving the environment,* Preamble.

10   Supreme Federal Court, http://www.iraqijudicature.com/. Not available in English.

11   *Law No. 53 on environmental protection* (1999), Articles 3, 45, 46, 47.

12   No jurisprudence available online for the Supreme Court of Kyrgyzstan.

13   *Environmental Protection and Preservation Act of Maldives* (1993). Predates constitutional recognition of the right to a healthy environment.

14   Maldives Supreme Court. No website available (court established in 2008).

15   *Environmental Protection Law of Mongolia,* (1995), Articles 1, 2, 4, 5, 20.

16   Constitutional Court of Mongolia, http://www.court-decision.gov.mn/. Search function not available in English. No cases on the Ecolex (http://www.ecolex.org) or Asian Legal Information Institute (http://www.asianlii.org) websites.

17   *Environment Protection Act 1997.*

18   Supreme Court, http://www.supremecourt.gov.np. Jurisprudence not searchable, but some cases are available on the Ecolex website (http://www.ecolex.org).

19 *Clean Air Act of 1999,* Articles 2, 4.

20 Supreme Court, http://sc.judiciary.gov.ph/. Thirty-eight hits for "right" and "balanced and healthful ecology."

21 *Framework Act on Environmental Policy* (1990, as amended), Articles 1, 2, 6, http://faolex. fao.org/.

22 Constitutional Court, http://english.ccourt.go.kr/; Supreme Court, http://eng.scourt. go.kr/eng/main/Main.work.

23 *National Health Act* (2007).

24 Supreme Administrative Court, http://www.admincourt.go.th/amc_eng/login_eng.aspx. No judgments available. Constitutional Court, http://www.constitutionalcourt.or.th. No hits for "environment" (although judgments in English are limited to those from 1998 to 2003). However, news reports in December 2009 indicated that Thailand's Supreme Administrative Court halted dozens of major projects at a petrochemicals hub due to violations of the Thai constitution arising from health and environmental concerns. Boonlai and Changplayngam (2009); Ahuja (2009).

25 *Law No. 5491 amending the Environmental Law No. 2872* (2006), Article 3.

26 Constitutional Court and Supreme Court, http://www.anayasa.gov.tr/ and http://www. yargitay.gov.tr/. Jurisprudence is not available in English as of 15 July 2009. However, several cases are available through Ecolex (http://www.ecolex.org).

27 *Law No. 600-XII on Environmental Protection* (1991), Articles 27-31.

28 The Supreme Court of Turkmenistan does not have an English website. No cases reported at the Ecolex site, http://www.ecolex.org.

9
Eastern Europe

Many of the nations in Eastern Europe recently underwent a transition from communism and authoritarian rule to capitalism and democracy.[1] Almost all of their constitutions have been written or substantially amended since 1989, with nineteen constitutions in the region now recognizing the right to live in a healthy environment. Many of these nations bear the scars of the communist era, when the Iron Curtain hid some of the most dramatic environmental abuses in the world.[2] The Chernobyl disaster had lasting regional repercussions in terms of environmental awareness, mistrust of the state, and the importance of access to information.[3] Carrying out environmental restoration in Eastern Europe will cost hundreds of billions of dollars and take decades to complete.[4]

Legislation

Environmental provisions, including the right to a healthy environment, in the new generation of Eastern European constitutions appear to have influenced the development of legislation in all nineteen nations (see Figure 9.1, and see Table 9.A at the end of this chapter). For example, according to the OECD, Slovakia's environmental legislation was strengthened subsequent to constitutional recognition of the right to a healthy environment in 1992.[5] New and improved Slovakian laws govern air quality, waste management, nature and landscape protection, environmental impact assessment, and access to environmental information. Similarly, Bulgaria passed new laws, including the *Environmental Protection Act* (1991), *Clean Air Act* (1996), *Law on Forests* (1997), *Law on Protected Areas* (1998), *Waters Act* (1999), and the *Public Access to Information Act* (1999), following constitutional recognition of the right to a healthy environment.[6] Russia's 1993 constitution acted as an important driver in the overhaul of environmental laws and policies during the 1990s.[7] Key legislative developments included the *Law Concerning*

Ecological Expertise (1995), *Law Concerning Specially Protected Natural Areas* (1995), *Law Concerning Wildlife* (1995), *Water Code* (1995), *Forestry Code* (1997), *Law Concerning Wastes of Production and Consumption* (1998), *Law Concerning Protection of the Atmosphere* (1999), *Law Concerning the Sanitary-Epidemiological Well-being of the Population* (1999), and the major revision of the *Law Concerning the Protection of the Environment* (2002).

In Georgia, the 1995 constitution is recognized as the basis for a new generation of environmental laws.[8] Georgia's *Framework Law on Environmental Protection*, adopted in 1996, lists citizens' environmental rights, including the right to live in a healthy environment; use natural resources; obtain full, true, and timely information on the state of the environment; join public environmental protection organizations; take part in decision making; receive compensation for environmental damage; and challenge decisions on new projects, or the construction, reconstruction, and use of facilities that create a risk to the environment. The UN Economic Commission for Europe describes the constitutions of Serbia and Montenegro, with their recognition of the right to a healthy environment, as the foundations of environmental legislation and institutions.[9] Following the incorporation of environmental considerations in the constitution in 1994, most of Moldova's environmental laws were written between 1995 and 1999.[10]

Constitutional provisions have clearly had a significant influence in strengthening environmental legislation in Eastern Europe, although there are other factors at play, such as the influence of the European Union (EU). The Czech Republic, Hungary, Latvia, Poland, Slovakia, and Slovenia joined the EU in 2004. Bulgaria and Romania became members in 2007. Each of these nations was required to upgrade environmental laws to EU standards as a prerequisite to membership. The Council of Europe drafted model environmental framework legislation in the early 1990s for Eastern European nations. It included the following provision:

> Everyone has the right to an ecologically stable and healthy environment. Such a right can be exercised not only in respect of any normative or administrative acts by the public authorities but also in respect of the actions of private persons which are likely to have a significant effect on the environment.[11]

The case of Hungary illustrates the extent of the EU's influence on environmental legislation, as it was required to adopt or amend roughly three hundred

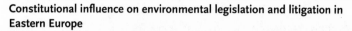

FIGURE 9.1

Constitutional influence on environmental legislation and litigation in Eastern Europe

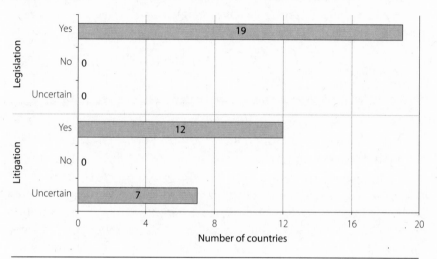

environmental laws, regulations, and standards.[12] The *Aarhus Convention* also has played an important role in advancing both procedural and substantive rights to a healthy environment in Eastern Europe.[13]

Litigation

The constitutional right to a healthy environment has been enforced by courts in at least twelve of nineteen Eastern European nations (see Table 9.A). As well, in at least one nation (Estonia), courts have recognized a constitutional right to a healthy environment in the absence of an explicit provision. This level of constitutional rights litigation is quite remarkable, for as Goldston observes, "PIL [public interest litigation] is a post-Communist phenomenon."[14] The full extent of litigation based on the constitutional right to a healthy environment in Eastern Europe is difficult to ascertain because of a lack of access to court decisions via the Internet.[15]

In some of the remaining seven Eastern European nations, citizens and ENGOS are using litigation as a tool, but less frequently, and it is unclear whether and to what extent they are invoking the right to a healthy environment. In other nations, litigation does not appear to be a viable strategy. In

Belarus, the UN Economic Commission for Europe observed, "cases of citizens challenging administrative decisions in courts or of public prosecutors pursuing environmental offenders are extremely rare. Similarly non-existent are cases of individual citizens or NGOs seeking a judicial review of the infringement of their environmental rights."[16]

HUNGARY

In Hungary, the constitution and legislation guarantee that ENGOs have standing to challenge environmental decisions in court.[17] There have been several precedent-setting decisions from Hungary's Constitutional Court regarding the interpretation and implementation of the constitutional right to a healthy environment. The first decision, in 1990, held that because of the right to a healthy environment, the state was required to establish and maintain the institutions and programs necessary to protect this right.[18] In the 1994 *Forests Case*, the Constitutional Court struck down provisions of a law that sought to privatize forested lands that had previously been declared protected, on the basis of citizens' rights to a healthy environment and the highest possible level of physical and spiritual health. The court interpreted the constitution as imposing upon the government a binding obligation to maintain a high level of environmental protection. This high level of environmental protection, according to the court, could only be diminished if necessary to fulfill other constitutional rights.[19] Legal experts believe that the decision of the Constitutional Court in the *Forests Case* "will certainly have a lasting significance on future Hungarian environmental legislation."[20] In recognition of the greater difficulties and higher costs associated with restoring damaged ecosystems, the Constitutional Court ruled in a 1997 nature conservation case that "the implementation of the right to environment requires not only keeping the present level of protection, but also that the state should not step backward towards liability based protection from the preventive measures."[21]

Hungarian courts review not only the procedural legality of an administrative decision, but also the scientific correctness of the decision and supporting technical documentation, particularly environmental impact statements.[22] In two recent cases – dealing with a luxury hotel to be built on a protected wetland and a proposed cement factory – courts have appointed independent experts to review the technical correctness of environmental impact statements prepared by project proponents.[23]

Despite these promising judicial developments, the leading Hungarian environmental law NGO warns that "there is no court in Hungary that would stop an investment worth several billions of forints [Hungarian currency] based on environmental arguments."[24] Economic concerns are paramount. In some cases, the Hungarian courts have used a narrow definition of what constitutes an environmental case in order to deny standing to NGOs.[25] However, an important milestone in the development of Hungarian jurisprudence was the *Uniformity Decision* of the Supreme Court in 2004, which provides that environmental NGOs may appeal decisions made (e.g., permits granted) by any government decision maker who has sought expert advice from the environmental authorities.[26]

LATVIA

The right to a healthy environment in the Latvian constitution is worded as follows:

> Art. 115. The State shall protect the right of everyone to live in a benevolent environment by providing information about environmental conditions and by promoting the preservation and improvement of the environment.

While the right to information is explicitly included, the Constitutional Court has also read in the rights to participate in environmental decision making and to bring legal challenges.[27] In the words of the court, these three "procedural elements form a part of the obligations of the State to ensure a benevolent environment for the next generations."[28] Latvia's Constitutional Court has been active in protecting the right to a healthy environment, which it applies directly and immediately, as it does all other fundamental rights.[29] In several cases, environmental laws – including the *Environmental Protection Law, Spatial Planning Law,* and *Protected Zones Law* – have been given forceful interpretations based on the constitutional right to a healthy environment.[30] The Constitutional Court has ruled that the right to a healthy environment imposes on public institutions, both national and local, "the duty to create and secure an effective system of environment protection."[31] Land use plans have been successfully challenged by concerned citizens and environmental groups for allowing building in floodplains, failing to conduct environmental assessments, and failing to protect ecologically valuable habitat.[32] All of these challenges have been based on violations of the constitutional right to a healthy environment.

RUSSIA

Russia's experience with the constitutional right to a healthy environment is mixed. In an important non-environmental case decided in 1995, the Supreme Court of the Russian Federation ruled that constitutional rights are directly enforceable, authorizing individuals to take complaints about breaches of basic rights to the ordinary courts.[33] Citizens and NGOs in Moscow filed a lawsuit in 1995 and applied repeatedly for injunctions to prevent the reduction in size of a municipal park and the felling of hundreds of old trees.[34] The lawsuit was based on, *inter alia*, the right to a healthy environment. While no injunction was ever granted, after a series of appeals the court ruled that the government had acted illegally and ordered construction halted and trees replanted.

Those precedents were followed by groundbreaking environmental rights cases involving the privatization of forests and offshore oil and gas drilling. The forest privatization cases involved a series of government decrees that downgraded strictly protected public forests to a status that permitted development. More than a hundred plaintiffs, including Russia's largest ENGOs, filed the case and were initially rebuffed. Following a series of appeals, the Supreme Court declared twelve government decrees, covering more than eighteen thousand hectares of forest, illegal.[35] This case is hailed as a major milestone in Russian constitutional and environmental jurisprudence.[36] The offshore oil and gas case involved a successful challenge to a government decree that would have permitted Exxon to discharge toxic drilling waste into the ocean, contrary to Russian environmental laws and conventional industry practice.[37]

Greenpeace, the Movement for Nuclear Safety, and citizens of the Chelyabinsk region filed a legal challenge against shipments of spent nuclear fuel from Hungary destined for disposal in Russia. The Supreme Court upheld the petition based on the claim the shipments would violate the right to a clean environment, as well as the rights to health and information.[38] Since then, Russian ENGOs have gone to court to challenge oil leasing, nuclear waste disposal, and a trans-Siberian pipeline.[39] For example, in 2007, a court ruled that a federal environmental impact review for a portion of the Siberia-Pacific Pipeline was inadequate and violated the constitutional right to a healthy environment.[40]

A number of citizens have challenged toxic pollution released from Russia's largest steel-manufacturing facility, the Severstal plant in Cherepovets, alleging violation of their right to live in a healthy environment.[41] The government had a longstanding but unfulfilled promise to relocate residents living near the steel plant to safer locations. Russian courts agreed that the government's failure to protect people from toxic pollution, by either reducing emissions or resettling nearby residents, violated their constitutional right to a favourable environment.[42] However, the Russian government's response was to place the residents on a waiting list for safe housing, leading residents to file appeals that were upheld by the European Court of Human Rights. The ECHR found that the levels of pollution violated Article 8 of the *European Convention on Human Rights*, which safeguards the right to respect for privacy, family life, and home.[43]

There has been political backlash against the successes of the Russian environmental movement. President Putin "has moved aggressively to curb environmental law and environmental civil society."[44] He abolished the Ministry of Environment (known as the State Committee on Ecology) and the Ministry of Forests (Federal Forest Service), transferring all responsibilities to the more commercially oriented Ministry of Natural Resources. These decisions were challenged in court, both in Russia and in the ECHR, without success.[45] Houck surveyed the anti-environmental actions taken by the Putin government and the courts' unwillingness to intervene, and concluded that "the Supreme Court temporarily found its voice in the forest cases but has since blown hot and cold on the idea of reviewing government decisions."[46]

SLOVAKIA

In 2009, the Supreme Court of Slovakia revoked the permits of a waste-processing landfill based on violations of constitutional environmental rights.[47] Other cases brought by Via Iuris (formerly the Center for Environmental Public Advocacy) – the leading Slovakian legal advocacy organization – have involved a planned dam, expansion of a polluting paper mill, operation of a landfill, and a gas station in a residential neighbourhood.[48]

Slovakia passed legislation in 2007 and 2008 that limited access to justice and participation in environmental decision making, meaning ENGOs were no longer allowed to challenge permit decisions in court.[49] Changes were made to the *Nature Protection Act, Environmental Impact Assessment Act,* and *Act on the Use of Genetically Modified Organisms.*[50] The European Commission commenced infringement proceedings against Slovakia because these laws were inconsistent with EU requirements for public participation.[51] In 2010, Slovakia responded by enacting legal changes that enhance access to justice in environmental assessment cases.[52]

SLOVENIA

Slovenia has been one of the most active Eastern European nations in terms of litigation invoking the constitutional right to a healthy environment, with at least twenty-four decisions reported on the Constitutional Court's website.[53] Because of the constitutional right to a healthy environment, "it has become ordinary for environmental matters to come to the Constitutional Court."[54] In a key 1995 case, the Slovenian Ecologists Society challenged the legality of a development plan for a small business/manufacturing zone in the hinterland of Lake Bled. The Constitutional Court annulled the development plan because it was inconsistent with municipal and state long-term plans. Based on the constitutional right to a healthy environment, the court articulated a broad conception of standing in which every person has a legal interest in protecting the environment, even if the harm is not imminent and the location of the harm is not close to where he or she lives.[55]

In a case challenging the legality of a tax on water pollution, the Constitutional Court held that the relevant provisions of the *Environmental Protection Act* were valid, based on the constitutional right to a healthy environment.[56] Other cases based on violations of the constitutional right to a healthy environment have involved electromagnetic radiation,[57] waste incineration,[58] noise,[59] and regulations governing wild species.[60]

In 2006, Slovenia passed a law that limits standing in administrative proceedings to NGOs that meet certain requirements.[61] As of 2008, no ENGOs had qualified.[62] However, ENGOs continue to have standing under other legislation and pursuant to the constitution, so it is unclear how these new standing rules will affect protection of the right to a healthy environment.

ROMANIA

Romania did not include the right to a healthy environment in its constitution until 2003, making it one of the most recent Eastern European nations to do so. The 2003 amendments were intended to ensure that Romania's constitution was compatible with accession to the European Union. A decision of Romania's Constitutional Court, based upon a review of the proposed constitutional amendments, directed the government to include the right to a healthy environment in the Fundamental Rights chapter of the revised constitution.[63] The original draft amendments included a government duty to protect the environment in the Fundamental Rights chapter of the constitution, but not an individual right, which the court found illogical.

Romania's 1991 constitution also included a government duty to protect the environment. In a 1997 case, the Supreme Court of Justice used this government duty as the basis for finding an implicit constitutional right to a healthy environment.[64] The court decided that construction of a hotel in a park that was established to protect ecological values violated the constitution. Based on the implicit constitutional right to a healthy environment, courts increased access to justice for ENGOs through generous standing rules. Four cases stemmed from a catastrophe in 2000 near the town of Baia Mare, when a mine's tailing dam broke, spilling water laced with cyanide and other toxic substances.[65] However, at least two cases decided by the ECHR indicate that Romanian courts are not adequately enforcing and protecting the constitutional right to a healthy environment. In the *Tatar* case, residents living near the Baia Mare mining operation, which was using sodium cyanide, were unable to secure a remedy. The ECHR noted the constitutional right to a healthy environment in Romania and concluded that the government had violated Article 8 of the *European Convention on Human Rights* by failing to take adequate measures to protect the rights of parties to respect for their privacy, their home, and, more generally, to the enjoyment of a healthy and protected environment.[66] In the *Branduse* case, the ECHR found that the Romanian government's failure to address the pollution from a landfill also violated Article 8 of the *European Convention*.[67]

CROATIA, MACEDONIA, AND BULGARIA
There appear to be relatively few cases in Croatia, Macedonia, and Bulgaria involving the right to a healthy environment. In Croatia, one unsuccessful lawsuit challenged the construction of a new electrical power station; another involved Green Action Zagreb's opposition to construction in a public park.[68] In both cases, the Constitutional Court ruled that the developments were proceeding in a manner consistent with the law and that adequate steps were being taken to mitigate environmental damage.

In a leading Macedonian case, the Constitutional Court ruled that proposed urban developments had the potential to harm the ecology of three lakes and were therefore contrary to the constitutional right to a healthy environment.[69] In the words of the court:

From the analysis of the constitutional and legal provisions mentioned, it derives that the basic function of the state is the establishment of a balance between man and nature, between economic and ecologic spheres. Hence, the development of the economy and industry may not take place in an uncontrolled manner and to the maximum without paying attention to the consequences to the environment and nature stemming from it. Namely, it concerns a fundamental value having a universal character and as such it should be safeguarded and protected in the environment we live in.[70]

Article 5 of the Bulgarian constitution states that constitutional rights are, in general, directly applicable and enforceable without implementing legislation. Lawsuits have challenged transportation laws favouring motor vehicles and amendments that weakened the environmental impact assessment law.[71] The Constitutional Court did not make a strong environmental ruling in either of these cases. Eventually, however, the law governing environmental impact assessment was strengthened to address the deficiencies introduced by the earlier amendments.[72] Overall, progress in implementing and enforcing the constitutional right to a healthy environment in Bulgaria is slow.[73]

Czech Republic

Despite the constitutional right to a healthy environment, Czech courts take a narrow view of standing, limiting it to those whose interests are directly affected, with few exceptions.[74] For example, Czech ENGOs seeking to limit logging in Sumava National Park were denied standing by both the High Court and the Constitutional Court.[75] When citizens allege that the government, by act or omission, has violated national environmental laws, they cannot enforce the law in court themselves but are limited to submitting informal applications to the Supreme State Prosecutor, the Czech Environmental Inspectorate, or the Ombudsman.[76] Even when ENGOs are granted standing, courts often limit their arguments to procedural issues and preclude consideration of substantive issues because, according to the Constitutional Court, ENGOs as non-biological or legal persons do not enjoy the substantive right to a healthy environment.[77] Lawsuits challenging the approval of nuclear plants, permission of mining in protected areas, and excessive noise have been rejected by the courts.[78]

Several decisions in the 1990s – in cases related to highway construction, limestone quarrying, and the failure to involve the public in environmental impact assessments – appeared to signal a more open and accessible approach from the courts.[79] However, recent decisions from both the Supreme Administrative and Constitutional Courts have reverted to narrow interpretations of both standing and the scope of judicial review.[80] In 2008, the Constitutional Court rejected a lawsuit alleging that the right to a healthy environment was violated by the proposed construction of a storage facility for spent nuclear waste.[81] A study prepared for the European Commission concluded that, in general, opportunities to protect the right to a healthy environment through the Czech courts are limited.[82] Nevertheless, Czech lawyers continue to file lawsuits asserting constitutional environmental rights.[83]

UKRAINE

The leading environmental law NGO in the Ukraine – Environment, People, Law (formerly Ecopravo) – has brought many court cases that invoke the constitutional rights to environmental information, participation in decision making, and a healthy environment.[84] These cases have involved air, water, and soil pollution from coal mining and processing, toxic hazards posed by a waste-processing plant, the import and incineration of hazardous wastes, construction of new highways, residential construction replacing a public garden, nuclear reactors, a cement plant, a steel factory, and a quarry. Other Ukrainian lawyers have also brought cases that cite the right to a healthy environment.[85]

Although the Ukraine's laws may appear strong on paper, the reality is that constitutional environmental rights are not being protected.[86] The UN Economic Commission for Europe recommended that the Ukraine improve public access to environmental information, enhance public participation in decision making, encourage citizens to pursue their environmental rights, and develop effective mechanisms to ensure citizens' access to justice.[87]

ARMENIA

There is little evidence available regarding litigation in Armenia based on the constitutional right to a healthy environment. In one publicized case, journalists frustrated by the government's refusal to release environmental information sued the Ministry of Ecology.[88] A mediated settlement was reached, and reports indicate that the Ministry of Ecology is now making environmental information more accessible.[89] The 2008 annual report of Armenia's Human Rights Defender makes it clear that many violations of the right to a healthy environment – from commercial exploitation of the ecologically vital Lake

Sevan to unconstrained construction that has turned the capital city of Yerevan into an "environmental disaster zone" – are ongoing but are not being addressed.[90] Armenia has also been criticized by the Compliance Committee of the Aarhus Convention for failing to disclose environmental information, provide adequate opportunities for public participation in environmental decision making, or provide access to justice.[91]

Poland

Poland's framework environmental law explicitly grants NGOs standing to challenge government decisions in court.[92] More than one hundred court cases dealing with access to environmental information, participation in decision making, or access to justice have been brought before administrative courts.[93] Poland's Environmental Law Center (and its predecessor, the Environmental Law Information Service) reportedly won almost one hundred administrative appeals and nearly fifty court cases between 1992 and 2002.[94] However, it is not known whether any of these cases explicitly referenced the right to live in a healthy environment. As discussed in Chapter 3, the Polish constitution's current provisions regarding the right to a healthy environment are ambiguous. Poland's 2008 implementation report to the *Aarhus Convention* states that "the law does presently not contain provisions on the right of every person to the [healthy] environment."[95] Overall, the constitutional status of the right to a healthy environment in Poland remains unclear.

Georgia, Moldova, Belarus, Montenegro

It is difficult to determine whether the constitutional right to a healthy environment is being enforced by courts in Georgia, Moldova, Belarus, and Montenegro. There were thirty-eight legal actions launched in Georgia between 2000 and 2004 in pursuit of environmental information, and two cases alleging violations of the public's right to participate in environmental decision making.[96] In Montenegro, the Constitutional Court has made rulings related to the unconstitutionality of urban development plans because of a lack of public participation.[97] Court cases seeking environmental protection have also been brought in Moldova and Belarus, but are rare.[98] Again, it is not known whether or to what extent the litigants or the courts relied on the constitutional right to a healthy environment.

Estonia

The Estonian constitution makes no explicit reference to the right to a healthy environment, although it does include a government duty to protect the environment. Nevertheless, Estonian courts now recognize that individuals enjoy a constitutional right to a healthy environment.[99] The courts reached their conclusion through an analysis of Estonia's constitution, the *Aarhus Convention*, and jurisprudence from the ECHR.[100] The recognition of an implicit constitutional right to a healthy environment has contributed to relaxation of previously restrictive standing requirements, enabling citizens and ENGOs to access the courts.[101] The Supreme Court has endorsed the concept of *actio popularis* in environmental cases.[102] On the other hand, Vaarmari contends that Estonia is still having difficulty meeting the requirements of the *Aarhus Convention*.[103]

Factors Affecting the Influence of the Constitutional Right to a Healthy Environment in Eastern Europe

A wide variety of historical, political, cultural, and legal factors affect the influence of constitutional provisions recognizing the right to a healthy environment in Eastern Europe (see Table 9.1). While some generalizations can be made about common challenges and opportunities, it is important to acknowledge that there are critical differences between nations. For example, the differing degree to which their former communist governments were authoritarian has contributed to different levels of NGO presence in nations such as Hungary and Romania.[104]

Among the overarching problems facing Eastern Europe are widespread poverty, weakness of the state, low levels of democracy in some nations, and institutional instability.[105] In some nations, corruption, concentrated wealth and power, and bureaucratic arbitrariness are deeply rooted in political culture.[106] The rule of law in some nations is fragile, with governments having trouble policing themselves, let alone industrial and commercial interests.[107] Where these problems are less severe, human rights – including the right to a healthy environment – are more likely to gain traction. Stec suggests that the European nations that belong to the Commonwealth of Independent States (i.e., Armenia, Belarus, Georgia, Moldova, Russia, and the Ukraine) are experiencing slower progress environmentally because of ongoing political instability and a penchant for anti-democratic responses to that instability.[108] Kravchenko concludes that full enjoyment of constitutional rights, including the right to a healthy environment, will not become a reality "without a firm commitment to the development of the rule of law in the region."[109]

Environmental concerns occupy a unique place in the modern history of many Eastern European nations. In Hungary, Latvia, and the Czech Republic, environmentalism played a critical role in mobilizing the public

TABLE 9.1

Factors influencing the extent of the environmental rights revolution in Eastern Europe

Factor	Generally positive	Generally negative	Mixed	Examples of positive influence	Examples of negative influence
Constitutional provisions			×	Hungary, Latvia	Armenia, Czech Republic, Poland
Prospective litigants			×	Hungary, Montenegro	Belarus, Romania
Access to justice			×	Hungary, Latvia, Slovenia	Armenia, Czech Republic, Slovakia
Resources for legal mobilization			×	Poland, Slovenia, Slovakia, Ukraine	Georgia, Moldova
Rule of law			×	Hungary	Russia
Responsive judiciary			×	Estonia, Latvia, Slovenia	Bulgaria, Croatia, Czech Republic
Social, economic, and political conditions		×			Russia, Serbia

to bring about the transformation to democracy.[110] In Hungary, citizens coalesced in opposition to the proposed Nagymaros Dam on the Danube River.[111] In Latvia, the public united against plans to dam the Daugava River.[112] In Estonia and the Czech Republic, citizens protested air pollution.[113] Green movements in these nations as well as in Poland, Bulgaria, and Romania provided a politically acceptable outlet for public dissatisfaction with the communist regimes because they were not perceived as a threat.[114]

In the early years of democratization there was a tidal wave of change, including new constitutions, new institutions, and substantial rewriting of environmental laws.[115] The challenge was immense. Both constitutions and environmental laws under communist regimes served a largely symbolic function.[116] In practice, the laws were unrealistically stringent, incomplete, and rarely enforced. Environmental decision making was a closed process, with information closely guarded by the state and little or no citizen involvement.[117] Salvo argues that Eastern European nations continue to be economically dependent on polluting, inefficient industries and cannot afford to enforce environmental laws, despite constitutional provisions.[118]

The economic, political, and social upheaval that occurred in the 1990s following the breakup of the Soviet Union meant that environmental protection became a lower priority. International financial institutions pressured governments to adopt liberalization packages, promote privatization, and encourage foreign investment (which targeted natural resource industries).[119] Achieving political stability and economic recovery became paramount. Environmental groups lost their "mobilizational utility," their mass support, and much of their influence.[120] For environmentalists, "expectations were often disappointed in the actual process of transition, which involved economic disruption, establishment of new power elites for whom environment was not a major concern, and continued problems with corruption."[121] The economic crisis "thwarted any moves extending beyond weak sustainability towards deeper, systemic reform."[122]

Many nations still lack detailed regulations, specific standards, permitting processes, and reporting requirements, and weak enforcement continues to be an Achilles' heel.[123] In some nations, regulations from the Soviet era are still in force.[124] According to the OECD, environmental agencies suffer from weak authority, scarce resources, outdated management approaches, high turnover of professionals, frequent restructuring, and lack of incentives.[125] Other problems include lack of leadership, limited access to key information, poor sequencing of reforms, limited public participation, and reform fatigue.[126]

On the positive side, the budgets of most environment ministries are increasing, national environmental standards and targets have been set, access to information and levels of public participation in decision making are improving, judiciaries are becoming more independent and environmentally aware, and training programs are in place for civil servants, enforcement officials, and judges.[127] The IUCN, UNEP, and other agencies have provided expert advice. A major source of financing for the improvement of environmental laws, institutions, policies, and programs is foreign aid, both bilateral assistance from Western nations and multilateral assistance from institutions, including the UN Development Programme, European Commission, European Bank for Reconstruction and Development, and the World Bank.[128] At the same time, the flow of funds for economic development projects that cause additional environmental damage has been much higher.[129]

The litigation support structure needed to enable a "rights revolution" is slowly taking shape, with growth in civil society, networks of environmental lawyers, and new sources of funding. There are hundreds of ENGOs, but many are small, cash-strapped, and weak compared to other societal actors. To make matters worse, some nations have passed laws that make it difficult to operate NGOs; in nations like Russia, the difficulties extend to harassment and intimidation.[130] For example, Belarus imposed very tight restrictions on the registration, operation, and financing of NGOs, which are scrutinized by judicial authorities.[131] As a result, the number of NGOs in Belarus, including environmental ones, is very low compared to that of many other Eastern European countries.[132] In contrast, Montenegro is enjoying rapid growth in civil society, in part due to a law that encourages these organizations instead of constraining them.[133] Goldston has identified three key factors contributing to the emergence of public interest environmental litigation in post-communist Europe.[134] First, the prospect of admission to the European Union, with its common economic rules and legal standards, "acted as a powerful incentive for post-Communist governments to rapidly professionalize their courts and bars and to enhance the independence of the judiciary."[135] Second, NGO movements, with their experience in protest and dissent, saw litigation as a potentially powerful tool. Third, there was an infusion of financial support from foreign donors. Goldston also identified a number of constraints: widespread distrust of the legal profession and courts because of their historical role supporting the state; high costs; procedural obstacles; long delays; and limited remedies.[136]

Competent legal assistance is critically important in a law-based society.[137] Public interest environmental law organizations are operating in many nations, including the Ukraine, Moldova, Armenia, Poland, Uzbekistan, Slovenia, Slovakia, Russia, and the Czech Republic.[138] International donors have played a major role in establishing and funding these organizations.[139] For example, USAID helped set up Environmental Public Advocacy Centers across Central and Eastern Europe in the 1990s.[140] Large US foundations, including Ford and Rockefeller, funded environmental law organizations in Hungary and Slovakia.[141] American NGOs, including ELAW and the Environmental Law Institute, have also provided assistance.

In less than two decades, significant advances have been made in terms of access to information, public participation in environmental decision making, and access to justice. Constitutional provisions guaranteeing the right to a healthy environment and related procedural rights appear to be a

driving force behind this progress.[142] Gravelle identifies public interest standing as the most important element in enforcing the right to a healthy environment.[143] Many nations have liberalized their rules regarding standing,
although the extent to which public interest standing is recognized varies
from open (e.g., Latvia) to restrictive (e.g., Czech Republic).[144]

The *Aarhus Convention* is also contributing to major advances in access
to environmental information, public participation in decision making, and
access to justice.[145] *Aarhus* raises the bar for all parties, but particularly for the
Eastern European nations. While citizen complaints, independent reports,
and determinations of the Compliance Committee of the Aarhus Convention
indicate there is still room for improvement, considerable progress has been
made.[146] The increased availability of procedural rights should be a major
boost to protection and enforcement of the substantive right to a healthy
environment.

However, there are still significant barriers to bringing court challenges,
including the lack of lawyers with environmental training, the costs, time
commitment, lack of public confidence in the judicial system, and lack of
environmental awareness and expertise in the judiciary.[147] Citizens in many
Eastern European nations have little knowledge regarding their environmental
rights.[148] Stec notes that "despite the concerted efforts over many years of
legions of legal professionals, particularly those engaged in international
assistance, to stimulate the bringing forward of test cases, these societies have
remained largely non-litigious."[149] Eastern European nations must overcome
a social tradition of disenfranchisement before citizens can fully engage in
environmental decision making and access to justice.[150] The number of lawsuits about gaining access to environmental information and securing participation in environmental decision making reflects ongoing problems with
governments using control of information as a form of power and a pater-
nalistic attitude toward public participation.[151]

Unlike the nations of Latin America, Eastern European nations have not
developed simplified and expedited judicial procedures for citizens and NGOs
whose constitutional rights have allegedly been violated. Lawsuits asserting
violation of the right to a healthy environment, to the extent that this right
is enforceable, must be pursued through the regular civil and administrative
court procedures. The consequences include high costs, delays, and the need
for professional legal assistance. There is often a fee imposed for filing a
lawsuit, and many courts require that a bond be posted if a litigant seeks
injunctive relief (e.g., seeks to halt construction on an allegedly unlawful

project).[152] The availability of interim relief ranges widely, from difficult to obtain (e.g., Czech Republic) to readily available upon proof of irreparable harm (e.g., Hungary, Latvia, and Slovenia).[153] Many Eastern European nations follow the loser-pays system, which requires unsuccessful litigants to pay the costs of opposing parties (which may be the government and sometimes businesses). Some nations have altered their rules of court so that NGOs and citizens are exempt from administrative legal fees.[154]

Conclusion

Perhaps because of the past experience of communist nations, some scholars were skeptical about whether the new constitutional environmental rights of the emerging democracies in Eastern Europe would be more effective than their historical antecedents.[155] On the other hand, Shemshuchenko and Kravchenko both see environmental rights in Eastern Europe as not mere social intention but as substantive rights that citizens can rely upon.[156] In some countries, such as Hungary, there is a sense of constitutional optimism, a belief that in a post-communist world, rules have to be obeyed.[157] Given that authoritarian governments ruled Eastern Europe for decades prior to the 1990s, the extent of progress in terms of environmental governance appears impressive. The challenge is to shift from a focus on procedural rights to fulfilling the substantive right to a healthy environment. Effective protection of environmental rights in Eastern Europe will require the development of a governance culture that offers newfound respect for both human rights and the environment.

TABLE 9.A

Constitutional influence on environmental legislation and litigation in Eastern Europe

Nation	Year*	Legislation	Litigation
Albania	1998	Yes[1]	N/A[2]
Armenia	1995	Yes[3]	Yes[4]
Belarus	1994	Yes[5]	N/A[6]
Bulgaria	1991	Yes[7]	Yes[8]
Croatia	1990	Yes[9]	Yes[10]
Czech Republic	1992	Yes[11]	Yes[12]
Georgia	1995	Yes[13]	N/A[14]
Hungary	1989	Yes[15]	Yes[16]
Latvia	1998	Yes[17]	Yes[18]
Macedonia	1991	Yes[19]	Yes[20]
Moldova	1994	Yes[21]	N/A[22]
Montenegro	2007	Yes[23]	N/A[24]
Poland	1997	Yes[25]	N/A[26]
Romania	2003	Yes[27]	Yes[28]
Russia	1993	Yes[29]	Yes[30]
Serbia	2006	Yes[31]	N/A[32]
Slovakia	1992	Yes[33]	Yes[34]
Slovenia	1991	Yes[35]	Yes[36]
Ukraine	1996	Yes[37]	Yes[38]

* Year when right to healthy environment was constitutionalized.

1 *Law No. 8934 on Environmental Protection* (2002), Articles 1, 7.

2 Constitutional Court of Albania, http://www.gjk.gov.al/ (available in English). Searched for "Article 56" and "environment." No hits for either.

3 *Law on Provision of Sanitary-Epidemiological Security of the Population* (1998), Articles 8(6), 10. See also *Law on Ecological Education of the Population* (2001), Article 12, and *Law No. ZR-21 of 1995 on Expertise of Environmental Impact*, Article 2.

4 Constitutional Court, http://www.concourt.am/. No case law available online as of 31 July 2009. However, *Association of Investigative Journalists v. Ministry of Environment* (2003) is cited in Goldston (2006, 522).

5 *Law on Protection of the Environment, No. 1982-XII* (1992), Preamble, Articles 2, 4, 7, 12-16.

6 Constitutional Court of Belarus, http://www.ncpi.gov.by/constsud/eng/.

7 *Law of Preservation of Environment* (2002), Article 1, 3, 17.

8 Constitutional Court, http://www.constcourt.bg. Decision No. 10, 10 July 1995, on CC No. 8/95. See also the Supreme Administrative Court, http://www.sac.government.bg/.

9 *Environmental Protection Act* (2007).

10 Constitutional Court, http://www.usud.hr/. Searched for "environment" and "Article 69" (the right to a healthy environment). For example, see Decision U-III/69/2002 and Decision U-II/4833/2005.

11 *Act on Environment* (1992).

12 Supreme Administrative Court, http://www.nssoud.cz/. Decisions are available only in

Czech. Constitutional Court, http://www.usoud.cz/clanek/interneten. No cases on right to favourable environment or Article 35. However, cases of the legal ENGO Environmental Law Services based on the constitutional right to a healthy environment are available at the Environmental Law Services website, http://www.i-eps.cz/en-us/.

13 *Law of 1996 on Environmental Protection*, Articles 2, 3, 6, 7.

14 Constitutional Court, http://www.constcourt.ge. Supreme Court of Georgia, http://www.supremecourt.ge/. Decisions not searchable in English.

15 Act LIII of 1995 on the *General Rules of Environmental Protection*, ss. 1, 12, 41, 54, 97, and 98.

16 Constitutional Court, http://www.mkab.hu/en/enmain.htm. Supreme Court, http://www.mkab.hu/. For an example of Constitutional Court decision, see 11/2005. (IV. 5.) AB Decision. See also Supreme Court No. 1/2004.

17 *Environmental Protection Law* (2006).

18 Constitutional Court, http://www.satv.tiesa.gov.lv/?lang=2. For example, see *Judgment of 21 December 2007* in case No. 2007-12-03 (http://www.satv.tiesa.gov.lv/upload/judg_2007-12-03.htm), *Judgment of 14 February 2003* in Case No. 2002-14-04, and *Judgment of 8 February 2007* in case No. 2006-09-03.

19 *Act on Environment and Nature Protection and Promotion* (1996), Article 1. *Law on Ambient Air Quality* (2004).

20 Constitutional Court, http://www.ustavensud.mk/domino/WEBSUD.nsf. For example, see No. 176/2004 (05/04/2005).

21 *Law on environmental protection* (1993, as amended), Articles 1, 2, 34.

22 Constitutional Court, http://www.constcourt.md/. Cases not available in English.

23 *Law on Environment* (2008).

24 Constitutional Court, http://www.ustavnisudcg.co.me. Very limited case law online. None related to environment.

25 *Environmental Protection Act* (2001). See also *Act on making information on environment and its protection available* (2008).

26 Constitutional Tribunal of Poland, http://www.trybunal.gov.pl/eng/index.htm. Summaries of cases available in English reviewed. No relevant cases found.

27 *Law on the Protection of the Environment* (1995), Article 5. See also *Government Emergency Ordinance No. 243/2000 on atmospheric protection* (2001), Article 1(2), and Act 195/2005 establishing broad procedural rights in environmental matters.

28 Constitutional Court, http://www.ccr.ro/default.aspx?lang=EN. Selected cases available from 1992 to 2009. No references to environment. However, see Supreme Court of Justice decision No. 1112 of 12 June 1997, cited in Dutu (2004).

29 *Federal Law No. 7-FZ on environmental protection* (2002), Preamble, Articles 2, 3, 11-13.

30 Supreme Court of the Russian Federation (http://www.supcourt.ru) and Constitutional Court (http://www.ksrf.ru). Neither offers access to cases in English. However, see Ruling No. 8, 31 October 1995 of the Supreme Court.

31 *Environmental Protection Law* (2004), Articles 1, 2, 7, 9.

32 Supreme Court, http://www.ustavni.sud.rs. No case law available.

33 *Environmental Protection Act* (1991).

34 Constitutional Court, http://www.concourt.sk/. Only 1992-2003 cases available in English. See Finding of the Constitutional Court of the Slovak Republic Ref. No. II. ÚS 58/01 of 31 October 2001 (No. 45/01).

35 *Environmental Protection Act* (2004), Articles 1, 13, 14.

36 Constitutional Court, http://www.us-rs.si/. Search for "healthy environment" yielded
    twenty-four cases (8 July 2009). For example, see Decision No. U-I-30/95-26, 1/15-1996.
    National Association of Ecologists.
37 *Law No. 1264-XII on environmental protection* (1995), Articles 9-12.
38 Constitutional Court, http://www.ccu.gov.ua. Searched English summaries of cases from
    each year, 2000 to 2009. No environmental cases. However, cases reported in secondary
    literature include those brought by the ENGO Environment, People, Law to protect the
    right to a healthy environment, available at the Environment, People, Law website, http://
    epl.org.ua/en/lawnbspnbspnbsp/access-to-justice/cases/.

10
...... Western Europe

Nine Western European nations have constitutions that explicitly recognize the right to a healthy environment. All of these countries are members of the European Union, except Andorra and Norway. In Western Europe, democratic traditions, strong adherence to the rule of law, well-established public access to judicial systems, and relatively high levels of economic development provide fertile ground for the development of constitutional environmental rights. Portugal (1976) and Spain (1978) were global pioneers in constitutional recognition of the right to a healthy environment, and their leadership had a significant influence on Latin America. Even Western European nations without constitutional recognition of the right have ratified the *Aarhus Convention on Access to Information, Public Participation in Decision-making and Access to Justice in Environmental Matters* and are bound by the jurisprudence of the European Court of Human Rights, which recognizes the right to a healthy environment (see Chapter 4).

Legislation
Western European nations are recognized for having some of the strongest environmental laws and policies in the world.[1] In eight of the nine nations whose constitutions recognize the right to a healthy environment, legislation reflects the influence of this right (see Figure 10.1, and see Table 10.A at the end of this chapter). For example, in Portugal, as the OECD observes, "the Constitution designates protection of the environment and conservation of natural resources as being among the *essential tasks of the Portuguese State,* and sets out the State's obligations regarding the prevention and control of pollution and its effects" (emphasis in original).[2] Portugal's *Framework Law on the Environment* reiterates the right to a healthy and ecologically balanced environment; outlines the state's responsibility to protect the right; guarantees

public participation in decision making; ensures access to courts to prevent environmental harm, seek compensation, or compel government action; and encourages the formation of and participation in ENGOs.

Although Spain recognized the right to a healthy environment in Article 45 of its constitution more than three decades ago (1978), that recognition continues to exert a major influence on the country's development of environmental legislation. For example, the *Environmental Responsibility Law* and the *Law on Natural Heritage and Biodiversity*, both from 2007, make repeated references to Article 45.[3] The OECD concluded that Spain's 1978 constitution prompted the "major revision and amplification of environmental policies ... [and] facilitated the development of inspection, monitoring and enforcement."[4]

According to Karacostas and Dacoronia, Article 24 of the Greek constitution has strengthened the application of provisions of the *Greek Civil Code* related to environmental protection.[5] Similarly, the *Belgian Civil Code* includes recognition of the right to live in a healthy environment and the responsibility to protect it.[6] In Finland, several important environmental laws have been strengthened to reflect the constitutional right to a healthy environment.[7] The OECD states that France has a "vast, coherent body of environmental legislation," which is further strengthened by the incorporation of the *Charter for the Environment* into the constitution in 2005.[8] A review process for proposed legislation, governed by France's Constitutional Council, will ensure that new laws are consistent with the *Charter*'s provisions.[9]

The only Western European nation in this study whose environmental legislation does not explicitly mention the constitution or the right to a healthy environment is the Netherlands. Nevertheless, Verschuuren argues that "environmental law has its foundation in the Dutch Constitution."[10]

Litigation

In eight of the nine Western European nations whose constitutions recognize the right to a healthy environment there has been litigation enforcing and interpreting the right (see Table 10.A). Norway is the exception. The environmental right provision in the Norwegian constitution is explicitly not self-executing, and Norway is not a litigious society. In at least one additional Western European nation, Italy, courts recognize the constitutional right to a healthy environment as implicit in other fundamental rights and therefore amenable to judicial enforcement.

FIGURE 10.1

Constitutional influence on environmental legislation and litigation in Western Europe

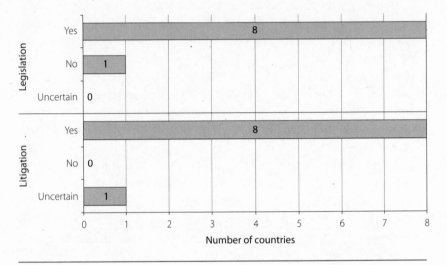

PORTUGAL

As mentioned earlier, Portugal's 1976 constitution was a pioneering document. In addition to recognizing the right to a healthy and ecologically balanced environment and imposing extensive responsibilities on government, it established the *actio popularis,* which enabled individuals and NGOs to protect collective rights through the judicial system without meeting the traditional standing requirement of a direct personal interest. A series of laws expand upon the environmental rights of Portuguese citizens.[11] For example, ENGOs and citizens are exempt from a number of fees usually imposed in judicial and administrative processes.[12] As a result of these progressive actions, Portugal is regarded as the EU country "with the widest accessibility to administrative and judicial remedies" in environmental matters.[13]

Portugal joined the EU in 1986, leading to higher environmental standards and access to the European court system. The EU accession process also led to a major infusion of funds for infrastructure projects, with significant environmental repercussions. According to Vasconcelos and Baptista, "During the last thirty years, the country has radically changed from a rural society, centered around traditional values, to late industrialization and chaotic urbanization, both of which have caused dramatic concern over the environment."[14]

A review of the jurisprudence available on the Constitutional Court's website identified thirty-nine decisions citing Article 66 of the constitution, which sets out the right to a healthy and ecologically balanced environment as well as the state's extensive duties to protect the environment. Additional cases have been decided by other courts and tribunals. Between 1995 and 2002, the *actio popularis* was used to bring 101 cases, mostly administrative appeals.[15] However, de Andrade suggests that the rate of success in administrative cases was fairly low, as these courts appear to resist the new values and principles of environmental law.[16]

The following are some examples of successful cases:[17]

- a court decision that a gas station could not be built beside an elementary school because the constitutional right to a healthy environment justifies preventive action[18]
- a prosecution for cutting down trees that held the nests of a legally protected species[19]
- a court order halting the construction of a landfill on the basis that the constitutional right to a healthy environment demands prevention, not compensation, and preventive action is warranted on a precautionary basis[20]
- court orders for the protection of bird habitat in an urban setting.[21]

Reis and Neves assert that lawsuits brought by ENGOs "have contributed to a growing awareness of environmental matters in the Portuguese courts."[22]

An earlier assessment found that although Portugal offers extensive legal procedures for both individuals and NGOs to protect the constitutional right to a healthy environment, there is a relatively low rate of use of these tools.[23] Possible explanations include a lack of public knowledge of rights and a general lack of faith in the judicial system (e.g., it takes too long, court decisions are too late, and environmental protection is not adequately valued).[24] Overall, da Cruz concludes that "environmental law, in general, and environmental protection, in particular, have become richer with the constitutional recognition of a right to a healthy and ecologically balanced environment."[25]

GREECE

In 1975, Greece was among the first countries in the world to make reference to the environment in its constitution. The right to a healthy environment was added to the Greek constitution in 2001, although courts had already recognized that it was implicit in Article 24 (which articulated the state's duty to protect the environment).[26] According to Karageorgou, it is "widely recognized that there has been a significant gap in the field of environmental protection" caused by the inadequate legislative framework.[27] The Council of State, Greece's supreme administrative court, has played an important role in filling that gap.[28] Based on Article 24 of the constitution, the Council of State has issued a series of strong decisions holding that the environment is not merely a factor to be considered but a core protected value to be disregarded only in exceptional cases where there is a compelling public purpose and no demonstrable alternative.[29] In 1992, a fifth division of the Council of State was created especially for environmental cases, a step that has contributed to innovative environmental jurisprudence.[30] According to the Greek government, "In environmental cases the scope of legal standing has been remarkably expanded as a result of the jurisprudence of the Council of State."[31] Sioutis and Gerapetritis report that "many legal provisions have been ruled unconstitutional and many regulations and administrative acts have been annulled."[32] Because the environment is a constitutionally protected value, the Council of State has repeatedly directed government to take preventive measures.[33]

The leading case involved the Council of State's repeated cancellation of permits for a major water-diversion project that would have dammed and rerouted the Acheloos River.[34] The first decisions, in 1994 and 1995, were based on inadequacies in the environmental assessment (the project was divided into pieces without assessment of the cumulative impacts).[35] Later decisions (in 2000 and 2005) were based on adverse effects on cultural and environmental heritage that violated the constitution.[36] In other important cases, the court cancelled the authorization of a major gold mine because of unacceptable environmental impacts and granted injunctions requiring removal of cellphone base stations because of concerns regarding electromagnetic radiation.[37] According to Papadopoulou, the constitutional provisions require precautionary action and remove some of the discretion that has long characterized administrative decision making.[38]

Greek courts have applied the principle of "practical harmony" or proportionality to balance the right to a healthy environment with other constitutional rights.[39] However, the Council of State has recognized that environmental protection must occasionally trump property rights.[40] For example, it has limited construction in areas important for the reproduction of sea turtles.[41] Concerns have been raised about whether the Council of State has overstepped its bounds and intruded upon the legislative and executive realms. The OECD observes that Council of State decisions to stop projects lacking proper, independent environmental impact assessments do not always lead to the cancellation of projects, as the legislature has occasionally ignored or overruled court decisions.[42]

In summary, the constitutional provisions for environmental protection have had significant legal effects in Greece. The Council of State has relied on the constitutional provisions requiring environmental protection "as the basis for a body of decisions that is playing an important role in pressing the executive branch to take the environment into account in its actions."[43] The strengthening of the constitution in 2001 to explicitly recognize the right to a healthy and ecologically balanced environment is expected to have an even greater effect, reaching "beyond the law."[44]

FRANCE

With the oldest constitution in Europe, France has the newest environmental provisions. The *Charter for the Environment* was added to the French constitution in 2005, following an extensive public consultation process led by the Coppens Commission.[45] The *Charter* recognizes the right to a healthy environment (and associated procedural rights), the responsibility to protect the environment, and the precautionary principle. It also requires that public policies promote sustainable development. In 2008, France passed another set of constitutional amendments. One of these established the position of Defender of Rights, giving citizens someone to whom they can refer complaints.[46] There has been an intense debate about whether the *Charter* is legally significant or merely intended as symbolic politics.[47] After reviewing the legislative history, French constitutional law, and the *Charter* itself, Prieur concludes that the creation of a substantive right to a healthy environment is sure to have substantial effects, though they may not be foreseeable today, just as the long-term effects of the first human rights instruments were unforeseeable.[48] One extra-legal effect of the *Charter* that has already occurred is the increased attention to environmental education in the curriculum of French primary and secondary schools.[49]

France offers broad access to justice in environmental matters although there are concerns that high costs may pose a barrier to individuals and ENGOs (for whom legal aid is generally not available).[50] Approximately three thousand civil cases seeking interim relief or damages for harm caused by an environmental nuisance reach the courts annually.[51] The *Charter* could have an upward influence on the number of civil cases.

Despite its recent vintage, the *Charter* has already had a marked effect on French law. France cited the *Charter's* precautionary principle in becoming the first nation in the world to pass legislation banning hydraulic fracturing (fracking), a destructive method of extracting natural gas and oil.[52] The Constitutional Council evaluated the consistency of a new law on genetically modified organisms (GMOs) and a proposed carbon tax with the *Charter*.[53] The Council of State (the highest administrative court in France) has based more than a dozen decisions on the *Charter* on issues ranging from nuclear power to the protection of mountain lakes.[54] In one case, a group of organic farmers asserted their right to a healthy environment in challenging the mandatory chemical treatment of their cattle for a disease.[55] Several lower courts have accepted that the right to a healthy environment can inform defences against criminal charges stemming from the destruction of GMO crops, although these decisions were overturned by appellate courts.[56] Similarly, several lower-court decisions based on the *Charter* that annulled authorizations to grow genetically modified crops were overturned by the Council of State.[57]

While it was anticipated that the *Charter* would increase the prominence of environmental issues in French law, Marrani asserts that "it has developed beyond all predictions during the first two years of enforcement."[58] Other scholars express disappointment at the conservative approach of the higher courts, particularly the Council of State.[59] Puechavy points out that to be made really effective, the right to a healthy environment needs to be elaborated through legislative and regulatory mechanisms that ensure the right to drink clean water, the right to breathe clean air, and the right to enjoy the benefits of biodiversity.[60] The scope of the right to a healthy environment has yet to be defined conclusively by the courts. On balance, although progress is being made, "there is still a long way to go."[61]

SPAIN

In the Spanish constitution, the right to a healthy environment is not found in "Chapter 2: Rights and Freedoms," but, rather, in "Chapter 3: Guiding Principles of Economic and Social Policy." Unlike the fundamental rights in Chapter 2, which are directly enforceable in courts, Chapter 3's "Guiding Principles" are explicitly not self-executing, enforceable rights. Instead, the right to a healthy environment is intended to guide legislators, judges, and public authorities in formulating, implementing, and enforcing laws, policies, judgments, and programs. As a result of the way these provisions are worded, there is a lively and ongoing debate about the legal and practical implications of Article 45 of the constitution.[62] The Constitutional and Supreme Courts have issued a number of decisions that refer to the right to a healthy environment – in cases on soil contamination, environmental taxes, conservation of biodiversity and natural areas, protection of the maritime shoreline, and noise pollution – but the status of the right remains uncertain.[63] Most experts conclude that the wording of the constitution precludes citizens and ENGOs from filing *amparo* cases before the Constitutional Court solely on the basis that their right to a healthy environment has been violated.[64] Other rights, such as the right to life or the right to privacy and respect for the home, need to be incorporated into lawsuits.[65] Figueroa Alegre warns that unless the uncertainty is clarified, the right to a healthy environment is at risk of becoming a "dead right."[66]

Spanish law does not provide any special legal procedures for environmental cases.[67] The country does recognize the *actio popularis* for ENGOs in cases involving environmental protection, so standing generally is not an obstacle,[68] and a recent law guarantees that ENGOs meeting certain criteria will be guaranteed legal aid in bringing lawsuits.[69] The main procedural obstacle facing defenders of the environment in Spain is a requirement for large financial undertakings when injunctive relief is sought.[70]

In 2007, based on the constitutional right to a healthy environment, the Supreme Court upheld a complaint about noise from machinery.[71] In its decision, the court referred to the decisions of the European Court of Human Rights in the *Lopez Ostra* and *Moreno Gomez* cases, where the ECHR found that Spain had violated the rights of its citizens in environmental cases.[72] Overall, the subordinate status for the right to a healthy environment in Spain has limited the role of courts in protecting the right.[73]

FINLAND

In 1995, the Finnish constitution was amended to include the right to a healthy environment. Nergelius suggested that it "would probably be difficult to base a legal claim before a court" on the right to a healthy environment in Finland's constitution.[74] Yet this constitutional right played a critical role in determining the outcome of one of the most prominent environmental controversies in Finnish history.[75] Plans to build a hydroelectric dam and reservoir in the headwaters of the Kemijoki River first emerged in the 1950s but were rejected repeatedly because of the high natural values of the area, internationally renowned as important habitat for migratory birds. In 1992, a company reapplied for permission to construct the dam and create a reservoir flooding 240 square kilometres. The application was approved in 2000, triggering a legal challenge by opponents of the plan. Based in part on the constitutional right to a healthy environment, the legal challenge was successful. The permit was quashed by the Vaasa Administrative Court in 2001. In 2002, the Supreme Administrative Court rejected the company's appeal.[76] The court asserted that the *Water Act* "must be interpreted in light of Article 20 of the Constitution, which guarantees the right to a decent environment."[77] The court noted that the constitutional provision was both a prescription to legislators and a principle for interpreting and applying the law. This case illustrates the important influence that constitutional environmental rights can have on the interpretation of other laws and policies.

In 2006, 288 of the 3,793 matters (7.6 percent) submitted to Finland's Supreme Administrative Court were environmental cases, while 2,829 out of 24,000 appeals (11.8 percent) filed with the lower administrative courts were environment-related.[78] It is not known whether and to what extent the constitutional right to a healthy environment played a role in these cases. Davies believes that, thanks in part to the influence of its constitutional provisions requiring environmental protection and participation in decision making, Finland has gone beyond the requirements of the *Aarhus Convention*.[79] The OECD agrees.[80] However, Kuusiniemi argues that there are still significant restrictions on the standing of ENGOs, particularly in cases involving forestry and mining.[81]

The Netherlands

The Dutch constitution does not create an explicit right to a healthy environment, but in the "Fundamental Rights" chapter, Article 21 imposes a duty upon the government to protect and improve the environment. In spite of the uncertainty, courts have treated Article 21 as a *de facto* constitutional right to a healthy environment in a wide range of cases, ordering the cleanup of hazardous wastes, placing restrictions on the operating hours of airports, protecting the habitat of an endangered species of salamander, and placing greater weight on environmental considerations than economic concerns.[82] As well, recognition of the constitutional right to a healthy environment has strengthened the rights of citizens to information and to participation in environmental decision making.[83]

Verschuuren notes that "standing for environmental NGOs is often considered to be a consequence of the constitutional right to environmental protection, laid down in Article 21 of the Dutch Constitution."[84] There are "ample possibilities for access to justice in environmental cases for individuals and NGOs alike."[85] However, disturbing trends in recent years include the elimination of the *actio popularis* (which allowed groups to defend diffuse or collective interests) and more self-regulation for industry (meaning fewer permits are issued that can be appealed).[86] Critics of environmental litigation have based their arguments on the impropriety of allowing nondemocratic ENGOs to mount legal challenges to the decisions of democratically elected governments and the adverse economic effects of projects being delayed or cancelled.[87] Although seen as a disturbing development, the elimination of the *actio popularis* is likely to have only a modest effect because ENGOs are generally considered to have a legitimate interest in environmental matters.[88] Another negative development in terms of access to justice in environmental matters is the creation of a list of decisions (e.g., airport expansion) that are no longer subject to administrative review.[89]

Factors contributing to the limited impact of Article 21 include the vague wording of the provision, the extensive Dutch environmental legislation (which courts rely on instead of the constitution), and the high level of deference courts grant to government decision makers.[90] Dutch courts focus on procedural issues and rarely address the substantive matters that are at the heart of most environmental litigation.[91] Roughly 70 percent of the victories in environmental cases are on formal, procedural grounds.[92]

There has been a decline in the number of environmental court cases in recent years, which is attributed to a hostile political climate (in part because an ENGO employee killed the high-profile leader of a new right-wing political party) and to ENGOs' frustration at winning cases on legal grounds only to see government reaffirm its decision or reissue a permit after correctly following the procedural requirements.[93] Litigation on constitutional rights also is more constrained in the Netherlands than in most nations because the courts do not have the authority to review acts of Parliament.[94]

Scholars of Dutch environmental policy assert that there has been a shift away from "formal constitutional-legal approaches to governance" toward a neo-liberal market-oriented approach.[95] As a result of the negative legal developments in the Netherlands, van Rijswick and Robbe conclude that Article 21 has been reduced to symbolic meaning and should be replaced with a classic enforceable right.[96]

BELGIUM

The drafters of Belgium's constitutional right to a healthy environment did not intend it to be an enforceable right.[97] Nevertheless, courts have developed a large body of jurisprudence about the right and have often relied on it to overturn government decisions. For example, a court overruled the government's approval of a waste incinerator because the decision ignored expert reports about the threats posed to human health and the environment.[98] The Constitutional Court overturned government attempts to evade the public participation requirements of municipal planning law.[99] Belgian jurisprudence has interpreted the right to a healthy environment broadly, not limited to protecting humans from pollution but also protecting nature and biodiversity.[100] Courts have held that the right to a healthy environment includes the right to water.[101] Approximately 8 percent of Constitutional Court cases and 22 percent of Council of State cases deal with the environment or municipal law and planning, although the proportion of these cases invoking the right to a healthy environment is not known.[102]

Two important principles enunciated by Belgian courts as a result of the constitutional right to a healthy environment are the standstill doctrine and *in dubio pro natura*. The crux of the standstill doctrine is that governments are precluded from weakening levels of environmental protection except in limited circumstances where there is a compelling public interest.[103] In other words, existing environmental laws and standards represent a baseline that can be improved but not weakened. For example, a court ruled that an attempt to relax rules for motor racing violated the standstill aspect of the right to a healthy environment.[104] The phrase *in dubio pro natura* (in doubt, favour Nature) means that where there is uncertainty or ambiguity, the interpretation that protects the environment should be chosen. Thus the right to a healthy environment can restrict the wide discretion that governments otherwise enjoy and force them to make decisions consistent with environmental protection.[105]

In Belgium, standing is at the discretion of courts, and this has resulted in restrictions and inconsistencies.[106] The Constitutional Court has adopted a liberal approach to standing in environmental matters, while the Council of State (the supreme administrative court) has taken a narrow view of standing.[107] The Council of State's jurisprudence was criticized by the Compliance Committee of the Aarhus Convention following a complaint filed by a Belgian ENGO.[108]

Because of the constitutional right to a healthy environment, the principles of precaution, prevention, and integration have a constitutional basis that strengthens their influence on court decisions, government policies, and administrative decisions.[109] The Council of State relied on the constitutional provisions when it used the precautionary principle to cancel a permit for proposed cellphone infrastructure.[110] Belgian courts also apply the fair balance or proportionality principle, meaning that there is no absolute right to a healthy environment; rather, any interference with the right is examined in light of all the circumstances to determine whether the infringement is excessive.[111] The Constitutional Court has rejected challenges to environmental laws and regulations based on property rights and freedom of commerce because of the compelling constitutional interest in environmental protection.[112]

ANDORRA

Andorra is a microstate with a population of 84,424 (2007) and an area of 468 square kilometres.[113] Andorra is one of the six nations identified in Chapter 3 whose constitution includes an ambiguous right to a healthy environment. However Andorra's Constitutional Court has resolved the ambiguity, treating the constitutional provision as a fundamental right. In 1996, the court ruled that the constitutional right to a healthy environment served as sufficient grounds to grant standing to the Association for the Protection of Animals, Plants and the Environment, an ENGO that sought to appeal the approval of a highway extension.[114] The constitutional provisions related to environmental protection have also been used to justify municipal environmental regulations challenged by the national government.[115] Environmental lawsuits are relatively rare in this small nation.

NORWAY

The right to a healthy environment in Norway's constitution is explicitly not self-executing but is subject to the caveat that "the State authorities shall issue further provisions for the implementation of these principles." As a result, Mestad suggests that it is "very unlikely" that anyone can base a legal action directly on the constitutional provision.[116] While it has long been established that ENGOs have legal standing, there is little environmental litigation in Norway.[117] ENGOs tend to have a cooperative rather than confrontational relationship with the state, lessening the motivation to use litigation.[118] Yet Lafferty, Larsen, and Ruud assert that Norway's constitutional provisions represent a powerful mandate for prioritizing environmental protection that the government has not yet acknowledged.[119]

ITALY

In Italy, there is no explicit constitutional right to a healthy environment. However, courts have interpreted the constitutional right to health as incorporating the right to live in a healthy environment.[120] The first recognition of this concept came from the Constitutional Court in 1987 when it held that with regard to Articles 9 (state's duty to safeguard natural beauty) and 32 (right to health) of the Italian constitution, "we must recognize the ongoing efforts to give specific recognition to the protection of the environment as a fundamental human right."[121] In 1990, the Constitutional Court held that environmental protection must take priority over economic considerations when acceptable limits for human health are exceeded.[122] Since then, many successful cases have invoked the right to a healthy environment.[123] Environmental rights can be defended in administrative courts, civil courts, and criminal courts. However, ENGOs in Italy are assured of standing only if the Minister of Environment has issued a decree recognizing their official status, and no such decree exists for the majority of ENGOs.[124]

Factors Affecting the Influence of the Constitutional Right to a Healthy Environment in Western Europe

Even within Western Europe, the most homogeneous of the five regions in this study, there are different legal systems, histories, cultures, and institutions (see Table 10.1). EU membership has accelerated the modernization and convergence of environmental laws and policies to some extent, but national factors – culture, history, institutions, and policies – continue to be more important in shaping environmental law.[125] Despite the unique national contexts, some general observations are possible regarding the influence of the constitutional right to a healthy environment on legislation and litigation.

The clarity and strength of constitutional provisions related to environmental protection can have a significant effect on their legal influence. Weak or ambiguous expressions of the right to a healthy environment (as in the Netherlands, Spain, and Belgium) have constrained the impact of the right in those nations. The Netherlands, with its ambiguous constitutional provision, is the only Western European nation in this study where there is no clear evidence of constitutional influence on environmental legislation. It is possible that one of the reasons Spanish and Belgian environmental laws and policies have lagged behind those in the rest of Europe is the ambiguous nature of their constitutional environmental provisions.[126]

The rule of law is more firmly entrenched in Western Europe than it is in any other region in this study. There is a consistently high degree of transparency regarding the law; the judicial branch of government is well established and independent; and governments generally respect the law.

TABLE 10.1

Factors influencing the extent of the environmental rights revolution in Western Europe

Factor	Generally positive	Generally negative	Mixed	Examples of positive influence	Examples of negative influence
Constitutional provisions			×	France, Portugal	Andorra, Belgium, Netherlands, Norway, Spain
Prospective litigants	×			All Western European nations	
Access to justice	×			France, Greece, Portugal	Belgium
Resources for legal mobilization	×			All Western European nations	
Rule of law	×			All Western European nations	
Responsive judiciary			×	Belgium (Constitutional Court), Greece, Netherlands	Belgium (Council of State)
Social, economic, and political conditions	×			Finland, France	Netherlands

As well, these nations generally enjoy a high standard of living, although per capita income is lower in the southern nations (Portugal, Spain, Italy, and Greece).

In terms of the litigation support structure, there is, again, a greater degree of homogeneity in Western Europe. In all nine nations covered by this study, ENGOs are numerous, well organized, and well funded.[127] There are many lawyers trained with a specialty in environmental law, as well as ENGOs dedicated specifically to providing environmental law advice and services, supported in many cases by experts from the academic sector. International networks enable these lawyers to share precedents, advice, and strategies.[128]

Access to information is widely available and there is generally ample opportunity for public participation in environmental decision making. These conclusions are buttressed by the paucity of public complaints lodged with the Compliance Committee of the Aarhus Convention against the nine Western European nations in this study.[129] Only Belgium, France, and Spain have been the subject of citizen submissions to the compliance committee. The complaint against Belgium was upheld based on limitations on access to justice. The complaint against France, for failing to provide adequate opportunities for public participation, was dismissed. The three complaints against Spain involved allegations of inadequate opportunities for public participation.

Access to justice is less consistent. Western European nations employ different rules on standing, costs, evidence, and types of proceedings. The leading nations are systematically eliminating the barriers that limit access to justice. There is broad public interest standing in Portugal, the Netherlands (although it is eroding), and Greece, whereas standing is narrowly based on private interests in nations such as Germany and Denmark, which do not recognize the constitutional right to a healthy environment.[130] Germany is described as a laggard among European nations in terms of environmental litigation because of its lack of recognition of the right to a healthy environment.[131]

One area where there is a high degree of variability among the Western European nations is that of judicial activism. At one end of the spectrum, Greece's Council of State has taken the most activist approach to interpreting and applying constitutional environmental provisions, on the basis of both the government's duty to protect the environment (1975) and the right to a healthy environment (added in 2001). At the other end of the spectrum, courts in Spain have taken a conservative approach to cases involving the assertion of environmental rights. Further research is required to ascertain the reasons behind these differences, although the relative youth of the Spanish Constitutional Court (established in 1979, compared to the Greek Council of State, which dates back to 1835) could be a factor.

Conclusion

Overall, constitutionalization of the right to a healthy environment has had a positive influence in Western Europe, contributing to stronger environmental laws, enhancing access to justice, and supporting the development of some environmentally friendly court decisions. Thus far, the constitutional right to a healthy environment appears to have been most influential in Greece and Portugal, with weaknesses in the wording of the right undermining its role in Belgium, the Netherlands, and Spain. The jurisprudence of the European Court of Human Rights, with its growing recognition of the right to a healthy environment, is likely to have a significant impact throughout Western Europe. Iceland has drafted a new constitution, pending parliamentary approval and possibly a public referendum, which includes the right to a healthy environment and other strong environmental provisions. The proposed protocol to the *European Convention on Human Rights* on the right to a healthy environment would extend the right to the remaining nations of Western Europe, requiring changes to domestic legislation and possibly constitutions.

TABLE 10.A

Constitutional influence on environmental legislation and litigation in Western Europe

Nation	Year*	Legislation	Litigation
Andorra	1993	Yes[1]	Yes[2]
Belgium	1994	Yes[3]	Yes[4]
Finland	1995	Yes[5]	Yes[6]
France	2005	Yes[7]	Yes[8]
Greece	2002	Yes[9]	Yes[10]
Netherlands	1983	No[11]	Yes[12]
Norway	1992	Yes[13]	N/A[14]
Portugal	1976	Yes[15]	Yes[16]
Spain	1978	Yes[17]	Yes[18]

* Year when right to healthy environment was constitutionalized.

1 *Decree on access to environmental information relating to waste management* (2008).
2 Constitutional Court, http://www.tribunalconstitucional.ad/.
3 *Law on the public access to environmental information* (2006).
4 Constitutional Court (known as the Court of Arbitration prior to 2007), http://www.const-court.be/. Decisions for dozens of cases related to the right to a healthy environment are on the website.
5 *Environmental Protection Act* (2000).
6 Supreme Court and Supreme Administrative Court, http://www.finlex.fi.
7 *Environmental Code* (2000), Book I Common Provisions, General Principles, Articles L110-2, L-124, L-125, and L-220.
8 Constitutional Council, http://www.conseil-constitutionnel.fr; Council of State, http://www.conseil-etat.fr/cde/; Court of Cassation, http://www.courdecassation.fr/.
9 *Law No. 3422/2005* (2005), *Law No. 1650/86 on the protection for the environment*, as amended by Law 3010/2002
10 Council of State, http://www.ste.gr/councilofstate/index_gr.jsp; Supreme Court of Civil and Penal Law (also known as the Court of Cassation), http://www.areiospagos.gr/en/INDEX.htm. Neither website has decisions available in English.
11 *Environmental Management Act* (2004).

12 Administration of Justice, http://www.rechtspraak.nl. Decisions are not available in English, but there were 314 hits in Dutch for "milieu" (environment). Council of State, http://www.raadvanstate.nl/. Also, not available in English, but there were 672 hits in Dutch for "milieu" (environment).

13 *Pollution Control Act* (1981, as amended). Procedural rights are provided in the *Environment Information Act* (2003).

14 Supreme Court of Norway, http://www.domstol.no. Search for "environment" yielded four English summaries of environmental cases, none involving the right to a healthy environment.

15 *Framework Act on the Environment* (1987), Articles 1, 2, 40.

16 Constitutional Court, http://www.tribunalconstitucional.pt. There were thirty-nine hits for a search containing all the following words: "Constituição," "artigo 66," "ambiente" (Constitution, Article 66, environment).

17 *Environmental Responsibility Law* (2007); *Law on Natural Heritage and Biodiversity* (2007).

18 Constitutional Court, http://www.tribunalconstitucional.es. Nine hits for a search on "el derecho a disfrutar de un medio ambiente adecuado" (the right to enjoy an adequate environment). Supreme Court, http://www.poderjudicial.es/. Fifty-nine hits for a search on the same phrase.

PART 3

Evaluating the Impacts of Environmental Provisions in Constitutions

11

Lessons Learned: Practical Experiences with the Right to a Healthy Environment

Chapter 2 described the prospective advantages and disadvantages of recognizing a constitutional right to a healthy environment. The analysis in this chapter revisits that debate in light of the experiences of over one hundred nations in implementing the right through legislation and litigation. The experiences of nations with an explicit constitutional right to a healthy environment and also of nations where courts have recognized the right as implicit in the rights to life or health are included. Consistent with the focus of Chapters 6 to 10, the emphasis is on the legal effects of constitutionalization, although some extra-legal effects are given brief consideration.

The Advantages of Constitutionalizing the Right to a Healthy Environment

STRONGER ENVIRONMENTAL LAWS

There is extensive evidence that constitutional recognition of the right to a healthy environment influences the development of national environmental legislation. In at least seventy-eight out of ninety-two nations, environmental laws were strengthened after the constitutionalization of environmental protection to incorporate substantive, and in many countries procedural, environmental rights (see Figure 11.1). This includes all surveyed nations in Eastern Europe (19 out of 19); almost all nations in Western Europe (8/9), Latin America and the Caribbean (16/18), and Asia (12/14); and a clear majority in Africa (23/32). In some nations, the constitutional right to a healthy environment has become a unifying principle, permeating not only national framework laws but also the entire body of environmental law and policy. This is most clearly the case in Argentina (where the right has been incorporated into national laws, provincial constitutions, and provincial legislation), Costa Rica, Brazil, Colombia, South Africa, Portugal, and the Philippines.

Among the small minority of nations where no constitutional influence on environmental laws could be discerned are countries whose constitutional environmental provisions are very recent (e.g., Dominican Republic, 2010; Jamaica, 2011) and countries that are wracked by civil war and other overriding social, economic, or political crises (e.g., Democratic Republic of the Congo). Environmental legislation was unavailable for two nations – Iran and Sudan. Eight of the twelve nations where there is no evidence of constitutional influence on environmental laws are in Africa.

Constitutional provisions clearly are not the only factor contributing to improved environmental laws. For example, the European Union accession process had a demonstrable influence on the environmental legislation of the nations of Eastern Europe. Other factors include public pressure, the migration of ideas and legislative approaches, and international assistance from agencies such as UNEP and the IUCN. However, the conclusion that constitutions have had a strong influence on national environmental laws is supported by the consistent inclusion in those laws of direct references to the constitution, the explicit acknowledgment of the right to a healthy environment, and the enactment of procedural environmental rights. This conclusion is shared by legal experts and organizations, including the OECD and the UN Economic Commission for Europe.

The constitutionalization of environmental protection provides another major benefit to environmental legislation in that courts appear more likely to defend environmental laws and regulations. Challenges to environmental laws based on property rights and freedom of commerce often fail. For example, Slovenia's Constitutional Court upheld a tax on water pollution based on the constitutional interest in environmental protection.[1] In contrast, in nations lacking a constitutional right to a healthy environment, such as Germany and the United States, litigation involving property rights and freedom of commerce is more likely to constrain government's ability to protect the environment and to have a chilling effect on future legislation.[2] The knowledge that environmental laws have a constitutional backstop may encourage governments to enact stronger environmental laws with confidence that the laws will withstand legal challenges.

Another benefit of constitutional recognition of the right to a healthy environment is that most, if not all, governments will employ lawyers to screen all prospective laws and regulations to ensure that they are consistent with the governmental duty to respect, protect, and fulfill the right. In some nations, this can be a formal process. For example, in France, the Constitutional

Council reviews proposed legislation prior to its enactment. In other nations, the screening process is informal. Cepeda Espinosa describes a phenomenon in Colombia called the "anticipation effect," in which close supervision by the Constitutional Court compels legislators to consider constitutional case law when drafting and debating the content of new legislation.[3]

The positive influence of the constitutional right to a healthy environment and other constitutional environmental provisions on legislation has been largely overlooked, with most of the scholarly literature focusing on litigation. Yet it may be by contributing to the enactment of stronger legislation that constitutional environmental provisions have their greatest impact. Studies indicate that legislation is more effective than litigation in achieving environmental protection.[4] Legislators can act proactively, whereas courts, by their very nature, can only respond to cases brought to them. Legislation benefits from the existence of institutions, such as environmental ministries or departments, with resources, experience, and technical expertise. As well, if implemented and enforced, legislation tackles all instances of a problem and applies nationally, as opposed to the generally *ad hoc* nature of litigation, where the effects may be limited to the parties. For example, legally binding national air quality standards should, if adequately implemented and enforced, result in cleaner air throughout an entire country. In contrast, a lawsuit will generally focus on improving air quality in a specific location or region. To be sure, litigation can have radiating effects, which are the indirect consequences of litigation that ripple outward through the legal system and into society.[5] Litigation can also be part of a broader strategy and is valued for its "mobilization potential," high public profile, and ability to demand a formal response from government.[6] But radiating effects occur under limited circumstances, whereas legislation is generally intended to have the equivalent of radiating effects.

SAFETY NET

In addition to providing an impetus for strengthening environmental laws, the constitutional right to a healthy environment has also been used by public interest litigants to close gaps in environmental law. Nepal and Costa Rica offer clear examples of courts ordering governments to enact legislation or regulations that would reduce air pollution and protect fisheries, respectively.[7] The courts do not spell out the details of the laws but merely clarify that legislation is an essential element if the government is to meet its obligation to respect, protect, and fulfill the right to a healthy environment. In other

FIGURE 11.1

Overall constitutional influence on environmental legislation and litigation

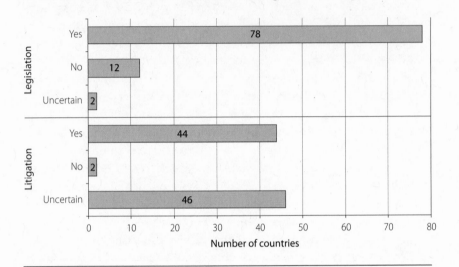

nations, courts refused to compel governments to enact laws but influenced states to take action (e.g., legislation governing plastic bags in Uganda, public smoking in India, and air quality standards in Sri Lanka).[8] Courts do not always side with citizens and NGOs seeking to fill legislative gaps. The Supreme Court of the Philippines, despite agreeing that air pollution from motor vehicles was a toxic threat to health, declined to order the government to convert all of its vehicles to compressed natural gas (CNG) because it believed this would have interfered with legislative and executive responsibilities.[9]

PREVENTS ROLLBACKS

Another theoretical advantage of constitutional recognition of the right to a healthy environment related to environmental law, which is being achieved in practice in some nations, is the prevention of rollbacks. Courts have articulated the principle, based on the constitutional right to a healthy environment, that current environmental laws and policies represent a baseline that can be improved upon but not weakened.[10] In society's quest for sustainable development, courts recognize that there is only one viable direction, and that is stronger environmental laws and policies. Known in Belgium and France as the standstill doctrine, this benefit has also been realized in Hungary, South Africa, and throughout many nations in Latin America.

IMPROVED IMPLEMENTATION AND ENFORCEMENT

Litigation based on the constitutional right to a healthy environment can facilitate increased implementation and enforcement of environmental laws and policies. Citizens, communities, and ENGOs in Latin America, Europe, and Asia have supplemented the enforcement efforts of the state, drawn attention to violations, and provided an impetus for the allocation of additional resources to environmental services and protection. A leading example is the cooperative approach taken in Brazil, where the public and ENGOs report alleged violations of constitutional rights and environmental laws to the independent Ministerio Publico, which can then conduct investigations, civil actions, and prosecutions.[11] Concerned citizens and communities also have the opportunity to enforce laws themselves when the right to a healthy environment is being violated or threatened, or when environmental laws are being broken. As noted earlier, there are over a thousand reported cases where citizen and community enforcement has supplemented the efforts of the state.

Although environmental laws have been strengthened in many nations, the capacity or political will to enforce them still appears to be lacking. As Pound wrote almost a century ago, the "complaint of non-enforcement of law is nothing new. It is as old as the law."[12] The environmental law implementation and enforcement gap is not limited to developing countries but is global in scope. This is illustrated by the fact that a disproportionate number of the European Commission's infringement cases are in the environmental field (as many as one-third in some years, despite environment being a relatively minor policy area compared to sectors such as agriculture, trade, and social policy).[13]

ENVIRONMENTAL JUSTICE

The constitutional right to a healthy environment should, in theory, promote environmental justice by ensuring a minimum standard of environmental quality for all members of society. Although this book offers extensive evidence of a trend toward stronger environmental laws, few of these laws prioritize the people most affected by environmental degradation – the poor, ethnic minorities, and other populations vulnerable to discrimination. However, some politically weak and marginalized communities have enjoyed success in the courts in enforcing their right to a healthy environment. Many cases, particularly in Latin America, deal with the provision of clean water, sewage treatment, and adequate waste management, environmental concerns more likely to confront the poor than middle or upper classes. An Argentine case involving Chacras de la Merced, a poor community whose drinking water was being contaminated by inadequate wastewater treatment in an upstream municipality, illustrates the potential for using the right to a healthy environment to advance environmental justice.[14] An ENGO brought an *amparo* action against the upstream municipality and the province on behalf of local residents, asserting a violation of their constitutional right to a healthy environment. The court agreed that there was a violation of the right and ordered the government to upgrade the wastewater treatment plant and, in the interim, provide a supply of clean water to the residents of Chacras de la Merced.[15] The court-ordered infrastructure improvements were completed, and in an interesting development, the municipality passed a law mandating that all future sewage and sanitation tax revenues must be reinvested in upgrading and maintaining the sewage system.[16] Many poor residents in Colombia, Costa Rica, and Argentina enjoy clean drinking water today because legislation and litigation based on the constitutional right to a healthy environment have compelled governments to make necessary investments in infrastructure and protecting water supplies. In contrast, consider the situation in Canada, a wealthy industrialized nation whose constitution is silent regarding environmental protection and where nearly one hundred communities (predominantly Aboriginal) either lack running water or face long-term boil-water advisories because of inadequate water treatment systems.[17]

Because of litigation based on their constitutional environmental rights, the people of La Oroya, Peru, are finally receiving medical treatment for their long-term exposure to lead and other heavy metals emitted by a nearby smelter.[18] Citizens in Russia, Romania, Chile, and Turkey have brought lawsuits based on their right to a healthy environment and received compensation for threats posed to their health by industrial pollution.[19] There are some situations where systemic changes are being produced by constitutions, legislation, and litigation. In Brazil, litigation based on the constitutional right to a healthy environment resulted in a new government policy that all citizens have the right to a core minimum of environmental services, including water, sanitation, and waste management.[20] In South Africa, constitutional recognition of the right to water has been translated into legislation, policy, and major infrastructure investments. Nelson Mandela has described the extension of clean drinking water to millions of South Africans (predominantly black and poor) since the mid-1990s as "amongst the most important achievements of democracy in our country."[21]

On the other hand, it is harder for the communities most affected by environmental degradation to influence the law- and policy-making process or take advantage of their constitutional right to a healthy environment. Barriers include lack of awareness of their rights, lack of financial resources, lack of access to legal assistance, and distrust of the judicial system. Some critics claim that environmental litigation brought by middle-class litigants to enforce their right to a healthy environment worsens the plight of the poor. For example, the closure or relocation of polluting factories in India is alleged to have displaced workers and caused adverse socio-economic effects.[22] More broadly, there are unresolved questions about "leakage," which occurs when legislation, litigation, or other societal forces displace environmentally harmful activities to poorer nations or regions.[23]

INCREASED PUBLIC INVOLVEMENT

Constitutional environmental provisions have substantially increased the public's role in environmental governance. The right to a healthy environment has been interpreted consistently by legislators, the executive, and the judiciary as including procedural environmental rights – e.g., access to information, participation in decision making, and access to justice. Citizens, in ever-increasing numbers, appear to be using these rights. Other major factors contributing to the growing public role in environmental governance include the enhanced importance of civil society, advances in communications technology (particularly the Internet), and in many nations the transition from closed, authoritarian types of government to open, participatory democracy. A key development in terms of access to justice has been the use of the constitutional right to a healthy environment (and legislation implementing this right) to rewrite traditional rules of standing to include collective and diffuse interests. In many of the nations studied here, administrative processes and courthouse doors are now open to citizens without a traditional economic or personal interest at stake. As a result, the state appears to have lost its monopoly in terms of representing the public interest.

Several Latin American nations – Costa Rica, Colombia, Argentina, and Brazil – are in a class of their own in terms of improving access to justice. Procedural innovations have radically increased the ability of citizens, communities, and ENGOs to seek judicial protection. Simplified, expedited actions include the *amparo, tutela, recurso de proteccion*, direct action of unconstitutionality, popular action, and public civil action. India's Supreme Court, with its simple writ petition procedure, is not far behind, and the Philippines, with its new writ of *kalikasan* and groundbreaking procedural rules for environmental litigation, is moving in the same direction. As M.C. Mehta, the prominent Indian lawyer, writes, "Ordinarily it is very difficult for a citizen to go to court for environmental relief under the existing laws. It is only under the constitutional provisions that it became possible ... to move the courts for judicial relief."[24]

Progress is not uniform across and within all regions. Africa lags behind on all indicators of public involvement due to the extensive social, economic, and political problems facing large swaths of that continent. There is high variability between nations within Eastern Europe and Asia, with a correlation between the overall health of democracy and the extent of public participation in environmental governance. Where authoritarian regimes maintain power, as in Turkmenistan, constitutional environmental provisions are more symbolic than effective. Where democracy is more robust, as in the Philippines and Slovenia, constitutional environmental provisions are more influential.

INCREASED ACCOUNTABILITY

The increased transparency associated with public participation in environmental governance provides a boost to accountability, as does more rigorous enforcement of environmental laws. It is vital to note that public interest litigation based on the constitutional right will be successful only if the government is proven to be violating the constitution through its actions or omissions. Protecting human rights from violations by the state is a legitimate role for the judiciary in a constitutional democracy. What is novel about judicial protection of the right to a healthy environment is that it can impose a positive duty on the state to take preventive or remedial action. In this sense, judicial protection of the right to a healthy environment is distinct from the court's historical role in protecting individuals and their property from state interference. Courts are protecting a collective public interest, which was historically the prerogative of the legislature. By constitutionalizing the right to a healthy environment, both the public and the judiciary are newly empowered to hold governments accountable for protecting the environment. The landmark court decisions regarding the restoration of the Matanza-Riachuelo River in Argentina and of Manila Bay in the Philippines are leading examples.[25] In both cases, a generation of political leaders repeatedly promised to clean up these environmental disasters but took few concrete steps. Litigation brought by concerned citizens, based on the right to a healthy environment, led to strict and detailed court-imposed obligations that will be difficult for current and future political leaders to avoid. In both of these cases, concerns about the non-enforcement of past court orders led courts to create independent monitoring bodies, impose special reporting requirements, and establish substantial penalties for non-compliance.

The influence of the constitutional right to a healthy environment on jurisprudence appears to be less pervasive than its influence on legislation. Court decisions based on the right to a healthy environment have been made in at least forty-four of ninety-two nations and are increasing in frequency and significance (see Figure 11.1). These decisions have been made in almost all surveyed nations in Western Europe (8 out of 9), most nations in Latin America and the Caribbean (13/18), a majority of nations in Eastern Europe (12/19), a minority of nations in Asia (6/14), and only a few nations in Africa (5/32). In at least twelve other nations, high courts have ruled that the right to a healthy environment is implicit in other constitutional rights and therefore directly enforceable. Well over one thousand reported cases are available, with the number per nation ranging from one in Malawi to hundreds in some Latin American, Asian, and European nations, led by Colombia, Costa Rica, Brazil, Argentina, India, the Philippines, Belgium, and Greece. The suggestion that constitutional environmental rights are enforceable in "only a few" or a "handful" of nations is clearly no longer accurate.[26]

Difficulties in accessing the jurisprudence of forty-six nations mean that the statistics presented here may underestimate the full extent of litigation based on the right to a healthy environment. In many nations, not all court decisions are published, which means that a substantial proportion of litigation is not easily accessible to researchers. In India, for example, hundreds of decisions of the Supreme Court are published annually, but these are only a small fraction of the tens of thousands of cases heard by the court.[27] Stec and Kravchenko both identify the difficulty of locating judicial decisions from courts in Central and Eastern Europe.[28]

Available data – from Europe, Brazil, Colombia, Costa Rica, and India – indicate that the majority of lawsuits based on the constitutional right to a healthy environment are successful.[29] In Brazil, it appears that environmental public civil actions are successful in 67.5 percent of cases.[30] In Colombia, applicants were successful in 53 percent of the *acciones populares* related to drinking water that were based on the right to a healthy environment and brought between 1991 and 2008.[31] In Costa Rica, it appears that roughly 66 percent of cases asserting violations of the right to a healthy environment are successful.[32] Jariwala estimated that nearly 80 percent of environmental cases brought in India up to 1999 were successful.[33]

Looking at the numbers on a regional basis, enforcement of the constitutional right to a healthy environment is common in Latin America and Western Europe, is becoming more frequent in parts of Eastern Europe and Asia (particularly South Asia), and remains rare in Africa. Twenty-seven of the forty-six nations for which no court decisions are available are in Africa. This regional pattern is broadly consistent with Epp's hypothesis about the rights revolution, which stipulates that certain conditions need to be present in order for courts to play a significant role in defending human rights.[34] The presence of these conditions – which include clear constitutional provisions, the rule of law, an independent and activist judiciary, and legal infrastructure supportive of rights-based litigation (e.g., lawyers, NGOs, networks, and funding) – appears to be positively correlated with the extent of court decisions about the right to a healthy environment in each of the five regions examined. Clear constitutional articulation of the right (as in, for example, Costa Rica, Brazil, Colombia, and Argentina) will generally lead to a larger role for courts than an ambiguous provision (e.g., that of Spain). India and other nations where courts have recognized an implicit constitutional right to a healthy environment are exceptions to this generalization. The absence of the rule of law, in combination with daunting social, economic, and political problems, dramatically reduces the potential influence of the constitutional right in Africa, although South Africa offers hope that the situation can be reversed.

One central element of Epp's hypothesis regarding the rights revolution may need rethinking in light of the evidence presented in Chapters 6 to 10. According to Epp, the litigation support structure – e.g., rights lawyers, NGOs, networks, and funding sources – is a prerequisite to the rights revolution.[35] Yet in several Latin American nations – Costa Rica, Colombia, and Brazil in particular – the environmental rights revolution has taken place without these elements playing a central role. Because of remarkable innovations in legal procedures, such as the *amparo* and *tutela*, that simplify and expedite cases involving constitutional rights, individuals and communities have been able to bring lawsuits without lawyers, funding, or support from NGOs. The Philippines is implementing a similar suite of procedural reforms, as well as the novel writ of *kalikasan* (nature) that incorporates remedies specifically designed for environmental cases. In Brazil, the constitutional changes that empowered the Ministerio Publico to enforce constitutional environmental provisions resulted in a dramatic increase in enforcement without relying on the litigation support structure described by Epp.[36]

Courts have ruled that the constitutional right to a healthy environment imposes three duties upon government: to respect the right by not infringing it through state action; to protect the right from infringement by third parties (which may require regulations, implementation, and enforcement); and to take actions to fulfill the right (e.g., by providing environmental services, including clean water, sanitation, and waste management). As well, courts have consistently held that laws, regulations, and administrative actions that violate the constitutional right to a healthy environment will be struck down. The Netherlands provides a limited exception, as courts are not permitted to review the constitutionality of legislation.

It is uncommon for courts to decide that the constitutional right to a healthy environment is not directly enforceable, although this is the case in South Korea, Spain, Mexico, the Czech Republic, Slovakia, and, because of a recent court decision that reversed earlier precedents, Paraguay. In most of these nations, the courts are following constitutional language that specifies that the right can only be enforced pursuant to enabling legislation (i.e., the right is not self-executing). However, these nations are exceptions to the general rule that the constitutional right to a healthy environment is a directly enforceable right. Even in nations where the constitutional right to a healthy environment does not appear to be directly enforceable or self-executing, it can still play an important role in litigation, as the experiences of Andorra, Belgium, and France demonstrate. Overall, constitutional principles related to the right to a healthy environment "have created the right conditions for courts of law ... to begin to play a more prominent role in protecting the environment."[37]

LEVEL PLAYING FIELD

Another theoretical advantage of the constitutional right to a healthy environment is the prospect of a level playing field with competing social and economic rights. The strengthening of environmental laws chronicled in Chapters 6 to 10 represents a significant advance in that direction. Environmental legislation often constrains the exercise of property rights, recognizing that there are circumstances in which the public interest should take precedence over private interests. There is case law in many nations where courts have rejected constitutional challenges against environmental laws or administrative decisions in which plaintiffs alleged that their property rights were violated. Courts have referred to constitutional protection of the environment as a compelling rationale that can justify the infringement of private property rights.[38] South Korea and Israel are rare examples of nations where courts have ruled that property rights continue to trump the right to a healthy environment.[39]

Rights can and do collide, in complex, multi-faceted disputes. A plan to run electricity lines through Canaima Park in Venezuela to reach Brazil caused

ENGOs to protest a violation of their environmental rights, indigenous people their cultural rights, and business its economic rights.[40] The constitutional right to a healthy environment is not applied as a systematic trump card. Courts go to great efforts to balance competing rights and conflicting social priorities. For example, in a Turkish case involving air pollution from coal-fired power plants, the courts ordered installation of pollution abatement equipment instead of requiring the plants to be closed.[41] Some would argue that courts have not gone far enough to level the playing field, particularly in cases involving powerful economic interests, such as India's Sardar Sarovar Dam, Peru's Camisea natural gas project, or French controversies involving genetically modified crops.[42] On the other hand, the constitutional right to a healthy environment played an instrumental role in the Greek Council of State's repeated decisions to strike down approvals for the Acheloos water diversion project,[43] the Finnish Supreme Administrative Court's decision blocking the Vuotos hydroelectric project,[44] Costa Rican court decisions blocking offshore oil and gas development,[45] the Ecuadorian Constitutional Court's rejection of the Baba Dam,[46] Hungarian and Russian court decisions preventing the privatization of public forests,[47] and the Thai Supreme Court's decision to block dozens of petrochemical projects.[48] All of these cases involved powerful actors and major economic consequences, yet courts took bold decisions.

Finally, the constitutionalization of the right to a healthy environment can have a systemic effect on the exercise of discretion by legislators, judges, and public authorities, pushing countless decisions in a more environmentally sustainable direction. At a minimum, constitutional provisions requiring environmental protection should ensure a better balancing of competing interests than has been the case in the past. For example, in Belgium, "courts are no longer inclined when facing conflicting interests, to automatically sacrifice environmental interests in favor of economic interests."[49]

EDUCATION

Among the many laws spurred, at least in part, by the constitutionalization of environmental protection are national laws related to environmental education in, for instance, the Philippines, Armenia, South Korea, and Brazil.[50] Courts in India, Argentina, and the Philippines have ordered governments to develop and implement environmental education programs.[51] The *Charter for the Environment* has reportedly revitalized environmental education in France.[52] Further research is required to determine whether the constitutional right to a healthy environment is contributing to increased ecological literacy.

The Theoretical Disadvantages of Constitutionalizing the Right to a Healthy Environment

Practical experience with the right to a healthy environment is debunking many of the theoretical criticisms and potential drawbacks associated with it, while lending some support to two important critiques – that it is undemocratic and ineffective – that continue to raise substantive concerns.

Vague, Absolute, and Redundant?

The argument has been made that the constitutional right to a healthy environment is too vague to be implemented and protected effectively. Yet at least seventy-eight national legislatures and courts in at least fifty-six nations have managed to interpret and implement the right, as hundreds of laws and more than a thousand court decisions demonstrate. There is an occasional exception, such as the 2008 Supreme Court decision in Paraguay that suggested that the impreciseness of the right was one reason for deferring to the legislature.[53] The variety of adjectives used to describe the right – healthy, clean, safe, favourable, etc. – does not appear to influence the outcome of litigation. Concerns that the right to a healthy environment would be applied in an absolutist fashion have not materialized in any of the nations whose constitutions recognize the right. Neither legislatures nor courts have used environmental rights to systematically trump other rights, opting instead for careful balancing. The extensive reliance upon the right to a healthy environment by legislators, citizens, communities, ENGOs, and judges should put to rest the notion that it duplicates the protection offered by other human rights or existing environmental laws.

Anthropocentric?

Among the seventy-eight nations where legislation has been influenced by constitutional environmental provisions, many laws intended to protect forests, oceans, wildlife, and biodiversity have been enacted. While an argument can be made that there are anthropocentric motives for the conservation and preservation of Nature, a growing number of these laws also include recognition of the intrinsic value of the natural world. In some cases this recognition is implicit, while in other cases it is explicit. For example, one of the general principles of Costa Rica's *Law of Biodiversity* is "Respect for all forms of life. All living things have the right to live, independently of actual or potential economic value."[54]

Citizens, NGOs, and prosecutors have brought many successful lawsuits to protect Nature itself – national parks, dolphins, sharks, lakes, forests, rivers, birds, sea turtles, salamanders, and other species.[55] A leading Portuguese case concerned swallows nesting on the outer wall of a courthouse. Workers claimed that dust from the nests was disturbing them, causing a nuisance and allergies, so the government planned to destroy the nests. Instead, a lawsuit was filed and the court ordered the protection of the birds' homes.[56] As Collins proposed, the right to a healthy environment is being "understood as encompassing both human-centred and eco-centric aspects, as in an environment that is both healthy for humans and healthy in its own right (e.g., a healthy lake, a healthy forest, a healthy ecosystem)."[57] Based on the enactment of new environmental laws and the rulings of courts, the constitutional right to a healthy environment, while technically a human right, is having positive ecocentric spillover effects.[58]

CULTURAL IMPERIALISM?

Evidence also undermines the critique of cultural imperialism. National legislatures in all regions of the world – South, North, East, and West – have enacted constitutions and laws that recognize the right to a healthy environment. Unlike deregulation, privatization, and other policies imposed on nations by international financial institutions, there is no powerful source of international pressure compelling nations to recognize environmental rights, apart from civil society. For example, in drafting its paradigm-shifting constitutional provisions recognizing the rights of Pachamama (Nature), the government of Ecuador took the initiative of seeking input from experts around the world. High courts in all regions of the world are directly applying and protecting the right to a healthy environment, again undermining the cultural imperialism argument. Ironically, it is Western nations – including the United States, the United Kingdom, Canada, and Australia – where constitutional protection for the environment, including the right to a healthy environment, lags behind. Further undermining the cultural imperialism argument is the fact that among the decisions cited most frequently by constitutional and supreme courts around the world are those of the Supreme Court of India.

UNENFORCEABLE OR UNJUSTICIABLE?

In practice, for the most part, the constitutional right to a healthy environment is treated as an enforceable right, unless the constitution itself clearly states that it is strictly a guiding principle (e.g., Spain) or requires enabling legislation in order for it to be implemented (e.g., the Czech Republic). As noted earlier, the right is enforceable in at least fifty nations. There are only a handful of countries – South Korea, Mexico, the Czech Republic, Slovakia, and Paraguay – where courts have declined to enforce the constitutional right to a healthy environment.

The argument that the right to a healthy environment, like other social and economic rights, should not be justiciable because policy decisions are the sole purview of the legislature also ought to be put to rest by the evidence in Chapters 6 to 10. This theoretical objection is largely extinguished by the willingness of courts to take a principled and pragmatic approach to the question of rights, balancing the interests of the individual with the interests of society in the context of specific facts and circumstances. Beatty concludes that recent "jurisprudence shows that a lot of judges think that the legal enforcement of social and economic rights isn't so different from the protection that is provided by the more traditional political and civil guarantees."[59] The same could be said regarding legal enforcement of environmental rights. Courts do not generally dictate environmental policy, except in exceptional circumstances, but they do critically scrutinize government policies and actions to determine whether they offer adequate protection for constitutional rights. The case involving the restoration of the Matanza-Riachuelo River in Argentina illustrates how today's judiciaries can undermine the objection that courts are not an appropriate arena for addressing polycentric disputes.[60] Argentina's Supreme Court opened its doors to multiple parties and *amici curiae* (friends of the court), held public hearings, and engaged independent experts. The Supreme Court of the Philippines employed a similar approach in the *Manila Bay* case.

Open the Floodgates to Litigation?

As Chapters 6 to 10 demonstrate, constitutional recognition of the right to a healthy environment does result in additional cases being brought to court. In some nations with very open rules regarding standing and expedited procedures, such as India, Brazil, Colombia, Argentina, and Costa Rica, courts face a huge caseload, resulting in backlogs and delays that may result in injustices.[61] However, cases based on the right to a healthy environment represent a very small fraction of the total number of constitutional cases in any given nation, according to empirical evidence from Europe and Latin America.[62] In Colombia, for example, since 1991 there have been over 300,000 lawsuits filed to enforce the constitutional right to health, which is roughly three hundred times the number of cases brought to enforce the right to a healthy environment.[63] Environmental lawsuits tend to have a relatively high success rate, negating the related argument that frivolous and vexatious lawsuits will proliferate if standing and procedural rules are relaxed.

UNDEMOCRATIC

The first drawback of constitutionalizing the right to a healthy environment that finds some support in the national experiences surveyed in Chapters 6 to 10 involves potentially undemocratic consequences. This argument does not apply to the right's influence on legislation, since duly enacted laws express the will of the people through their democratically elected representatives. The critique focuses on the role of the judiciary and the potential judicialization of politics. For the most part, courts are well aware of the separation of powers and act conscientiously to avoid crossing the line into legislative and executive action. This is especially true in new democracies, where courts recognize that an excessively ambitious judicial agenda may cause undue politicization and undermine both the legitimacy of the courts and the foundation of the rule of law.[64]

In some nations, however, judges have taken an activist stance in interpreting and applying social and economic rights as well as the constitutional right to a healthy environment. Excessive judicial activism can remove contentious issues from the democratic arena and create a risk that governments responsible for environmental protection will be unable to properly establish priorities or allocate resources. The argument of the critics is perhaps particularly forceful in the twelve nations where courts have enforced the right to a healthy environment despite the absence of explicit constitutional language guaranteeing the right.[65] The most notorious example is the Supreme Court of India, which has been accused of crossing the line in several high-profile cases, including the Delhi motor vehicle case, the Ganges water pollution case, and the forest conservation case.[66] Some of the court's orders in these controversial cases may have trespassed into the legislative or executive realms. On the other hand, the court's actions can be justified on the basis of government's persistent failure to implement and enforce India's environmental laws, as mandated by the constitution.

There are two compelling rebuttals to the charge that the constitutional right to a healthy environment is undemocratic. The first lies in the expansion and enforcement of procedural environmental rights. Improving access to information and participation in environmental decision making can actually enhance democracy by enabling more people to play a hands-on role in shaping the policies and decisions that affect their lives.[67] The survey of legislation and litigation in Chapters 6 to 10 demonstrates that the constitutional right to a healthy environment is contributing to democracy by providing a robust legal basis for the enjoyment of these procedural rights. In general, constitutional recognition of environmental rights in Latin America and Europe, and to a lesser extent in other regions, has "created a vehicle for new and more democratic relations to resolve conflicts between the state and civil society."[68]

The second rebuttal is that excessive judicial activism is rare and must be distinguished from cases where courts are fulfilling their legitimate roles as constitutional guardians. Constitutions empower courts to safeguard human rights, so the judiciary is fulfilling one of its basic functions by protecting the right to a healthy environment. A judge from the Supreme Court of the Philippines responded to criticism of the *Manila Bay* judgment by stating, "Surely, it is not judicial activism when courts carry out their constitutionally assigned function of judicial review and in the process enjoin those charged with implementing a law to so implement the law."[69] South Africa has gained worldwide renown for the seemingly constructive democratic dialogue between judges and legislators, with courts telling governments that they must make best efforts to fulfill social and economic rights (e.g., housing, water) without necessarily spelling out in detail how to do so, except in compelling circumstances (e.g., requiring nationwide provision of nevirapine to pregnant women with HIV/AIDS).[70] Corder and other experts have concluded that "an admirable balance has been struck between activism and restraint" in South African courts.[71]

INEFFECTIVE

The second substantive criticism directed at constitutionalizing the right to a healthy environment is that it will be ineffective because it fails to address the underlying political economy of environmental degradation. There is undoubtedly some truth to this claim, as neither constitutions nor human rights can magically solve deep-rooted societal problems related to capitalism, globalization, and the growing gap between rich and poor. However, experience indicates that the right can act as a countervailing force to some of the factors identified as key drivers of unsustainability, including deregulation and privatization. For example, the standstill doctrine (described earlier in this chapter and in Chapter 10 under Belgium) effectively blocks deregulation unless there is a compelling societal justification for rolling back environmental laws. Courts from Costa Rica to Russia have struck down efforts to privatize public resources, from forests to the seabed.[72] In fact, Costa

Rica's Constitutional Court has even reversed the process of privatization by mandating the expropriation of privately owned land that provides critical habitat for endangered sea turtles.[73] Critics should bear in mind that the main reason environmental legislation is ineffective is a lack of implementation and enforcement. Constitutionalizing the right to a healthy environment, as demonstrated in Chapters 6 to 10, provides multiple means for improving implementation and enforcement.

Critics of constitutional rights argue that civil and political rights have been appropriated by societal elites to entrench and extend their power (e.g., corporations have used the right to free speech to strike down government regulation of advertising).[74] However, the right to a healthy environment has been used predominantly to advance public, not private, interests. The only prominent example to the contrary is the South African case where the Fuel Retailers Association used the right to a healthy environment to protect itself from competition.[75] In general, the right to a healthy environment and other constitutional environmental provisions impose positive obligations on the state and are thus pro-government rather than anti-government. In Latin America, and particularly in the leading nations of Costa Rica, Colombia, Argentina, and Brazil, constitutional litigation (including but not limited to the right to a healthy environment) is beginning to alter some of the structural inequalities and power relations that are at the heart of unsustainability.[76]

A second concern about effectiveness that arises from the legislation and litigation reviewed in Chapters 6 to 10 is the danger of proceduralization.[77] Koskenniemi describes "proceduralization" as a process in which courts seek outcomes that are broadly acceptable to parties by focusing on process rather than substantive outcomes. In nations where there is a major emphasis on procedural environmental rights – which is particularly the case in Europe, as a result of the *Aarhus Convention* – there is a possibility that substantive outcomes will go unchallenged or unchanged. In the Netherlands, one of the main reasons for the decline in environmental litigation is that courts focus almost exclusively on the procedural aspects of government decision making and are reluctant to scrutinize the substantive rationale for decisions, or their potential consequences.[78] Many lawsuits in Eastern Europe based on the right to a healthy environment appear to fall into the same category. Cases are brought to force the disclosure of environmental information or require greater public participation in environmental decision making, but environmentally harmful projects and policies continue after procedural shortcomings have been rectified. A common occurrence, for example, is opponents of an environmentally damaging project filing a lawsuit alleging deficiencies in the environmental assessment process, winning the lawsuit, and then watching as the procedural deficiencies are remedied and approval is granted for the project to proceed.

A third concern about the effectiveness of litigation based on the constitutional right to a healthy environment is that some governments do not respect or implement court orders. A notorious example is gas flaring in Nigeria, which continues despite a court's conclusion that this practice violates the right to a healthy environment. Citizens in Peru, Turkey, Romania, and Russia have won cases in court based on their constitutional right to a healthy environment, only to see governments circumvent the courts' decisions, forcing citizens to take their cases to the Inter-American Commission on Human Rights and the European Court of Human Rights. There are also instances where, in the dialogue between courts and legislatures, the latter insist on having the last word even though courts have determined that a project violates constitutional rights. For example, the OECD reports that the government of Greece has passed legislation overturning environmental decisions of the Council of State.[79]

Conclusion

Four key findings emerge from this review of legislation and litigation in the ninety-two nations whose constitutions explicitly recognize the right to live in a healthy environment. First, the majority (seventy-eight out of ninety-two) of these nations have taken the important step of incorporating the right to live in a healthy environment in their major environmental laws. While largely overlooked in previous analyses, this influence on legislation may represent the most important effect of constitutionalizing environmental rights, although litigation garners far more media and scholarly attention. Second, constitutions are having a less pervasive but growing influence on the filing and adjudication of environmental lawsuits. Third, procedural environmental rights – to information, participation in decision making, and access to justice – are almost universally recognized as complements to the substantive right to a healthy environment. Thus the suggestion, often encountered in the literature, that a choice must be made between substantive and procedural environmental rights is outdated.

Fourth, the foregoing examination of national environmental laws and jurisprudence provides a fairly robust and extensive body of empirical evidence that constitutional environmental rights are delivering many of the anticipated benefits and few of the potential drawbacks forecast by legal experts. To some degree, this may not be surprising, given that constitutions are intended to create meta-rules that guide legislators, administrative decision makers, and judges. For practical purposes, there are still some nations, predominantly in Africa, and to a lesser extent in Asia and Eastern Europe, where the rule of law and a functioning legal order are still not present. In some nations, democracy is still in its infancy and "the political and legal climates do not tolerate litigation and political activism."[80]

This research also reveals extensive synergy between constitutional provisions, environmental legislation, and litigation. Constitutional provisions can spur stronger, more comprehensive legislation and create unprecedented opportunities for public participation. Litigation can be used to compel governments to fill gaps, implement laws, enforce laws, and exercise their discretion in more environmentally friendly ways. The constitutional basis of environmental laws can insulate them to some degree from legal and political challenges, potentially contributing to greater certainty in their application. Increasing the enforcement of environmental laws, and applying them more consistently, can lead to enhanced respect for both the environment and the rule of law.

It should be reiterated that stronger environmental laws, increased public participation, and ecologically conscious court decisions are merely means toward the ultimate objective of reducing environmental degradation and improving human well-being. Whether the constitutional right to a healthy environment is effective is ultimately a question that goes beyond legal considerations and requires assessment of environmental outcomes such as cleaner air, cleaner water, and reduced pressure on natural resources. The question of whether constitutionalizing environmental protection has a systemic, quantifiable effect on environmental performance is the focus of the next chapter.

12

Do Environmental Provisions in Constitutions Influence Environmental Performance?

> The appropriate strategy for research in this area is to remove
> the strong ideological lenses and systematically to examine the
> evidence in an effort to distinguish the rhetoric from the reality.
>
> – J.J. Donohue, "The Legal Response to
> Discrimination: Does Law Matter?"

The majority of nations (147 out of 193) have incorporated environmental protection provisions into their constitutions. The right to a healthy environment is entrenched in the constitutions of ninety-two nations. Legislatures in at least seventy-seven nations have rewritten environmental laws to reflect constitutional recognition of the right. Courts in at least fifty-six countries have made decisions interpreting and enforcing the right. In light of these developments, it is essential to assess whether, and to what extent, the right to a healthy environment is affecting the environmental performance of nations – improving environmental quality, decreasing the prevalence of adverse effects on human health, and reducing pressure on ecosystems.

There are two types of quantitative studies used in comparative constitutional law – basic and advanced. Basic quantitative studies are exploratory, asking if there is a relationship between a constitutional feature and another variable of interest. For example, Montenegro found a negative correlation between the length of a constitution and economic performance (as measured by GDP per capita).[1] Kinney and Clark found no correlation between constitutional recognition of the right to health and per capita health care expenditures.[2] Hirschl found no correlation between the constitutionalization of rights and improvements in the status of disadvantaged groups in terms of education, access to health care, housing, employment, and income.[3] Basic quantitative studies can only demonstrate correlation; they do not imply causation.

In contrast, advanced quantitative studies are more sophisticated, using multiple regression models to determine if there is a causal relationship between a constitutional feature or provision and one or more dependent variables. For example, Barrett and Graddy sought to determine whether civil and political freedoms affect environmental quality. Their hypothesis was that environmental outcomes depend on

> citizens being able to acquire information about the quality of their environment, to assemble and organize, and to give voice to their preferences for environmental quality; and on governments having an incentive to satisfy these preferences by changing policy, perhaps the most powerful incentive being the desire to get elected or re-elected. In short, they will depend on civil and political freedoms.[4]

Barrett and Graddy conducted a sophisticated regression analysis using income, population density, industrial structure, geography, and civil/political freedoms as explanatory variables, and several measures of environmental quality as the dependent variables. They found that increasing civil and political freedoms has a demonstrable, beneficial effect on environmental quality.[5]

This chapter takes the basic approach, asking whether there is a relationship between constitutional provisions requiring environmental protection and environmental performance. The results of this analysis, to be clear, are not capable of demonstrating conclusively that constitutionalizing environmental protection does (or does not) cause improved environmental performance. As noted in Chapter 1, Hayward discounted the possibility of conducting such an examination because of methodological difficulties.[6] Shelton also observed that "causality is difficult to demonstrate."[7] The crux of the problem is that there are many factors that can influence environmental performance. Because of multiple causality, it is difficult to disentangle the effects of constitutional provisions related to the environment from other potentially influential factors, including a nation's geographic size, population density, wealth, economic structure, level of urbanization, income inequality, international trade profile (i.e., types of imports and exports), public opinion, history, climate, natural resource endowment, and socio-economic status.[8]

As well, the time frame required to observe differences in environmental performance flowing from the implementation of constitutional provisions is difficult to establish and will vary from nation to nation depending on legislative and judicial processes as well as political, social, economic, and cultural factors. For example, it will take time to strengthen environmental legislation, create and implement detailed regulations, and enhance the capacity of the public service. Similarly, it will take time for concerned citizens or civil society to identify violations of constitutional rights or duties and then file lawsuits. The judicial process, including appeals, can contribute to additional delay. All of these factors could result in a significant lag before constitutional provisions related to the environment have an effect. To isolate the effects of constitutionalization and conclude that environmental provisions in constitutions cause changes in environmental outcomes is possible but would require advanced quantitative analysis that is beyond the scope of this book.

Challenges in Measuring Environmental Performance

There is no ideal approach to making cross-national comparisons of environmental performance.[9] Gleditsch and Sverdrup observe that "compared to existing data sets for economic performance, demographic developments, political rights, democratization, or armed conflict, international data sets for environmental issues are still in their infancy."[10] There are countless potential sources of data that could be used to evaluate the environmental performance of nations, all of which have advantages and disadvantages.[11] Data on environmental performance are often plagued by problems, including differences in definition (e.g., the definition of municipal waste may include commercial and construction waste or merely household waste); data quality problems (e.g., unaudited self-reporting of toxic releases by industry); and gaps in data (e.g., emissions data for some air pollutants may be unavailable for some years).

Indicators used to measure environmental performance can be divided into three categories: pressure, state, and response.[12] Greenhouse gas emissions, water consumption, and pesticides used per square kilometre of arable land are pressure indicators. Ambient levels of air pollutants and the number of endangered species are state indicators. Pollution abatement and control expenditures, proportion of tax revenues from environmental taxes, and ratification of international agreements are response indicators.

It is important to acknowledge that different approaches to measuring environmental performance can produce disparate, even contradictory, results.[13] A nation like Denmark fares reasonably well according to some environmental indices (e.g., third of 30 OECD nations according to environmental rankings compiled by researchers at Simon Fraser University) and poorly on other indices (e.g., fourth-largest per capita ecological footprint among 150 nations, 32nd of 163 nations on Yale University's Environmental Performance Index).[14] No single indicator or index is optimal, and their limitations and biases should be made clear when using them. The use of several indices (triangulation) may be helpful in overcoming the weaknesses of a single index. This chapter focuses on environmental performance, not the broader issue of sustainability, which incorporates social and economic considerations.

Constitutions and Environmental Performance

To minimize the problems associated with individual environmental indicators, this chapter relies on three indices and four indicators that measure environmental performance. Specifically, this chapter examines the following data:

- the ecological footprints of 150 nations
- the ranking of 30 nations in the Organisation for Economic Co-operation and Development (OECD) based on twenty-nine environmental indicators, conducted by researchers at Simon Fraser University
- the ranking of the 17 largest and wealthiest OECD nations based on fifteen environmental indicators selected by the Conference Board of Canada
- the ratification of major international environmental agreements
- time-series data related to nitrogen oxide emissions (1980-2005), sulphur dioxide emissions (1980-2005), and greenhouse gas emissions (1990-2005).

For purposes of comparison, nations were divided into three groups:

- nations with no constitutional provisions related to environmental protection
- nations with constitutional provisions requiring the government to protect the environment but no explicit recognition of the right to live in a healthy environment
- nations whose constitutions include both a government duty to protect the environment and the right to a healthy environment.

This approach enables not only a comparison between nations with and without environmental provisions in their constitutions but also a comparison of the relative effects of different types of constitutional provisions.

THE ECOLOGICAL FOOTPRINT

The ecological footprint measures how much of the regenerative capacity of the biosphere is used by human activities.[15] Based primarily on UN statistics, the ecological footprint is defined as "the area of biologically productive land and water required to produce the resources consumed and to assimilate the wastes generated by humanity, under the predominant management and production practices in any given year."[16] Calculations of the ecological footprint include the area of land and water needed to produce crops, livestock, fish, wood products, and energy, as well as the area needed to absorb the carbon dioxide produced by burning fossil fuels. Footprints are generally compared with biological capacity to determine whether a nation is living within its means or whether the Earth can sustain a particular nation's or individual's level of impact. Overshoot (exceeding biocapacity) at the national level is not necessarily unsustainable, as international trade provides a means of appropriating biocapacity from other nations. Overshoot at the global level is inherently unsustainable.

Like any composite environmental metric, the ecological footprint has strengths and weaknesses.[17] One of the main strengths is that it reflects strong sustainability, which is based on the premise that not all ecological functions and resources can be substituted with technological or other anthropogenic replacements, whereas weak sustainability assumes universal substitution.[18] In other words, the ecological footprint "highlights the reality of the limited biological carrying capacity of the planet."[19] Ferguson concludes that the ecological footprint is "the best method available for making a quantitative assessment of the extent to which consumption is exceeding biocapacity."[20] Another strength is that the ecological footprint aggregates in a single unit (hectares) a large number of heterogeneous impacts, which makes it a simple and understandable metric.[21] Its proponents argue that the ecological footprint has become "a leading biophysical accounting tool for comparing present aggregate human demand on the biosphere with the Earth's gross ecological capacity to sustain human life."[22]

Its creators acknowledge that the ecological footprint is exclusively a measure of anthropogenic pressure on the environment and does not measure the state of the environment or ecosystem health; depletion of nonrenewable materials; problems associated with the release of persistent bioaccumulative toxic chemicals; or non-ecological aspects of sustainability.[23] The ecological footprint also has methodological limitations in terms of how it deals with freshwater use, nuclear power, non-carbon dioxide greenhouse gas emissions, and waste flows (except to the extent that these factors contribute to reduced bioproductivity).[24]

The ecological footprint has been the subject of extensive methodological critiques. Noted weaknesses include the potential inadequacy of the assumptions required to convert consumption data into land area and convert energy use into land area used to absorb carbon dioxide emissions. Critics have noted that there are other ways to sequester carbon dioxide emissions beyond absorption by forests. The ecological footprint has also been criticized for the following weaknesses:

● pays inadequate attention to the oceans[25]
● fails to acknowledge that trade, technological change, and substitution can increase biocapacity[26]
● exaggerates energy and land use impacts[27]
● fails to incorporate variability within nations.[28]

Some criticisms have been addressed through improvements in the methodology of calculating the ecological footprint.[29] A review of six widely used environmental metrics found that the ecological footprint came the closest to approximating strong sustainability.[30] An increasing number of governments are incorporating the ecological footprint into their planning and monitoring programs.[31] Although it clearly has weaknesses, the ecological footprint provides a useful single measure for assessing the relative ecological sustainability of different nations.[32]

Data published by the Global Footprint Network in 2008 were used to compare the ecological footprints of 150 nations.[33] Overall, the 34 nations without any environmental protection provisions in their constitution had an ecological footprint averaging 3.58 hectares per capita, while the 116 nations with environmental protection provisions in their constitution had an ecological footprint averaging 2.36 hectares per capita (see Figure 12.1). In each of the five regions (Africa, Americas, Asia-Pacific, Europe, and Middle East/Central Asia), the ecological footprints of nations with constitutional environmental provisions were smaller (see Table 12.1). Analysis indicates that the difference in average ecological footprints is statistically significant

FIGURE 12.1

Constitutions and ecological footprints: Global

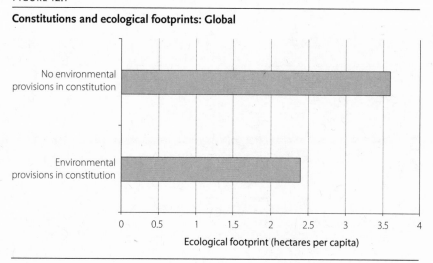

Ecological footprint (hectares per capita)

globally and in the Asia-Pacific, Europe, and Middle East/Central Asia regions (see Appendix 1 for additional details on statistical methods).

ENVIRONMENTAL RANKINGS OF OECD NATIONS

In 2005, researchers at Simon Fraser University (SFU) compared the environmental performance of the nations in the Organisation for Economic Co-operation and Development (OECD) on a suite of twenty-nine indicators.[34] The OECD regularly publishes comprehensive environmental data for its member nations and employs an extensive due diligence process to ensure reliability and comparability of data.[35] Despite the OECD's best efforts, there are still differences in the quality of data collected by member nations, conflicting definitions, and variation in data availability.[36] The SFU study is weighted toward pressure indicators (eighteen), with fewer state (four) and response (seven) indicators.[37] The twenty-nine indicators are listed in Table 12.2.

The SFU study is distinct from the ecological footprint comparison in several ways. First, the ecological footprint data involved a heterogeneous group of 150 nations large and small, rich and poor. The thirty OECD nations are more homogeneous, including twenty-seven wealthy industrialized nations and three newly industrializing countries (i.e., Poland, Mexico, and Turkey).[38] Second, the SFU data include a mixture of pressure, state, and

TABLE 12.1

Constitutional provisions and ecological footprints

	Nations without EPIC	Nations with duty	Nations with duty/rights	Regional average
Africa	1.8 (n = 11)	1.4 (n =13)	1.3 (n = 23)	1.4 (n = 47)
Asia-Pacific	3.7 (n = 8)	1.3 (n = 9)	2.0 (n = 6)	2.3 (n = 23)
Americas	4.2 (n = 5)	2.3 (n = 4)	2.4 (n = 15)	2.8 (n = 24)
Middle East/ Central Asia	4.8 (n = 6)	2.5 (n = 8)	1.6 (n = 7)	2.9 (n = 21)
Europe	5.6 (n = 4)	4.8 (n = 7)	3.9 (n = 24)	4.3 (n = 35)
Global average	3.6 (n = 34)	2.2 (n = 41)	2.4 (n = 75)	2.6 (n = 150)

Note: All mean ecological footprint measurements are given in hectares per capita.
EPIC – Environmental provisions in constitutions
Duty – Government has obligation to protect the environment
Rights – Individuals have right to live in a healthy environment

response indicators, whereas the ecological footprint focuses exclusively on pressure indicators. Although there is some overlap, the reliance on different indicators is likely to result in different assessments of environmental performance.

The SFU study ranked each country from 1 (best) to 30 (worst) for each indicator. The average rank for each country was calculated based on equal weighting for all twenty-nine indicators, and that average was used to provide an overall country rank. The advantage of this approach is its simplicity. The disadvantage is that the ordinal scale measures only whether one nation is ahead of another nation; it does not measure the magnitude of the difference. Nations far apart in ranks may still be relatively close in environmental performance, whereas countries close in ranking may be far apart in environmental performance.

A clear pattern is evident from the ranking of OECD nations (see Table 12.3). Fourteen of the fifteen top-performing nations have constitutions that include protection for the environment. Denmark is the sole exception. Conversely, nine of the fifteen nations making up the bottom half of the OECD rankings lack constitutional environmental provisions. Among the seven nations with the worst environmental records, only Belgium has constitutional provisions related to the environment. (The reasons Denmark and Belgium are outliers are explored later in this chapter.) The average ranking of the twenty nations with environmental rights and/or responsibilities in their constitutions is 12.2 (where 1 is the top-performing nation and 30 is

TABLE 12.2

Indicators used in SFU's environmental comparison of OECD nations

Indicator	Measured by
Energy consumption	Tonnes of oil equivalent per capita annually
Energy intensity	Tonnes of oil equivalent per US$1,000 of GDP
Water consumption	Cubic metres per capita annually
Environmental pricing	Environmental taxes as percent of GDP
Greenhouse gas emissions	Tonnes of carbon dioxide equivalent per capita annually.
Renewable energy including hydro	Percent of electricity supply
Renewable energy excluding hydro	Percent of electricity supply
Sulphur oxides	Kilograms per capita emitted annually
Nitrogen oxides	Kilograms per capita emitted annually
Volatile organic compounds	Non-methane kilograms per capita emitted annually
Carbon monoxide	Kilograms per capita emitted annually
Ozone-depleting substances	Kilograms per capita released annually
Municipal waste	Kilograms per capita produced annually
Recycling of municipal waste	Percent of municipal waste recycled annually
Nuclear waste	Kilograms per capita produced annually
Pollution abatement and control expenditures	Percent of GDP
Municipal sewage treatment	Percent of population served by treatment
Pesticide use	Kilograms per square kilometre of arable land
Fertilizer use	Tonnes per square kilometre of arable land
Livestock	Sheep equivalent per square kilometre of arable land and grassland
Species at risk	Number
Species at risk	Percent
Protected areas	Percent of land base
Timber harvest	Cubic metres per square kilometre of forestland
Timber harvest	Ratio to forest growth
Capture fisheries	Kilograms per capita
Fisheries	As percentage of world catch
Distance travelled	Vehicle kilometres per capita
Official development assistance	Percent of Gross National Income

Source: Simon Fraser University Sustainable Planning Research Group (2005).

Table 12.3

Constitutions and environmental performance of OECD nations

OECD environmental ranking	Government duty to protect	Government duty and individual right
1. Turkey	Y	Y
2. Switzerland	Y	N
3. Denmark	N	N
4. Poland	Y	Y
5. Slovak Republic	Y	Y
6. Germany	Y	N
7. Austria	Y	N
8. Sweden	Y	N
9. Italy	Y	N
10. Netherlands	Y	Y
11. Portugal	Y	Y
12. Czech Republic	Y	Y
13. Mexico	Y	Y
14.5T. Norway	Y	Y
14.5T. Hungary	Y	Y
16. Japan	N	N
17. Finland	Y	Y
18.5T. France	Y	Y
18.5T. United Kingdom	N	N
20. Greece	Y	Y
21. Spain	Y	Y
22. Luxembourg	N	N
23. South Korea	Y	Y
24. Iceland	N	N
25.5T. New Zealand	N	N
25.5T. Australia	N	N
27. Ireland	N	N
28. Canada	N	N
29. Belgium	Y	Y
30. United States	N	N

T = Tie
Y = Yes, constitution includes specified environmental provision
N = No, constitution does not include specified environmental provision

the worst-performing nation), while the average ranking of the ten nations with constitutions silent on the environment is 21.8. Overall, nations whose constitutions include a government obligation to protect the environment and/or an individual right to live in a healthy environment perform better on the suite of twenty-nine environmental indicators. Analysis confirms that the difference in environmental performance is statistically significant (see Appendix 1 for additional details on statistical methods).

CONFERENCE BOARD OF CANADA ENVIRONMENTAL PERFORMANCE RANKINGS
In 2008, the Conference Board of Canada compared the performance of seventeen wealthy industrialized nations across six domains: environment, economy, education and skills, health, innovation, and society.[39] The Conference Board selected the seventeen nations from among the thirty-eight nations deemed "high income" by the World Bank, because "this is the group of countries likely to have achieved a high and sustainable quality of life, and would therefore serve as a worthy peer group."[40] The Conference Board then applied three filters: removing nations with populations smaller than 1 million (e.g., Iceland and Luxembourg); eliminating nations with an area smaller than ten thousand square kilometres (e.g., Singapore); and dropping nations whose per capita income was below the mean income (based on a five-year average of GDP per capita). The seventeen remaining nations represent a relatively homogeneous subset of OECD nations.

The Conference Board's environmental comparison covers fifteen indicators in six areas: air quality; waste; water quality and quantity; natural resource management; biodiversity and conservation; and climate change and energy efficiency (see Table 12.4). Within these broad areas, the Conference Board focused on what it describes as "outcome" indicators, which measure what nations are achieving, rather than the type or extent of effort being undertaken. Six of the Conference Board's indicators overlap with SFU's ranking of OECD nations.[41]

Again, a clear pattern can be observed by looking at the rankings of environmental performance in Table 12.5. Eight of the nine top-ranked nations have environmental protection provisions in their constitutions. Conversely, six of the eight lowest-ranked nations do not. The average ranking of the seven nations with no constitutional protection for environment is 12.6 (where 1 is the best-performing nation and 17 is the worst). In contrast, the average ranking for the five nations with only government duty to protect the environment is 5.8. The average ranking of the five nations with a government

TABLE 12.4

Indicators in the Conference Board of Canada's environmental rankings

Indicator	Measure
Urban particulate matter concentration (PM 10)	Micrograms per cubic metre
Urban nitrogen dioxide concentration	Micrograms per cubic metre, weighted by population
Urban sulphur dioxide concentration	Micrograms per cubic metre, weighted by population
Volatile organic compounds	Emissions per capita (kg)
Water consumption	Annual water withdrawals measured in million cubic metres (withdrawals refer to the gross amount of water extracted from any source, either permanently or temporarily, for a given use)
Water quality index	Amount of dissolved oxygen, pH, conductivity, total nitrogen, and total phosphorus, reflecting eutrophication, nutrient pollution, acidification, and salinization
Municipal waste generated per capita (kg)	Waste from households, including bulky waste; similar waste from commerce and trade, office buildings, institutions and small businesses, yard and garden waste, street sweepings, the contents of litter containers, and market cleansing waste
Greenhouse gas emissions per capita	Total CO_2 equivalent emissions measured in tonnes of CO_2 equivalent per capita, including the offset effects of land use, land-use change, and forestry (LULUCF)
Energy intensity	The change in total primary energy supply per unit of gross domestic product (GDP) from 2000 to 2005, measured by the change in tonnes of oil equivalent (toe) per US$1,000 GDP
Low-emitting electricity production	The share of low-emitting electricity production (nuclear, hydro, geothermal, wind, solar, and other renewables) in total domestic electricity production
Threatened species	Mammals, birds, and vascular plants listed by the International Union for Conservation of Nature as critically endangered, endangered, or vulnerable, as a proportion of known species
Use of forest resources	Timber harvest as a percent of the forest's annual growth
Forest cover change	Change in land area covered by forest between 2000 and 2005
Organic farming	Share of organic agricultural land out of total agricultural land
Marine trophic index	The degree to which countries are fishing down the food web

Source: Conference Board of Canada (2009).

TABLE 12.5

Constitutions and the Conference Board of Canada's environmental rankings

Conference Board ranking	Government duty to protect	Government duty and individual right
1. Sweden	Y	N
2. Finland	Y	Y
3. Norway	Y	Y
4. Switzerland	Y	N
5. United Kingdom	N	N
6. France	Y	Y
7. Italy	Y	N
8. Austria	Y	N
9. Germany	Y .	N
10. Ireland	N	N
11. Denmark	N	N
12. Belgium	Y	Y
13. Netherlands	Y	Y
14. Japan	N	N
15. Canada	N	N
16. Australia	N	N
17. United States	N	N

Y = Yes, constitution includes specified environmental provision
N = No, constitution does not include specified environmental provision

duty and constitutional recognition of the right to live in a healthy environment is 7.2. Overall, nations whose constitutions include a government obligation to protect the environment and/or an individual right to live in a healthy environment perform better on a suite of fifteen environmental indicators. Analysis confirms that the difference in environmental performance is statistically significant (see Appendix 1 for additional details on statistical methods).

RATIFICATION OF INTERNATIONAL ENVIRONMENTAL CONVENTIONS AND TREATIES

Another metric that can be used to assess the environmental performance of nations is the extent of participation in international environmental agreements. Signing and ratifying such agreements is, at least on its face, a reflection of commitment to improved environmental protection.[42] Because of the general lack of enforcement mechanisms in international environmental law, it could be argued that ratification does not necessarily imply a commitment to comply with the terms of an agreement. For example, it has been suggested that Canada's ratification of the *Kyoto Protocol* in 2002 was a symbolic gesture rather than an indication that Canada genuinely intended to take the steps necessary to reduce greenhouse gas emissions.[43]

For some agreements, such as the *Vienna Convention on the Protection of the Ozone Layer* and the associated *Montreal Protocol on Substances that Deplete the Ozone Layer*, international participation is universal, so these agreements were excluded from the analysis. The following assessment examines the ratification status of five major environmental treaties and protocols:

- the *Kyoto Protocol* to the *United Nations Framework Convention on Climate Change*
- the *Stockholm Convention on Persistent Organic Pollutants*
- the *Rotterdam Convention on the Prior Informed Consent Procedure for Certain Hazardous Chemicals and Pesticides in International Trade*
- the *Cartagena Protocol on Biosafety* to the *United Nations Convention on Biological Diversity*
- the *Ban Amendment to the Basel Convention on the Control of Transboundary Movements of Hazardous Wastes and their Disposal*.

The *Kyoto Protocol* commits a group of industrialized nations to self-selected limits on greenhouse gas emissions.[44] The *Stockholm Convention* bans or severely restricts the manufacture, use, and release of more than a dozen persistent toxic substances.[45] The *Cartagena Protocol* protects biological diversity from the risks associated with genetically modified living organisms produced by biotechnology.[46] The *Rotterdam Convention* establishes a process for listing hazardous chemicals (including pesticides) and requires exporting nations to obtain the prior informed consent of importing nations for trade in the listed substances.[47] The *Ban Amendment* is intended to restrict international trade in hazardous waste.[48]

Eleven of the seventeen relatively wealthy and large OECD nations in the Conference Board of Canada's comparison group have signed and ratified all five of these international environmental laws (see Table 12.6). Of the ten nations whose constitutions require environmental protection, only Italy has failed to ratify one of the international environmental agreements. Of the seven nations without environmental provisions in their constitutions, five have failed to ratify one or more of the international environmental

TABLE 12.6

Constitutions and ratification of international environmental laws

Nation	Constitutional Duty	Right	Kyoto	Stockholm	Cartagena	Rotterdam	Ban
Sweden	Yes	No	Y	Y	Y	Y	Y
Finland	Yes	Yes	Y	Y	Y	Y	Y
Norway	Yes	Yes	Y	Y	Y	Y	Y
Switzerland	Yes	No	Y	Y	Y	Y	Y
United Kingdom	No	No	Y	Y	Y	Y	Y
France	Yes	Yes	Y	Y	Y	Y	Y
Italy	Yes	No	Y	N	Y	Y	Y
Austria	Yes	No	Y	Y	Y	Y	Y
Germany	Yes	No	Y	Y	Y	Y	Y
Ireland	No	No	Y	N	Y	Y	Y
Denmark	No	No	Y	Y	Y	Y	Y
Belgium	Yes	Yes	Y	Y	Y	Y	Y
Netherlands	Yes	Yes	Y	Y	Y	Y	Y
Japan	No	No	Y	Y	Y	Y	N
Canada	No	No	Y	Y	N	Y	N
Australia	No	No	Y	Y	N	Y	N
United States	No	No	N	N	N	N	N

Y = Yes, the agreement has been ratified
N = No, the agreement has not been ratified

agreements. The United States stands out because of its failure to ratify any of the five agreements included in this assessment. Canada and Australia have each failed to ratify two of the five international agreements. Overall, this comparison suggests that nations whose constitutions require environmental protection are more likely to ratify international environmental agreements. Other explanations should not be ruled out, however, such as the added complexity of achieving ratification in federal nations such as Canada, the United States, and Australia.

Constitutions and Progress in Addressing Air Pollution and Climate Change

Thus far, the quantitative evidence has consisted of snapshots of environmental performance at a given point in time. Examining patterns of performance over time while taking into account the enactment of constitutional environmental provisions is also vital. However, problems related to data quality, consistency, and reliability for environmental indicators become more acute further back in time. The following assessment focuses on three specific indicators: nitrogen oxides, sulphur dioxides, and greenhouse gas emissions. Air pollution has been the focus of remedial efforts in all major industrialized nations since the years prior to 1980. The OECD has published data for nitrogen oxide and sulphur dioxide emissions for the period 1980-2005. OECD data on greenhouse gas emissions are available for a shorter time period (1990-2005) because climate change did not appear on the public policy radar screen until the late 1980s. The assessment of time-series data in this chapter focuses on the seventeen relatively large and wealthy nations used in the Conference Board of Canada's rankings, applying the "most similar cases" approach to comparative constitutional law to increase the explanatory power of the independent variable.[49] For purposes of the comparative analysis, France was included among the nations without constitutional environmental protection provisions because its *Charter for the Environment* did not come into force until 2005 (i.e., at the end of the data set).

Comparative trends in environmental performance between countries must be interpreted with caution because the changes recorded depend on the starting point. The choice of a particular year as a starting point could penalize so-called early movers, the nations that acted first to address a particular problem. A country may demonstrate a seemingly large increase in emissions because of particular political or economic circumstances associated with the base year. On the other hand, countries may show a major improvement because they recorded an unusually high volume of emissions in the base year. Environmental performance could still be relatively poor or good, despite the reported statistical changes. Nevertheless, international comparisons can yield valuable insights into factors affecting national environmental performance.

CONSTITUTIONS AND PROGRESS IN REDUCING NITROGEN OXIDE EMISSIONS

Nitrogen oxides (NOx) are produced by the combustion of fossil fuels and contribute to acid precipitation, ozone, smog, and particulate matter. Exposure to elevated levels of NOx can contribute to eye, nose, and throat irritation; respiratory illness; aggravation of asthma; decreased lung function; increased risk of respiratory infection; and reduced lung growth in children.

When one examines the progress of the seventeen wealthy industrialized nations in reducing emissions of NOx, an interesting pattern again emerges (see Table 12.7). Among the eight nations with no environmental provisions

TABLE 12.7

Constitutions and changes in nitrogen oxide emissions

		Change in NOx emissions (%)	Annual change (%)
No environmental provisions in constitutions			
Australia	1990-2005	12.9	0.86
Canada	1980-2005	21.4	0.86
Denmark	1980-2005	−31.9	−1.28
France	1980-2005	−26.7	−1.07
Ireland	1980-2005	58.9	2.36
Japan	1990-2005	−6.4	−0.43
United Kingdom	1980-2005	−32.1	−1.28
United States	1980-2005	−20.9	−0.84
Average		**−3.1**	**−0.10**
Constitutional duty for government to protect the environment			
Austria	1980-2005	−8.5	−0.34
Germany	1990-2005	−47.4	−3.16
Italy	1980-2005	−29.7	−1.19
Sweden	1980-2005	−54.8	−2.19
Switzerland	1980-2005	−56.1	−2.24
Average		**−39.3**	**−1.82**
Constitutional duty for government to protect the environment and individual right to live in a healthy environment			
Belgium	1990-2005	−26.8	−1.79
Finland	1980-2005	−33.3	−1.33
Netherlands	1980-2005	−41.1	−1.64
Norway	1980-2005	7.1	0.28
Average		**−23.5**	**−1.12**
Combined average of nations with EPIC		**−32.3**	**−1.51**

EPIC = Environmental provisions in constitution

in their constitutions, total NOx emissions fell an average of 3.1 percent over the twenty-five-year period from 1980 to 2005. The average annual decrease in NOx emissions among these nations was 0.1 percent.

During the same period, total NOx emissions declined by an average of 32.3 percent among the nine nations that have environmental protection provisions in their constitutions. The average annual decrease among these nations was 1.5 percent. In other words, NOx emissions fell ten times faster between 1980 and 2005 in nations where constitutional provisions required environmental protection. Not all of the nations that have environmental provisions in their constitutions today had those provisions in place in 1980. Among the seven nations that incorporated environmental protection provisions in their constitutions during this time span (Austria, Belgium, Finland, Germany, Netherlands, Norway, and Sweden), NOx emissions declined by an average of 1.1 percent per year prior to the incorporation of these provisions and by an average of 1.9 percent per year after the incorporation of these provisions. In Switzerland and Sweden, the rate of decline in NOx emissions also accelerated after their constitutions' environmental provisions were strengthened in 1999 and 2002 respectively. It must be noted that there are other potential factors for the widespread decline in NOx emissions, including technological advances and the UN's *Convention on Long-Range Transboundary Air Pollution* (to which fifteen of these seventeen nations became parties in the early 1980s).[50]

CONSTITUTIONS AND PROGRESS IN REDUCING SULPHUR DIOXIDE EMISSIONS

Sulphur dioxide (SO_2) emissions are produced by the production, processing, and combustion of fossil fuels, as well as by metal smelting and refining. Sulphur dioxide contributes to acid precipitation, which damages forests, soils, and aquatic ecosystems. Sulphur dioxide also reacts with other air pollutants to form particulate matter. Exposure to SO_2 can cause severe problems for people with asthma and is linked to increased risks of lung cancer and chronic bronchitis.[51]

Data on SO_2 emissions for fourteen of the seventeen countries are available from the OECD for the twenty-five-year period from 1980 to 2005. Data for Australia, Belgium, and Germany are available only from 1990 to 2005.[52] The eight nations without environmental protection provisions in their constitutions achieved an average total reduction in SO_2 emissions of 52.8 percent, an average annual reduction of 1.9 percent (see Table 12.8). In comparison, the nine nations with environmental provisions in their constitutions achieved an average total reduction in SO_2 emissions of 84.8 percent over 25 years (an average reduction of 3.8 percent per year). These results are consistent with the other empirical evidence examined in this chapter. Nations with constitutional provisions requiring environmental protection demonstrate superior environmental performance.

Looking at emission trends prior to and after the enactment or strengthening of constitutional environmental provisions yields unanticipated results. Among the eight nations that enacted or strengthened environmental

TABLE 12.8

Constitutions and changes in sulphur dioxide emissions

		Change in SO_2 emissions (%)	Annual change (%)
No environmental provisions in constitutions			
Australia	1990-2005	53.7	3.6
Canada	1980-2005	−55.5	−2.2
Denmark	1980-2005	−95.1	−3.8
France	1980-2005	−86.1	−3.4
Ireland	1980-2005	−68.5	−2.7
Japan	1990-2005	−40.7	−1.6
United Kingdom	1980-2005	−85.6	−3.4
United States	1980-2005	−44.2	−1.8
Average		**−52.8**	**−1.9**
Constitutional duty for government to protect the environment			
Austria	1980-2005	−93.4	−3.7
Germany	1990-2005	−86.0	−5.7
Italy	1980-2005	−87.0	−3.5
Sweden	1980-2005	−92.1	−3.7
Switzerland	1980-2005	−86.5	−3.5
Average		**−89.0**	**−4.0**
Constitutional duty for government to protect the environment and individual right to live in a healthy environment			
Belgium	1990-2005	−59.4	−4.0
Finland	1980-2005	−88.3	−3.5
Netherlands	1980-2005	−87.3	−3.5
Norway	1980-2005	−83.0	−3.3
Average		**−79.5**	**−3.6**
Combined average of nations with EPIC		**−84.8**	**−3.8**

EPIC = Environmental provisions in constitution

provisions in their constitutions between 1980 and 2005, the annual rate of emissions reductions declined subsequent to the constitutional changes. A potential explanation is that the most cost-effective steps to reduce SO_2 emissions were taken in earlier years (i.e., the low-hanging fruit hypothesis). An examination of emission trends across all seventeen nations supports this hypothesis, as the rate of decline of SO_2 emissions slowed over time. Sweden was the sole exception. The rate of decline in Swedish SO_2 emissions fell after

1987 when environmental provisions were initially inserted in the Swedish constitution, from −7.9 percent per year (1980-87) to −5.0 percent per year (1987-2002). However, the rate of decline increased after the environmental provisions in the Swedish constitution were strengthened in 2002, from −5.0 percent per year (1987-2002) to −10.3 percent per year (2002-05).

CONSTITUTIONS AND CHANGES IN GREENHOUSE GAS EMISSIONS

Climate change was recognized as a global environmental problem in the late 1980s. In 1992 the *United Nations Framework Convention on Climate Change* was established. Data for the fifteen-year period from 1990 to 2005 are available from the OECD.[53] Between 1990 and 2005, the eight nations without environmental protection provisions in their constitutions saw total GHG emissions increase by 9.6 percent, equal to an average annual increase of 0.6 percent (see Table 12.9). In comparison, the nine nations with environmental provisions in their constitutions saw total GHG emissions increase by 1.2 percent, equal to an average annual increase of 0.08 percent. In other words, total GHG emissions in nations without constitutional environmental provisions grew eight times faster than emissions in nations with constitutional environmental provisions.

It might be tempting to suggest that constitutional environmental provisions are responsible for superior performance in reducing greenhouse gas emissions. Instead, there are reasons to believe that GHG emission trends illustrate the difficulty of making causal inferences. First, although the *UN Framework Convention on Climate Change* was created in 1992, the *Kyoto Protocol* was not completed until 1997 and did not come into force until 2005. Thus there was no binding obligation under international law to reduce GHG emissions until the end of the period for which emission trends are being assessed. In many nations, potentially effective laws and policies to reduce emissions were not established until the later years in the 1990-2005 period, or are still lacking. Second, there are competing explanations for the variability in GHG emissions, including economic trends, population growth, and policies aimed at energy conservation and energy security rather than reducing GHG emissions. The largest reductions in GHG emissions came from two nations without constitutional protection for the environment. In the United Kingdom, fuel switching (from coal to natural gas) was the key factor, while in Germany, reunification had a major effect on the rate of GHG emissions. Despite the correlation between constitutional provisions related to environmental protection and reductions in GHG emissions between 1990 and 2005, there may not be a causal relationship.

Table 12.9

Constitutions and changes in greenhouse gas emissions (GHG)

Nation	EPIC	R2HE	Change in GHG emissions, 1990-2005 (%)	Annual change (%)
Canada	N	N	25.3	1.7
United States	N	N	16.2	1.1
Japan	N	N	6.9	0.5
Australia	N	N	25.6	1.7
Austria	Y	N	18.0	1.2
Belgium	Y	Y	−1.3	−0.1
Denmark	N	N	−7.4	−0.5
Finland	Y	Y	−2.7	−0.2
France	N	N	−1.6	−0.1
Germany	Y	N	−18.4	−1.2
Ireland	N	N	26.3	1.8
Italy	Y	N	12.1	0.8
Netherlands	Y	Y	−0.4	0.0
Norway	Y	Y	8.8	0.6
Sweden	Y	N	−7.3	−0.5
Switzerland	Y	N	1.7	0.1
United Kingdom	N	N	−14.7	−1.0
Average			5.1	0.34

EPIC = Environmental provisions in constitution
R2HE = Right to a healthy environment in constitution

Discussion

The results of this basic quantitative analysis are surprising in their degree of consistency. Across three indices and four indicators, there is a consistent relationship between constitutional environmental provisions and superior environmental performance. Nations with environmental provisions in their constitutions have smaller ecological footprints, rank higher on comprehensive indices of environmental indicators, are more likely to ratify international environmental agreements, and made faster progress in reducing emissions of sulphur dioxides, nitrogen oxides, and greenhouse gases than nations without such provisions. Although correlation does not imply causation, the consistency of the association suggests that such a relationship exists and warrants further investigation, using advanced quantitative techniques.

There are two outliers in these comparisons: Denmark and Belgium. Despite the absence of environmental provisions in the Danish constitution, Denmark ranks third-best among OECD nations according to the SFU index. Many factors may be responsible for this anomaly. The Danish constitution is among the most difficult in the world to amend and has not been amended since it was enacted in 1953 (well before the first incorporation of environmental considerations into national constitutions). According to section 88 of the constitution: any proposed changes must be passed by the national legislature (the Folketing); a general election must be called and the proposed changes approved again by the newly reconstituted national legislature; and the proposed changes must be endorsed by the majority in a public referendum, which must constitute at least 40 percent of all eligible voters.[54] This latter condition may be difficult to fulfill in an era of declining voter turnout.

Despite the static nature of its constitution, Denmark's environmental policies have been influenced by its membership in the European Union and its cultural and geographic connections to the Scandinavian nations renowned for environmental leadership. The OECD praises Denmark's "excellent environmental policies," including some "innovative policy instruments."[55] However, Denmark does not fare as well on other indices of environmental performance. Denmark is among the fifteen nations identified by Wilson, Tyedmers, and Pelot as ranking among the best in the world on some sustainability metrics and among the worst in the world on others, such as the ecological footprint (fourth-largest out of 150 nations).[56] The OECD concluded that despite strong showings in reducing SO_2 emissions, improving wastewater treatment, and reducing energy intensity, "Denmark's environmental policies have not always been strong enough to counter the pressures exerted on the environment from transport, agriculture, fisheries and other economic activities, as well as from consumption patterns."[57]

Belgium is an outlier in the opposite direction. Despite having recognized the right to a healthy environment in its constitution since 1994, Belgium's environmental record ranks at the bottom of industrialized nations (second-worst among OECD countries). A contributing factor to Belgium's relatively poor environmental performance may be that the environmental provisions in the Belgian constitution are weak and ambiguous.[58] However, other factors are likely to blame for Belgium's poor environmental record. First, during the 1980s and 1990s, Belgium undertook an extended process of political and institutional reforms associated with the country's transition to federalism. According to the OECD, this lengthy process was a major impediment to the creation and implementation of environmental laws and policies, resulting in a backlog of environmental problems.[59] Furthermore, Belgium is a relatively small nation that is densely populated and heavily industrialized. More than one-quarter of the geographic area of Belgium is built up or covered with dense networks of roads, railways, and navigation canals. As the OECD observes, "industry, heavy freight and passenger traffic, and intensive livestock production and crop cultivation also put pressure on the air, soil, water resources, and nature."[60]

The problems created by the lack of attention to environmental challenges during the transition to federalism and the dense, industrialized, resource-intensive economy are compounded by barriers to environmental information and constraints on access to justice. Environmental information is scattered amongst a wide range of government agencies at the federal, regional, and provincial levels. Belgian citizens, according to the OECD, are not well informed about their rights of access to information and access to courts. The OECD recommended that Belgium "increase citizens' access to justice in environmental matters."[61]

A final factor contributing to Belgium's poor environmental performance is unfavourable judicial interpretation of the constitutional provision.[62] Some Belgian courts have limited NGOs' access to the judicial system through a restrictive interpretation of "interest." The Council of State has limited standing to bring legal actions to parties that can show a direct personal, physical, or financial interest. As a result, a Belgian NGO filed a complaint with the Compliance Committee of the Aarhus Convention, alleging that Belgium is violating the *Convention*.[63] In adjudicating the complaint, the compliance committee concluded that the jurisprudence of Belgian courts was excessively restrictive, effectively limiting access to judicial remedies for environmental organizations.[64] The compliance committee recommended that Belgium

(a) Undertake practical and legislative measures to overcome the previous shortcomings reflected in the jurisprudence of the Council of State in providing environmental organizations with access to justice in cases concerning town planning permits as well as in cases concerning area plans;
(b) Promote awareness of the Convention, in particular the provisions concerning access to justice, among the Belgian judiciary.

Belgium responded to these recommendations with several actions, including a publicity campaign and federal legislation that broadens the definition of standing to include parties defending collective interests (such as environmental protection).[65] Belgium also amended its constitution in 2007 to strengthen its environmental provisions.[66]

Conclusion

The evidence presented in this chapter indicates that nations with constitutional provisions related to environmental protection have superior environmental records.

- Such nations have smaller per capita ecological footprints (both among 150 nations globally and within five broad geographic regions including Africa, the Americas, Asia-Pacific, Europe, and the Middle East/Central Asia).
- They rank higher on several comprehensive indices of environmental performance.
- They are more likely to have ratified international environmental agreements.
- They have achieved deeper cuts in emissions of nitrogen oxides and sulphur dioxide.
- They have experienced slower growth in greenhouse gas emissions.

There are other potential explanations for this pattern. For example, it might be that the causal relationship works in the other direction – a nation with strong environmental policies and broad public support for environmental protection may be more likely to entrench constitutional provisions related to environmental protection. In such circumstances, the costs of implementing constitutional environmental responsibilities would be perceived as small. The consistency of the relationship between nations with constitutional provisions requiring environmental protection and superior environmental performance across three indices and four indicators reduces the likelihood that this relationship is merely the result of chance. The relationship was consistent in a heterogeneous group of 150 nations from across the world and in two smaller, more homogeneous groups of nations (thirty OECD nations and seventeen large, wealthy democracies). Further research is required to substantiate these initial results and determine whether there is a cause-and-effect relationship. Researchers should incorporate constitutional provisions as an explanatory or independent variable in multiple regression analysis to identify the factors driving environmental performance over time.[67] However, when the consistent relationship between constitutional provisions and superior environmental performance is combined with the evidence of strengthened environmental legislation, enhanced opportunities for public participation in environmental governance, and increasing judicial enforcement of the right to a healthy environment, the case in favour of constitutionalizing environmental protection is quite persuasive.

13
...... An Idea Whose Time Has Come

Located at the convergence of constitution making, human rights, and the global environmental crisis, the environmental rights revolution is well underway in most regions of the world. The right to a healthy environment is a relatively recent legal concept but has become widely recognized in international, constitutional, and environmental law. The theoretical advantages and disadvantages of constitutionalizing the right to a healthy environment have been extensively debated, but far less attention has been paid to evaluating the practical consequences.

Although law exerts a pervasive influence on our daily lives, to trace, quantify, and prove the extent of that influence is a complex and contentious endeavour.[1] As Young observed in the context of evaluating the effectiveness of international environmental law, "Complex relationships between institutions, ideas, and material conditions make it virtually impossible to arrive at simple conclusions."[2] The challenges, while daunting, are not insurmountable. This book employed pragmatic approaches to identify the effects of constitutionalizing the right to a healthy environment: a review of national environmental legislation; an assessment of court decisions based on the right; and an evaluation of the relationship between constitutional environmental protection and national environmental performance.

This research generated the following key findings:

- Constitutional environmental protection, including the right to a healthy environment, is widespread and steadily increasing.
- The constitutional right to a healthy environment is exerting extensive influence on national environmental legislation.
- The constitutional right to a healthy environment is enforceable in many more nations than previously recognized.
- Courts are playing a greater role in environmental governance because of increased public access to the judicial system.

- Latin America, the Philippines, and India have emerged as global hotspots of innovation in constitutional and environmental law.
- Constitutional environmental protection provisions appear to be consistently correlated with superior environmental performance.

The Rapid Spread of Constitutional Environmental Protection

Since the landmark *Stockholm Declaration* in 1972, more than half of the world's nations have recognized the constitutional right to a healthy environment. Ninety-two nations have explicitly incorporated the right into their constitutions, while high courts in another 12 nations have ruled that the right is implicit in the constitutional rights to life and health. A total of 147 national constitutions include environmental protection provisions, including one or more of the following provisions: a government duty to protect the environment (140 nations); an individual right to a healthy environment (92 nations); an individual duty to protect the environment (83 nations); and procedural environmental rights (30 nations). This represents a remarkably rapid evolution of law. Indeed, only civil and political rights achieved such widespread legal recognition in such a short time.[3]

A map of the world reflecting constitutionalization of environmental protection is predominantly green except for North America, the Caribbean, and Oceania. It is in China, Japan, and the common-law nations, including the United Kingdom, the United States, Canada, and Australia, that the environmental rights revolution has not yet taken hold. The peak of constitutionalization occurred in the 1990s as many Eastern European and African nations drafted new constitutions, but the flow of nations recognizing the right to a healthy environment continues unabated. The Dominican Republic (2010), Kenya (2010), Jamaica (2011), Morocco (2011), and South Sudan (2011) are the latest nations to join the environmental rights revolution. The editors of *Constitutions of the Countries of the World*, the leading compendium of national constitutions, now regard the right to a healthy environment as one of the standard rights included in contemporary constitutions.[4] It is important to acknowledge, however, that dozens of nations have amended their constitutions in recent years without including the right to a healthy environment or other environmental provisions.

Below the Radar Screen: The Constitutional Influence on Legislation

The most underrated effect of the constitutional right to a healthy environment has been its influence on environmental legislation. In seventy-eight out of ninety-two nations studied, national environmental laws have been strengthened, incorporating substantive and procedural environmental rights. Hundreds of laws have been affected. In a growing number of nations, led by Argentina, Brazil, Colombia, Costa Rica, the Philippines, Portugal, and South Africa, the right to a healthy environment is a fundamental element of environmental governance. In these nations, the right is a unifying principle that permeates legislation, regulations, policies, and administrative decision making. Although litigation based on the right to a healthy environment has garnered more attention from scholars, activists, and the media, it is likely that legislation has a larger impact. Numerous studies comparing the importance of legislation and litigation in environmental protection have concluded that legislation is more effective because of its ability to be preventive and comprehensive. Legislation also has the advantage of relying on government agencies with resources to ensure its implementation and enforcement.

The Last Line of Defence: Judicial Enforcement of the Right to a Healthy Environment

In more than fifty nations – spanning Latin America, Western Europe, Eastern Europe, Asia, and Africa – there is a growing body of court decisions interpreting and enforcing the constitutional right to a healthy environment. As Yang and Percival observe, "Even in countries with very different legal traditions like India and Argentina, the judiciary has used constitutional provisions relating to the environment to intervene when the other branches of government fail to respond adequately to severe pollution problems."[5] Court decisions based on the right to a healthy environment represent a remarkable evolution for the judiciary, whose focus for centuries has been the protection of private interests, while the protection of public interests was the exclusive domain of the legislature.[6] It is likely that this tectonic shift contributed to the initial reluctance of courts to defend environmental interests. Today's judges are more receptive to environmental issues than their predecessors, as the hundreds of decisions referred to in Chapters 6 to 10 demonstrate.[7] The constitutional right to a healthy environment has been used as a sword to attack government and corporate actions that cause environmental damage, and as a shield to defend environmental laws from attacks based on property rights and freedom of commerce. In some nations, the constitutionalization of environmental protection has led to the creation of the standstill doctrine, where courts have ruled that governments cannot weaken environmental laws or current levels of protection unless there is a compelling justification for taking such an unconstitutional action.

Until recently, the leading precedents on the constitutional right to a healthy environment tended to be symbolic victories like the eloquent endorsement of the rights of future generations in the Philippines' *Minors Oposa* case (a decision on standing in a case that never actually went to trial on its merits), the Russian forest privatization case whose seemingly bright light has been cloaked in shadows by subsequent events, or the Nigerian gas flaring case, where the judgment has yet to be enforced. Today there are so many cases from so many nations that it is challenging to identify leading decisions. Hundreds of cases can be cited as proof that the constitutional right to a healthy environment is having positive practical consequences. Two recent court decisions based on the constitutional right to a healthy environment stand out: the *Manila Bay* case from the Philippines and the *Matanza-Riachuelo River* case from Argentina. In each case, a group of concerned citizens took a stand on behalf of important water bodies damaged by decades of abuse, using their constitutional rights to secure remarkable Supreme Court judgments. In both cases a host of government agencies and corporations were ordered to perform a series of cleanup, restoration, and pollution-prevention activities that will cost billions of dollars. The legal processes were open and flexible, and relied on independent experts for scientific assistance. The court orders incorporated innovative mechanisms to ensure compliance, including third-party supervision, mandatory progress reports to the court, and substantial court-imposed fines for non-compliance. The successful implementation of these court orders will mark a watershed in the judicial role in environmental protection.

Constitutions and Environmental Performance

Comparative analysis using seven sets of data revealed a consistent relationship between constitutional environmental protection and superior environmental performance. Globally, nations with environmental provisions in their constitutions have smaller ecological footprints than nations without such provisions. This relationship is consistent on a regional basis across Africa, Asia-Pacific, the Americas, Europe, and the Middle East/Central Asia. Nations with environmental provisions in their constitutions also ranked higher on comprehensive indices of environmental indicators, were more likely to ratify international environmental agreements, and made faster progress in reducing emissions of sulphur dioxides, nitrogen oxides, and greenhouse gases. While these assessments demonstrate correlation and only suggest a potential causal relationship, they raise a tantalizing possibility that should be explored through more sophisticated quantitative analysis.

Regional Differences: Latin America Leads the World

There are major regional differences in the extent to which the constitutional right to a healthy environment is exerting influence. The most far-reaching changes have taken place in Latin America, where nations such as Brazil, Costa Rica, Argentina, and Colombia are experiencing broad rights revolutions that include environmental rights. If one is looking for creative ideas at the convergence of constitutions, human rights, and environmental protection, these nations are at the top of the list. Courthouse doors have been thrown wide open by the elimination of traditional standing requirements. To overcome the barriers of costs, delays, and lack of legal representation, these nations have adopted simplified and expedited procedures for the enforcement of constitutional rights. The result of these innovations is a level of access to judicial protection that is globally unprecedented. The rights revolution is occurring without the extensive litigation support structure previously believed to be necessary. In addition, Bolivia and Ecuador recently passed the most ecologically advanced constitutions in the world, with provisions recognizing not only the human right to a healthy environment but also rights for Nature. The collective aspect of the right to a healthy environment seems to reflect the politics of Latin America, where there is still a strong class consciousness.[8] At least four presidents elected in recent years are advocates of radical social transformation (Morales in Bolivia, Correa in Ecuador, Chavez in Venezuela, and Lula in Brazil). The four nations at the forefront of the Latin American rights revolution (Costa Rica, Colombia, Brazil, and Argentina) are among the top fifteen nations on the Happy Planet Index, which ranks 143 nations based on life expectancy, life satisfaction, and ecological footprints.[9]

The constitutional right to a healthy environment is recognized across most of Europe. Major differences persist between Western and Eastern European nations despite the rapid growth in EU membership. In Eastern Europe, the constitutionalization of the right to a healthy environment reflects an ecological consciousness that played a central role in the democratic transformation of the region two decades ago. However, the process of change has been so politically, socially, and economically turbulent that greater progress in environmental law and policy has been made on paper than in practice. Nevertheless, Kravchenko concludes, "the seeds of participatory democracy, after being sown, are now growing."[10] It will be essential to ensure that the procedural gains being made in Eastern Europe are translated into substantive improvements in environmental quality. In Western Europe, the constitutional right to a healthy environment appears to play more of a complementary role. Environmental legislation, already the strongest in the world, grows ever stronger, with an occasional push from litigation. In Portugal and Greece, the constitutionalization of environmental protection has played a more prominent role, in part because of the strength of the environmental provisions in the Portuguese constitution and the judicial activism of the Greek Council of State.

Asia generally lags behind Latin America and Europe in constitutional protection for the environment, with several remarkable exceptions. The Philippines is among global leaders in terms of legislation and litigation that have been deeply influenced by the right to a healthy environment, and is moving further ahead by simplifying procedural requirements and creating specialized environmental courts. India's Supreme Court is unrivalled in terms of building a comprehensive jurisprudence around the right to a healthy environment despite the lack of explicit reference to such a right in the Indian constitution. Courts in Pakistan, Bangladesh, and Sri Lanka have been influenced by the Supreme Court of India's pioneering decisions. Despite high levels of judicial activism, there are limits to what the courts in these nations can accomplish without the legislative and executive branches of government taking adequate steps to develop, implement, and enforce environmental laws, policies, and programs. China represents a major gap in the diffusion of the right to a healthy environment, a gap that takes on added significance in light of this superpower's huge population, massive economy, rapid growth, and immense environmental challenges.

In Africa, the right to a healthy environment is widely recognized in constitutions and legislation but daunting social, political, and economic challenges have, for the most part, prevented its implementation and enforcement. There are promising signs in South Africa, Uganda, and Kenya – in the form of stronger legislation and progressive court decisions – but for most of the continent the right to a healthy environment remains primarily an aspiration.

In North America, neither Canada nor the United States has constitutionalized environmental protection, although Canada's Supreme Court has on several occasions made positive references to the concept of a right to a healthy environment.[11] In fact, all twenty-five nations with common-law systems, including the United States, the United Kingdom, and Canada (with the exception of Quebec), trail the rest of the world in constitutional recognition of social, economic, and environmental rights. The rationale generally offered is that these kinds of rights are not justiciable, as they involve issues best left to democratically elected legislatures. This argument is steadily losing its credibility as more and more nations enjoy successful experiences with the constitutional protection and enforcement of these rights.

The Globalization of the Right to a Healthy Environment

While there is not yet a global treaty explicitly recognizing the right to a healthy environment, there is a renewed push for such an agreement, driven by recognition of the connection between climate change and human rights.[12] The UN Development Programme describes climate change as a "systematic violation of the human rights of the world's poor and future generations."[13] In 2011, the UN General Assembly held a debate on the proposed Universal Declaration of the Rights of Mother Earth. At the regional level, the right to a healthy environment is recognized in four binding agreements covering 115 nations in the Americas, Europe, Africa, and the Middle East. Including nations that explicitly recognize the right to a healthy environment in their constitutions or framework environmental laws, nations whose high courts have ruled that the right is implicit in their constitutions, nations that have signed binding regional treaties, and nations that signed the *Male' Declaration* on climate change, at least 178 out of 193 UN member nations support the right to a healthy environment. In other words, at least 92 percent of the countries in the world endorse legally recognizing that people possess the right to live in a healthy environment.

The right to a healthy environment is becoming an accepted part of the landscape of international law, both on paper and, more importantly, in practice. International courts and commissions – the African Commission on Human and Peoples Rights, the Inter-American Commission on Human Rights, the Inter-American Court of Human Rights, the European Court of Human Rights, and the European Social Committee – have moved in the direction of explicitly recognizing the right to a healthy environment. The UN's handbook on preparing national action plans for human rights instructs governments to treat the right to a healthy environment as one of the fundamental human rights.[14]

The globalization of the right to a healthy environment has been fuelled by the wave of constitution making, the rights revolution, and growing environmental concerns. Other key factors have been an iterative dialogue between international law and national law; processes of transplantation, harmonization, integration, and convergence; and yeoman efforts from actors including judges, parliamentarians, prosecutors, lawyers, ENGOs, local communities, and their respective networks. Constitutional provisions, laws, and judicial precedents have been shared and emulated. The increasing accessibility of legal information via the Internet means that this process will become even more prominent in the future. Lasser's observation that European courts are engaged in a race to the top in terms of human rights decisions is likely to be repeated in other regions and at the global level.[15]

Implications of This Research

> Often it is only comparison that can indicate to us that something may be wrong with our usual way of explaining things.
>
> – M.A. Glendon, M.W. Gordon, and C. Osakwe,
> *Comparative Legal Traditions*

This book focuses on the experiences of nations that already recognize the constitutional right to live in a healthy environment, but its implications are relevant for all nations. For those in the process of implementing this right, the experiences of other nations can offer ideas, insights, and guidance. For nations that have not yet recognized constitutional environmental rights, Hirschl's observation on social and economic rights is relevant:

> By expanding our knowledge of the possibilities to advance progressive notions of distributive justice through constitutional and interpretive innovation ... comparative studies not only elevate the level of sophistication in discussing the concept of positive constitutional entitlements, but also inject new life into the near-moribund issue of welfare rights in North American constitutional law.[16]

In a similar vein, but referring directly to constitutional protection for the environment, Yang and Percival state that "there is much that the United States can learn about governance systems that take environmental human rights seriously enough to back them specifically in the law."[17] This statement applies with equal force to the United Kingdom, Canada, Australia, and other nations that have not yet constitutionalized environmental protection. As

Portuguese environmental lawyer Branca Martins da Cruz argues, in order to achieve a sustainable future "the recognition to all of a right to the environment becomes an imperative and, with all due respect, the nations that haven't it yet in their fundamental laws live with a crippled [sic] Environmental Law System."[18]

Priorities for Future Research

Many of the academic debates about the implications of constitutional recognition of the right to a healthy environment have been answered, to varying degrees, by four decades of practical experience. For example, the distinctions between generations of rights, positive and negative rights, and civil and political rights on the one hand and social and economic rights on the other are gradually eroding.[19] In a growing number of nations, governments and courts treat all human rights as interdependent and indivisible, not hierarchical. The debate about substantive versus procedural environmental rights has been resolved by recognition that they are both necessary and complementary. In practice, substantive environmental rights almost always include procedural environmental rights. Most of the anticipated benefits of constitutionalizing the right to a healthy environment are being realized to some extent, including stronger environmental laws, improved access to information and public participation in environmental decision making, increased access to justice, more ecologically conscious court decisions, barriers to rollbacks in environmental law, and a greater effort by both governments and courts to give adequate weight to environmental considerations. To be clear, no one is advancing the claim that the constitutional right to a healthy environment has single-handedly delivered these benefits, or that they are universally enjoyed. However, the evidence suggests that the constitutional right is making a significant contribution to these positive outcomes, both through the legal channels studied in this book as well as through extra-legal effects that are more difficult to quantify and that require additional research.

On the other hand, few of the potential disadvantages of the right to a healthy environment are being borne out by experience. Theoretical concerns related to vagueness, redundancy, absolutism, and cultural imperialism lack credibility in the face of the available evidence. The debate about the judicialization of environmental politics will continue, but scholars should recognize that environmental rights actually enhance democracy by enabling more people to participate in shaping environmental policies and decisions that affect their lives.

Given these developments, scholars need to direct their focus away from the question of whether the right to a healthy environment merits legal and constitutional protection. That horse, with respect, has left the barn. The central research questions that need to be answered involve evaluating the most effective, efficient, and equitable means of ensuring that everyone's right to a healthy environment is respected, protected, and fulfilled.

There is a large body of work on the effectiveness, or lack thereof, of law. Many scholars argue that legal tactics are never sufficient on their own to bring about transformative social change.[20] That argument seems to attack a straw person. Nobody is suggesting that the constitutional right to a healthy environment is a silver bullet capable, on its own, of securing a sustainable future. Instead, constitutional recognition of the right to a healthy environment should be viewed as a useful additional tool for the societal actors engaged in the process of attempting to transform today's unsustainable societies. Because of the constitution's paramount place in contemporary legal systems, constitutionalizing environmental protection is a potentially powerful change.

Future research in this field should focus on evaluating, both within nations and in comparative studies, the extent of influence that constitutional provisions have on environmental performance (tracing the steps in the causal chain from constitution to on-the-ground outcomes); assessing the relative effectiveness of the various types of constitutional environmental provisions (i.e., individual rights versus government duties); evaluating the relative roles of legislation and litigation in contributing to environmental progress; and identifying contextual factors that influence the fulfillment of constitutional rights and responsibilities related to environmental protection. The focus needs to be on quantitative evidence about the consequences of environmental law, an area that is notoriously difficult but vitally important.[21]

These overarching research questions raise many more specific issues. How do constitutional provisions affect environmental agencies and the entities they regulate? Does constitutional recognition of the right to a healthy environment affect the distribution of environmental harms and benefits? How do constitutional environmental provisions affect the attitudes and decisions of legislators, civil servants, and judges? Are court orders related to environmental protection being complied with and enforced? Is judicial involvement in environmental governance interfering with the government's ability to rationally set priorities and allocate resources? Do constitutional environmental provisions constrain economic growth? Does explicit constitutional recognition of the right to a healthy environment provide greater benefits than implicit inclusion as part of the right to life?

The focus of this book has been on the instrumental effects of the constitutional right to a healthy environment. What are the constitutive effects of constitutionalizing environmental protection? Do society's values and attitudes toward environmental protection and environmental policy change? More importantly, does behaviour change? How does the constitutionalization of environmental protection affect civil society? Does the right to a healthy environment serve as a mobilizing tool or does it impede mobilization by focusing energy and resources on legal processes that are inaccessible to the majority of people?

The composition of the judiciary is a crucial factor influencing the role of courts and needs to be examined on a country-by-country basis. What is the pool of people from which judges are appointed? Who makes the appointments and on what basis? What kind of legal training do they receive? What are the judges' perspectives on environmental protection? What is the legal and political culture in which they make decisions? According to Goldsworthy, these may be the determining factors in constitutional interpretation, as "judges somehow find ways of adjusting their constitutions to the felt necessities of the time."[22] These factors play a major role in explaining why the level of judicial activism in domestic courts varies significantly between nations (e.g., conservative in Chile and Spain, activist in Greece and Colombia) and within nations at different times.[23]

This book revealed a major difference between nations employing common-law and civil law legal systems, raising several important questions. Why do common-law nations lag behind in recognizing the right to a healthy environment? Are common-law nations simply emulating the British and American approach to constitutional rights, which is averse to social, economic, and cultural rights as well as the right to a healthy environment? Is the objection based on the issue of justiciability, or do powerful elites in these nations block progress because of fears related to the redistribution of power and resources? Is the common-law legal system an impediment to environmental sustainability? If so, how can this systemic institutional weakness be overcome?

Scholarly opinion is divided about whether litigation-focused strategies have been effective in securing other social and economic rights.[24] There is also a body of evidence about regulatory enforcement in industrialized countries, which indicates that a legalistic approach to environmental enforcement may lead to uncertainty, high compliance-related costs, and adversarial relationships.[25] In light of the extraordinary constitutional developments taking place in Argentina, Brazil, Colombia, Costa Rica, and the Philippines, are these observations applicable? As McAllister observes, "The subject of environmental regulation and enforcement in most developing countries remains intellectual *tierra incognita*."[26]

If the evidence proves that constitutionalizing environmental protection is effective in reducing environmental impacts within a nation, a new set of questions arises. Are the environmental pressures actually being decreased, or are they merely being exported to other nations? For example, if constitutional provisions requiring a government to protect the environment result in reductions in the volume of wood being harvested in a given nation, but there is no concurrent decline in demand for wood and paper products, then imports will necessarily rise. The overall environmental impact could be negative from a global perspective if the replacement wood and paper products come from forests that have high biodiversity values and are not being sustainably managed.

Another fascinating line of inquiry, not explored in this book, involves the conditions and processes that give rise to constitutional changes related to environmental protection. Is recognition of the right to a healthy environment the product of grassroots campaigns and broad public support? Or do such provisions owe their existence to academic and policy elites engaged in transnational processes of constitutional reform? These questions will be of greatest interest to those nations whose constitutions remain silent on environmental protection.

A final aspect of the constitutionalization of environmental protection that deserves greater attention is the individual duty to protect the environment.[27] As Wolfrum and Grote note, France's *Charter for the Environment* "puts the obligations of the individual with regard to the environment on an equal footing with his/her rights."[28] More than eighty constitutions incorporate this duty but it has been almost completely overshadowed by the right to a healthy environment. The importance of the duty gains additional weight when the intergenerational aspect of environmental protection is taken into consideration.

An investigation into the extent and effectiveness of the right to a healthy environment when recognized in subnational constitutions or regular legislation would also be a useful addition to the field.[29] Several provincial and territorial governments in Canada and a number of American states recognize the right to a healthy environment despite a lack of recognition at the national level. In nations such as Argentina, provincial constitutions include the right, reinforcing national recognition, but the additional benefits and drawbacks do not appear to have been studied.

Final Thoughts

In less than fifty years, the right to a healthy environment has gone from an idea articulated by Rachel Carson to a concept that is legally recognized in most of the world. The remarkably rapid proliferation of environmental rights and responsibilities in the world's national constitutions is a hopeful sign for the future well-being of the Earth and its inhabitants. The presence of these constitutional provisions demonstrates an important commitment to environmental protection, given that constitutions represent our most deeply held and cherished values and are the supreme law of nations. As Hiskes concludes, "The power of human rights is uniquely suited to assisting us in gathering the collective will necessary to preserve the planet."[30]

At the end of the day, however, human rights matter only if they make a difference in people's lives. Measured by this yardstick, the constitutional right to a healthy environment is beginning to matter. There are hundreds of inspiring stories of individuals, NGOs, and communities seizing the eloquent words printed in their national constitutions and bringing them to life. The right to a healthy environment is gaining momentum, law by law, case by case, place by place, and nation by nation. As a result of the right to a healthy environment, people in many communities have gained access to safe drinking water. Millions of people are breathing cleaner air. Law-breaking polluters and despoilers have been hauled into court, fined, and forced to clean up their act. And while the right to a healthy environment is focused primarily on people, Nature too has benefited. The habitats of endangered species – sea turtles in Greece, green macaws in Costa Rica, salamanders in the Netherlands, and many others – have been protected. Damaged ecosystems from Argentina to the Philippines are being restored.

While constitutional environmental law slowly spreads its wings, the ongoing environmental challenges facing the world – climate change, toxic pollution, resource depletion, and the decline of biological diversity – indicate that we have a long way to go in achieving a sustainable future. Environmental protection remains more an aspiration than a goal that has been achieved. A parallel can be drawn with the fact that despite the long history of human rights, people throughout the world still experience inequality, poverty, oppression, and hunger. The right to a healthy environment recognizes that humanity's most common link is that we all share this small planet. We all breathe the same air. We all cherish our children's future. Constitutional protection for the environment, especially the right to a healthy environment, has the legal and symbolic power to both change the rules of the game and alter our vision of the world, bringing us closer to the elusive goal of achieving sustainability.

APPENDIX 1

Research Methods

The Prevalence and Enforceability of Environmental Provisions in National Constitutions

A two-stage approach to reviewing the constitutions of the 193 nations belonging to the UN was undertaken to ensure the accuracy of the analysis. First, the most recent published versions of all constitutions were reviewed, as provided by the leading subscription service, *Constitutions of the Countries of the World*.[1] Then online versions of current constitutions were identified and reviewed to confirm that the documents in *Constitutions of the Countries of the World* were up to date. Approximately 10 percent of the 193 constitutions included in this study were not available in their most recent version in *Constitutions of the Countries of the World*.[2] For these nations, constitutions published on official government websites were used whenever possible. Current versions of all constitutions under consideration were found on the Internet, although significant numbers were available only in languages other than English (predominantly Spanish and French). Spanish and French versions were translated by the author, while Google's online translation tool was used for constitutions in other languages.

Both *Constitutions of the Countries of the World* and Internet sources have advantages and disadvantages, but by relying on both, their respective weaknesses can be minimized and the rigour of the analysis maximized. *Constitutions of the Countries of the World* is the acknowledged authority in comparative constitutional law and strives to achieve a consistent approach to translation. However, it can be out of date with respect to recent constitutional amendments and revisions. Internet sources are often as current as possible but can suffer from higher degrees of inaccuracy.

All 193 constitutions were initially searched for a series of ten keywords and phrases: biodiversity, ecology, environment, future generations, natural resources, nature, sustainable, sustainability, toxic, and water. A search for equivalent terms in other languages was used for constitutions where English translations were unavailable (again using Google's online translation tool). All constitutional provisions containing these terms were reviewed to answer the following questions:

(a) Was a specific provision related to environmental protection? Occasionally, some of the ten keywords and phrases are used in other constitutional contexts. For example, pursuant to Article 69(2) of Portugal's constitution, "The state shall ensure special protection for children who are orphaned, abandoned or deprived of a normal family environment in any way." These kinds of provisions, unrelated to protection of the biophysical environment, were excluded from this study. The only constitutional provisions related to the biophysical environment that were excluded from this analysis were those that merely *authorized* one or more levels of government to enact environmental legislation, regulations, policies, or programs (as opposed to requiring action) or simply *allocated* jurisdiction over environmental matters between different levels of government. For example, Article 117 of the constitution of Italy states:

> 117. (1) Legislative power belongs to the state and the regions in accordance with the Constitution and within the limits set by European Union law and international obligations.
> (2) The state has exclusive legislative power in the following matters:
> ...
> > s) protection of the environment, of the ecosystem and of the cultural heritage.

(b) When were environmental provisions first incorporated into the constitution? If applicable, when was the right to a healthy environment recognized?

(c) What was the nature or type of the provisions? Five categories of environmental provisions were identified: a substantive individual right to a healthy environment; procedural environmental rights; government's duty to protect the environment; individual environmental responsibilities; and miscellaneous other provisions.

All constitutions with provisions related to protection of the biophysical environment were then reviewed a second time. Keywords employed in this phase of the research were commission, court, defend, enforce, justiciable, ombudsman, and rights (or their equivalents in other languages). The purpose of the second review was twofold: first, to identify limits (if any) imposed on the extent of substantive rights to a healthy environment; and second, to identify constitutional provisions that either explicitly authorized or constrained the enforceability of environmental provisions.

The Legal Influence of the Constitutional Right to a Healthy Environment

ENVIRONMENTAL LEGISLATION

The UN Food and Agriculture Organization's FAOLEX database was used to search for national environmental legislation in each of the ninety-two nations whose constitution explicitly recognizes the right to a healthy environment.[3] The Advanced Search feature of the FAOLEX database allows the specification of parameters, including the type of legal instrument (e.g., legislation, regulation, or agreement) and subject matter (e.g., forestry, water, or general).

Once the relevant environmental laws of a specific nation were identified, they were searched for two key words: "right" and "constitution." For documents in Spanish and French, the keywords used for searching were "derecho" and "constitución," and "droit" and "constitution," respectively. For legislation in other languages, Google's online translation function was used to generate translations of "right" and "constitution."[4] After legislative provisions containing the words "right" and/or "constitution" were identified, they were reviewed to confirm that they were directly related to either the right to a healthy environment and/or other constitutional provisions requiring environmental protection. Spanish and French provisions were translated by the author, while legislative provisions in other languages were converted into English using Google Translate.

For a handful of countries, national environmental legislation was not available on FAOLEX or was available but not in a format that was searchable or translatable. For these nations (e.g., Iran), an additional effort was made using official government websites; an array of other legal databases, including ECOLEX, the World Legal Information Institute (WORLDLII),[5] the World Law Guide,[6] and the Global Legal Information Network;[7] and consultation with other scholars.

Court Decisions

To identify court decisions based on the constitutional right to a healthy environment in the ninety-two nations, a three-pronged approach was taken. First, a search for court decisions in each nation was undertaken on ECOLEX, the environmental law database jointly operated by the UN Food and Agriculture Organization, the UN Environment Programme, and the International Union for Conservation of Nature.[8] Second, searches for court decisions in each nation were conducted on the relevant legal information databases, including the following:

- the World Legal Information Institute
- the Global Legal Information Network
- the Common Legal Information Institute
- Asian Legal Information Institute
- Droit Francophone
- Southern Africa Legal Information Institute.

Boolean commands were used to search for the phrase "right to a healthy environment" and each of the words "right," "healthy," and "environment." In nations where a different phrase is used in the constitution, the appropriate language was substituted. For example, in the Philippines, the constitution refers to the right to a "balanced and healthful ecology." Third, individual searches were conducted on the websites of national courts, generally the Supreme Court and the Constitutional Court. Again, these searches looked for the phrase "right to a healthy environment" (or its nation-specific equivalent), as well as both the words "right" and "environment." Where the search function was not available in English, Spanish, or French, a search was conducted on the specific number of the constitutional provision (article or section) that refers to the right to a healthy environment.

These structured and systematic searches were supplemented by an opportunistic sampling of the secondary legal literature, where court decisions are frequently discussed and analyzed. The purpose of combining these multiple searches was to ensure the most comprehensive coverage possible. There is no single, comprehensive repository of environmental or constitutional jurisprudence. Each of the databases used in this research has gaps in coverage. Higher courts (i.e., supreme or constitutional courts) were the primary focus because their decisions carry the greatest weight, but lower-court decisions are far more numerous. In many nations, not all court decisions are published. Although the more important court decisions are generally published, this practice means that a substantial proportion of litigation is not easily accessible to researchers. As well, there may be difficulties arising from the translation of many different languages into English. The bottom line is that for some nations, the assessment of litigation in Chapters 6 to 10 represents the tip of the iceberg of case law regarding the right to a healthy environment.

Also included in this study are nations whose high courts have recognized a constitutional right to a healthy environment despite the absence of an explicit right in the national constitution. These nations are Bangladesh, Estonia, Guatemala, India, Israel, Italy, Malaysia, Nigeria, Pakistan, Sri Lanka, Tanzania, and Uruguay. The rationale used by these courts is that the right to live in a healthy environment is an essential element of the constitutional right to life or right to health. The Indian courts, in particular, are globally recognized for their constitutional jurisprudence related to the right to live in a healthy environment. Court decisions from these twelve nations were identified using the same methods outlined above.

It should also be noted that this survey of court decisions includes cases where the plaintiff or applicant asserting a violation of the right to a healthy environment was successful or unsuccessful, or where the outcome could not easily be categorized (e.g., a court agrees that there has been a violation of the right but refuses to grant all or part of the remedy being sought). Where data are available regarding the proportion of environmental cases that are successful (e.g., Brazil, Colombia, Costa Rica, India, and the Netherlands), they are provided.[9] As well, this analysis includes cases where the constitutional right to a healthy environment was not the basis of the lawsuit but was relied upon by the court in reaching its decision. For example, there are numerous cases in which courts rejected legal challenges to environmental laws, regulations, and taxes and justified their decisions in whole or in part because of the constitutional basis for environmental protection.

Do Environmental Provisions in Constitutions Influence Environmental Outcomes? A Preliminary Assessment

For each of the snapshots comparing environmental performance between nations with and without constitutional environmental provisions, basic analysis was conducted to determine whether the differences in observed performance were statistically significant. In each comparison, nations were divided into three groups: those without constitutional provisions requiring environmental protection; nations whose constitutions recognize the constitutional right to a healthy environment; and nations whose constitutions include both the right to a healthy environment and an explicit government responsibility to protect the environment. Because the comparisons used different types of data, different statistical tests were applied.

ECOLOGICAL FOOTPRINT COMPARISON

A one-way analysis of variance (ANOVA) was calculated on the per capita ecological footprints of nations with various constitutional provisions.[10] An alpha level of 0.05 was used for all statistical tests. There were thirty-four nations without constitutional environmental provisions, forty-one nations with a government duty to protect the environment, and seventy-five nations with both a government duty and an individual right to a healthy environment. The analysis of variance revealed a significant difference in the means of the three groups F (2, 147), p = 0.004. Nations without constitutional provisions related to environmental protection have larger ecological footprints (M = 3.58, SD = 2.89) than nations with either constitutional government duties to protect the environment (M = 2.24, SD = 1.64) or government duties and individual rights to live in a healthy environment (M = 2.42, SD = 1.39). Multiple comparisons (calculated using the Tukey HSD Test) indicated that the ecological footprints of nations with no constitutional provisions related to the environment were significantly different from both nations with a government duty to protect the environment and nations with a government duty and an individual right.[11] Comparisons also indicated that the ecological footprints of nations with only a government duty to protect the environment were not significantly different from the footprints of nations with both a government duty and an individual right.

Similarly, in each of the five global regions (Africa, Americas, Asia-Pacific, Europe, and Middle East/Central Asia), the ecological footprints of nations with constitutional environmental provisions were smaller. A one-way ANOVA was calculated for each region. An alpha level of 0.05 was used for all statistical tests. The results were significant for the Asia-Pacific region F (2, 20), p = 0.049, Europe F (2, 32), p = 0.026, and the Middle East/Central Asia F (2, 18), p = 0.044. The results were not significant for Africa F (2, 44), p = 0.196 or the Americas F (2, 21), p = 0.172.

OECD COMPARISON

Because the OECD index uses rankings, it is necessary to use a Kruskal-Wallis test for nonparametric data, instead of one-way ANOVA.[12] The Kruskal-Wallis test is applied under the same conditions as one-way ANOVA, except that the dependent variable need not be normally distributed. In applying the

Kruskal-Wallis test, the thirty OECD nations were sorted into three separate samples based on their constitutional provisions (or lack thereof) related to environmental protection. The first group consisted of the nations with no environmental protection provisions in their constitutions ($n = 10$). The second group consisted of the nations whose constitutions impose a duty upon the government to protect the environment ($n = 5$). The third group included nations whose constitutions include both a government duty and an individual right to live in a healthy environment ($n = 15$). The null hypothesis stipulates that there are no differences in the mean ranks of the three groups.

The results of a Kruskal-Wallis test were significant ($H = 11.02$, d.f. $= 2$, $p = 0.004$). The test indicates that there is a statistically significant difference between the rankings of OECD nations based on whether their constitutions contain provisions requiring environmental protection. Nations whose constitutions include a government obligation to protect the environment and/ or an individual right to live in a healthy environment performed better on a suite of twenty-nine environmental indicators.

CONFERENCE BOARD OF CANADA COMPARISON

Because the Conference Board appraisal of environmental performance uses rankings, it is again necessary to use a Kruskal-Wallis test for nonparametric data, instead of one-way ANOVA. In applying the Kruskal-Wallis test, the seventeen nations in the Conference Board comparison were sorted into three separate samples based on their constitutional provisions (or lack thereof) related to environmental protection. The first group consisted of the nations with no environmental protection provisions in their constitutions ($n = 7$). The second group consisted of the nations whose constitutions impose a duty upon the government to protect the environment ($n = 5$). The third group included nations whose constitutions include both a government duty and a individual right to live in a healthy environment ($n = 5$). The null hypothesis stipulates that there are no differences in the mean ranks of the three groups.

The results of the Kruskal-Wallis test were significant ($H = 6.14$, d.f. $= 2$, $p = 0.046$). The test indicates that there is a statistically significant difference between the rankings of nations based on whether their constitutions contain provisions requiring environmental protection. Nations whose constitutions include a government obligation to protect the environment and/or an individual right to live in a healthy environment performed better on a suite of fifteen environmental indicators.

Online Database: All Current Environmental Provisions from National Constitutions

http://hdl.handle.net/2429/36469

Notes

CHAPTER 1: CONSTITUTIONS, HUMAN RIGHTS, AND THE ENVIRONMENT

1   Hirschl (2004); Ackerman (1997).
2   Beatty (2004).
3   Wolfrum and Grote (2011).
4   McHugh (2002).
5   Monahan (2006, 3).
6   Chemerinsky (2006).
7   Buchanan (2000).
8   *State v. Acheson* (1991, 813).
9   Dworkin (1996).
10 Alexander (1998).
11 Tamanaha (2004, 141).
12 Waldron (1993).
13 Vallinder (1995, 13); Forsyth (2000).
14 Tate (1995).
15 Hirschl (2004).
16 Hirschl (2000); Tate and Vallinder (1995a).
17 Stotzky (2004, 198).
18 Sunstein (1994, 384); Dicey (1961, 198-202).
19 Beatty (2004, 181).
20 Bellamy (2007); Waldron (2006).
21 Tate and Vallinder (1995b, 527).
22 Waldron (1999).
23 Beatty (2004); Sunstein (2001).
24 Hogg and Bushell (1997).
25 Ginsburg (2003).
26 G.W. Anderson (2005).
27 Hirschl (2004, 213-14).
28 Davenport (1996).
29 Epp (1998).
30 Ibid.
31 Walker (1998); Sunstein (1990).
32 Clement (2009); B.M. Wilson (2007).

33 Steiner, Alston, and Goodman (2008); Weissbrodt and de la Vega (2007); Freeman and van Ert (2004); Smith (2003); Jayawickrama (2002).
34 *UN Charter* (1945).
35 *Universal Declaration of Human Rights* (1948); *International Covenant on Civil and Political Rights* (1966); *International Covenant on Economic, Social and Cultural Rights* (1966).
36 Mahoney (2007); Martin et al. (2006).
37 McHugh (2002, 27).
38 Henkin (1990, xvii).
39 Boutros-Ghali (1993).
40 Mahoney (2007, 64).
41 Shue (1996).
42 Ignatieff (2000, 2).
43 Risse, Copp, and Sikkink (1999).
44 Dworkin (1978).
45 Shapiro (2004, 18); Dworkin (1996).
46 Waldron (2006).
47 MacIntyre (1981).
48 Bellamy (2007).
49 Glendon (1991, 177).
50 Bork (1990, 9, 11).
51 Baxi (2005, 234).
52 Baxi (2005).
53 Falk (2000, 56).
54 Carson (1962).
55 Zalasiewicz et al. (2008).
56 UN Population Fund (2002).
57 Rockström et al. (2009).
58 Lancet Editorial Board (2009).
59 Intergovernmental Panel on Climate Change, Working Group I (2007).
60 Intergovernmental Panel on Climate Change (2007); Thomas et al. (2004).
61 Scheffer et al. (2001); US National Research Council (2001).
62 Patz et al. (2005).
63 McMichael et al. (2003).
64 Chivian and Bernstein (2008).
65 Heywood and Watson (1995); E.O. Wilson (1992).
66 World Wildlife Fund, Zoological Society of London, and Global Footprint Network (2010).
67 Millennium Ecosystem Assessment (2005).
68 Myers and Worm (2003).
69 Worm et al. (2006).
70 Berkes et al. (2006).
71 UN Environment Programme (2010).
72 Environmental Defence Canada (2005); US Centers for Disease Control (2005).
73 Environmental Working Group (2005).

74 Commission on Environmental Cooperation (2006). These figures cover only a small subset of the toxic chemicals used in large volumes by North American industry and are unaudited figures reported by corporations.

75 Prüss-Üstün and Corvalán (2006).

76 Ibid.

77 Wigle (2003).

78 Mitchell (2003); Nanda and Pring (2003).

79 Gormley (1976).

80 Carson (1962, 12-13).

81 Carson is quoted in Cronin and Kennedy, Jr. (1997, 235).

82 *Stockholm Declaration* (1972).

83 Hiskes (2009, 70).

84 The December 2007 issue of the *Review of European Community and International Environmental Law* 16 (3), was dedicated to the right to a healthy environment. See also Turner (2009); Hlako (2008); Pedersen (2008); Schall (2008); Collins (2007); Hunter, Salzman, and Zaelke (2007); May (2006); Hayward (2005); Giorgetta (2004); Atapattu (2002a); Giorgetta (2002); Hancock (2003); Handl (2001); Rodriguez-Rivera (2001); Shelton (2001); J. Lee (2000); Tucker (2000); Eleftheriadis (1999); Pevato (1999); Cullet (1995); Nickel (1993); Brandl and Bungert (1992); Shelton (1991); Gormley (1990).

85 Kravchenko and Bonine (2008); Collins (2007); Shelton (2006); Hayward (2005); Giorgetta (2004); Pathak (1992).

86 Eleftheriadis (2007); Brownlie (2003, 540-41); Alston (2001b, 281); Handl (2001, 312); Dias (1999, 400); Eleftheriadis (1999); Pevato (1999); Ruhl (1999); Miller (1998); Robertson and Merrills (1989); Sax (1971).

87 Hayward (2005, 162-63, 182).

88 Shelton (2004b).

89 Law (2010); Congleton (2007); Hirschl (2004); Epp (1998); Bakan (1997); Strauss (1996); Greenberg et al. (1993); Rosenberg (1991); Finer (1979).

90 Congleton (2007, xiii).

91 Epp (1998).

92 Perry (1982).

93 Bakan (1997); Rosenberg (1991); Scheingold (1989).

94 Dershowitz (2004); Ignatieff (2001).

95 Farber (2002).

96 Weaver and Rockman (1993).

97 Ginsburg (2005).

98 Garth and Sarat (1998).

99 For contrasting perspectives on the effects of this decision, see Donohue (1998); Rosenberg (1991).

100 Carlson (2005).

101 Persson and Tabellini (2003); Berggren and Kurrild-Klitgaard (2002); Leschke (2000); Elster (1995); Montenegro (1995); De Vanssay and Spindler (1994).

102 Cooter (2000).

103 Kinney and Clark (2004).

104　Arthurs and Arnold (2005); Hirschl (2004).

105　Arthurs and Arnold (2005).

106　Hirschl (2004, Chapter 5).

107　Carlson (2005).

108　Montenegro (1995).

109　Spindler and De Vanssay (2002); De Vanssay and Spindler (1994).

110　Gleditsch and Sverdrup (2002).

111　Bernauer and Koubi (2009); Beckerman (1999); Torras and Boyce (1998).

112　Kinney and Clark (2004).

113　Palmer and Robb (2005); DeMarco and Campbell (2004); M. Anderson and Galizzi (2002).

114　Pallemaerts (2002, 11-12).

115　Revkin (2008).

116　Joint Committee on Human Rights, House of Commons and House of Lords (2008).

117　Mr. Lluis Maria de Puig made the statement on 28 March 2008, in a speech given in Athens at the Fourth Plenary Session of the Euro-Mediterranean Parliamentary Assembly (translated by author), http://assembly.coe.int//Mainf.asp?link=http://assembly.coe.int/President/dePuig/Discours/2008/20080327_EMPA-Athenes.htm.

118　Limon (2009, 472); Shaheed (2009).

119　Gauri and Brinks (2008); Baderin and McCorquodale (2006).

CHAPTER 2: THE RIGHT TO A HEALTHY ENVIRONMENT

1　Cranston (1973; 1962, 40).

2　Cullet (1995, 26).

3　Hiskes (2009); Collins (2007); Hayward (2005); Giorgetta (2004); Shelton (2001); Shue (1996); Pathak (1992); Gormley (1976).

4　Hayward (2000, 568; 2005).

5　Shue (1996, 23).

6　Birnie and Boyle (2002, 255).

7　Miller (1998, 92).

8　Robertson and Merrills (1989, 259).

9　Alston (1999); *International Covenant on Civil and Political Rights* (1966).

10　*International Covenant on Economic, Social and Cultural Rights* (1966).

11　Downs (1993).

12　Nanda and Pring (2003, 455).

13　Rogge (2001, 37).

14　*Vienna Declaration on Human Rights and Programme of Action* (1993).

15　Shue (1996).

16　UN Committee on Economic, Social and Cultural Rights (1998, 1990).

17　Hayward (2005, 182).

18　May (2006).

19　*R. (on the application of Limbuela) v. Secretary of State for the Home Department* [2006]. See also Ramcharan (2005).

20 UN Food and Agriculture Organization (2006, 77).

21 Fredman (2008, 240). See also Sachs (2007).

22 Holmes and Sunstein (1999).

23 *Optional Protocol* to the *International Covenant on Economic, Social and Cultural Rights,* opened for signature 24 September 2009. As of 5 April 2010, the *Optional Protocol* had thirty-two signatories but no parties. It will come into force when ten nations have ratified it.

24 Giagnocavo and Goldstein (1990).

25 For example, see the Constitution of Colombia, Article 79.

26 *Caso de la Comunidad Mayagna (Sumo) Awas Tingni* (2001); *Case of Yanomani Indians* (1985).

27 *African (Banjul) Charter on Human and Peoples' Rights,* Article 24.

28 Hiskes (2009).

29 Law Reform Commission of Canada (1985).

30 Articles 19, 21, and 8, respectively, of the *Universal Declaration of Human Rights* and Articles 2, 19, and 25 of the *International Covenant on Civil and Political Rights.*

31 De Sadeleer, Roller, and Dross (2005).

32 Hunter, Salzman, and Zaelke (2007).

33 Bruch, Coker, and VanArsdale (2007, 2).

34 Eckersley (1996, 230).

35 Douglas-Scott (1996).

36 Fitzmaurice and Marshall (2007, 106).

37 Hayward (2005, 180).

38 M.R. Anderson (1996a, 10).

39 Hayward (2005, 63).

40 Ibid., 126.

41 *Marbury v. Madison* (1803, 177).

42 *Constitution Act, 1982,* s. 52.

43 Dworkin (1978).

44 Stevenson (1983, 391).

45 Shue (1996).

46 For example, weak enforcement in Canada and Brazil is detailed in two books: McAllister (2008) and Boyd (2003).

47 Stevenson (1983, 391).

48 De Sadeleer (2002, 278).

49 "Let us be clear: no current health or environmental regulatory program squarely addresses nanotechnology." Segal (2004, 295). See also Bowman and Hodge (2007).

50 Bruch, Coker, and VanArsdale (2007).

51 Stone (1972).

52 Hayward (2005, 129).

53 Prieur (2011).

54 Brandl and Bungert (1992, 87).

55 De Sadeleer (2004).

56 Stephens (2009, 116).

57   Du Bois (1996, 157).
58   Cranor (2006); Saxe (1990, 11).
59   Chiappinelli (1992).
60   Eckersley (1996, 213).
61   Bryner (1987, 7).
62   Bullard (2005); Byrne, Martinez, and Glover (2002); Hofrichter (2002).
63   Fredman (2008, 32-33).
64   Cha (2007, 12).
65   Fredman (2008).
66   Brandl and Bungert (1992, 4-5).
67   A. Kiss (1993, 559).
68   May (2006, 118).
69   Birnie and Boyle (2002, 255).
70   Handl (2001).
71   Wolfe (2003); Pevato (1999).
72   Alston (2001).
73   Handl (2001); Pevato (1999).
74   A. Kiss and Shelton (2004, 710).
75   Michaels (2008).
76   M.R. Anderson (1996b, 224).
77   Lazarus (2004, 28).
78   Beatty (2004, 137).
79   Eleftheriadis (1999); Tilleman (1995, 399).
80   Malone and Pasternack (2006).
81   Atapattu (2006).
82   Wood (2009a, 2009b); Boyd (2003).
83   Hayward (2005, 165).
84   Waldron (1993).
85   Barry (1996).
86   Sax (1971).
87   Brandl and Bungert (1992, 94).
88   Fisher (2001); Fuller (1978).
89   Eleftheriadis (1999).
90   *Rhodes et al. v. E.I. Du Pont* (2009).
91   Rodriguez-Rivera (2001).
92   Nedelsky (2008); Hogg and Bushell (1997).
93   Fredman (2008).
94   Dershowitz (2004, 109).
95   May (2006).
96   Garner (2004).
97   Sunstein (1993); Davis (1992).
98   Steiner, Alston, and Goodman (2008); Waldron (1999).
99   Fried (1973).
100 Sunstein (1993, 35).
101 Davis (1992).

102 Fredman (2008); Gauri and Brinks (2008); Sachs (2007); Baderin and McCorquodale (2006); Wiles (2006); Beatty (2004); Tushnet (2002).

103 Beatty (2004); Tushnet (2002).

104 Beatty (2004, 129); *South Africa et al. v. Grootboom et al.* (2000).

105 *South Africa et al. v. Grootboom et al.* (2000).

106 Davis (2008, 2004); Davis, Macklem, and Mundlak (2002); Sunstein (2001).

107 Ramcharan (2005, 3).

108 Schwartz (1992).

109 Ruhl (1997).

110 Hayward (2005, 100).

111 Alston (1984, 1982).

112 Miller (1998, xi).

113 Etzioni (1993, 5).

114 Alston (1984, 611).

115 Cancado Trindade (1993).

116 UN General Assembly (1986).

117 Redgwell (1996).

118 Pallemaerts (1994).

119 Bridge and Laytner (2005).

120 Stone (1972). See also Morris (1964); Leopold (1949, 203-4).

121 *Sierra Club v. Morton* (1972).

122 Nash (1989).

123 Sunstein (1999).

124 Collins (2007, 137); Kellenberger (2003); Mowery (2002); Ledewitz (1998, 583); Taylor (1998a, 1998b); Elder (1984); Emond (1984); Livingston (1984); Tribe (1974).

125 Livingston (1994).

126 Eckersley (1995, 194).

127 Shelton (2004b).

128 Collins (2007); Redgwell (1996, 87).

129 Steiner, Alston, and Goodman (2008); C. Brown (1999).

130 Boyle (1996, 50).

131 Mushkat (2009).

132 See the book series "Religions of the World and Ecology," published by the Center for the Study of World Religions and distributed by Harvard University Press, 1997-2009.

133 Donnelly (2007); Subedi (1999, 70).

134 Sandel (1982).

135 Glendon (1991).

136 Handl (2001).

137 Weiss (1989, 105).

138 Boutaud, Gondran, and Brodhag (2006); Swaigen and Woods (1981, 199).

139 Raz (1986, 258).

140 Cranston (1973).

141 Handl (2001).

142   Bakan (1997); Pound (1917).
143   Ruhl (1999, 281).
144   Hancock (2003); Bakan (1997); M.R. Anderson (1996a, 22).
145   Galanter (1974).
146   Scheingold (1974).
147   Epp (1998, 205).
148   Beatty (2004); Epp (1998).
149   Hill, Wolfson, and Targ (2004).
150   Cullet (1995).
151   N. Gibson (1990, 5).
152   Carter and Turnock (2002).
153   Brandl and Bungert (1992, 29).

CHAPTER 3: THE PREVALENCE AND ENFORCEABILITY OF ENVIRONMENTAL PROVISIONS IN NATIONAL CONSTITUTIONS
1   Weiss (1989).
2   Ksentini (1994).
3   Anton (1998).
4   Earthjustice Legal Defense Fund (2008); May (2006).
5   Hayward (2005, 22).
6   Brandl and Bungert (1992, 7).
7   A complete list of UN members is at http://www.un.org/members/list.shtml. It should be noted that three nations – the United Kingdom, Israel, and New Zealand – lack the kind of unitary written constitution found in the overwhelming majority of the world's nations. Nevertheless, these nations do have legal documents that are considered to have constitutional status and were included in this research.
8   Article 9, Constitution of Italy, and Article 9, Constitution of Malta, in Wolfrum and Grote (2011). Article 108, Constitution of Guatemala, available in Spanish at http://www.bibliojuridica.org/libros/5/2210/26.pdf. In San Marino, pursuant to the constitution, "the Republic protects the historic and artistic heritage and the natural environment." The Constitution of San Marino can be found online (in Italian) at http://www.consigliograndeegenerale.sm/new/index.php3.
9   Wolfrum and Grote (2011). All further references to constitutions are from Wolfrum and Grote (2011), unless otherwise specified.
10 Examples of environmental provisions in the constitutions of the communist nations of Eastern Europe include Czechoslovakia (1960), East Germany (1968), Bulgaria (1971), Hungary (1972), Yugoslavia (1974), Albania (1976), Poland (1976), and the Union of Soviet Socialist Republics (USSR) (1977). Grandbois (1988).
11 Hirschl (2004).
12 Grubb (1993).
13 The forty-six nations without environmental protection provisions in their constitutions are Antigua and Barbuda, Australia, Bahamas, Barbados, Bosnia and Herzegovina, Botswana, Brunei Darussalam, Canada, Cyprus, Denmark, Djibouti, Dominica, Fiji, Grenada, Guinea-Bissau, Iceland, Ireland, Israel, Japan, Jordan,

Kiribati, Lebanon, Liberia, Libya, Liechtenstein, Malaysia, Marshall Islands, Mauritius, Monaco, Nauru, New Zealand, Pakistan, Saint Kitts and Nevis, Saint Lucia, Saint Vincent and the Grenadines, Samoa, Sierra Leone, Singapore, Solomon Islands, Tonga, Trinidad and Tobago, Tunisia, Tuvalu, the United Kingdom, the United States, and Zimbabwe.

14 The twenty-nine former British colonies (including nations that were part of British colonies) are Antigua and Barbuda, Australia, Bahamas, Barbados, Botswana, Brunei Darussalam, Canada, Cyprus, Dominica, Fiji, Grenada, Ireland, Kiribati, Malaysia, Mauritius, New Zealand, Pakistan, Saint Kitts and Nevis, Saint Lucia, Saint Vincent and the Grenadines, Samoa, Sierra Leone, Singapore, Solomon Islands, Tonga, Trinidad and Tobago, Tuvalu, United States, and Zimbabwe.

15 The eleven English-speaking nations of the Americas are Antigua and Barbuda, the Bahamas, Barbados, Canada, Dominica, Grenada, Saint Kitts and Nevis, Saint Lucia, Saint Vincent and the Grenadines, Trinidad and Tobago, and the United States.

16 Argentina, Bolivia, Brazil, Chile, Colombia, Costa Rica, Cuba, Dominican Republic, Ecuador, El Salvador, Guatemala, Guyana, Haiti, Honduras, Mexico, Nicaragua, Panama, Paraguay, Peru, Suriname, Uruguay, and Venezuela.

17 The twenty-four small island nations are Antigua and Barbuda, Bahamas, Barbados, Brunei Darussalam, Cyprus, Dominica, Fiji, Grenada, Iceland, Ireland, Kiribati, Marshall Islands, Mauritius, Nauru, New Zealand, Saint Kitts and Nevis, Saint Lucia, Saint Vincent and the Grenadines, Samoa, Singapore, Solomon Islands, Tonga, Trinidad and Tobago, and Tuvalu.

18 For a breakdown of countries by legal system, see the JuriGlobe – World Legal Systems Research Group website, http://www.juriglobe.ca/eng/syst-onu/rep-sys-juridique.php#syst1.

19 The only common-law mono-systems with environmental provisions in their constitutions are Belize, Jamaica, and Palau.

20 Olowu (2006).

21 The only civil law mono-systems without environmental provisions in their constitutions are Bosnia and Herzegovina, Denmark, Iceland, Liechtenstein, and Monaco.

22 The only mixed civil and customary law nations without environmental provisions in their constitutions are Guinea-Bissau and Japan.

23 The exception is Muslim mono-systems, as all three nations in this category (Afghanistan, Maldives, and Saudi Arabia) have environmental provisions in their constitutions.

24 Soveroski (2007); Shelton (2001); Taylor (1998a, 204).

25 The nations that did not include environmental provisions in constitutions revised in the 1970s and 1980s are Antigua and Barbuda, Brunei Darussalam, Canada, Grenada, Jordan, Liberia, Libya, Saint Kitts and Nevis, Saint Lucia, Saint Vincent and the Grenadines, and Tuvalu.

26 The nations that did not include environmental provisions in constitutions revised since 1990 are Bahamas, Barbados, Bosnia and Herzegovina, Botswana, Cyprus, Djibouti, Dominica, Fiji, Guinea-Bissau, Iceland, Ireland, Israel, Kiribati, Lebanon,

Liechtenstein, Malaysia, Marshall Islands, Mauritius, Monaco, Pakistan, Samoa, Sierra Leone, Singapore, Solomon Islands, Tonga, Trinidad and Tobago, Tunisia, Yemen, and Zimbabwe.

27 Constitution Review Group, All-Party Oireachtas Committee on the Constitution (1996).

28 The Citizens Information Board (Government of Ireland) provides the text of the Irish constitution on its website: http://www.citizensinformation.ie/categories/government-in-ireland/irish-constitution-1.

29 This is the case in the constitutions of Belgium, Central African Republic, Comoros, and Senegal.

30 Hohfeld (1923).

31 The new constitution of Bhutan (2008) is available at http://www.constitution.bt/TsaThrim%20Eng%20(A5).pdf.

32 Article 34, Constitution of El Salvador.

33 Article 19, Constitution of Burundi.

34 Article II(2), Constitution of Bosnia and Herzegovina.

35 The nine nations are Cameroon, Guyana, Malawi, Namibia, Nepal, Philippines, South Africa, Sudan, and Uganda.

36 Government of Kazakhstan, *Environmental Code*, Law No. 212-Z, 9 January 2007.

37 See the Green Salvation website (http://www.greensalvation.org/en/index.php?page=legal-proceedings), which includes a summary of the organization's lawsuits by year.

38 There are some disagreements among geographers as to what continent some countries belong to, with Russia being an obvious example. See the World Atlas website (http://www.worldatlas.com/cntycont.htm).

39 The countries in Africa are Angola, Benin, Burkina Faso, Burundi, Cameroon, Cape Verde, Central African Republic, Chad, Comoros, Congo-Brazzaville, Congo (Democratic Republic of the), Cote d'Ivoire, Egypt, Ethiopia, Gabon, Guinea, Kenya, Malawi, Mali, Mauritania, Morocco, Mozambique, Niger, Rwanda, São Tomé and Príncipe, Senegal, Seychelles, South Africa, South Sudan, Sudan, Togo, and Uganda.

40 The countries in Asia are Azerbaijan, East Timor, Indonesia, Iran, Iraq, Kyrgyzstan, Maldives, Mongolia, Nepal, Philippines, South Korea, Thailand, Turkey, and Turkmenistan.

41 The countries in Europe are Albania, Andorra, Armenia, Belarus, Belgium, Bulgaria, Croatia, Czech Republic, Finland, France, Georgia, Greece, Hungary, Latvia, Macedonia, Moldova, Montenegro, Netherlands, Norway, Poland, Portugal, Romania, Russia, Serbia, Slovakia, Slovenia, Spain, and Ukraine.

42 The countries in Latin America are Argentina, Bolivia, Brazil, Chile, Colombia, Costa Rica, Ecuador, El Salvador, Guyana, Honduras, Mexico, Nicaragua, Panama, Paraguay, Peru, and Venezuela.

43 The Caribbean countries are the Dominican Republic and Jamaica.

44 The total number of descriptive words and phrases used adds up to more than ninety-two because many constitutions use more than one word or phrase to describe the right to an environment.

45 The forty-one nations with generic limits are Albania, Angola, Armenia, Belarus, Bulgaria, Burundi, Cape Verde, Chile, Croatia, Czech Republic, Dominican Republic, East Timor, Greece, Guinea, Honduras, Hungary, Indonesia, Iraq, Jamaica, Kenya, Kyrgyzstan, Malawi, Maldives, Moldova, Montenegro, Mozambique, Poland, Portugal, Romania, Russia, Rwanda, São Tomé and Príncipe, Serbia, Slovakia, Slovenia, South Africa, South Korea, Thailand, Togo, Turkey, and Uganda.

46 The forty-six nations are Albania, Andorra, Angola, Armenia, Azerbaijan, Belarus, Cape Verde, Chad, Colombia, Congo (Democratic Republic of the), Croatia, Dominican Republic, East Timor, Ethiopia, Finland, Georgia, Honduras, Hungary, Jamaica, Kenya, Macedonia, Maldives, Mexico, Mongolia, Montenegro, Mozambique, Nepal, Nicaragua, Panama, Peru, Poland, Portugal, Romania, Russia, São Tomé and Príncipe, Senegal, Seychelles, Slovenia, South Africa, Spain, Sudan, Turkey, Turkmenistan, Uganda, Ukraine, and Venezuela.

47 The four nations are Costa Rica, Latvia, Netherlands, and Spain.

48 The six nations are Central African Republic, Gabon, Malawi, Maldives, South Africa, and Turkey.

49 Articles 9(d) and 23, Constitution of the Maldives.

50 US Department of State (2009); Grote (2008b).

51 The twenty-three nations are Argentina, Benin, Bolivia, Brazil, Burkina Faso, Cameroon, Comoros, Congo (Democratic Republic of the), Costa Rica, Cote d'Ivoire, Ecuador, El Salvador, France, Guyana, Iran, Latvia, Mali, Mauritania, Netherlands, Niger, Norway, Paraguay, and Philippines.

52 The fifty-four countries that include the right to a healthy environment with other fundamental human rights are Angola, Armenia, Azerbaijan, Belarus, Belgium, Benin, Bolivia, Bulgaria, Burundi, Chad, Chile, Congo-Brazzaville, Cote d'Ivoire, Dominican Republic, Ecuador, Finland, Gabon, Georgia, Greece, Guinea, Guyana, Honduras, Indonesia, Jamaica, Kenya, Kyrgyzstan, Latvia, Maldives, Mali, Mexico, Moldova, Mongolia, Montenegro, Morocco, Mozambique, Nepal, Netherlands, Niger, Panama, Paraguay, Peru, Romania, Russia, Rwanda, Senegal, Serbia, Seychelles, Slovakia, South Africa, South Korea, Thailand, Togo, Turkmenistan, Uganda, Ukraine, and Venezuela.

53 The seventeen countries that group the right to a healthy environment with economic, social, and cultural rights are Albania, Andorra, Burkina Faso, Cape Verde, Costa Rica, Croatia, Czech Republic, East Timor, El Salvador, Ethiopia, Iraq, Macedonia, Nicaragua, Poland, Portugal, São Tomé and Príncipe, and Turkey.

54 The eleven nations are Brazil, Central African Republic, Hungary, Iran, Malawi, Norway, Philippines, Slovenia, South Sudan, Spain, and Sudan.

55 Shemshuchenko (1995).

56 Articles 191-94, Constitution of El Salvador.

57 Article 91, Constitution of Namibia.

58 The six nations are Algeria, Estonia, Laos, Papua New Guinea, Syrian Arab Republic, and Vanuatu.

59 Monahan (2006, 3).

60 Article 220, Constitution of Gambia.

61 The constitution of Andorra can be found at http://www.andorramania.com/ constit_gb.htm.

62 The sixteen countries are Armenia, Article 31; Belarus, 44(6); Chile, 24; Croatia, 50; Czech Republic, 11(3) of the Charter; Kenya, 40(1); Mexico, 27; Moldova, 46(5); Romania, 44(7); Russia, 36(2); Slovakia, 20(3); Slovenia, 67; Thailand, 42; Ukraine, 41; Uzbekistan, 54; and Serbia, 83 and 88.

63 Article 44(7), Constitution of Romania.

64 Article 15(3)(a), Jamaica, *Charter of Fundamental Rights and Freedoms*.

65 Antigua and Barbuda – Article 9(4), Bahamas – 27(2), Barbados – 16(2), Botswana – 8(5), Dominica – 6(6), Grenada – 6(6), Kiribati – 8, Mauritius – 8, Saint Kitts and Nevis – 8, Saint Lucia – 6, Saint Vincent and the Grenadines – 6, Samoa – 14, Sierra Leone – 21, Solomon Islands – 8, and Tuvalu – 20. However, these nations are not included in this study because the constitutional provisions do not *require* government action to protect the environment but merely *authorize* such action.

66 Article 225(1)(V), Constitution of Brazil.

67 Article 41(3), Constitution of Argentina.

68 Article 66(2)(h), Constitution of Portugal.

69 Article XIII, Section 2, Constitution of Micronesia.

70 Brewer-Carias (2009).

71 Grote (2008c).

72 Constitution of Ecuador, Article 71, Constitution of Bolivia, Article 33.

73 Constitution of Ecuador, Articles 395(4), 397(1), 401, and 415.

74 The nations that include constitutional references to the rights, health, or well-being of future generations are Albania, Andorra, Argentina, Armenia, Bhutan, Bolivia, Brazil, Burundi, Cuba, Czech Republic, Dominican Republic, East Timor, Ecuador, Eritrea, France, Gambia, Georgia, Germany, Ghana, Guyana, Iran, Jamaica, Kenya, Lesotho, Luxembourg, Madagascar, Malawi, Maldives, Moldova, Morocco, Namibia, Norway, Papua New Guinea, Poland, Portugal, Qatar, Russia, Seychelles, South Africa, South Sudan, Swaziland, Sweden, Switzerland, Tajikistan, Uganda, Uzbekistan, Vanuatu, Venezuela, and Zambia.

75 The exceptions, which include generic references to the interests of future generations or "posterity," include Moldova, Russia, Seychelles, Tajikistan, and Uzbekistan.

76 Article 225, Constitution of Brazil.

77 Article 5(4), Constitution of Bhutan; Article 66(2)(d), Constitution of Portugal.

78 Article 27, Constitution of South Africa.

79 The seventeen other nations with provisions addressing clean water are Bolivia, Article 16(I); Colombia, 366; Congo (Democratic Republic of the), 48; Dominican Republic, 15 and 16; Ecuador, 12; Ethiopia, 90(1); Gambia, 216(4); Kenya, 43(1)(d); Maldives, 23; Morocco, 31; Panama, 110 and 118; Swaziland, 215; Switzerland, 76; Uganda, XIV(b) and XXI; Uruguay, 47; Venezuela, 127 and 304; and Zambia, 112(d).

80 Intergovernmental Working Group for the Elaboration of a Set of Voluntary Guidelines to Support the Progressive Realization of the Right to Adequate Food in the Context of National Food Security (2004, 73).

81 Bullard (2005); Hofrichter (2002).

82 Takahashi (2002).

83 Countries with constitutions that appear to have an enforceable right to a healthy environment include Albania, Angola, Argentina, Azerbaijan, Belarus, Bolivia, Brazil, Bulgaria, Burkina Faso, Burundi, Cape Verde, Central African Republic, Chad, Chile, Colombia, Comoros, Congo-Brazzaville, Congo (Democratic Republic of the), Costa Rica, Cote d'Ivoire, Croatia, Dominican Republic, East Timor, Ecuador, El Salvador, Ethiopia, Finland, Gabon, Georgia, Greece, Guyana, Honduras, Iran, Iraq, Jamaica, Kenya, Kyrgyzstan, Latvia, Macedonia, Maldives, Mexico, Moldova, Mongolia, Montenegro, Morocco, Mozambique, Nepal, Nicaragua, Niger, Panama, Paraguay, Peru, Philippines, Portugal, Romania, Russia, São Tomé and Príncipe, Serbia, Seychelles, Slovenia, South Africa, Thailand, Turkey, Turkmenistan, Uganda, Ukraine, and Venezuela.

84 The twelve nations that restrict the right to a healthy environment (and the relevant section of the constitution) are Andorra, Article 39; Armenia, 117; Belgium, 23, 134; Czech Republic, 41; Egypt, 59; France, 34; Poland, 81; Senegal, 8; Slovakia, 51; South Korea, 35(2); South Sudan, 44; Spain, 53(3); and Sudan, 22.

85 Grote (2008a, 14).

86 The nations with constitutional environmental rights but no provisions related to enforceability are Benin, Cameroon, Guinea, Indonesia, Mali, Mauritania, Norway, Rwanda, and Togo. Five of these nations are former French colonies with very similar constitutions (Benin, Cameroon, Guinea, Mali, and Togo).

87 Constitution of the Netherlands, Articles 17 and 120.

88 Constitution of Austria, Articles 19(4) and 24(h)(8). Plesser and Luiki (1996, 10).

89 National constitutions in which the government's duty to protect the environment appears to be enforceable include those of Afghanistan, Angola, Argentina, Azerbaijan, Bahrain, Belarus, Bolivia, Brazil, Bulgaria, Burkina Faso, Burundi, Cambodia, Cape Verde, Chad, Chile, Colombia, Comoros, Congo-Brazzaville, Congo (Democratic Republic of the), Costa Rica, Cote d'Ivoire, Croatia, Dominican Republic, East Timor, Ecuador, Egypt, El Salvador, Eritrea, Finland, Georgia, Greece, Guatemala, Guyana, Haiti, Honduras, Hungary, Iran, Iraq, Italy, Jamaica, Kazakhstan, Kenya, Kuwait, Kyrgyzstan, Latvia, Lithuania, Macedonia, Madagascar, Mexico, Moldova, Mongolia, Montenegro, Mozambique, Myanmar, Netherlands, Nicaragua, Niger, Oman, Panama, Paraguay, Peru, Philippines, Portugal, Qatar, Romania, Russia, San Marino, São Tomé and Príncipe, Saudi Arabia, Serbia, Seychelles, Slovenia, Somalia, Suriname, Sweden, Switzerland, Tajikistan, Turkmenistan, Ukraine, Uzbekistan, Venezuela, and Yemen.

90 The nations with constitutional environmental responsibilities for government but no explicit provisions related to enforceability include Austria, Belize, Benin, Cameroon, China, Cuba, Equatorial Guinea, Guinea, Indonesia, Luxembourg, Mali, Mauritania, Morocco, North Korea, Norway, Palau, Rwanda, South Korea, Togo, United Arab Emirates, Uruguay, and Vietnam.

91 Government duties to protect the environment are not directly enforceable because they are framed as directive principles of state policy in Bangladesh, Gambia, Ghana, Lesotho, Malawi, Malta, Namibia, Nigeria, South Sudan, Spain, Sri Lanka, Sudan, Swaziland, Tanzania, and Zambia.

92   Constitution of Gambia, Article 211.

93   Olowu (2006, 56).

94   These six nations are Armenia, Central African Republic, Gabon, Maldives, South Africa, and Turkey.

95   Constitution of Gabon, Article 1(8).

96   The fifteen nations are Albania, Andorra, Belgium, Bhutan, Czech Republic, Ethiopia, France, Germany, India, Nepal, Poland, Senegal, Slovakia, Thailand, and Uganda.

97   Constitution of Germany, Articles 19(4) and 20a.

98   Constitution of India, Article 32.

99   Ibid., Articles 37 and 48A.

100 Beatty (2004, 137).

101 Law and Versteeg (2011, 36-37).

102 Kinney and Clark (2004); UN Food and Agriculture Organization (n.d.).

103 View the constitution of Kenya at http://www.kenyalaw.org/.

104 See Jamaica's *Charter of Fundamental Rights and Freedoms* at http://www.japarliament. gov.jm/. See Morocco's new constitution at: http://www.parlement.ma/fe/ _textesdebase1.php?filename=201108181122510. See South Sudan's new constitution at: http://www.sudantribune.com/IMG/pdf/The_Draft_Transitional_ Constitution_of_the_ROSS2-2.pdf.

105 See Iceland's draft constitution at http://stjornlagarad.is/other_files/stjornlagarad/ Frumvarp-enska.pdf.

106 Zimbabwe Lawyers for Human Rights and National Constitutional Assembly (2009, 80).

CHAPTER 4: THE INFLUENCE OF INTERNATIONAL LAW

1   Shelton (2006, 130).

2   Wiener (2001).

3   Yang and Percival (2009).

4   Atapattu (2006, 21).

5   Malone and Pasternack (2006).

6   Article 59 of the *Statute of the International Court of Justice* states that "the decision of the Court has no binding force except between the parties and in respect of that particular case."

7   *Statute of the International Court of Justice* (1945), http://www.icj-cij.org/documents/ index.php?p1=4&p2=2&p3=0.

8   Currie, Forcese, and Oosterveld (2007, 156).

9   Kindred and Saunders (2006).

10 Boyle (2006).

11 Ibid.; Cassese (2005, 196); Janis (2003).

12 Boyle (2006, 144).

13 Guzman (2008); Boyle (2006).

14 Weil (1983, 417).

15 Szekely (1997).

16 Nanda and Pring (2003, 7).

17 Cassese (2005).
18 Boyle (2006, 142).
19 Kindred and Saunders (2006).
20 *Vienna Convention for the Protection of the Ozone Layer* (1985).
21 Sands (2003).
22 *Kyoto Protocol* (1997); *United Nations Framework Convention on Climate Change* (1992).
23 Kennedy Cuomo (1993, 227).
24 Article 24(2)(c), *Convention on the Rights of the Child* (1989).
25 Ibid., Article 29.
26 Article 14(2)(h), *Convention on the Elimination of All Forms of Discrimination against Women* (1979).
27 Articles 26 and 46 of the *Geneva Convention (III) Relative to the Treatment of Prisoners of War* (1949); Articles 89 and 127 of the *Geneva Convention (IV) Relative to the Protection of Civilian Persons in Time of War* (1949).
28 *Additional Protocol to the Geneva Conventions of 12 August 1949, and relating to the Protection of Victims of International Armed Conflicts (Protocol I)* (1977), Article 55.
29 Weissbrodt and de la Vega (2007, 189).
30 Kindred and Saunders (2006, 866).
31 Article 6, *International Covenant on Civil and Political Rights;* Article 3, *Universal Declaration of Human Rights.*
32 Weiss (1992).
33 Boyd (in press).
34 Article 12.1, *International Covenant on Economic, Social and Cultural Rights.*
35 UN Committee on Economic, Social and Cultural Rights (2000).
36 Ibid., para. 51.
37 Toebes (1999).
38 Shelton (2006).
39 The *African Charter* has been ratified by fifty-three nations, of which fifty-two are UN members. The *San Salvador Protocol* has been ratified by fifteen nations. The *Aarhus Convention* has been ratified by forty-three nations, although the United Kingdom filed a reservation with its ratification refusing to acknowledge that there is a substantive right to a healthy environment. The *Arab Charter* has been ratified by ten nations. Algeria and Libya have ratified both the *African Charter* and the *Arab Charter,* while Palestine is not a UN member. All ratification data are current to 1 August 2011.
40 Article 3.2 of the 1998 *Asian Human Rights Charter,* reproduced in Shelton (2008, 1079). Articles 1(9) and 2(2)(i) of the *Charter of the Association of Southeast Asian Nations* (2007).
41 Article 24, *African Charter on Human and Peoples' Rights* (1982).
42 A list of countries that have signed or ratified the charter is available on the African Commission on Human and Peoples' Rights website, http://www.achpr.org/english/ratifications/ratification_african%20charter.pdf.
43 Birnie and Boyle (2002, 254).
44 *Social and Economic Rights Action Centre (SERAC) et al. v. Nigeria* (2001).

45 Article 18, *Protocol to the African Charter on Human and Peoples' Rights on the Rights of Women in Africa* (2005).

46 Nwobike (2005, 145).

47 Viljoen and Louw (2007).

48 The *Protocol to the African Charter of Human and Peoples' Rights on the Establishment of an African Court on Human and Peoples' Rights* (2004). A list of countries that have signed or ratified the protocol is available on the African Commission on Human and Peoples' Rights website, http://www.achpr.org/english/ratifications/ratification_court.pdf.

49 See the court's website at http://www.african-court.org/.

50 A list of countries that have signed or ratified the convention, along with information on declarations, reservations, denunciations, and withdrawals, is available on the Organization of American States, Department of International Law website, http://www.oas.org/juridico/english/Sigs/b-32.html. Trinidad and Tobago originally ratified the convention in 1991 but filed a denunciation (i.e., withdrawal) in 1998.

51 *Additional Protocol to the American Convention on Human Rights in the Area of Economic, Social, and Cultural Rights* (1988).

52 A list of countries that have signed or ratified the convention is available on the Organization of American States, Department of International Law website, http://www.oas.org/juridico/English/sigs/a-52.html. Four additional nations (Chile, Dominican Republic, Haiti, and Venezuela) have signed the *San Salvador Protocol* but had not ratified it as of 1 August 2011.

53 Although Article 11 cannot be enforced through an individual petition, it is arguably incorporated, through Article 29 of the convention, into the existing rights in the convention and declaration. Hunter, Salzman, and Zaelke (2007, 1378).

54 Taillant (2003).

55 Article 37 of the charter, proclaimed by the European Parliament, the Council of the European Union, and the European Commission, 7 December 2000.

56 There are extensive environmental provisions in the draft *European Constitution* but none of them refer to a right to a healthy environment.

57 Miller (1998, 23).

58 *Declaration on the Management of the Natural Environment in Europe*, cited in Sohn (1973, 452n88).

59 Recommendation 1130 on the Formulation of a Draft European Charter and a European Convention on Environmental Protection and Sustainable Development (1990), from the Parliamentary Assembly of the Council of Europe, 42nd Assembly, reprinted in *Yearbook of International Environmental Law* 1 (1990): 484.

60 Parliamentary Assembly of the Council of Europe, Committee of Ministers (2010).

61 Stec (2003a).

62 Pallemaerts (2002, 18).

63 *Aarhus Convention*, Status of Ratifications in UN Treaties Database, Chapter 27: Environment, http://treaties.un.org/Pages/ViewDetails.aspx?src=TREATY&mtdsg_no=XXVII-13&chapter=27&lang=en.

64 Eleftheriadis (2007).

65 Pedersen (2008, 99).
66 *Arab Charter on Human Rights* (2004). As of 1 January 2011, the Arab Charter had
    been ratified by ten nations (Algeria, Bahrain, Jordan, Libya, Palestine, Qatar,
    Saudi Arabia, Syrian Arab Republic, United Arab Emirates, and Yemen).
67 Orakhelashvili (2006); American Law Institute (1987, para. 702).
68 Brownlie (2003, 6).
69 Currie, Forcese, and Oosterveld (2007).
70 Birnie and Boyle (2002, 15).
71 Currie, Forcese, and Oosterveld (2007, 141).
72 *Legality of the Threat or Use of Nuclear Weapons, Advisory Opinion* (1996, 241),
    International Court of Justice.
73 Kelly (2000).
74 Janis (2003, 44).
75 Brownlie (2003).
76 A.E. Roberts (2001, 758).
77 Guzman (2008, 214).
78 UN General Assembly (1968).
79 *Stockholm Declaration* (1972). See Popovic (1995-96).
80 A. Kiss and Shelton (2004, 667).
81 Preparatory Committee for the United Nations Conference on the Human Environ-
    ment, UN Doc. A/Conf.48/PC/17 at para. 77 (1972), cited in Sohn (1973, 429).
82 Gormley (1976).
83 Pallemaerts (2002, 11-12).
84 Organization of the Islamic Conference (1990).
85 UN Human Rights Commission (2005, 2003, 2001, 1991).
86 Earth Charter, Article 9(a). See the text of the charter and information about the
    initiative at the Earth Charter website, http://www.earthcharter.org.
87 Alliance of Small Island States (2007).
88 Pallemaerts (2003); *Rio Declaration on Environment and Development* (1992).
89 Acevedo (2000); Boyle (1996, 43); Wirth (1994-95).
90 Shelton (1993, 75).
91 J. Lee (2000).
92 Ibid., 3089.
93 Pevato (1999).
94 Ibid., 314.
95 Guzman (2008); Boyle (2006).
96 Inter-American Commission on Human Rights (2010).
97 Currie, Forcese, and Oosterveld (2007).
98 Malone and Pasternack (2006, 67).
99 These seven nations are Iceland, Ireland, Liechtenstein, Monaco, San Marino,
    Switzerland, and the United Kingdom.
100 This includes the ninety-two nations that recognize the right to a healthy environ-
    ment explicitly in their constitutions, the twelve nations recognizing the right
    through high court decisions, and the following thirty-nine nations that lack

constitutional recognition of the right but have ratified one of the four binding regional treaties: Algeria, Austria, Bahrain, Bosnia and Herzegovina, Botswana, Cyprus, Denmark, Djibouti, Equatorial Guinea, Eritrea, Gambia, Germany, Ghana, Guinea-Bissau, Jordan, Kazakhstan, Lesotho, Liberia, Libya, Lithuania, Luxembourg, Madagascar, Malta, Mauritius, Namibia, Qatar, Saudi Arabia, Sierra Leone, Somalia, Suriname, Swaziland, Sweden, Syrian Arab Republic, Tajikistan, Tunisia, United Arab Emirates, Yemen, Zambia, and Zimbabwe.

101 The small island states that do not provide constitutional recognition of the right to a healthy environment but have signed the *Male' Declaration* are Antigua and Barbuda, Bahamas, Barbados, Belize, Cuba, Dominica, Fiji, Grenada, Haiti, Kiribati, Marshall Islands, Micronesia, Nauru, Palau, Papua New Guinea, Saint Kitts and Nevis, Saint Lucia, Saint Vincent and the Grenadines, Samoa, Singapore, Solomon Islands, Tonga, Trinidad and Tunisia, Tuvalu, and Vanuatu.

102 Three additional nations whose environmental laws explicitly recognize the right to a healthy environment are Bhutan, Uzbekistan, and Vietnam.

103 In Canada, Northwest Territories, Nunavut, Ontario, Quebec, and Yukon recognize the right to a healthy environment, as do Hawaii, Illinois, Massachusetts, Montana, Pennsylvania, and Rhode Island in the United States.

104 Brownlie (2003).

105 A. Kiss and Shelton (2004, 682).

106 Since 1947, the International Court of Justice has adjudicated approximately 140 cases, including 116 "contentious cases" referred to it by the mutual consent of states, and 25 advisory opinions requested by authorized UN organs. For the docket of cases referred to the ICJ since 1946, see the court's website, http://www.icj-cij.org/docket/index.php?p1=3&p2=2 (accessed 1 February 2009).

107 Shaw (2003, 754).

108 *Case Concerning the Gabčíkovo-Nagymaros Project* (1997, 204-6).

109 *Optional Protocol to the International Covenant on Civil and Political Rights* (1976).

110 *Optional Protocol to the International Covenant on Economic, Social and Cultural Rights* (2009).

111 A. Kiss and Shelton (2004, 683).

112 United Nations Human Rights Committee, Communication No. 1331/2004: Sri Lanka. CCPR/C/87/D/1331/2004, 14 September 2006.

113 Taylor (1998a, ch. 5).

114 United Nations Human Rights Committee, *E.H.P. v. Canada*, 27 October 1982, Communication 67/1980, UN Doc. CCPR/C/OP 1, para. 8.

115 *Case of Yanomani Indians* (1985).

116 Picolotti and Cordonnier-Segger (2005).

117 Inter-American Commission on Human Rights (1997).

118 Ibid., 88.

119 Scott (2000, 236).

120 *Association of Lhaka Honhat Aboriginal Communities v. Argentina* (2000).

121 *Maya Indigenous Communities of the Toledo District (Belize Maya)* (2004).

122 *Community of San Mateo de Huanchor and its members v. Peru* (2004).

123 Petition to the IACHR on Human Rights Seeking Relief from Violations Resulting from Global Warming Caused by Acts and Omissions of the United States, 7 December 2005. The text of the petition is available online at the Earthjustice website, http://www.earthjustice.org/library/legal_docs/petition-to-the-inter-american-commission-on-human-rights-on-behalf-of-the-inuit-circumpolar-conference.pdf.

124 Documents related to the case are available from the Center for International Environmental Law, http://www.ciel.org/Hre/HRE_Cacataibo.html.

125 Inter-American Commission on Human Rights (2007).

126 *Community of La Oroya v. Peru* (2009).

127 *Maya People of the Sipacapa and San Miguel Ixtahuacán Municipalities v. Guatemala* (2010).

128 Inter-American Court of Human Rights (2008).

129 *Caso de la Comunidad Mayagna (Sumo) Awas Tingni* (2001).

130 *Kichwa Peoples of the Sarayaku Indigenous Community v. Ecuador* (2004).

131 *Case of the Sarayaku Indigenous Community v. Ecuador* (2004).

132 IACHR Application to the Inter-American Court in the case of *Kichwa People of Sarayaku v. Ecuador*, Case 12.465, 26 April 2010.

133 *Case of the Yakye Axa Indigenous Community v. Paraguay* (2005).

134 *Sawhoyamaxa Indigenous Community of the Enxet People v. Paraguay* (2006).

135 *Twelve Saramaka Clans v. Suriname* (2007).

136 The European Commission on Human Rights was disbanded in 1988, and the European Court on Human Rights is now responsible for adjudicating individuals' cases. The European Court has made rulings in more than eight thousand admissible cases in its fifty-plus-year history. Only a small fraction of these cases have involved environmental degradation or hazards. Guzman (2008).

137 *Lopez Ostra v. Spain* (1994).

138 Sands (1996).

139 *Guerra et al. v. Italy* (1998).

140 *Ledyayeva, Dobrokhotova, Zolotareva et Romashina v. Russia* (2006); *Fadeyeva v. Russia* (2005).

141 *Moreno Gomez v. Spain* (2004).

142 *Giacomelli v. Italy* (2006).

143 *Grimkovskaya v. Ukraine* (2011).

144 *Tatar and Tatar v. Romania* (2009); *Taskin and Others v. Turkey* (2004).

145 *Hatton and Others v. United Kingdom* (2003).

146 *Oneryildiz v. Turkey* (2004).

147 Ibid., para. 71.

148 Ibid., para. 89.

149 *Zander v. Sweden* (1993).

150 *Okyay et al. v. Turkey* (2005).

151 Ibid., paras. 51-52.

152 *Taskin and Others v. Turkey* (2004).

153 *Alatulkkila and Others v. Finland* (2005); *Pine Valley Development Ltd. et al. v. Ireland* (1991).

154 *Fägerskiöld v. Sweden* (2008).
155 *Vides Aizsardzibas Klubs v. Latvia* (2004); *Bladet Tromso and Stensaas v. Norway* (1999).
156 *Tebieti Mühafize Cemiyyeti and Israfilov v. Azerbaijan* (2010); *Zeleni Balkani v. Bulgaria* (2007).
157 *Hatton and Others v. United Kingdom* (2003, para. 96).
158 Ibid., Dissenting Judgment, paras. 2, 4.
159 *Kyrtatos v. Greece* (2003) was decided by a 6-1 vote. The dissenting judge found a violation of Article 8 based on environmental deterioration leading to adverse effects on quality of life.
160 *Kyrtatos v. Greece* (2003, para. 52).
161 Ibid., para. 53.
162 *Fadeyeva v. Russia* (2005, para. 68).
163 *Tatar and Tatar v. Romania* (2009).
164 Ibid., para. 109.
165 Ibid., paras. 107, 112.
166 *Atanasov v. Bulgaria* (2011).
167 *Grimkovskaya v. Ukraine* (2011).
168 Shelton (2008, 205).
169 Boyle (2009).
170 Trilsch (2009).
171 *Marangopoulos Foundation for Human Rights v. Greece* (2006).
172 Trilsch (2009, 534).
173 *Centre for Minority Rights Development on behalf of Endorois Community v. Kenya* (2010); *Social and Economic Rights Action Centre (SERAC) et al. v. Nigeria* (2001, para. 52).
174 *SERAC et al. v. Nigeria* (2001, para. 52).
175 A. Kiss and Shelton (2004, 716).
176 Shelton (2004a, 206); Chirwa (2002).
177 Ebuku (2007).
178 World Commission on Environment and Development (1987, 348).
179 Ksentini (1994).
180 World Health Organization (1989).
181 *Johannesburg Principles on the Role of Law and Sustainable Development* (2003).
182 Schrijver and Weiss (1995, para. 31).
183 Commission on Environmental Law of the IUCN, in cooperation with the International Council of Environmental Law (1995).
184 UN Educational, Scientific and Cultural Organization and the UN High Commissioner for Human Rights (1999).
185 Dejeant-Pons and Pallemaerts (2002, 91).
186 Shelton (2009); UN High Commissioner for Human Rights and UN Environment Programme (2002, para. 15).
187 Prepared at the Experts Meeting held in Oslo, 29-31 October 1990. Reprinted in *Environmental Policy and Law* (1991): 81.
188 UN Educational, Scientific and Cultural Organization and the UN High Commissioner for Human Rights (1999).
189 International Centre of Comparative Environmental Law (2001, 1990).

190 Center for Human Rights and Environment and the Center for International Environmental Law (2002).
191 McCallion and Sharma (2000); Thorme (1991, 332-33).
192 Atapattu (2006, 34); Nanda and Pring (2003, 17, 29, 475).
193 Pedersen (2008); Collins (2007); Fitzmaurice and Marshall (2007); Hill, Wolfson, and Targ (2004); Downs (1993); Nickel (1993); Marks (1981).
194 Singh (1997, 210).
195 Brownlie (2003, 540-41); Alston (2001, 281); Dias (1999, 400); Eleftheriadis (1999, 549); Pevato (1999); Robertson and Merrills (1989).
196 Handl (2001, 312).
197 Currie, Forcese, and Oosterveld (2007); Louka (2006); Martin et al. (2006); Cassese (2005).
198 Steiner, Alston, and Goodman (2008); Hunter, Salzman, and Zaelke (2007, 1378); Merrills (2007); Brownlie (2003, 540-41); Janis (2003).
199 Freeman and van Ert (2004, 30).
200 Weissbrodt and de la Vega (2007, 189, 192); Atapattu (2006, 21, 23); Kindred and Saunders (2006, 1038); Cordonier-Segger and Khalfan (2004, 72); A. Kiss and Shelton (2004, 709); Nanda and Pring (2003, 17, 29, 475); Sands (2003, 294, 297); Shaw (2003, 756-57); Smith (2003, 342); Birnie and Boyle (2002, 254).
201 Palmer and Robb (2005); DeMarco and Campbell (2004); M. Anderson and Galizzi (2002).
202 Pallemaerts (2002, 11-12).
203 Sarlet and Fensterseifer (2009); Hancock (2003).
204 Davies (2007).
205 Nimushakavi (2006, 23, 156-57). For example, see *Virender Gaur v. State of Haryana* (1995); *M.C. Mehta v. Union of India* (1988, Ganges pollution).
206 *P.K. Waweru v. Republic of Kenya* (2006).
207 Sala Constitucional de Costa Rica, resolución nos. 2003-04654 (2003) and 2007-02154 (2007).
208 Lasser (2009, 1).
209 European Court of Human Rights (2008).
210 *Tatar and Tatar v. Romania* (2009).
211 Hottelier and Martenet (2006).
212 *Tatar and Tatar v. Romania* (2009); *Fadeyeva v. Russia* (2005); *Okyay et al. v. Turkey* (2005); *Taskin and Others v. Turkey* (2004).
213 Schall (2008).
214 Yang and Percival (2009).
215 Watson (1993).
216 *Advocates Coalition for Development and Environment v. Attorney General* (2004); Razzaque (2004).
217 *WALHI v. PT Inti Indorayon Utama* (1989), cited in Koesnadi (1997).
218 Nelken (1995); Slaughter (1994, 99);
219 Choudhry (2006); McCrudden (2000).
220 Yang and Percival (2009).

221 *Beatriz Silvia Mendoza and others v. National Government and Others* (2008); *Concerned Residents of Manila Bay et al. v. Metropolitan Manila Development Authority et al.* (2008).

222 Liefferink and Jordan (2004).

223 Slaughter (2000).

224 Lavrysen (2005).

225 Agcaoili (2009, 4).

226 *Johannesburg Principles on the Role of Law and Sustainable Development* (2002).

227 Information on the Judges Programme is available on the UNEP website, http://www.unep.org/Law/Programme_work/Judges_programme/index.asp.

228 Bankobeza (2003).

229 Kameri-Mbote (2009).

230 Greenwatch (2007a); Greenwatch and UNEP (2006).

231 Mechlem (2006).

232 Greenwatch (2007b).

233 Pendergrass (2006).

234 Bedner (2007, 122).

235 Chernaik (1998). For more on ELAW, see the organization's website, http://www.elaw.org.

236 The GUTA Association's website is at http://epl.org.ua/en/guta/history/.

237 Justice and Environment's website is http://www.justiceandenvironment.org.

238 Epp (1998, 6).

239 For more information on the Community Environmental Legal Defense Fund, see the organization's website, http://www.celdf.org.

240 For more information on the IUCN Commission on Environmental Law, see http://www.iucn.org/about/union/commissions/cel/.

241 For more on the IUCN Academy of Environmental Law, see http://www.iucnael.org/.

242 For more information on INECE, see http://www.inece.org/.

243 For information on UNEP, see http://www.unep.org/law/About_prog/introduction.asp.

244 For information on IUCN projects in Nepal, see http://www.iucn.org/about/union/secretariat/offices/asia/asia_where_work/nepal/projects/.

245 For information on COHRE, see http://www.cohre.org.

246 *Lindiwe Mazibuko et al. v. The City of Johannesburg et al.* (2010).

247 Shelton (2009).

248 Rodriguez-Rivera (2001).

249 Eleftheriadis (2007).

250 Ibid.

251 Yang and Percival (2009, 664).

CHAPTER 5: A FRAMEWORK FOR ASSESSING THE LEGAL INFLUENCE OF THE RIGHT TO A HEALTHY ENVIRONMENT

1 Hirschl (2004, ch. 5).

2 Bruch, Coker, and VanArsdale (2007, 38).

3   Hill, Wolfson, and Targ (2004, 382); May (2006, 114); May and Daly (2009).
4   Gloppen (2006); Epp (1998).
5   Krygier and Czarnota (1999); Raz (1979).
6   Chavez (2004, 1).
7   Beatty (2004, 154).
8   Gloppen (2006).
9   Epp (1998).
10   Dickson (2007a, 14).

CHAPTER 6: LATIN AMERICA AND THE CARIBBEAN

1   McAllister (2005).
2   A.F. Aguilar and Arnal (2002); A.F. Aguilar (1994).
3   Repetto (2003, 16).
4   Ankersen (2003, 819).
5   Walsh (2007, 505).
6   *System of Free Public Access to Environmental Information* (2003); *Water Law* (2003); *General Law on the Environment* (2002); *Minimum Standard Law Regarding Industrial Waste* (2002); *Minimum Standard Law Regarding Management and Elimination of PCBs* (2002).
7   Sabsay (2003, 3).
8   An example of a provincial law that incorporates the right to a healthy environment as a guiding principle is Rio Negro's *Environmental Impact Assessment Law* (1998). Sabsay (n.d.).
9   Examples include the *Toxic Substances Control Act, Water Act, Environmental Crimes Act,* and *National Environmental Education Policy Act.* Sarlet and Fensterseifer (2009).
10   Organisation for Economic Co-operation and Development (2005a, 91, 125-26).
11   For Colombian environmental legislation and regulations post-1991, see the ECOLEX database at http://www.ecolex.org.
12   Colombia Ministry of Environment, Housing, and Territorial Development (2011).
13   Eljuri and Quintero (2009, 21).
14   *Organic Law on the Environment* (2006), Articles 1, 4, 39, and 43.
15   Eljuri and Quintero (2009).
16   *Law of the Rights of Mother Earth* (2010).
17   Barrera-Hernandez (2002).
18   *General Law on the Environment,* 2005, Law No. 28611, repairs damage to framework environmental law.
19   Turner (2009).
20   Ibid., 106.
21   Turner (2009).
22   *Sanctioning Crimes against the Environment* (1996).
23   Abed (2009); Sobrevivencia and Amigas de la Tierra Paraguay (2006).
24   Abed (2009).
25   Bynoe (2006).
26   World Bank (2009).

27　Martinez (2001, 51).

28　UN Economic Commission for Latin America and the Caribbean (2002, 163). See also Garcia-Guadilla (2006).

29　Martinez (2000); Programa de las Naciones Unidas para el Medio Ambiente (2000); A.F. Aguilar (1994).

30　A.F. Aguilar (1994).

31　Martinez (2001).

32　Rojas and Iza (2009, 123).

33　Brewer-Carias (2009).

34　Ferrada Borquez, Bordali Salamanca, and Cazor Aliste (2004).

35　*Sociedad Peruana de Derecho Ambiental v. Ministerio de Energía y Minas* (1996).

36　B.M. Wilson (2009); Gargarella, Domingo, and Roux (2006).

37　Carballo (2009, 270).

38　Di Paola, Duverges, and Esain (2006, 5).

39　Smulovitz (2005).

40　Defensor del Pueblo (2008).

41　Carballo (2009); Martinez (2001).

42　*Margarita v. Copetro* (1993).

43　See, for example, details of the Chacras de la Merced case on the Centro de Derechos Humanos y Ambiente website (http://www.cedha.org.ar) and the Paynemil Mapuche Community case on the Rights to Water and Sanitation website (http://www.righttowater.info/legal-approach-case-studies).

44　*General Law on the Environment* (2002).

45　Dug and Faggi (2003, 100).

46　*Maria del Carmen Cosimi, v. Direccion Provincial de Energia de Corrientes* (2005).

47　*Beatriz Silvia Mendoza and others v. National Government and Others in regards to damages suffered* (2008).

48　*Beatriz Silvia Mendoza and Others v. National Government and Others* (2006).

49　Dug and Faggi (2003).

50　Carballo (2009, 285).

51　World Bank (2009).

52　Yang and Percival (2009).

53　*Law on the Matanza-Riachuelo Watershed* (2006).

54　Matanza-Riachuelo Watershed Authority (2011).

55　World Bank (2009, 15).

56　Walcacer (2002).

57　Constitution of Brazil, Article 225; McAllister (2008).

58　Constitution of Brazil, Articles 127-29.

59　*Public Civil Action Law* (1985).

60　*Environmental Crimes Act* (1998).

61　McAllister (2005).

62　Arantes (2005, 248).

63　McAllister (2008, 91-92).

64　Daibert (2007).

65　Cappelli (2003).

66 Passos de Freitas (2003, 62).
67 McAllister (2008, 99).
68 Fearnside (2006).
69 Sarlet and Fensterseifer (2009, 261).
70 Supreme Court of Justice (SCJ) Appeal No. 575.998 (Minas Gerais), 16 November 2004; SCJ Appeal No. 70011759842 (Rio Grande do Sul), 1 December 2005; SCJ Appeal No. 70012091278 (Rio Grande do Sul), 25 January 2006.
71 Vieira (2008).
72 Hochstetler and Keck (2007, 55).
73 Daibert (2007, 97).
74 McAllister (2008, 2).
75 Hirakuri (2003).
76 J.T. Roberts and Thanos (2003, 201).
77 Arantes (2005).
78 McAllister (2008).
79 Decision T-411 (1992).
80 Cepeda Espinosa (2005, 75).
81 Barrera-Hernandez (2002, 612-13).
82 Yepes (2006).
83 Constitution of Colombia, Article 277.
84 Defensoria del Pueblo (2009a, 292).
85 Ibid., 293.
86 Ibid., 294-95.
87 Ibid., 299.
88 Defensoria del Pueblo (2007, 26).
89 Defensoria del Pueblo (2009b, 583-84).
90 See Decisions T-411 (1992), C-519 (1994), C-524 (1995), C-431 (2000), C-595 (2010), and C-366/11 (2011). Decisions are available through the website of the Constitutional Court, http://www.corteconstitucional.gov.co/. Lower courts have also made many decisions in cases involving the constitutional right to a healthy environment, e.g., *Victor Ramon Castrillon Vega y otros v. La Federacion Nacional de Algonoderos y CORPOCESAR* (1997).
91 *Antonio Mauricio Monroy Cespedes* (1993).
92 Decision C-519 (1994).
93 *Fundepúblico v. Mayor of Bugalagrande and others* (1992); *Fundepúblico v. La Compania Maritima de Transporte Croatia Line y Comar S.A., Tradenet S.A y otros* (1994).
94 See Decision T-115 of 1997 and Decision T-099 of 1998, cited in Cepeda Espinosa (2005).
95 A.F. Aguilar (1996, 262-63).
96 Rojas and Iza (2009, 312).
97 B.M. Wilson (2005, 47). The Constitutional Court is technically a special *sala*, or chamber, of the Supreme Court. See also Grote (2007b).
98 See the website of the Constitutional Court, http://www.poder-judicial.go.cr/salaconstitucional/.
99 B.M. Wilson (2007).

100 B.M. Wilson and Rodriguez Cordero (2006).
101 *Carlos Roberto García Chacón* (1993).
102 *Presidente de la sociedad MARLENE S.A. v. Municipalidad de Tibás Marlene* (1994).
103 Vote No. 5393 of 1995.
104 The website of the Constitutional Court of the Supreme Court of Justice includes a Constitutional Review (http://www.poder-judicial.go.cr/salaconstitucional/REVISTADIGITAL2009/D.html), with a selection of cases from 1989 to 2009 in various categories. Sixty-two cases are listed under the heading "Right to a Healthy and Ecologically Balanced Environment." In forty-one of those cases, the court found a violation of the right.
105 For example, see Sala Constitucional N° 18442 (2008).
106 Vote No. 2812 de 20 de abril de 1999.
107 Sala Constitucional N° 02154 (2007).
108 *M.M. Levy y Asociacion Ecologista Limonense v. Ministerio del Ambiente y Energia* (2001).
109 Carminati (2007).
110 Ibid.
111 *Caribbean Conservation Corporation et al. v. Costa Rica* (1999). See also Sala Constitucional, resolución número 2002-2486 (2002).
112 Expediente 01-011865-0007-CO, Resolución 2002-2486 (2002).
113 *A. Cederstav and Others v. National Technical Secretary for the Environment, Municipality of Santa Cruz and Others* (2008).
114 Rojas and Iza (2009, 132-36).
115 Sala Constitucional de Costa Rica, resolución no. 2004-01923 (2004).
116 *Asociación Interamericana para la Defensa del Ambiente (AIDA) y otros Recurso de Amparo* (2009).
117 See Article 200, Constitution of Peru.
118 *Jose Clemente y Arqueno Garay* (2009). *Asociacion de Propietarios del Sector Imperial del Asentamiento Humano Pamplona Alta v. Comision de Formalizacion de la Propiedad Informal* (2005); *Proterra v. Metropolitan Municipality of Lima* (2005).
119 *Colegio de Abogados del Santa* (2001); *Sociedad Peruana de Derecho Ambiental v. Direccion Regional Del Ministerio de Pesqueria* (1993).
120 *Pablo Miguel Fabián Martínez and Others v. Minister of Health and Director General of Environmental Health* (2006). See also Mesa Suarez (2006).
121 *Community of La Oroya v. Peru* (2007). See documents at the International Association for Environmental Defense website, http://www.aida-americas.org/en/project/laoroya_en.
122 *Sandro Chavez Vasquez and Channels Lopez v. Provincial Municipal Council of Pisco* (2004).
123 Turner (2009).
124 Dougnac Rodriguez (2009).
125 *Comunidad de Chañaral v. CODELCO* (1988). See Hillstrom and Hillstrom (2004).
126 *Comunidad de Chañaral v. CODELCO* (1988).
127 Ibid.
128 Asenjo (1989).

129 Houck (2008).
130 Bruch, Coker, and VanArsdale (2007, 26).
131 See details on the Fiscalía del Medio Ambiente (FIMA) website, http://www.fima.cl/2009/10/08/defensa-de-los-deerechos-humanos-caso-contaminacion-en-arica/.
132 *Municipalidad de Calbuco v. Empresa de Servicios Sanitarios de Los Lagos* (2007).
133 Biggs (2009).
134 See details on the FIMA website, http://www.fima.cl/2009/08/15/caso-celco -valdivia/.
135 See details on the FIMA website, http://www.fima.cl/2009/10/06/caso-pelambres -2005-2008/.
136 Organisation for Economic Co-operation and Development (2005a, 172).
137 Couso (2005).
138 *Confederation of Indigenous Nations v National Assembly et al.* (2010).
139 *R.F. Wheeler and E.G. Huddle v. Attorney General of the State of Loja* (2011). See Professor Erin Daly's blog on this judgment at http://blogs.law.widener.edu/ envirolawblog/2011/07/12/ecuadorian-court-recognizes-constitutional-right -to-nature/.
140 *Fundacion Natura v. Petro Ecuador* (1998).
141 *Arco Iris v. Ecuador Mineral Institute* (1993).
142 *Baba Dam Case* (2008).
143 Organic Code of the Judicial Function, Article 246. CÓDIGO ORGÁNICO DE LA FUNCIÓN JUDICIAL. Registro Oficial Suplemento No. 544: 09/03/2009.
144 *Maria Aguinda et al. v. Chevron Corporation* (2011).
145 *Manuel Zurita Sanchez et al. v. Justino Orellana Carballo* (2010).
146 La Sala Tercera de lo Contencioso Administrativo y Laboral de la Corte Suprema de Justicia, 30 de Junio, 2009. La Sala Tercera de la Corte Suprema de Justicia, 9 de Julio 2009. *Luis González et al. v. General Directorate of Health of Veraguas* (2010).
147 No. 242-2001. Sala de lo Constitucional de la Corte Suprema de Justicia: Mejia (2009); San Salvador (2003).
148 Perez Perdomo (2005).
149 Supreme Court of Justice, Judgment of 6 May 2009. Appeal by Deputy Attorney for the Defense of the Environment and Natural Resources against sentence rendered by Criminal Chamber of the Court of Appeal in San Cristobal, 27 November 2008. See also Judgment No. 024-2009 of the Tax and Administrative Law Court in Case No. 030-09-00209, 19 June 2009.
150 *Northern Jamaica Conservation Association et al. v. Natural Resources Conservation Authority et al.* (2006).
151 *Pedro Viudes v. Ley No. 816/96* (1997).
152 Agreement and Sentence No. 426, 8 July 1999; Agreement and Sentence No. 98 (1999).
153 Interlocutory Order No. 21 of 20 March 2003, Court of Appeals, San Juan Bautista, Misiones.
154 Agreement and Sentence No. 78, 19 August 2003, Court of Appeal de Asuncion.
155 *Federacion de Asociacion Organizacion de Afectados por La Represa y Acyreta de Itapua y Misiones – Fedayin S/ Amparo Constitucional* (2008).

156   Ibid.
157   Abed (2009, 311).
158   Diez (2006, 108-9).
159   Domingo (2005); López Ramos (2003).
160   Organisation for Economic Co-operation and Development (2005c, 213).
161   Ojeda-Mestre (2007, 142).
162   Ojeda-Mestre (2007).
163   *Concesiones otorgadas por el Ministerio de Energía y minas a Empresas Petroleras* (1998).
164   *Fundación Defensores de la Naturaleza v. Particular,* cited in Bruch, Coker, and VanArsdale (2007, 75).
165   Viana Ferreira (2003); Blengio Valdes (2003); Mantero de San Vicente (1993).
166   *Law of Environmental Protection* (2000), Section 2.
167   Sieder, Schjolden, and Angell (2005); Ankersen (2003, 808-9).
168   The websites for these groups are as follows: CEDARENA, http://www.cedarena.org; CEDHA, http://www.cedha.org.ar; FIMA, http://www.fima.cl/; SPDA, http://www.spda.org.pe.
169   See the AIDA website at http://www.aida-americas.org/aida.php.
170   Bonine (2009).
171   For example, Sala Constitucional de Costa Rica, resolución no. 2003-04654 (2003); Sala Constitucional de Costa Rica, resolución no. 2007-02154 (2007).
172   Sikkink (2005).
173   B.M. Wilson (2009).
174   Organisation for Economic Co-operation and Development (2005c, 108).
175   Gargarella, Domingo, and Roux (2006).
176   Couso (2006).
177   B.M. Wilson (2005).
178   Cepeda Espinosa (2005).
179   Lorenzetti, C.J., cited in Percival (2009, 455-56).
180   Couso (2005, 2004).
181   Rojas and Iza (2009, 33).
182   McAllister (2008, 2005).
183   Ojeda-Mestre (2007).
184   Walsh (2007).
185   Holley (1998).
186   Ruiz Mendoza and Martinez Torres (2003).
187   Chavez (2004).
188   G. Aguilar and Iza (2005).
189   Salazar (2004, 282).

CHAPTER 7: AFRICA
1   Kotze (2007b).
2   *National Environmental Management Act, 1998,* Preamble, ss. 2(4)(a)(viii), 31, and 32.
3   *National Environmental Management: Air Quality Act* (2004), Articles 2, 3; *National Environmental Management of Biodiversity Act* (2004), Article 3; *Local Government*

Municipal Systems Act (2000); National Water Act (1998), Preamble, Article 4; Local Government Municipal Structures Act (1998).

4   Promotion of Access to Information Act (2000), and Promotion of Administrative Justice Act (2000).

5   Decree 2005-437 organizing Environmental Inspections for Benin; Decree 2001-094 establishing Drinking Water Quality Standards for Benin; Decree 2001-110 establishing Air Quality Standards for Benin; Decree 2001-235 establishing Environmental Impact Study Regulations for Benin.

6   Kasimbazi (2009).

7   Environmental Impact Assessment Proclamation (2002), Preamble; Environmental Protection Organs Establishment Proclamation (2002), s. 6.

8   Constitution of Kenya, Article 261(1), Fifth Schedule.

9   Government of the Republic of South Africa and Others v. Grootboom and Others (2000).

10   Corder (2007, 341).

11   Kotze and Paterson (2009).

12   Khabisi NO and Another v. Aquarella Investment 83 (Pty) Ltd and Others [2007]; Harmony Gold Mining Company Limited v. Regional Director Free State Department of Water Affairs and Forestry and Another [2006]; Chief Pule Shadrack VII Bareki NO and Another v. Gencor Limited and Others (2005); Earthlife Africa (Cape Town) v. Director General Department of Environmental Affairs and Tourism and Another (2005); Wildlife and Environment Society of South Africa v. MEC for Economic Affairs, Environment and Tourism, Eastern Cape Provincial Government and Others (2005); Pretoria City Council v. Walker (1998); Minister of Health v. Woodcarb (Pty) Ltd and Another (1996).

13   Kotze and Paterson (2009).

14   Director, Mineral Development, Gauteng Region and Another v. Save the Vaal Environment and Others (1999).

15   Khabisi NO and Another v. Aquarella Investment 83 (Pty) Ltd and Others [2007].

16   BP South Africa v. MEC for Agriculture, Conservation and Land Affairs [2004].

17   Ibid.

18   Fuel Retailers Association of South Africa v. Director-General: Environmental Management, Department of Agriculture, Conservation and Environment, Mpumalanga Province, et al. (2007).

19   Ibid., Sachs J, dissenting, para. 109.

20   Ibid., Ngcobo J, para. 102.

21   Biowatch Trust v. Registrar, Genetic Resources et al. (2009).

22   Lindiwe Mazibuko v. The City of Johannesburg et al. (2010).

23   This was in the 2008 Ibrahim Index of African Governance from the Mo Ibrahim Foundation, http://www.moibrahimfoundation.org/en/media/get/20091002 _061008-index-global-press-release.pdf.

24   Glazewski (2002, 197).

25   Kotze (2007a).

26   Kasimbazi (2009).

27   Greenwatch v. Uganda Wildlife Authority and the Attorney General (2004); Uganda Electricity Transmission Co. Ltd. v. De Samaline Ltd. (2004); British American Tobacco

Ltd. v. the Environmental Action Network (2003); Greenwatch v. Attorney General and National Environmental Management Authority (2002); Environmental Action Network v. Attorney General and National Environmental Management Authority (2001); Greenwatch v. Attorney General and National Environmental Management Authority (2001); National Association of Professional Environmentalists v. AES Nile Power Ltd. (1999).

28 A.G. Nyakana v. National Environmental Management Authority et al. (2009).
29 The Environmental Action Network Ltd. v. Joseph Eryau, National Environmental Management Authority and the Attorney General (2008).
30 National Environmental (Control of Smoking in Public Places) Regulations (2004).
31 Greenwatch v. Attorney General and NEMA (2002).
32 Greenwatch (2007a).
33 Advocates Coalition for Development and Environment v. Attorney General (2004) citing M.C. Mehta v. Union of India and Others (1988) AIR 1037 (Supreme Court).
34 Greenwatch (2007a, 2007b); Greenwatch and UNEP (2006).
35 Grace Sentongo v. Yakubu Taganza (2003); B.G. Thaddeus v. Mukwano Industries (2000).
36 Twinomugisha (2007).
37 Kasimbazi (2009).
38 Okidi (2007).
39 Twinomugisha (2007, 246-47).
40 Wangari Maathai v. Kenya Times Media Trust (1989).
41 P.K. Waweru v. Republic of Kenya (2006); Rodeers Muema Nzioka and Others v. Tiomin Kenya Limited (2001), cited in Akiwomi (2002).
42 Kameri-Mbote (2009).
43 Ibid.
44 R. v. Marengo, Azemia, Antat et al. (2004).
45 Indian Council for Enviro-Legal Action v. Union of India (1996) AIR 1446 (S.C.) and M.C. Mehta v. Union of India (1997) AIR 761 (S.C.), cited at pp. 14-15 of R. v. Marengo et al. (2004).
46 Kamuzu (Administrator of Deceased Estate) v. Attorney General [2004].
47 Ibid.
48 Mwafongo and Kapila (1999).
49 Gloppen and Kanyongolo (2007).
50 Ebuku (2007).
51 Jonah Gbemre v. Shell Petroleum Development Company Nigerian Limited and Others (2005).
52 Okidi (2007); Obasanjo (2006).
53 Nwobike (2005); Oronto Douglas v. Shell Petroleum Development Company (1999). See also Gani Fawehinmi v. Abacha (1996).
54 Ladan (2009).
55 Joseph Kessy et al. v. Dar es Salaam City Council (1998); Festo Balegele et al. v. Dar es Salaam City Council (1991).
56 Environmental Management Act (2002), s. 4(1).
57 Pallangyo (2007, 39).

58 Mubangizi (2007, 2006); Darkoh and Rwomire (2003).
59 For specific examples, see Djeri-Alassani (2003); Gaba Boko (2003); Ly (2003).
60 Keeley and Scoones (2003, 116).
61 Mechlem (2006).
62 Okoth-Ogendo (1993).
63 Ihonvbere (2005, 100).
64 Moseley (2004).
65 Okidi (2007).
66 Obasanjo (2006).
67 Mba et al. (2004).
68 Moseley (2004, 233).
69 Hatchard, Ndulo, and Slinn (2004).
70 Dibie and Umeh (2008).
71 Ibid.
72 J.E. Gibson, Hager, and Pires (1994).
73 Zakane (2008).
74 Dibie (2008); Mohamed Salih (1999).
75 *P.K. Waweru v. Republic of Kenya* (2006); *Jonah Gbemre v. Shell Petroleum Development Company Nigerian Limited and Others* (2005).
76 Doumbe Bille and Ali Mekouar (2008, 213-14).
77 Ihonvbere (2005, 101-2).
78 Gnangui (2003).
79 Amechi (2009, 72).
80 Bruch, Coker, and VanArsdale (2007).

CHAPTER 8: ASIA

1 Lack of English translation of Iran's environmental laws confirmed by Professor Said Mahmoudi of Stockholm University (email received 6 April 2010).
2 Mushkat (2004, 40); Heng (2002).
3 *Clean Air Act of 1999.*
4 *Clean Water Act* (2004).
5 *Ecological Solid Waste Management Act* (2001).
6 *National Environmental Awareness and Education Act of 2008*, s. 2.
7 *Climate Change Act of 2009*, s. 2.
8 Executive Order No. 446, *Mandating the Phase-Out of Leaded Gasoline as One of the Means of Solving Air Pollution* (1997).
9 *Local Government Code* (1991), s. 16.
10 UN Economic Commission for Europe, Committee on Environmental Policy (2004, 14).
11 Kim (2006).
12 Organisation for Economic Co-operation and Development (2008b).
13 Hassan and Azfar (2004, 216).
14 *Minors Oposa v. Factoran, Jr., Secretary of the Department of the Environment and Natural Resources* [1993].
15 Gatmaytan (2003).

16   Houck (2007).
17   C and M Timber Corporation v. A.C. Alcala, Secretary of the Department of Environment and Natural Resources (1997).
18   Agcaoili (2009, 4).
19   J.C. Reyes et al. v. Republic of the Philippines (2006); A.L. Momongan v. R.B. Omipon (1995); Laguna Lake Development Authority v. Court of Appeals (1994).
20   Alfredo Tano and Others v. Hon. Gov. Salvador P. Socrates and Others (1997).
21   Concerned Residents of Manila Bay et al. v. Metropolitan Manila Development Authority, Department of Environment and Natural Resources and Others (2008).
22   The court cited M.C. Mehta v. Union of India, 4 SC 463 (1987).
23   Manila Bay.
24   Executive Order 829, Forming a Task Force on the Manila Bay Cleanup. Signed by President Arroyo, 25 August 2009. Official Gazette 105(44) 2 November 2009, p. 6472.
25   Metropolitan Manila Development Authority et al. v. Concerned Residents of Manila Bay (2011).
26   Supreme Court of the Philippines. 2008. Resolution A.M. No. 07-11-12, authorized by the Constitution of the Philippines, Art. VIII, s. 5.
27   Rules of Procedure for Environmental Cases (2010).
28   H.M. Henares, Jr. et al. v. Land Transportation Franchising and Regulatory Board et al. (2006).
29   Suray Prasad Sharma Dhungel v. Godavari Marble Industries and Others (1995).
30   Prakash Mani Sharma v. His Majesty's Government Cabinet Secretariat and Others (1990).
31   Suray Prasad Sharma Dhungel v. Godavari Marble Industries and Others (1995).
32   Subedi (2007).
33   K.B. Shrestha and Others v. HMG, Department of Transport (1999).
34   Gajurel (2001).
35   Belbase and Thapa (2007).
36   Cha (2007).
37   Belbase and Thapa (2007).
38   Subedi (2007).
39   Adaman and Arsel (2005, 1-2).
40   Günes and Coskun (2005).
41   Adaman and Arsel (2005).
42   Arsel (2005, 269); S. Ozay v. Ministry of the Environment and Eurogold (1996).
43   Taskin and Others v. Turkey (2004).
44   Okyay et al v. Turkey (2005).
45   Ginsburg (2003, 207).
46   West and Yoon (1992).
47   Ginsburg (2003, 206-46).
48   Excessive Audits Case [2003].
49   Constitutional Complaint against Article 21 of the Urban Planning Act [1998].
50   Ibid.
51   Busan University Case (1995).

52 *Revocation of a Corrective Order et al.* (2006).

53 *Naewonsa Temple, Mitaam and the Friends of Salamanders v. Korea Rail Network Authority* (2006).

54 Kim (2006).

55 *Saemangeum Case* (2006).

56 Cheongju District Court (1997). See also Busan High Court (1995) and Seoul Civil District Court (1994).

57 Eder (1996).

58 Cho (2002).

59 Ginsburg (2003, 243-44).

60 Cho (2002).

61 Ibid., 48.

62 Al'Afghani (2005).

63 *Environmental Management Act* (1997), Article 38.

64 International Development Law Foundation (2006).

65 *Mandalawangi Landslide Class Action Case* (2003).

66 *WALHI v. PT Inti Indorayon Utama* (1989), cited in Koesnadi (1997).

67 *Judicial Review of the Law No. 7 of 2004 on Water Resources* (2005).

68 Bedner (2007).

69 International Development Law Foundation (2006); Mulyono (2006); Craig, Robinson, and Koh (2003).

70 Heng (2002, 673).

71 Fawzia (2008).

72 Bedner (2007, 121).

73 Ratnawati (2008).

74 Heringa (2006, 12).

75 Asia Pacific Forum of National Human Rights Institutions (2007, 180).

76 Ibid.

77 Ahuja (2009); Boonlai and Changplayngam (2009).

78 Nimushakavi (2006).

79 *Rural Litigation and Entitlement Kendra v. Uttar Pradesh* (1987).

80 *T. Damodar Rao v. Municipal Corp. of Hyderabad* (1987).

81 *L.K. Koolwal v. State of Rajasthan* (1988).

82 *Subhash Kumar v. State of Bihar* (1991).

83 *Virender Gaur v. State of Haryana* (1995).

84 A search of the Supreme Court of India's Judgment Information System (http://judis.nic.in/supremecourt/chejudis.asp) for the words "right" and "environment" and "Article 21" produced 201 hits. See also Nimushakavi (2006); Razzaque (2004, 48-58).

85 *M.C. Mehta v. Union of India* 2002 (4) SCC 356.

86 *M.C. Mehta v. Union of India* AIR 1988 SC 1037, 1115.

87 *M.C. Mehta v. Union of India* (Taj Trapezium case) AIR 1997 SC 735.

88 *M.C. Mehta v. Union of India* (1997) 11 SCC 327.

89 Ibid., 312; *M.C. Mehta v. Union of India* 2004 (12) SC 118.

90 *AP Pollution Control Board v. M.V. Nayudu* (1999).

91 *Th. Majra Singh v. Indian Oil Corporation* (1999).

92 *M.C. Mehta v. Union of India* (1996).

93 *T.N. Godavarman Thirumulpad v. Union of India* (1999).

94 *Indian Council for Enviro-Legal Action v. Union of India* (1996).

95 *Narmada Bachao Andolan v. Union of India* (1999).

96 *UP Pollution Board v. Mohan Meakins Ltd.* (2000).

97 *Aruna Rodrigues v. Union of India*, WP. No. 260 of 2005, Order dated 22/09/2006.

98 *Murli S. Deora v. Union of India* (2001).

99 Panjwani (2008, 98-99). See *Tarun Bharat Sangh, Alwar v. Union of India* (1992).

100 *Ramasubramnayam v. Member Secretary, Chennai Metropolitan DA* (2002).

101 Jariwala (2000).

102 Cullet (2007, 39).

103 *Ramgopal Estates v. State of Tamil Nadu* [2007]; *Karnataka Industrial Areas Development Board v. Sri C. Kenchappa and Others* (2006); *Research Foundation for Science Technology and Natural Resources Policy v. Union of India* (2005); *Deepak Nitrite Ltd. v. State of Gujarat* (2004); *Essar Oil Ltd. v. Halar Utkarsh Samiti and Others* (2004).

104 Divan and Rosencranz (2001).

105 *Milk Producers Association, Orissa v. State of Orissa and Others* (2006); *N.D. Jayal and Others v. Union of India and Others* (2004).

106 Iyer (2007).

107 *State of Himachal Pradesh v. Ganesh Wood Products* (1995).

108 *M.C. Mehta v. Kamal Nath* 1997 (1) SCC 388.

109 *M.C. Mehta v. Union of India* (Oleum Gas case) AIR 1987 SC 1086.

110 *M.C. Mehta v. Kamal Nath* AIR 2000 SC 1997; 2002 SCC 653.

111 *AP Pollution Control Board v. M.V. Nayudu* (1999).

112 *Vellore Citizens Welfare Forum v. Union of India* (1996).

113 *M.C. Mehta v. Union of India* (Ganges pollution) AIR 1988 SC 1037; *T.N. Godavarman Thirumulpad v. Union of India* (1999); *M.C. Mehta v. Union of India* (motor vehicles) 2002(4) SCC 356.

114 Writ Petition 13029 of 1985. See also Padhy (2008).

115 Padhy (2008).

116 *M.C. Mehta v. Union of India* 1991 2 SCC 353. *M.C Mehta v. Union of India* Orders dated 12 August 1994, 21 October 1994, and 28 March 1995 reported at 1997 4 SCALE 4, 1997 4 SCALE 5 (SP), and 1997 4 SCALE 6 (SP).

117 *M.C. Mehta v. Union of India* 1998 (8) SCC 206.

118 World Bank (2005).

119 *M.C. Mehta v. Union of India* 2002(4) SCC 356.

120 World Bank (2005, 34).

121 The Energy and Resources Institute (2006, 19).

122 Kandlikar (2007); Narain and Krupnick (2007); Ravindra et al. (2006); Kathuria (2004); Goyal and Sidhartha (2003).

123 World Bank (2005, 28).

124 Cassels (1989).

125 *M.C. Mehta v. Union of India* (1987) 4 SCC 463 2 SCALE 611; *M.C. Mehta v. Union of India* AIR 1988 SC 1037; *M.C. Mehta v. Union of India* (1997) 2 SCC 411.

126 *T.N. Godavarman Thirumulpad v. Union of India* (1999).

127 The case is so complex that it has its own website. See http://www.forestcaseindia. org.

128 Rosencranz, Boenig, and Dutta (2007).

129 R. Sharma (2008).

130 Jariwala (2000).

131 Sahu (2008). For example, in 1997 the Supreme Court ordered seven states to each pay 20,000 rupees to M.C. Mehta, *Jagannath v. Union of India* (1997).

132 *M.C. Mehta v. Union of India* 2000 (9) SCC 411.

133 *M.C. Mehta v. Union of India* AIR 1988 SC 1031.

134 *M.C. Mehta v. Union of India* AIR 1992 SC 382.

135 *N.D. Jayal and Others v. Union of India and Others* (2004).

136 *Animal and Environment Legal Defence Fund v. Union of India* (1997).

137 *T.N. Godavaraman v. Union of India and Others* (2007).

138 Ramesh (2010, 15).

139 *Animal and Environment Legal Defence Fund v. Union of India* (1997).

140 C. Sharma (2007); Leelakrishnan (1999).

141 R. Sharma (2005, 12).

142 Dresler and Marks (2006).

143 World Bank (2005, 1).

144 Law Commission of India (2003, 25).

145 Narain and Bell (2006, 2).

146 R. Sharma (2008, 52).

147 Dam and Tewary (2005, 385).

148 Cassels (1989).

149 Iyer (2007).

150 Dutta et al. (2000).

151 Galanter and Krishnan (2004).

152 Rosencranz and Lele (2008).

153 Rosencranz, Boenig, and Dutta (2007, 10032).

154 Sahu (2008).

155 Rosencranz and Jackson (2003).

156 *P.N. Kumar v. Municipal Corp. of Delhi* (1987).

157 Krishnan (2008).

158 Ibid.

159 Gill (2010); *National Green Tribunal Act of 2010.*

160 Epp (1998, 71).

161 M.R. Anderson (1996b, 211).

162 M.R. Anderson and Bluck (2000, 106).

163 *Shehla Zia v. WAPDA* (1994).

164 *General Secretary West Pakistan Salt Miners Labour Union v. Director Industries and Mineral Development* (1994).

165 Hassan (2006).

166 For example, in *Shehla Zia v. WAPDA*, Pakistan's Supreme Court referred to *M.C. Mehta v. Union of India*, AIR 1988 SC 1115 and AIR 1988 SC 1037.

167 *Shehri v. the Province of Sindh* (2001); *Dr. Zahir Ansari v. Karachi Development Authority* (2000); *Syed Mansoor Ali Shah v. Government of the Punjab and Others* (1997), cited in Razzaque (2004, 113-14); Human Rights Case No. 20-K/92, discussed in Lau (1996); *Environment Pollution in Balochistan* (1994); *Sheri-CBE Human Rights Case* (1993), cited in Lau (2007).

168 Hassan (2003b).

169 *Muhammad Yousuf and Others v. Province of the Punjab through Secretary, Local Government and Others* (2003).

170 Hassan (2006).

171 *Syed Mansoor Ali Shah v. Government of the Punjab and Others* (1997).

172 Hassan (2007b); Hassan and Azfar (2004); Akhund and Qureshi (1998).

173 Hassan (2003a, 18).

174 *Anjum Irfan v. LDA* (2002).

175 Hassan and Hassan (2009).

176 Lau (2007).

177 Hassan (2007a).

178 *Dr. M. Farooque v. Bangladesh* (1997), cited in Razzaque (2004, 107).

179 See the list of public interest litigation cases brought by the Bangladesh Environmental Lawyers Association on the BELA website (http://www.belabangla. org/html/pil.htm); for example, Writ Petition No. 6025/05. See also May and Daly (2009, 402).

180 A search for cases using the search terms "Sri Lanka" and "right to a healthy environment" at the Commonwealth Legal Information Institute (http://www. commonlii.org) yielded no hits on 12 December 2009.

181 *Lalanath de Silva v. Minister of Forestry and Environment* (1998), cited in Puvimana-singhe (2004).

182 *National Environmental (Air, Fuel and Vehicle Importation Standards) Regulations* (2003).

183 *Bulankulama et al. v. The Secretary, Minister of Industrial Development et al.* (2000).

184 Atapattu (2002b).

185 Levinson and Page (2004).

186 *Adam, Teva ve'Din (Human Being, Nature, and Law) v. Prime Minister of Israel et al.* (2004).

187 Levinson and Page (2004, 25).

188 Malaysia, Ministry of Science, Technology, and Environment (1993).

189 *Malaysian Vermicelli Manufacturers (Melaka) Sdn Bhd v. PP* [2001]; *Tan Tek Seng v. Suruhanjaya Perkhidmatan Pendidikan* [1996]. Both are cited in Asia Pacific Forum of National Human Rights Institutions (2007).

190 *Pihak Berkuasa Negeri Sabah v. Sugumar Balakrishnan and Anor* [2002]; *Ketua Pengarah Jabatan Alam Sekitar and Anor v. Kajing Tubek and Ors* [1997].

191 Sharom (2002).

192 Harding and Sharom (2007).

193 Craig, Robinson, and Koh (2003).

194 Boer, Ramsay, and Rothwell (1998).

195 Richardson (2004, 178).

196　Heng (2002).

197　Pompe (2005); Tan (2004).

198　Mehta (2006).

199　Adeel and Nakamoto (2003, 223).

200　Tookey (1999, 362).

201　Richardson (2004); Johnston (1998).

202　Harding (2007, 12).

203　Richardson (2004).

204　Tan (2004).

205　Mulyono (2006); Mushkat (2004); Tan (2004); Adeel and Nakamoto (2003); Bolla and McDornan (1999).

206　Robinson (2003).

207　Boer (1999).

208　Pompe (2005).

209　Boer, Ramsay, and Rothwell (1998).

210　Nimushakavi (2006, 23, 156-57). For example, see *Virender Gaur v. State of Haryana* (1995) and *M.C. Mehta v. Union of India* (Ganges pollution) AIR 1988 SC 1037.

211　Heng (2002).

212　Prominent examples include Antonio Oposa in the Philippines and M.C. Mehta in India.

213　Kravchenko (2007).

214　Compliance Committee of the Aarhus Convention (2005).

215　*Tebieti Mühafize Cemiyyeti and Israfilov v. Azerbaijan* (2010).

216　Harding (2007).

217　Boer (1999, 1552).

CHAPTER 9: EASTERN EUROPE

1　It is acknowledged that Eastern Europe is an imprecise term. For purposes of this section, it includes nations from the former Soviet Union (Belarus, Moldova, Russia, Ukraine), Central Europe (Czech Republic, Hungary, Poland, Slovakia, Slovenia), Southeastern Europe (Albania, Bulgaria, Croatia, Macedonia, Montenegro, Romania), the Baltic Region (Estonia and Latvia), and the Transcaucasus (Armenia and Georgia).

2　Peterson (1993).

3　Stec (1998).

4　Serafin (1991).

5　Organisation for Economic Co-operation and Development (2002, 18).

6　Staddon and Cellarius (2002).

7　Oldfield (2005).

8　UN Economic Commission for Europe, Committee on Environmental Policy (2003).

9　Ibid. (2007b, 40; 2007a).

10　Ibid. (2005).

11　Bandi (2004).

12　Organisation for Economic Co-operation and Development (2008a, 127).

13　Eighteen of the nineteen Eastern European nations studied in this chapter have ratified the *Aarhus Convention*. Russia is the only exception. For information on this convention and its signatories, see the relevant page of the UN Treaty Collection website: http://treaties.un.org/Pages/ViewDetails.aspx?src=TREATY&mtdsg_no= XXVII-13&chapter=27&lang=en.

14　Goldston (2006).

15　Stec (2009).

16　UN Economic Commission for Europe, Committee on Environmental Policy (2006).

17　*Environmental Protection Act* (1995), Article 98.

18　Constitutional Court, decision No. 996/G/1990. Cited in Bandi (1993).

19　Judgment 28/1994.

20　Bandi (2003, 111).

21　Judgment 48/1997, cited in Majtenyi (2006).

22　Cerny (2009a).

23　C. Kiss (2009).

24　Environmental Management and Law Association (2003, 29).

25　See for example, the *Balaton Highway* case cited in Stec (2003a).

26　*Uniformity Decision* No.1/2004. Cited by Organisation for Economic Co-operation and Development (2008a, 174-75).

27　*Judgment of 21 December 2007* in the case No. 2007-12-03, Para. 13; *Judgment of 8 February 2007* in the case No. 2006-09-03, Para. 11; *Judgment of 14 February 2003* in the case No. 2002-14-04, Para. 1 of the Motives.

28　*Judgment of 17 January 2008* in the Case No. 2007-11-03.

29　The reference to "directly and immediately" comes from *Judgment of 5 December 2001* in the case No. 2001-07-0103, Para. 1 of the Concluding Part.

30　*Judgment of 21 December 2007*.

31　From "Conformity of Part of Garkalne Parish Territorial Planning with respect to Construction on Baltezers Lake Floodplain," *Judgment of 8 February 2007*, Para. 11.

32　Decisions of the Latvian Constitutional Court are available in English at the court's website, http://www.satv.tiesa.gov.lv/?lang=2&mid=19.

33　No. 8, 31 October 1995, Supreme Court of the Russian Federation.

34　Stec (2003b).

35　*T.V. Zlotnikova, K.E. Lebedeva et al. v. Russian Federation* (1998). See also Mischenko and Rosenthal (1999).

36　Powell (2002, 146).

37　Mischenko and Rosenthal (2002); Mischenko (2001).

38　Vinogradov (2004, 594-95).

39　Houck (2007).

40　Pacific Environment (2007).

41　*Ledyayeva, Dobrokhotova, Zolotareva et Romashina v. Russia* (2006); *Fadeyeva v. Russia* (2005).

42　Vologda Regional Court opinion in *Ledyayeva v. Russia* (2002).

43　*Ledyayeva, Dobrokhotova, Zolotareva et Romashina v. Russia* (2006); *Fadeyeva v. Russia* (2005).

44 Houck (2007, 365-66).

45 Kravchenko (2004).

46 Houck (2007, 372).

47 The case is described on the Via Iuris website, http://www.viaiuris.sk/en/activities/ strategic-litigation/older-concluded-cases/pezinok-landfill-case.html.

48 Details of these and other cases can be found in the news archive of the Via Iuris website, http://www.viaiuris.sk/en/news/archiv.html.

49 Wilfling (2009, 1).

50 See *Act 454/2007 amending the Nature and Landscape Conservation Act.*

51 Citizen and Democracy Association (2008).

52 Justice and Environment (2010).

53 The Constitutional Court's website is http://www.us-rs.si. A search for the term "healthy environment" yielded twenty-four cases on 8 July 2009. For example, see *National Association of Ecologists* (1996).

54 Bonine (2002, 536).

55 Decision No U-I-30/95, cited in Stec, Antypas, and Steger (2006).

56 *Pavel Ocepek, Breg pri Komendi* (1999).

57 Case No. U-I-254/99.

58 Case No. U-I-113/00.

59 Case U-I-80-04, Official Gazette RS, No. 109/2005, Doc. No. AN02813.

60 Case No. U-I-386/06, Decision O3/13/2008, Official Gazette RS, No. 32/2008.

61 Milieu Ltd. (2007d).

62 Slovenia (2008).

63 Decision 148 of 16 April 2003, Constitutional Court of Romania (available at http://www.ccr.ro/decisions/pdf/en/2003/D148_03.pdf).

64 Supreme Court of Justice decision No. 1112 of 12 June 1997, cited in Dutu (2004).

65 *Asociatia Aurarilor Alburnus Maior in Rosia Montana v. Inspectoratul de Protectie a Mediului Alba* (2006); *Asociatia Aurarilor Alburnus Maior in Rosia Montana v. Alba Local Council* (2005); *Asociatia Aurarilor Alburnus Maior in Rosia Montana v. Inspectoratul de Protectie a Mediului Alba* (2005).

66 *Tatar and Tatar v. Romania* (2009).

67 *Branduse v. Romania* (2009).

68 Decision U-III/69/2002; Decision U-II/4833/2005.

69 No.176/2004 (05/04/2005). See also No. 152/2004, No. 192/2004, and No. 197/2004.

70 No.176/2004 (05/04/2005).

71 Decision No. 3 of 13 April 2006, CC No. 4/2006; Decision No. 10 of 10 July 1995, CC No. 8/95.

72 Stec, Antypas, and Steger (2006).

73 Medarova and Antypas (2006).

74 Cerny (2009b).

75 *Hnuti Duha v. Sumava National Park Authority* (1996), cited in Stec (2003a).

76 Milieu Ltd. (2007a).

77 Decision of the Constitutional Court (ÚS 282/97).

78 Cerny (2009b).

79 Beckmann (1999).
80 Relevant decisions of the Supreme Administrative Court include 1 As 39/2006-55; 2 As 59/2005-136; 3 As 38/2007-81; 5 As 19/2006-59. The Constitutional Court denied the complaint against Decision 2 As 12/2006-111 of the Supreme Administrative Court. Cited in Jancarova (2009).
81 Czech News Agency (2008).
82 Milieu Ltd. (2007a).
83 For details, see the Ekologicky Pravni Servis (Environmental Law Service) website (http://www.i-eps.cz/en-us/).
84 There is a list of cases brought by Environment, People, Law on the organization's website (http://epl.org.ua/en/lawnbspnbspnbsp/access-to-justice/cases/). See also the EPL annual report for 2007-08 at http://epl.org.ua/en/annual-reports/.
85 Kravchenko (2004).
86 Kravchenko (2005).
87 UN Economic Commission for Europe, Committee on Environmental Policy (2007c, 142).
88 *Association of Investigative Journalists v. Ministry of Environment* (2003), cited in Goldston (2006, 522).
89 Goldston (2006).
90 Human Rights Defender of the Republic of Armenia (2009).
91 Compliance Committee of the Aarhus Convention (2006a).
92 *Environmental Protection Law*, Article 323.
93 Bar and Jendroska (2009).
94 Bonine (2002). For more information on the work of the Environmental Law Center, see the organization's website at http://cpe.eko.org.pl/cpe_ang.html.
95 Poland (2008).
96 Georgia (2008).
97 Regional Environmental Center (n.d.).
98 Iordanov (2007); UN Economic Commission for Europe, Committee on Environmental Policy (2005, 27); Bushmovich (2001).
99 Veinla and Relve (2005).
100 Administrative Court of Tallinn (19 January 2004); Administrative Court of Tartu (14 May 2004); Circuit Court of Tallinn (15 December 2004); Administrative Court of Tallinn (3 June 2002); Administrative Court of Tallinn (5 June 2002).
101 Andersson (2003, 147).
102 Szuniewicz-Wenzel (2008).
103 Vaarmari (2009).
104 Botcheva (1996).
105 Organisation for Economic Co-operation and Development (2007d).
106 Friedberg and Zaimov (1994).
107 Mendelson and Glenn (2002).
108 Stec (2009).
109 Kravchenko (2002, 503).
110 Hunter and Bowman (1992).
111 Harper (2005).

112   Scwartz (2006, 9).
113   Snajdr (2008).
114   Pearce (2009).
115   Tickle and Welsh (1998).
116   Klarer and Moldan (1997).
117   Hunter and Bowman (1992).
118   Salvo (1997).
119   Scrieciu and Stringer (2008).
120   Scwartz (2006, 70).
121   Stec (2005, 5).
122   Tickle and Welsh (1998, 171).
123   Bandi (2004).
124   Schrage, Bull, and Karadjova (2008).
125   Organisation for Economic Co-operation and Development (2007d).
126   Ibid.
127   Ibid.
128   Regional Environmental Center (2009).
129   Hunter and Bowman (1992).
130   Powell (2002).
131   See the 1999 amendments to the *Law on Public Associations*. See also UN Economic Commission for Europe, Committee on Environmental Policy (2006).
132   UN Economic Commission for Europe, Committee on Environmental Policy (2006).
133   *Law on Non-Governmental Organizations* (1999).
134   Goldston (2006).
135   Ibid. 493.
136   Ibid. 497-500.
137   Stec (1998).
138   Bonine (2002); Kravchenko (2002).
139   Regional Environmental Center (2007).
140   Rekosh (2008).
141   Ibid.
142   Kravchenko (2002).
143   Gravelle (1997).
144   Milieu Ltd. (2007f).
145   Zaharchenko and Goldenman (2004).
146   Milieu Ltd. (2007f).
147   UN Economic Commission for Europe, Committee on Environmental Policy (2003, 41-42).
148   UN Economic Commission for Europe, Committee on Environmental Policy (2003).
149   Stec (2009, 160).
150   E. Brown (1993).
151   Stec (2005).

152   Milieu Ltd. (2007f).
153   Ibid.
154   For example, see Montenegro's *Law on Administrative Fees* (2006).
155   Sunstein (1993).
156   Kravchenko (2002); Shemshuchenko (1995).
157   Pickvance (2003).

CHAPTER 10: WESTERN EUROPE

1   Kramer (2006); Jordan (2005); Demmke (2003).
2   Organisation for Economic Co-operation and Development (2001, 41-42).
3   *Environmental Responsibility Law* (2007); *Law on Natural Heritage and Biodiversity* (2007). See also Law 27/2006, which regulates the rights of access to information, public participation, and access to justice in environmental matters.
4   Organisation for Economic Co-operation and Development (2004, 122).
5   Karacostas and Dacoronia (2006).
6   Haumont and Bodart (2006).
7   Milieu Ltd. (2007f).
8   Organisation for Economic Co-operation and Development (2005b, 18).
9   Marrani (2008).
10   Verschuuren (2009, 57).
11   *Environmental NGOs Law* (1998); *Popular Action Law* (1995).
12   Reis and de Andrade Neves (2002).
13   Milieu Ltd. (2007f, 7).
14   Vasconcelos and Baptista (2002, 112).
15   Carinhas de Andrade (2004).
16   Ibid.
17   Cited in Aragao (2004).
18   *Maia Petrol Pump case* (1996).
19   *Coruche Stork Nests case* (1990).
20   *Povoa de Lanhoso Landfill case II* (2001); *Povoa de Lanhoso Landfill case I* (1998).
21   *Nisa Swallow Nests case* (2000).
22   Reis and de Andrade Neves (2002, 413).
23   Pureza, Frade, and Dias (1997).
24   Carinhas de Andrade and Cavalheiro (2005); Organisation for Economic Co-operation and Development (2001).
25   Martins da Cruz (2007, 56).
26   Sioutis and Gerapetritis (2002).
27   Karageorgou (2007).
28   For example, the Council of State filled gaps in environmental legislation in decisions 772/98, 4503/1997, 6500/1995, 1784/1993, 2844/1993.
29   Papadopoulou (2006).
30   Sioutis and Gerapetritis (2002).
31   Greece (2008, 34).
32   Sioutis and Gerapetritis (2002, 264).

33 For example, the Council of State directed government to take preventive measures in decisions 1468/2004, 613/2002, 1675/99, 2818/97, 2281/92, 2196/82, 1362/81, 2034/78.

34 Karakostas and Vassilopoulos (1999).

35 *Hellenic Society for Protection of Environment & Cultural Heritage et al. v. Minister for the Enviroment* (1995); *Hellenic Ornithological Society et al. v. Minister of National Economy and Tourism* (1994).

36 Council of State decision 3478/2000.

37 Injunction Order 4531/2004, also First Instance Court of Piraeus 187/2004; Council of State decision 613/2002. Cited in Karacostas and Dacoronia (2006, 486).

38 Papadopoulou (2006, 529).

39 Nikolopolous and Haidarlis (2005); Sioutis and Gerapetritis (2002).

40 Sioutis (2006).

41 Council of State decision 695/1986.

42 Organisation for Economic Co-operation and Development (2000, 102).

43 Ibid., 114.

44 Nikolopolous and Haidarlis (2005, 72).

45 France, Minister of Ecology and Sustainable Development (2003).

46 Wolfrum and Grote (2011).

47 Bourg and Whiteside (2007); Bioy (2006); Lepage (2003, 15).

48 Prieur (2008).

49 Marrani (2008).

50 Milieu Ltd. (2007b).

51 France (2008, 28).

52 Patel (2011).

53 Decision No. 2008-564 DC–19 June 2008, *Law on Genetically Modified Organisms.*

54 *L'Association France Nature Environnement, Commune d'Annecy.*

55 *Groupement des Agriculteurs Biologistes et Biodynamistes de Maine-et-Loire.*

56 Marrani (2008).

57 Conseil d'État, No. 295918 (2007).

58 Marrani (2008, 25).

59 Huten and Cohendet (2007a, 2007b).

60 Puechavy (2006).

61 The author's translation of the original French "Il reste toutefois encore beaucoup de chemin a parcourir." Puechavy (2006, 426).

62 Ibanez Macias (2007); Lopez Ramon (2005).

63 Examples of Constitutional Court decisions include Sentencia 247/2007; Sentencia 179/2006; Auto 351/2005; Sentencia 173/2005; Sentencia 194/2004; Sentencia 195/2003. Examples of Supreme Court decisions include STS 274/2008; STS 4076/2008; STS 5364/2007; and STS 5964/2006.

64 Instituto Internacional de Derecho y Medio Ambiente (2005).

65 Milieu Ltd. (2007e).

66 Figueroa Alegre (2008).

67 Herrero de la Fuente (2002).

68   Milieu Ltd. (2007e).

69   Law 27/2006 *on Access to Information, Public Participation and Access to Justice in Environmental Matters* (2006).

70   Milieu Ltd. (2007e).

71   Supreme Court decision STS 8509/2007.

72   *Moreno Gomez v. Spain* (2004); *Lopez Ostra v. Spain* (1994).

73   Constitutional Court decisions 199/1996, 102/1995.

74   Nergelius (2006).

75   Koivurova (2004a).

76   Koivurova (2004b, 482-83).

77   Koivurova (2004a, 57).

78   Finland (2008, 23).

79   Davies (2007).

80   Organisation for Economic Co-operation and Development (2009, 25).

81   Kuusiniemi (2002).

82   Council of State, 31 January 1991, *Kort geding* (Interim measures) 1991-181; Council of State, 18 July 1991, *Administratieve beslissingen* (Administrative decisions) 1991-591; Council of State, 22 April 1991, *Administratieve beslissingen* (Administrative decisions) 1991-592; Council of State, 29 May 1992, *Milieu en Recht* (Environment and Law) 1992, p. 477; Supreme Court, 14 April 1989, *Milieu en Recht* (Environment and Law) 1989, p. 258.

83   Milieu Ltd. (2007c).

84   Verschuuren (2005, 101).

85   Backes (2002, 396).

86   Verschuuren (2005); Backes (2002).

87   Bergkamp (2001).

88   Verschuuren (2009).

89   Milieu Ltd. (2007c).

90   Smorenburg-van Middelkoop (2004); Verschuuren (1993).

91   Milieu Ltd. (2007c).

92   Verschuuren (2009).

93   Verschuuren (2005).

94   Alkema (2006).

95   Van Tatenhove and Goverde (2002, 47).

96   Van Rijswick and Robbe (2007).

97   Lavrysen and Theunis (2007).

98   Stec (2003a, 74).

99   *Inter-Environnement Wallonie v. Walloon Government* (2005).

100   Haumont and Bodart (2006).

101   Judgment No. 36/98 (1998).

102   Lavrysen (2009).

103   Constitutional Court, no. 135/2006; Constitutional Court, no. 137/2006; Constitutional Court, no. 145/2006. Cited in Lavrysen (2007).

104   *Jacobs v. Flemish Region* (1999). See also *Venter* (1999).

105   Lavrysen (2004).

106 De Sadeleer and Sambon (2005).
107 Jadot (2007).
108 Compliance Committee of the Aarhus Convention (2005).
109 *Cornelis and Others* (2005); *Van Doren and Others* (2005); *Commune Woluwe-Saint-Pierre and Others* (2003).
110 *SA Mobistar* (2003). See also *De Becker and Others* (2005).
111 Lavrysen and Theunis (2007).
112 Lavrysen (2009); *N.V. Hazegras v. Flemish Government* (1995).
113 Government of Andorra, Department of Statistics (2009).
114 *Association for the Protection of Animals, Plants and the Environment* (1996).
115 Causa 2003-1-CC, No. 43-2003.
116 Mestad (2002).
117 Grendstad et al. (2006).
118 Ibid.
119 Lafferty, Larsen, and Ruud (2004).
120 De Sadeleer, Roller, and Dross (2002).
121 Decision 210/1987.
122 Decision 127/1990.
123 Nespor (2005).
124 Zito, d'Orsogna, and Giordano (2002).
125 Jordan and Liefferink (2004).
126 Fernandez (2004).
127 Ebbesson (2002).
128 Examples include the European Environmental Law Association and Justice and Environment, as well as global networks, including ELAW and INECE.
129 A total of forty-four citizen communications have been received by the compliance committee, mainly directed at Eastern European nations, according to the UN Economic Commission for Europe. For details, see the UNECE website, http://www.unece.org/env/pp/pubcom.htm.
130 Dette (2004).
131 Schaffrin and Mehling (2007).

CHAPTER 11: LESSONS LEARNED

1 *Pavel Ocepek, Breg pri Komendi* (1999).
2 Rehbinder (2009); Robinson (2009).
3 Cepeda Espinosa (2005).
4 Bogart (2002); Rosenberg (1991).
5 Galanter (1983).
6 Gloppen (2006).
7 *Asociación Interamericana para la Defensa del Ambiente y otros* (2009, Costa Rica); *Suray Prasad Sharma Dhungel v. Godavari Marble Industries and Others* (1995, Nepal).
8 *Greenwatch v. Attorney General and NEMA* (2002, Uganda); *Murli S. Deora v. Union of India* (2001); *Lalanath de Silva v. Minister of Forestry and Environment* (1998, Sri Lanka).

9   H.M. Henares, Jr. et al. v. Land Transportation Franchising and Regulatory Board et al.
(2006, Philippines). See also Anjum Irfan v. LDA (2002, Pakistan).
10 Belgian Constitutional Court, no. 135/2006; no. 137/2006; no. 145/2006 – cited
in Lavrysen (2007). Constitutional Court of Hungary, Judgment 48/1997.
11 McAllister (2008).
12 Pound (1917, 160).
13 M. Lee (2005).
14 Picolotti (2005).
15 Ibid.
16 Ibid.
17 Lin (2009).
18 Pablo Miguel Fabián Martínez and Others v. Minister of Health and Director General
of Environmental Health (2006).
19 Tatar and Tatar v. Romania (2009); Fadeyeva v. Russia (2005). The Chilean case is
described in "Defensa de los Derechos Humanos: Caso contaminación en Arica"
on the FIMA website, http://www.fima.cl/2009/10/08/defensa-de-la-deerechos
-humanos-caso-contaminacion-en-arica/.
20 SCJ Appeal No. 70012091278 (Rio Grande do Sul), 2006; SCJ Appeal No.
70011759842 (Rio Grande do Sul), 2005; SCJ Appeal No. 575.998 (Minas Gerais),
16 November 2004.
21 Mandela (2002).
22 Alley and Meadows (2004, 15); Dutta et al. (2000).
23 Ghertner and Fripp (2006).
24 Mehta (1997).
25 Beatriz Silvia Mendoza and Others v. National Government and Others in regards to
damages suffered (2008); Concerned Residents of Manila Bay et al. v. Metropolitan
Manila Development Authority, Department of Environment and Natural Resources and
Others (2008).
26 Bruckerhoff (2008, 625); May (2006).
27 Epp (1998, 90).
28 Stec (2009); Kravchenko (2002).
29 Regarding Europe, see de Sadeleer, Roller, and Dross (2005).
30 Hochstetler and Keck (2007, 55).
31 Defensoria del Pueblo (2009a).
32 The website of the Constitutional Chamber of the Supreme Court of Justice offers
a "Constitutional Review," with cases from 1989 to 2009 in various categories
(http://www.poder-judicial.go.cr/salaconstitucional/REVISTADIGITAL2009/D.
html). Sixty-two cases are listed under the heading "Right to a Healthy and
Ecologically Balanced Environment," and forty-one indicate that the court found
a violation of the right.
33 Jariwala (2000).
34 Epp (1998).
35 Ibid.
36 McAllister (2008).
37 UN Economic Commission for Latin America and the Caribbean (2002, 163).

38   Dougnac Rodriguez (2009); *Sioutis* (2006); *Pedro Viudes v. Ley No. 816/96* (1997, Paraguay); *N.V. Hazegras v. Flemish Government* (1995, Belgium); Council of State decision 695/1986 (Greece).

39   *Constitutional Complaint against Article 21 of the Urban Planning Act* (1998, South Korea); *Adam, Teva ve'Din (Human Being, Nature, and Law) v. Prime Minister of Israel et al.* (2004).

40   Garcia-Guadilla (2006).

41   *Okyay et al. v. Turkey* (2005).

42   Turner (2009); Cullet (2007).

43   Council of State decisions 3478/2000, 2759/1994, 2760/1994.

44   Koivurova (2004a).

45   *M.M. Levy y Asociacion Ecologista Limonense v. Ministerio del Ambiente y Energia* (2001).

46   *Baba Dam Case* (2008).

47   *T.V. Zlotnikova, K.E. Lebedeva et al., 1998* (Russia); Judgment 28/1994 (Hungary).

48   Ahuja (2009); Boonlai and Changplayngam (2009).

49   Lavrysen (2009, 114).

50   *Environmental Education Promotion Act* (2008); *National Environmental Awareness and Education Act of 2008; Law on Ecological Education of the Population* (2001); *National Environmental Education Policy Act* (1999).

51   *M.C. Mehta v. Union of India* AIR 1992 SC 382; *M.C. Mehta v. Union of India* 2000 (9) SCC 411; and *M.C. Mehta v. Union of India* AIR 1988 SC 1031. *Concerned Residents of Manila Bay et al. v. Metropolitan Manila Development Authority, Department of Environment and Natural Resources and Others* (2008); *Beatriz Silvia Mendoza and Others v. National Government and Others* (2006).

52   Marrani (2008).

53   *Federacion de Asociacion Organizacion de Afectados por La Represa y Acyreta de Itapua y Misiones – Fedayin* (2008).

54   *Law on Biodiversity* (1998), Article 9.

55   *Khabisi NO and Another v. Aquarella Investment 83 (Pty) Ltd and Others* (2007, South Africa); *National Association of Ecologists* (1996, Slovenia); *Arco Iris v. Ecuador Mineral Institute* (1993, Ecuador); Council of State decision 695/1986 (Greece); *Caribbean Conservation Corporation et al. v. Costa Rica* (1983).

56   *Nisa Swallow Nests case* (2000).

57   Collins (2007, 137).

58   Redgwell (1996, 87).

59   Beatty (2004, 129).

60   *Beatriz Silvia Mendoza and Others v. National Government and Others in regards to damages suffered* (2008).

61   Krishnan (2008); Arantes (2005).

62   McAllister (2008); De Sadeleer, Roller, and Dross (2005).

63   Yamin and Parra-Vera (2009).

64   Couso (2004); Ginsburg (2003).

65   In addition to India, these nations include Bangladesh, Estonia, Guatemala, Israel, Italy, Nigeria, Pakistan, Sri Lanka, Tanzania, and Uruguay.

66 *M.C. Mehta v. Union of India* 2002 (4) SCC 356 (Motor vehicles); *T.N. Godavarman Thirumulpad v. Union of India* 1999 (Forest conservation); *M.C. Mehta v. Union of India* AIR 1988 SC 1115 (Ganges pollution).

67 Stephens (2009).

68 Garcia-Guadilla (2006, 14).

69 Velasco, Jr. (2009).

70 Davis (2008).

71 Corder (2007, 361).

72 *M.M. Levy y Asociacion Ecologista Limonense v. Ministerio del Ambiente y Energia* (2001, Costa Rica); *T.V. Zlotnikova, K.E. Lebedeva et al. v. Russian Federation* (1998).

73 *A Cederstav and Others v. National Technical Secretary for the Environment, Municipality of Santa Cruz and Others* (2008).

74 Bakan (1997).

75 *Fuel Retailers Association of South Africa v. Director-General: Environmental Management, Department of Agriculture, Conservation and Environment, Mpumalanga Province, et al.* (2007).

76 Gargarella, Domingo and Roux (2006).

77 Koskenniemi (1991).

78 Milieu Ltd. (2007c).

79 Organisation for Economic Co-operation and Development (2000, 102).

80 Weinthal and Jones Luong (2002, 168).

CHAPTER 12: DO ENVIRONMENTAL PROVISIONS IN CONSTITUTIONS INFLUENCE ENVIRONMENTAL PERFORMANCE?

1   Montenegro (1995).

2   Kinney and Clark (2004).

3   Hirschl (2004).

4   Barrett and Graddy (2000, 434).

5   See also Torras and Boyce (1998).

6   Hayward (2005, 162-63, 182).

7   Shelton (2004b).

8   Jorgenson, Rice, and Crowe (2005); Jorgenson (2003); York, Rosa, and Dietz (2003); Vogel (1993).

9   Mayer (2008); J. Wilson, Tyedmers, and Pelot (2007); Morse and Fraser (2005).

10 Gleditsch and Sverdrup (2002, 57).

11 There is an entire journal, *Ecological Indicators*, devoted to issues related to the measurement of environmental performance.

12 Organisation for Economic Co-operation and Development (2003).

13 Mayer (2008).

14 Ewing et al. (2008); Simon Fraser University Sustainable Planning Research Group (2005).

15 Wackernagel and Rees (1996).

16 Wackernagel et al. (2002, 9266).

17 Caviglia-Harris, Chambers, and Kahn (2009); Ness et al. (2007).

18 Rees (2002).

19   Moran et al. (2008, 471).
20   Ferguson (2002, 312).
21   Herendeen (2000).
22   Moran et al. (2008, 472).
23   Ewing et al. (2008).
24   Ibid.
25   Ayres (2000).
26   Van Kooten and Bulte (2000).
27   Van den Bergh and Verbruggen (1999).
28   Fiala (2008).
29   Wackernagel (2009); Kitzes and Wackernagel (2009); Stoehglener and Narodoslawsky (2008).
30   J. Wilson, Tyedmers, and Pelot (2007).
31   Venetoulis and Talberth (2008); Chen et al. (2007).
32   Caviglia-Harris, Chambers, and Kahn (2009).
33   Ewing et al. (2008).
34   Simon Fraser University Sustainable Planning Research Group (2005).
35   Organisation for Economic Co-operation and Development (2006).
36   Simon Fraser University Sustainable Planning Research Group (2005, 11). This study represented a refined and updated version of Boyd (2001).
37   The pressure indicators are energy consumption, energy intensity, water consumption, GHG emissions, sulphur oxide emissions, nitrogen oxide emissions, volatile organic compounds (VOC) emissions, carbon monoxide emissions, ozone-depleting substances, municipal waste, nuclear waste, pesticide use, fertilizer use, livestock, timber harvest, capture fisheries, fisheries as percent of world catch, and distance travelled. State indicators are number of species at risk, percent of species at risk, protected areas, and timber harvest to forest growth ratio. Response indicators are environmental pricing, renewable energy including hydro, renewable energy excluding hydro, recycling of municipal waste, pollution abatement and control expenditures, municipal sewage treatment, and official development assistance.
38   The OECD has since expanded to thirty-three members.
39   Conference Board of Canada (2008).
40   Ibid; Conference Board of Canada (2009).
41   Overlapping indicators are VOC emissions, water consumption, municipal waste, low-emission energy production, threatened species, and use of forest resources.
42   Guzman (2008).
43   Simpson, Jaccard, and Rivers (2007).
44   *Kyoto Protocol* (1997).
45   *Stockholm Convention on Persistent Organic Pollutants* (2001).
46   *Cartagena Protocol on Biosafety* (2000).
47   *Rotterdam Convention on the Prior Informed Consent Procedure for Certain Hazardous Chemicals and Pesticides in International Trade* (1999).
48   *Ban Amendment to the Basel Convention on the Control of Transboundary Movements of Hazardous Wastes and Their Disposal* (1995).

49   Hirschl (2007).
50   *UN Convention on Transboundary Air Pollution* (1979). Australia and Japan are not parties.
51   Curtis et al. (2006).
52   Data were assembled from a series of OECD publications. The most recent was Organisation for Economic Co-operation and Development (2007a). Other volumes were published in 1999, 1997, 1995, 1993, 1991, and 1989.
53   See also Organisation for Economic Co-operation and Development (2007a).
54   *The Constitutional Act of Denmark,* 5 June 1953, s. 88.
55   Organisation for Economic Co-operation and Development (2007c, 16-17).
56   J. Wilson, Tyedmers, and Pelot (2007).
57   Organisation for Economic Co-operation and Development (2007c, 17).
58   Martens (2007).
59   Organisation for Economic Co-operation and Development (2007b).
60   Ibid., 15.
61   Ibid., 170.
62   Martens (2007).
63   Bond Beter Leefmilieu Vlaanderen VZW (2005).
64   Compliance Committee of the Aarhus Convention (2006b).
65   See Annex 1 to Belgium's report on the implementation of the committee's recommendations, available as a PDF file on the UN Economic Commission for Europe website, http://www.unece.org/env/pp/compliance/C2005-11/Update/mailing %20of%202008.02.27/BillOf2007.03.16.pdf.
66   Neuray and Pallemaerts (2008).
67   Jorgenson, Rice, and Crowe (2005).

CHAPTER 13: AN IDEA WHOSE TIME HAS COME

1   Sarat and Kearns (1993).
2   Young (1999, 249).
3   Law and Versteeg (2011).
4   Wolfrum and Grote (2008, 7). See also Grote (2007a, 10).
5   Yang and Percival (2009, 635).
6   Merryman (1985).
7   Prieur (2008).
8   Millett, Holmes, and Perez (2009).
9   New Economics Foundation (2009).
10   Kravchenko (2002, 467).
11   *R. v. Hydro-Quebec* [1997]; *Ontario v. Canadian Pacific Ltd* [1995].
12   Knox (2009); Limon (2009); McInerney-Lankford (2009); Oxfam International (2008).
13   UN Development Programme (2008, 4).
14   UN High Commissioner for Human Rights (2002).
15   Lasser (2009).
16   Hirschl (2007, 45).
17   Yang and Percival (2009, 661).

18 Martins da Cruz (2007, 57).
19 International Commission of Jurists (2008).
20 McCann (1996); Rosenberg (1991).
21 See, for example, Mickwitz (2006).
22 Goldsworthy (2006, 343).
23 Dickson (2007b).
24 Epp (1998); Bogart (2002); Rosenberg (1991).
25 Kagan (2003).
26 McAllister (2009).
27 Babcock (2009).
28 Wolfrum and Grote (2005, vi).
29 Gardner (2008); Thompson (2006); Tarr, Williams, and Marko (2004).
30 Hiskes (2009, 117).

APPENDIX 1: RESEARCH METHODS
1 Wolfrum and Grote (2011).
2 Among the constitutions not yet available or incomplete in *Constitutions of the Countries of the World* as of 1 January 2011 were Andorra, Angola, Austria, Bhutan, Cape Verde, Ecuador, Guyana, Luxembourg, Maldives, Montenegro, San Marino, Turkmenistan, Uruguay, and Yemen.
3 See this database on the FAOLEX website, http://faolex.fao.org/faolex/.
4 This tool is available at the Google Translate website, http://translate.google.com.
5 The WORLDLII website is at http://www.worldlii.org.
6 The World Law Guide website is at http://www.lexadin.nl/wlg/legis/nofr/legis.php.
7 The Global Legal Information Network website is at http://www.glin.gov.
8 The ECOLEX website is at http://www.ecolex.org.
9 Defensoria del Pueblo (2009a, 2009b); Verschuuren (2009); Hochstetler and Keck (2007); Jariwala (2000).
10 Gravetter and Wallnau (2008).
11 Howell (2008).
12 Gravetter and Wallnau (2008).

References

BOOKS, ARTICLES, AND REPORTS

Abed, S. 2009. "Paraguay." In Kotze and Paterson 2009a, 295-320.

Acevedo, M.T. 2000. "The Intersection of Human Rights and Environmental Protection in the European Court of Human Rights." *New York University Environmental Law Journal* 8: 437-96.

Ackerman, B.A. 1997. "The Rise of World Constitutionalism." *Virginia Law Review* 83: 771-97.

Adaman, F., and M. Arsel. 2005. "Introduction." In *Environmentalism in Turkey: Between Democracy and Development?* edited by F. Adaman and M. Arsel, 1-11. Aldershot, UK: Ashgate.

Adeel, Z., and N. Nakamoto. 2003. "The Future of Environmental Governance in East Asia." In *East Asian Experience in Environmental Governance: Response in a Rapidly Developing Region*, edited by Z. Adeel, 217-32. Tokyo: UN University Press.

Agcaoili, A.D. 2009. "Role of the Philippine Judicial Academy in Environmental Law Dissemination, Enforcement, and Adjudication." Speech at the Forum on Environmental Justice: Upholding the Right to a Balanced and Healthful Ecology, University of the Cordilleras, Baguio City, 16-17 April 2009.

Aguilar, A.F. 1994. "Enforcing the Right to a Healthy Environment in Latin America." *Review of European Community and International Environmental Law* 3, 4: 215.

–. 1996. "Indigenous Peoples, Environmental Degradation, and Human Rights: A Case Study." In Boyle and Anderson 1996, 245-63.

Aguilar, A.F., and E. Arnal. 2002. *Review of Jurisprudence on Human Rights and the Environment in Latin America*. Background Paper No. 6 for the Joint UNEP-OHCHR Expert Seminar on Human Rights and the Environment, Geneva, Switzerland, 14-16 January 2002.

Aguilar, G., and A. Iza, eds. 2005. *Manual de derecho ambiental en Centroamérica*. Moravia, Costa Rica: IUCN.

Ahuja, A. 2009. "Thai Environmental Group Takes Aim at More Firms." Reuters, 4 December 2009.

Akhund, N., and Z. Qureshi. 1998. *You Can Make a Difference: A Lawyer's Reference to Environmental Public Interest Cases in Pakistan*. Karachi, Pakistan: IUCN.

Akiwomi, A.M. 2002. "The Court of Justice of the Common Market for Eastern and Southern Africa (COMESA) and the Sustainable Development of Its Member States."

Speech delivered at the Global Symposium on Sustainable Development and the Role of Law, Johannesburg, South Africa, 18-20 August 2002.

Al'Afghani, M.M. 2005. "Constitutional Court's Review and the Future of Water Law in Indonesia." *Law, Environment and Development Journal* 2, 1: 1-18.

Alexander, L., ed. 1998. *Constitutionalism: Philosophical Foundations.* Cambridge: Cambridge University Press.

Alkema, E.A. 2006. "Constitutional Law." In *Introduction to Dutch Law*, edited by J.M.J. Chorus, P.H.M. Gerver, and E.H. Hondius, 301-42. The Hague: Kluwer Law International.

Alley, K.D., and D. Meadows. 2004. "Workers' Rights and Pollution Control in Delhi." *Human Rights Dialogue*, Spring: 15.

Alliance of Small Island States. 2007. *Male' Declaration on the Human Dimension of Climate Change.* November 2007. On the Center for International Environmental Law website, http://www.ciel.org/Publications/Male_Declaration_Nov07.pdf.

Alston, P. 1982. "A Third Generation of Solidarity Rights: Progressive Development or Obfuscation of International Human Rights Law." *Netherlands International Law Review* 29: 307-22.

–. 1984. "Conjuring Up New Human Rights: A Proposal for Quality Control." *American Journal of International Law* 78: 607-21.

–. 1999. *Protecting Human Rights through Bills of Rights: Comparative Perspectives.* Oxford: Clarendon Press.

–. 2001. "Peoples' Rights: Their Rise and Fall." In *Peoples' Rights*, edited by P. Alston, 259-94. Oxford: Oxford University Press.

Amechi, E.P. 2009. "Enhancing Environmental Protection and Socio-Economic Development in Africa: A Fresh Look at the Right to a General Satisfactory Environment under the African Charter on Human and Peoples' Rights." *Law, Environment and Development Journal* 5, 1: 58-72.

American Law Institute. 1987. *Restatement of the Law (Third), Foreign Relations Law of the United States.* Philadelphia: ALI.

Anderson, G.W. 2005. *Constitutional Rights after Globalization.* Oxford: Hart Publishing.

Anderson, M., and P. Galizzi, eds. 2002. *International Environmental Law in National Courts.* London: British Institute of International and Comparative Law.

Anderson, M.R. 1996a. "Human Rights Approaches to Environmental Protection: An Overview." In Boyle and Anderson 1996, 1-24.

–. 1996b. "Individual Rights to Environmental Protection in India." In Boyle and Anderson 1996, 199-225.

Anderson, M.R., and S. Bluck. 2000. "Environmental Rights of the Child." In *The Right of the Child to a Clean Environment*, edited by A. Fijalkowski and M. Fitzmaurice, 105-31. Burlington, VT: Ashgate.

Andersson, T.K. 2003. "The Role of Basic Rights in Environmental Protection: Basic Right to Environment *de lege ferenda* in the Estonian Constitution." *Juridica International* 8: 147.

Ankersen, T.T. 2003. "Shared Knowledge, Shared Jurisprudence: Learning to Speak Environmental Law Creole *(Criollo)*." *Tulane Environmental Law Journal* 16: 807-30.

Anton, D.K. 1998. *Comparative Constitutional Language for Environmental Amendments to the Australian Constitution.* http://www.elaw.org/node/1512.

Aragao, A. 2004. "The Application and Interpretation of the Core Environmental Principles by the Portuguese Courts." In Macrory 2004, 159-77.

Arantes, R.B. 2005. "Constitutionalism, the Expansion of Justice and the Judicialization of Politics in Brazil." In Sieder, Schjolden, and Angell 2005b, 231-62.

Arsel, M. 2005. "The Bergama Imbroglio." In *Environmentalism in Turkey: Between Democracy and Development?* edited by F. Adaman and M. Arsel, 263-76. Aldershot, UK: Ashgate

Arthurs, H., and B. Arnold. 2005. "Does the Charter Matter?" *Review of Constitutional Studies* 11, 1: 37-117.

Asenjo, R. 1989. "Innovative Environmental Litigation in Chile: The Case of Chanaral." *Georgetown International Environmental Law Review* 2, 2: 99-110.

Asia Pacific Forum of National Human Rights Institutions. 2007. *Human Rights and the Environment: Reference Paper.* Sydney: Asia Pacific Forum.

Atapattu, S. 2002a. "The Right to a Healthy Life or the Right to Die Polluted? The Emergence of a Human Right to a Healthy Environment under International Law." *Tulane Environmental Law Journal* 16, 1: 65-126.

–. 2002b. "Sustainable Development: Myth or Reality? A Survey of Sustainable Development under International Law and Sri Lankan Law." *Georgetown International Environmental Law Review* 14: 265-300.

–. 2006. *Emerging Principles of International Environmental Law.* Ardsley, NY: Transnational Publishers.

Ayres, R.U. 2000. "Commentary on the Utility of the Ecological Footprint Concept." *Ecological Economics* 32: 347-49.

Babcock, H.M. 2009. "Assuming Personal Responsibility for Improving the Environment: Moving Toward a New Environmental Norm." *Harvard Environmental Law Review* 33, 1: 117-75.

Backes, C.W. 2002. "Netherlands." In Ebbesson 2002, 379-98.

Baderin, M.A., and R. McCorquodale, eds. 2006. *Economic, Social and Cultural Rights in Action.* Oxford: Oxford University Press.

Bakan, J. 1997. *Just Words: Constitutional Rights and Social Wrongs.* Toronto: University of Toronto Press.

Bandi, G. 1993. "The Right to Environment in Theory and Practice: The Hungarian Experience." *Connecticut Journal of International Law* 8: 439-62.

–. 2003. "Enlargement and Its Consequences for EU Environmental Law." In *The European Convention and the Future of European Environmental Law: Proceedings of the Avosetta Group of European Environmental Lawyers,* edited by J. Jans, 97-113. Amsterdam: Europa Law Publishing.

–. 2004. "Environmental Principles: Experiences of Transition Countries." In Macrory 2004, 213-22.

Bankobeza, S. 2003. "Latin American Needs Assessment and Judges and Prosecutors Planning Meeting." In Di Paola 2003, 67-70.

Bar, M., and J. Jendroska. 2009. "Access to Environmental Justice in Poland." In Justice and Environment 2009, 40-46.

Barrera-Hernandez, L.K. 2002. "The Legal Framework for Indigenous Peoples' and Other Public's Participation in Latin America: The Cases of Argentina, Colombia, and Peru." In Zillman, Lucas, and Pring 2002, 589-628.

Barrett, S., and K. Graddy. 2000. "Freedom, Growth, and the Environment." *Environment and Development Economics* 5: 433-56.

Barry, B. 1996. *Justice as Impartiality.* Oxford: Oxford University Press.

Baxi, U. 2005. *The Future of Human Rights.* 2nd ed. Oxford: Oxford University Press.

Beatty, D.M. 2004. *The Ultimate Rule of Law.* Oxford: Oxford University Press.

Beckerman, W. 1999. "Sustainable Development and Our Obligations to Future Generations." In *Fairness and Futurity,* edited by A. Dobson, 71-92. Oxford: Oxford University Press.

Beckmann, A. 1999. "A Quiet Revolution: The Influence of Environmental Organizations in the Czech Republic." *Central Europe Review* 1, 12. http://www.ce-review.org/99/12/beckmann12.html.

Bedner, A. 2007. "Access to Environmental Justice in Indonesia." In Harding 2007a, 89-124.

Belbase, N., and L.B. Thapa. 2007. "Nepal." In *Environmental Justice and Rural Communities: Studies from India and Nepal,* edited by P. Moore and F. Pastakia, 65-108. Gland, Switzerland: IUCN.

Bellamy, R. 2007. *Political Constitutionalism: A Defence of the Constitutionality of Democracy.* Cambridge: Cambridge University Press.

Berggren, N., and P. Kurrild-Klitgaard. 2002. "Economic Effects of Political Institutions with Special Reference to Constitutions." In *Why Constitutions Matter,* edited by N. Berggren, N. Karlson, and J. Nergelius, 167-212. Stockholm: City University Press.

Bergkamp, L. 2001. "Are Standing Rights for Environmental Groups in the Public Interest?" *Tijdschrift voor Milieuaansprakelijkheid (TMA)* 6: 153-57.

Berkes, F., T.P. Hughes, R.S. Steneck, J.A. Wilson, D.R. Bellwood, B. Crona, C. Folke, et al. 2006. "Globalization, Roving Bandits, and Marine Resources." *Science* 311: 1557-58.

Bernauer, T., and V. Koubi. 2009. "Effects of Political Institutions on Air Quality." *Ecological Economics* 68: 1355-65.

Biggs, G. 2009. "Chile's Environmental Law and Jurisprudence." *International Environmental Law Newsletter* (American Bar Association Section of Energy, Environment and Natural Resources) 12, 1: 8-14.

Bioy, X. 2006. "L'environnement, nouvel objet du droit constitutionnel ou qu'est-ce que constitutionnaliser?" In *Les nouveaux objets du droit constitutionnel,* edited by H. Roussillon, X. Bioy, and S. Mouton, 25-58. Toulouse: Presses universitaires des sciences sociales.

Birnie, P., and A. Boyle. 2002. *International Law and the Environment.* 2nd ed. Oxford: Oxford University Press.

Blengio Valdes, M. 2003. "Derecho humano a un medio ambiente sano." In *El derecho humano a un medio ambiente sano: Sexto certamen de ensayo sobre derechos humanos,* 181-203. Toluca, Mexico: Commission of Human Rights of the State of Mexico.

Boer, B. 1999. "The Rise of Environmental Law in the Asian Region." *University of Richmond Law Review* 32, 5: 1503-53.

Boer, B., R. Ramsay, and D.R. Rothwell. 1998. *International Environmental Law in the Asia Pacific.* London: Kluwer Law International.

Bogart, W.A. 2002. *Consequences: The Impact of Law and Its Complexity.* Toronto: University of Toronto Press.

Bolla, A.J., and T.L. McDornan. 1999. *Comparative Asian Environmental Law Anthology.* Durham, NC: Carolina Academic Press.

Bond Beter Leefmilieu Vlaanderen VZW. 2005. Communication to the Aarhus Convention's Compliance Committee. Reference No. ACCC/C/2005/11.

Bonine, J.E. 2002. "The Construction of Participatory Democracy in Central and Eastern Europe." In Zillman, Lucas, and Pring 2002, 505-48.

–. 2009. *Best Practices – Access to Justice.* Washington, DC: World Resources Institute. http://www.accessinitiative.org/.

Boonlai, K., and P. Changplayngam. 2009. "Thai Court Halts Many New Plants in Big Industrial Zone." Reuters, 3 December 2009.

Bork, R.H. 1990. *The Tempting of America: The Political Seduction of the Law.* New York: Free Press.

Botcheva, L. 1996. "Focus and Effectiveness of Environmental Activism in Eastern Europe: A Comparative Study of Environmental Movements in Bulgaria, Hungary, Slovakia, and Romania." *Journal of Environment and Development* 5, 3: 292-308.

Bourg, D., and K.H. Whiteside. 2007. "France's Charter for the Environment: Of Presidents, Principles, and Environmental Protection." *Modern and Contemporary France* 15, 2: 117-33.

Boutaud, A., N. Gondran, and C. Brodhag. 2006. "(Local) Environmental Quality versus (Global) Ecological Carrying Capacity: What Might Alternative Aggregated Indicators Bring to the Debates about Environmental Kuznets Curves and Sustainable Development?" *International Journal of Sustainable Development* 9, 3: 297-310.

Boutros-Ghali, B. 1993. Address of the Secretary-General of the United Nations at the opening of the World Conference on Human Rights in Vienna, Austria, 14 June 1993.

Bowman, D.M., and G.A. Hodge. 2007. "A Small Matter of Regulation: An International Review of Nanotechnology Regulation." *Columbia Science and Technology Review* 8: 1-36.

Boyd, D.R. 2001. *Canada vs. the OECD: An Environmental Comparison.* Victoria: University of Victoria.

–. 2003. *Unnatural Law: Rethinking Canadian Environmental Law and Policy.* Vancouver: UBC Press.

–. In press. "The Implicit Constitutional Right to Live in a Healthy Environment." *Review of European Community and International Environmental Law.*

Boyle, A.E. 1996. "The Role of International Human Rights Law in the Protection of the Environment." In Boyle and Anderson 1996, 43-65.

–. 2006. "Soft Law in International Law-making." In *International Law,* edited by M.D. Evans, 141-58. 2nd ed. Oxford: Oxford University Press.

–. 2009. *Human Rights and the Environment: A Reassessment.* Nairobi: UNEP.

Boyle, A.E., and M.R. Anderson, eds. 1996. *Human Rights Approaches to Environmental Protection.* Oxford: Clarendon Press.

Brandl, E., and H. Bungert. 1992. "Constitutional Entrenchment of Environmental Protection: A Comparative Analysis of Experiences Abroad." *Harvard Environmental Law Review* 16, 1: 1-100.

Brewer-Carias, A.R. 2009. *Constitutional Protection of Human Rights in Latin America: A Comparative Study of Amparo Proceedings.* Cambridge: Cambridge University Press.

Bridge, D., and A. Laytner, trans. 2005. *The Animals' Lawsuit against Humanity: An Illustrated 10th Century Iraqi Fable.* Louisville, KY: Fons Vitae.

Brown, C. 1999. "Universal Human Rights: A Critique." In *Human Rights in Global Politics,* edited by T. Dunne and N.J. Wheeler, 103-27. Cambridge: Cambridge University Press.

Brown, E. 1993. "Comment. In Defense of Environmental Rights in East European Constitutions." *University of Chicago Law School Roundtable* 1: 191-217.

Brownlie, I. 2003. *Principles of Public International Law.* 6th ed. Oxford: Oxford University Press.

Bruch, C., W. Coker, and C. VanArsdale. 2007. *Constitutional Environmental Law: Giving Force to Fundamental Principles in Africa.* 2nd ed. Washington, DC: Environmental Law Institute.

Bruckerhoff, J.J. 2008. "Giving Nature Constitutional Protection: A Less Anthropocentric Interpretation of Environmental Rights." *Texas Law Review* 86: 616-46.

Bryner, G.C. 1987. "Constitutionalism and the Politics of Rights." In *Constitutionalism and Rights,* edited by G.C. Bryner and N.B. Reynolds, 7-32. Albany, NY: State University Press.

Buchanan, J. 2000. "Why Do Constitutions Matter?" In *Why Constitutions Matter,* edited by N. Berggren, N. Karlson, and J. Nergelius, 1-17. London: Transaction Publishers.

Bullard, R.D., ed. 2005. *The Quest for Environmental Justice: Human Rights and the Politics of Pollution.* San Francisco: Sierra Club Books.

Bushmovich, A. 2001. *Access to Justice in Environmental Matters.* Amsterdam: Milieukontact Oost Europa.

Bynoe, M.L. 2006. "Citizen Participation in the Environmental Impact Assessment Process in Guyana: Reality or Fallacy?" *Law, Environment and Development Journal* 2, 1: 35-49.

Byrne, J., C. Martinez, and L. Glover, eds. 2002. *Environmental Justice: Discourses in the International Political Economy.* New Brunswick, NJ: Transaction Publishers.

Cancado Trindade, A.A. 1993. "Environmental Protection and the Absence of Restrictions on Human Rights." In *Human Rights in the Twenty-First Century: A Global Challenge,* edited by K.E. Mahoney and P. Mahoney, 561-93. Dordrecht, Netherlands: Martinus Nijhoff.

Cappelli, S. 2003. "Environmental Public Civil Action: The Brazilian Experience and Analysis of Jurisprudence." In Di Paola 2003, 111-26.

Carballo, J. 2009. "Argentina." In Kotze and Paterson 2009a, 269-94.

Carinhas de Andrade, I. 2004. "Access to Justice in Environmental Matters: The Portuguese Actio Popularis – Law and Practice." *Environmental Law Network International Review* 1: 11-16.

Carinhas de Andrade, I., and G. Cavalheiro. 2005. "Portugal." In de Sadeleer, Roller, and Dross 2005, 121-38.

Giorgetta, S. 2002. "The Right to a Healthy Environment, Human Rights, and Sustainable Development." *International Environmental Agreements: Politics, Law and Economics* 2: 173-94.

–. 2004. "The Right to a Healthy Environment." In *International Law and Sustainable Development: Principles and Practice*, edited by N. Schrijver and F. Weiss, 379-404. Leiden, Netherlands: Martinus Nijhoff.

Glazewski, J. 2002. "The Rule of Law: Opportunities for Environmental Justice in the New Democratic Legal Order." In *Environmental Justice in South Africa*, edited by D.A. McDonald, 171-98. Athens: Ohio University Press.

Gleditsch, N.P., and B.O. Sverdrup. 2002. "Democracy and the Environment." In *Human Security and the Environment*, edited by M. Redclift and E.A. Page, 45-70. Cheltenham, UK: Edward Elgar.

Glendon, M.A. 1991. *Rights Talk: The Impoverishment of Political Discourse*. New York: Free Press.

Glendon, M.A., M.W. Gordon, and C. Osakwe. 1985. *Comparative Legal Traditions*. St. Paul, MN: West Publishing.

Gloppen, S. 2006. "Courts and Social Transformation: An Analytical Framework." In Gargarella, Domingo, and Roux 2006, 35-60.

Gloppen, S., R. Gargarella, and E. Sklaar, eds. 2004. *Democratization and the Judiciary: The Accountability Function of Courts in New Democracies*. London: Frank Cass.

Gloppen, S., and F.E. Kanyongolo. 2007. "Courts and the Poor in Malawi: Economic Marginalization, Vulnerability and the Law." *International Journal of Constitutional Law* 5, 2: 258-93.

Gnangui, A. 2003. "Cote d'Ivoire." In Centre International de Droit Comparé de l' Environnement 2003, 361-64.

Goldston, J.A. 2006. "Public Interest Litigation in Central and Eastern Europe: Roots, Prospects, and Challenges." *Human Rights Quarterly* 28, 2: 492-527.

Goldsworthy, J., ed. 2006. *Interpreting Constitutions: A Comparative Study*. Oxford: Oxford University Press.

Gormley, W.P. 1976. *Human Rights and Environment: The Need for International Co-Operation*. Netherlands: A.W. Sijthoff.

–. 1990. "The Legal Obligation of the International Community to Guarantee a Pure and Decent Environment: The Expansion of Human Rights Norms." *Georgetown International Environmental Law Review* 3, 1: 85-116.

Government of Andorra (Department of Statistics). 2009. "Society and Population." http://www.estadistica.ad/.

Goyal, P., and Sidhartha. 2003. "Present Scenario of Air Quality in Delhi: A Case Study of CNG Implementation." *Atmospheric Environment* 37, 38: 5423-31.

Grandbois, M. 1988. "Le droit a l'environnement dans les pays de l'Est." *McGill Law Journal* 33, 3: 540-54.

Gravelle, R.K. 1997. "Enforcing the Elusive: Environmental Rights in East European Constitutions." *Virginia Environmental Law Review* 16: 633-60.

Gravetter, F.J., and L.B. Wallnau. 2008. *Essentials of Statistics for the Behavioral Sciences*. 6th ed. Belmont CA: Thomson Wadsworth.

Greece. 2008. *National Implementation Report (Aarhus Convention)*. ECE/MP.PP/IR/2008/ GRC. 9 June 2008.

Greenberg, D., S.N. Katz, S.C. Wheatley, and M.B. Oliviero. 1993. *Constitutionalism and Democracy: Transitions in the Contemporary World*. New York: Oxford University Press.

Greenwatch. 2007a. *Report on the Proceedings of the Judicial Symposium on International Environmental Law for Judges in Uganda*. Kampala, Uganda: Greenwatch.

–. 2007b. *Report on the Proceedings of the Training Workshop to Enhance Enforcement of Environmental Laws for Chief Magistrates*. Kampala, Uganda: Greenwatch.

Greenwatch and UNEP. 2006. *Handbook on Environmental Law in Uganda*. Kampala, Uganda: Greenwatch.

Greiber, T. 2006. *Judges and the Rule of Law: Creating the Links; Environment, Human Rights and Poverty*. Gland, Switzerland: IUCN.

Grendstad, G., P. Selle, K. Stromsnes, and O. Bortne. 2006. *Unique Environmentalism: A Comparative Perspective*. New York: Springer.

Grote, R. 2007a. "The Hashemite Kingdom of Jordan: Introductory Note." In Wolfrum and Grote 2011.

–. 2007b. "The Republic of Costa Rica: Introductory Note." In Wolfrum and Grote 2011.

–. 2008a. "The Republic of Korea: Introductory Note." In Wolfrum and Grote 2011.

–. 2008b. "The Republic of Maldives: Introductory Note." In Wolfrum and Grote 2011.

–. 2008c. "The United Mexican States: Introductory Note." In Wolfrum and Grote 2011.

Grubb, M. 1993. *The Earth Summit Agreements: A Guide and Assessment*. London: Earthscan.

Günes, Y., and A.A. Coskun. 2005. "Legal Structure of Public Participation in Environmental Issues in Turkey." *Journal of Environmental Assessment Policy and Management* 7, 3: 543-68.

Guzman, A.T. 2008. *How International Law Works: A Rational Choice Theory*. Oxford: Oxford University Press.

Hancock, J. 2003. *Environmental Human Rights: Power, Ethics, and Law*. Aldershot, UK: Ashgate.

Handl, G. 2001. "Human Rights and Protection of the Environment." In *Economic, Social and Cultural Rights: A Textbook*, edited by A. Eide, C. Krause, and A. Rosas, 303-28. 2nd ed. Dordrecht, Netherlands: Martinus Nijhoff.

Harding, A.J., ed. 2007a. *Access to Environmental Justice: A Comparative Study*. Leiden, Netherlands: Martinus Nijhoff.

–. 2007b. "Access to Environmental Justice: Some Introductory Perspectives." In Harding 2007a, 1-20.

Harding, A.J., and A. Sharom. 2007. "Access to Environmental Justice in Malaysia." In Harding 2007a, 125-56.

Harper, K. 2005. "Wild Capitalism and Ecocolonialism: A Tale of Two Rivers." *American Anthropologist* 107, 2: 221-33.

Hassan, P. 2003a. "Environmental Rights as Part of Fundamental Human Rights: The Leadership of the Judiciary in Pakistan." Paper presented at the Global Judges Symposium on Sustainable Development and the Role of Law at Johannesburg, South Africa, 18-20 August 2002, organized by UNEP.

–. 2003b. "Judicial Activism toward Sustainable Development in South Asia." *Pakistan Law Journal* 31: 39-59.

–. 2006. "The Role of Judiciary and Judicial Commissions on Sustainable Development Issues in Pakistan." Paper presented at the International Judicial Conference organized by the Supreme Court of Pakistan during its Golden Jubilee celebrations, 11-14 August 2006.

–. 2007a. "Environmental Protection, Rule of Law, and the Judicial Crisis in Pakistan." Paper presented at the International Congress on Environmental Law held in Rio de Janeiro, Brazil, on 22-24 May 2007 in tribute to Professor Charles O. Okidi.

–. 2007b. "Urbanization and Environmental Challenges in Pakistan." In Chalifour, Kameri-Mbote, Lye, and Nolon 2007, 334-51.

Hassan, P., and A. Azfar. 2004. "Securing Environmental Rights through Public Interest Litigation in South Asia." *Virginia Environmental Law Journal* 22, 3: 216-36.

Hassan, P., and J. Hassan. 2009. "Pakistan." In Kotze and Paterson 2009a, 381-410.

Hatchard, J., N. Ndulo, and P. Slinn. 2004. *Comparative Constitutionalism and Good Governance in the Commonwealth: An Eastern and Southern African Perspective.* Cambridge: Cambridge University Press.

Haumont, F., and J. Bodart. 2006. "Le droit a un environnement sain: Le cas de la Belgique." *Annuaire international des droits de l'homme* 1: 449-78.

Hayward, T. 2000. "Constitutional Environmental Rights: A Case for Political Analysis." *Political Studies* 48, 3: 558-72.

–. 2005. *Constitutional Environmental Rights.* Oxford: Oxford University Press.

Heng, L.L. 2002. "Public Participation in the Environment: A South-East Asian Perspective." In Zillman, Lucas, and Pring 2002, 651-78.

Henkin, L. 1990. *The Age of Rights.* New York: Columbia University Press.

Herendeen, R.A. 2000. "Ecological Footprint Is a Vivid Indicator of Indirect Effects." *Ecological Economics* 32-33: 357-58.

Heringa, A.W. 2006. "Human Rights and General Principles and Their Importance as a Legislative Technique. Do They Matter in Legislation? An Analysis with Specific Reference to Environmental Protection." In *Environmental Law in Development: Lessons from the Indonesian Experience,* edited by M. Faure and N. Niessen, 9-23. Cheltenham, UK: Edward Elgar.

Herrero de la Fuente, A.A. 2002. "Spain." In Ebbesson 2002, 421-42.

Heywood, V., and R. Watson, eds. 1995. *Global Biodiversity Assessment.* Cambridge: Cambridge University Press/UNEP.

Hill, B.E., S. Wolfson, and N. Targ. 2004. "Human Rights and the Environment: A Synopsis and Some Predictions." *Georgetown International Environmental Law Review* 16, 3: 359-402.

Hillstrom, K., and L.C. Hillstrom. 2004. *Latin America and the Caribbean: A Continental Overview of Environmental Issues.* Santa Barbara, CA: ABC-CLIO.

Hirakuri, S.R. 2003. *Can Law Save the Forest? Lessons from Finland and Brazil.* Jakarta, Indonesia: Center for International Forestry Research (CIFOR).

Hirschl, R. 2000. "The Political Origins of Judicial Empowerment through the Constitutionalization of Rights: Lessons from Four Polities." *Law and Social Inquiry* 25: 91-149.

–. 2004. *Towards Juristocracy: The Origins and Consequences of the New Constitutionalism.* Cambridge, MA: Harvard University Press.

–. 2007. "On the Blurred Methodological Matrix of Comparative Constitutional Law." In *The Migration of Constitutional Ideas*, edited by S. Choudhry, 39-66. Cambridge: Cambridge University Press.

Hiskes, R.P. 2009. *The Human Right to a Green Future: Environmental Rights and Intergenerational Justice*. Cambridge: Cambridge University Press.

Hlako, C. 2008. "The Environmental Rights Entered in the Constitution: A Critique." *U.S.-China Law Review* 5, 1: 1-14.

Hochstetler, K., and M.E. Keck. 2007. *Greening Brazil: Environmental Activism in State and Society*. Durham, NC: Duke University Press.

Hofrichter, R., ed. 2002. *Toxic Struggles: The Theory and Practice of Environmental Justice*. Salt Lake City: University of Utah Press.

Hogg, P.W., and A.A. Bushell. 1997. "The Charter Dialogue between Courts and Legislatures (or Perhaps the Charter Isn't Such a Bad Thing After All)." *Osgoode Hall Law Journal* 35: 75-124.

Hohfeld, W.N. 1923. *Fundamental Legal Concepts as Applied in Judicial Reasoning*. New Haven, CT: Yale University Press.

Holley, M. 1998. "Sustainable Development in Central America: Translating Regional Environmental Accords into Domestic Enforcement Action." *Ecology Law Quarterly* 25, 1: 89-119.

Holmes, S., and C.R. Sunstein. 1999. *The Cost of Rights: Why Liberty Depends on Taxes*. New York: W.W. Norton.

Hottelier, M., and V. Martenet. 2006. "Le droit de l'homme a un environnement sain: Perspectives suisses." *Annuaire international des droits de l'homme* 1: 427-47.

Houck, O.A. 2007. "Light from the Trees: The Stories of Minors Oposa and the Russian Forest Cases." *Georgetown International Environmental Law Review* 19: 321-73.

–. 2008. "A Case of Sustainable Development: The River God and the Forest at the End of the World." *Tulsa Law Review* 44, 1: 275-316.

Howell, D.C. 2008. *Fundamental Statistics for the Behavioral Sciences*. 6th ed. Belmont, CA: Thomson Wadsworth.

Human Rights Defender of the Republic of Armenia. 2009. *Annual Report 2008*. Yerevan, Armenia. http://www.ombuds.am/main/en/10/31/0/12.

Hunter, D., and M. Bowman. 1992. "Environmental Reforms in Post-Communist Central Europe: From High Hopes to Hard Reality." *Michigan Journal of International Law* 13: 921-80.

Hunter, D., J. Salzman, and D. Zaelke. 2007. *International Environmental Law and Policy*. 3rd ed. New York: Foundation Press.

Huten, N., and M.-A. Cohendet. 2007a. "La charte de l'environnement deux ans après: Chronique d'une anesthésie au palais-royal (1 partie)." *Revue juridique de l'environnement* 3: 277-94.

–. 2007b. "La charte de l'environnement deux ans après: Le conseil d'état hésite, les autres juridications tranchent (2e partie)." *Revue juridique de l' environnement* 4: 425-45.

Ibanez Macias, A. 2007. "El medio ambiente como derecho fundamental." *Revista de derecho urbanistico y medio ambiente* 231: 141-88.

Idllalène, S. 2010. "La charte marocaine de l'environnement et du développement durable sera-t-elle une loi fondamentale?" *VertigO: La revue électronique en sciences de l'environnement*. http://vertigo.revues.org/9956.

Ignatieff, M. 2000. *The Rights Revolution (CBC Massey Lectures)*. Toronto: Anansi.

–. 2001. *Human Rights as Politics and Idolatry*. Princeton, NJ: Princeton University Press.

Ihonvbere, J.O. 2005. "Constitutionalism and Governance in Africa." In *Sustainable Development in Africa: A Multifaceted Challenge*, edited by O. Ukaga and O.G. Afoaku, 93-118. Trenton, NJ: Africa World Press.

Instituto Internacional de Derecho y Medio Ambiente. 2005. *Mecanismos legales para la defensa del medio ambiente*. Madrid: IIDMA.

Inter-American Commission on Human Rights. 1997. *Report on the Human Rights Situation in Ecuador*. OEA/Ser.L/V/II.96, Ch. 9.

–. 2010. *Admissibility Decision Regarding Petition of Mossman Environmental Action Now against the United States*. Petition 242-05. Decision dated 17 March 2010.

Inter-American Court of Human Rights. 2008. *Annual Report of the Inter-American Court of Human Rights*. San Jose, Costa Rica: IACHR.

Intergovernmental Panel on Climate Change. 2007. *Climate Change 2007: Synthesis Report*. Cambridge: Cambridge University Press.

Intergovernmental Panel on Climate Change, Working Group I. 2007. *Climate Change 2007: The Physical Science Basis, Summary for Policy-Makers*. Cambridge: Cambridge University Press.

Intergovernmental Working Group for the Elaboration of a Set of Voluntary Guidelines to Support the Progressive Realization of the Right to Adequate Food in the Context of National Food Security. 2004. *Justiciability of the Right to Food*. Rome: FAO.

International Centre of Comparative Environmental Law. 1990. *Declaration de Limoges*. World Conference of Environmental Law Organizations. Limoges, France: ICCEL.

–. 2001. *Declaration de Limoges II: Towards a New Environmental Law*. World Conference of Environmental Law Organizations. Limoges, France: ICCEL.

International Commission of Jurists. 2008. *Courts and the Legal Enforcement of ISC Rights: Comparative Experiences of Justiciability*. Geneva: ICJ.

International Development Law Foundation. 2006. "Strengthening Environmental Law Enforcement and Compliance in Indonesia: Towards Improved Environmental Stringency and Environmental Performance." *Development Law Update 6*.

Iordanov, I.-R. 2007. *Scientific Basis and Normative Regulation of Environmental Human Rights in Republic of Moldova*. Doctoral thesis, Moldova State University.

Iyer, V. 2007. "The Supreme Court of India." In B. Dickson 2007b, 121-68.

Jadot, B. 2007. "La cour d'arbitrage ne cache plus l'obligation de standstill resultant de l'article 23 de la constitution." *Aménagement-environnement: Urbanisme et droit foncier* 1: 10-12.

Jancarova, I. 2009. *Recent Developments in Member State Environmental Law: Czech Republic*. http://www-user.uni-bremen.de/~avosetta/czechreport2009.pdf.

Janis, M.W. 2003. *An Introduction to International Law*. 4th ed. New York: Aspen Publishers.

Jariwala, C.M. 2000. "The Directions of Environmental Justice: An Overview." In *Fifty Years of the Supreme Court of India: Its Grasp and Reach*, edited by S.K. Verma and K. Kusum, 469-94. New Delhi: Oxford University Press.

Jayawickrama, N. 2002. *The Judicial Application of Human Rights Law: National, Regional, and International Jurisprudence*. Cambridge: Cambridge University Press.

Johannesburg Principles on the Role of Law and Sustainable Development. 2003. Adopted at the Global Judges Symposium held in Johannesburg, South Africa, 18-20 August 2002. *Journal of Environmental Law* 15: 107-10.

Johnston, D.M. 1998. "Environmental Law as Sacred Text: Western Values and Southeast Asian Prospects." In *Asia-Pacific Trends in Legal Development: Sectoral and Cross-Sectoral Studies*, edited by G.A. Ferguson and D.M. Johnston, 405-65. Vancouver: UBC Press.

Joint Committee on Human Rights, House of Commons and House of Lords. 2008. *Twenty-Ninth Report*. London: House of Lords.

Jordan, A., ed. 2005. *Environmental Policy in the European Union: Actors, Institutions and Processes*. 2nd ed. London: Earthscan.

Jordan, A., and D. Liefferink, eds. 2004. *Environmental Policy in Europe: The Europeanization of National Environmental Policy*. New York: Routledge.

Jorgenson, A.K. 2003. "Consumption and Environmental Degradation: A Cross-National Analysis of the Ecological Footprint." *Social Problems* 50, 4: 374-94.

Jorgenson, A.K., J. Rice, and J. Crowe. 2005. "Unpacking the Ecological Footprint of Nations." *International Journal of Comparative Sociology* 46: 241-60.

Justice and Environment. 2010. *Access to Justice in Environmental Matters*. Brno, Czech Republic: Justice and Environment.

–. 2009. *Selected Problems of the Aarhus Convention Application Based on Experience and Court Practice of NGOs in 7 EU Countries*. International Visegrad Fund and Ministry for Housing, Spatial Planning and Environment of the Netherlands. http://www.justiceandenvironment.org/_files/old-uploads-wordpress/2009/12/access-to_justice-selected_problems_2009-apr-conference.pdf.

Kagan, R.A. 2003. *Adversarial Legalism: The American Way of Law*. Cambridge, MA: Harvard University Press.

Kameri-Mbote, P. 2009. "Kenya." In Kotze and Paterson 2009a, 451-78.

Kandlikar, M. 2007. "Air Pollution at a Hotspot Location in Delhi: Detecting Trends, Seasonal Cycles and Oscillations." *Atmospheric Environment* 41, 28: 5934-47.

Karakostas, I., and E. Dacoronia. 2006. "Environment and Private Law in Greece." *Annuaire international des droits de l'homme* 1: 479-93.

Karakostas, I., and I. Vassilopoulos. 1999. *Environmental Law in Greece*. The Hague: Kluwer Law International.

Karageorgou, V. 2007. *Hellenic Constitution and Environmental Protection*. Unpublished paper, on file with author.

Kasimbazi, E. 2009. "Nigeria." In Kotze and Paterson 2009a, 479-504.

Kathuria, V. 2004. "Impact of CNG on Vehicular Pollution in Delhi: A Note." *Transportation Research Part D – Transport and Environment* 9, 5: 409-17.

Keeley, J., and I. Scoones. 2003. *Understanding Environmental Policy Processes: Cases from Africa*. London: Earthscan.

Kellenberger, J. 2003. "Human Rights, Environmental Rights, and Religion." In *Human Rights and Responsibilities in the World Religions*, edited by J. Runzo, N.M. Martin, and Arvind Sharma, 115-28. Oxford: Oneworld.

Kelly, P. 2000. "The Twilight of Customary International Law." *Virginia Journal of International Law* 40, 2: 449-543.

Kennedy Cuomo, K. 1993. "Human Rights and the Environment: Common Ground." *Yale Journal of International Law* 18, 1: 227-33.

Kim, R.-H. 2006. "Principles of Sustainable Development in Korean Environmental Law: Towards the Earth Charter Principles." *New Zealand Postgraduate Law E-Journal* 4: 1-44.

Kindred, H.M., and P.M. Saunders, eds. 2006. *International Law Chiefly as Applied and Interpreted in Canada.* 7th ed. Toronto: Emond Montgomery.

Kinney, E.D., and B.A. Clark. 2004. "Provisions for Health and Health Care in the Constitutions of the Countries of the World." *Cornell International Law Journal* 37, 2: 285-355.

Kiss, A. 1993. "Concept and Possible Implications of the Right to Environment." In *Human Rights in the Twenty-First Century: A Global Challenge,* edited by K.E. Mahoney and P. Mahoney, 551-59. Dordrecht, Netherlands: Martinus Nijhoff.

Kiss, A., and D. Shelton. 2004. *International Environmental Law.* 3rd ed. Ardsley, NY: Transnational Publishers.

Kiss, C. 2009. "Selected Problems of the Implementation of the Aarhus Convention in Hungary." In Justice and Environment 2009, 33-39.

Kitzes, J., and M. Wackernagel. 2009. "Answers to Common Questions in Ecological Footprint Accounting." *Ecological Indicators* 9: 812-17.

Klarer, J., and B. Moldan, eds. 1997. *The Environmental Challenge for Central European Economies in Transition.* Chichester, UK: John Wiley and Sons.

Knox, J.H. 2009. "Linking Human Rights and Climate Change at the UN." *Harvard Environmental Law Review* 33, 2: 477-98.

Koesnadi, H. 1997. "Environmental Management and Law in Indonesia." In *Environmental Law and Policy in Asia: Issues and Enforcement,* edited by Y. Nomura and N. Sakumoto, Chapter 7. Tokyo: Institute of Developing Economies.

Koivurova, T. 2004a. "The Case of Vuotos: Interplay between International, Community, and National Law." *Review of European Community and International Environmental Law* 13, 1: 47-60.

–. 2004b. "Finland: Country/Region Reports." *Yearbook of International Environmental Law 2002* 13: 481-84.

Koskenniemi, M. 1991. "Peaceful Settlement of Environmental Disputes." *Nordic Journal of International Law* 60: 73-92.

Kotze, L.J. 2007a. "The Judiciary, the Environmental Right and the Quest for Sustainability in South Africa: A Critical Reflection." *Review of European Community and International Environmental Law* 16, 3: 298-311.

–. 2007b. "Strategies for Integrated Environmental Governance in South Africa: Toward a More Sustainable Environmental Governance and Land Use Regime." In Chalifour, Kameri-Mbote, Lye, and Nolon 2007, 219-39.

Kotze, L.J., and A.R. Paterson, eds. 2009a. *The Role of the Judiciary in Environmental Governance: Comparative Perspectives.* The Hague: Kluwer Law International,

–. 2009b. "South Africa." In Kotze and Paterson 2009a, 557-602.

Kramer, L. 2006. "Thirty Years of Environmental Governance in the European Union." In *Reflections on 30 Years of EU Environmental Law: A High Level of Protection?* edited by R. Macrory, 553-77. Amsterdam: Europe Law Publishing.

Kravchenko, S. 2002. "New Laws on Public Participation in the Newly Independent States." In Zillman, Lucas, and Pring 2002, 467-503.

–. 2004. "Citizen Enforcement of Environmental Law in Eastern Europe." *Widener Law Review* 10, 2: 475-502.

–. 2005. "The Role of Civil Society." In *The Law of Energy for Sustainable Development*, edited by A.J. Bradbook, R. Lyster, R.L. Ottinger, and W. Xi, 521-39. Cambridge: Cambridge University Press.

–. 2007. "The Aarhus Convention and Innovations in Compliance with Multilateral Environmental Agreements." *Colorado Journal of International Environmental Law and Policy* 18: 1-50.

Kravchenko, S., and J.E. Bonine. 2008. *Human Rights and the Environment: Cases, Law, and Policy*. Durham, NC: Carolina Academic Press.

Krishnan, J.K. 2008. "Scholarly Discourse, Public Perceptions and the Cementing of Norms: The Case of the Indian Supreme Court and a Plea for Research." *Journal of Appellate Process and Practice* 9, 2: 255-90.

Krygier, M., and A.W. Czarnota, eds. 1999. *The Rule of Law after Communism: Problems and Prospects in East-Central Europe*. Aldershot, UK: Ashgate.

Ksentini, F.Z. 1994. *Review of Further Developments in Fields with Which the Sub-Commission Has Been Concerned: Human Rights and the Environment; Final Report of the UN Sub-Commission on Prevention of Discrimination and Protection of Minorities*. UN Doc. E/CN.4/Sub.2/1994/9. 6 July 1994.

Kuusiniemi, K. 2002. "Finland." In Ebbesson 2002, 177-202.

Ladan, M. 2009. "Nigeria." In Kotze and Paterson 2009a, 527-66.

Lafferty, W.M., O.M. Larsen and A. Ruud. 2004. "Institutional Provisions for Environmental Policy Integration in Norway." Paper presented at the Berlin Conference on the Human Dimensions of Global Environmental Change, 4 December 2004.

Lancet Editorial Board. 2009. "A Commission on Climate Change." *The Lancet* 373, 9676: 1659.

Larmusea, I., ed. 2007. *Constitutional Rights to an Ecologically Balanced Environment*. Ghent, Belgium: VVOR.

Lasser, M. de S.-O.-l'E. 2009. *Judicial Transformations: The Rights Revolution in the Courts of Europe*. Oxford: Oxford University Press.

Lau, M. 1996. "Islam and Judicial Activism: Public Interest Litigation and Environmental Protection in the Islamic Republic of Pakistan." In Boyle and Anderson 1996, 285-301.

–. 2007. "Access to Environmental Justice: Karachi's Urban Poor and the Law." In Harding 2007a, 177-204.

Lavrysen, L. 2004. "European Environmental Law Principles in Belgian Jurisprudence." In Macrory 2004, 73-92.

–. 2005. "The Role of National Judges in Environmental Law." http://www.inece.org/newsletter/12/lavrysen.pdf.

–. 2007. "Presentation of Aarhus-Related Cases of the Belgian Constitutional Court." *Environmental Law Network International Review* 2007/2: 5-8.

–. 2009. "Belgium." In Kotze and Paterson 2009a, 85-122.

Lavrysen, L., and J. Theunis. 2007. "The Right to the Protection of a Healthy Environment in the Belgian Constitution: Retrospect and International Perspective." In Larmusea 2007, 9-29.

Law Commission of India. 2003. *One Hundred Eighty-Sixth Report: On Proposal to Constitute Environment Courts.* New Delhi: Law Commission of India.

Law, D.S. 2010. "Constitutions." In *The Oxford Handbook of Empirical Legal Research,* edited by P. Cane and H. Kritzer, Chapter 16. Oxford: Oxford University Press.

Law, D.S., and M. Versteeg. 2011. "The Evolution and Ideology of Global Constitutionalism." *California Law Review* (in press).

Law Reform Commission of Canada. 1985. *Crimes against the Environment.* Working Paper No. 44. Ottawa: The Law Commission.

Lazarus, R. 2004. *The Making of Environmental Law.* Chicago: University of Chicago Press.

Ledewitz, B. 1998. "Establishing a Federal Constitutional Right to a Healthy Environment in the United States and in Our Posterity." *Mississippi Law Journal* 68: 565-673.

Lee, J. 2000. "The Underlying Legal Theory to Support a Well-Defined Right to a Healthy Environment as a Principle of Customary International Law." *Columbia Journal of Environmental Law* 25, 2: 283-346.

Lee, M. 2005. *EU Environmental Law: Challenges, Change, and Decision-Making.* Oxford: Hart Publishing.

Leelakrishnan, P. 1999. *Environmental Law in India.* New Delhi: Butterworths.

Leopold, A. 1949. *A Sand County Almanac and Sketches Here and There.* New York: Oxford University Press.

Lepage, C. 2003. "Une Charte qui fait régresser le droit de l'environnement." *Le Monde* 16 (April): 15.

Leschke, M. 2000. "Constitutional Choice and Prosperity: A Factor Analysis." *Constitutional Political Economy* 11: 265-79.

Levinson, T., and T.J. Page. 2004. "A Constitutional (or Basic Law) Right to 'Minimum Environmental Quality.'" *International Environmental Law Newsletter* (American Bar Association Section of Energy, Environment and Natural Resources) 6, 1: 24-25.

Liefferink, D., and A. Jordan. 2004. "Europeanization and Policy Convergence: A Basis for Comparative Analysis." In Jordan and Liefferink 2004, 15-31.

Limon, M. 2009. "Human Rights and Climate Change: Constructing a Case for Political Survival." *Harvard Environmental Law Review* 33, 2: 439-76.

Lin, B. 2009. "Too Many Canadians without Safe Water." *UBC Reports* 55, 4: 1, 6.

Livingston, J. 1984. "Rightness or Rights?" *Osgoode Hall Law Journal* 22, 2: 309-21.

–. 1994. *Rogue Primate: An Exploration of Human Domestication.* Toronto: Key Porter.

Lopez Ramon, F. 2005. "El medio ambiente en la constitucion Española." *Revista de derecho urbanistico y medio ambiente* 222: 183-98.

López Ramos, N. 2003. "Análisis de la constitución mexicana en materia ambiental y obstáculos para su eficacia." In *Resumenes de sentencias judiciales en materia ambiental: Pronunciadas por organos jurisdiccionales de paises de America Latina,* edited by N.

López Ramos, 153-73. Mexico City: UN Regional Office for Latin America and the Caribbean.

Louka, E. 2006. *International Environmental Law: Fairness, Effectiveness, and World Order.* Cambridge: Cambridge University Press.

Ly, I. 2003. "Senegal." In Centre international de Droit Comparé de l' Environnement 2003, 562-75.

MacIntyre, A. 1981. *After Virtue.* London: Duckworth.

Macrory, R., ed. 2004. *Principles of European Environmental Law: Proceedings of the Avosetta Group of European Environmental Lawyers.* Amsterdam: Europa Law Publishing.

Mahoney, J. 2007. *The Challenge of Human Rights: Origin, Development, and Significance.* Oxford: Blackwell.

Majtenyi, B. 2006. "The Institutional System of Hungarian Environmental Law." *Gazzetta Ambiente* 5: 149-54.

Malaysia, Ministry of Science, Technology, and Environment. 1993. *The Report of the Environmental Law Review Committee.* Kuala Lumpur: Ministry of Science, Technology, and Environment.

Malone, L.A., and S. Pasternack. 2006. *Defending the Environment: Civil Society Strategies to Enforce International Environmental Law.* 2nd ed. New York: Transnational Publishing.

Mandela, N. 2002. "No Water, No Future." Speech at the World Summit on Sustainable Development, Johannesburg, South Africa, 28 August 2002.

Mantero de San Vicente, O. 1993. "Uruguay." In *International Encyclopedia of Laws,* edited by R. Blanpain. Vol. 3, Supp. 7, *Environmental Law,* edited by K. Deketelaere. The Hague: Kluwer Law International.

Marks, S.P. 1981. "Emerging Human Rights: A New Generation for the 1980s." *Rutgers Law Review* 33, 1: 435-52.

Marrani, D. 2008. "The Second Anniversary of the Constitutionalisation of the French Charter for the Environment: Constitutional and Environmental Implications." *Environmental Law Review* 10, 1: 9-27.

Martens, M. 2007. Constitutional Right to a Healthy Environment in Belgium." *Review of European Community and International Environmental Law* 16, 3: 287-97.

Martin, F.F., S.J. Schnably, R.J. Wilson, J.S. Simon, and M.V. Tushnet. 2006. *International Human Rights and Humanitarian Law: Treaties, Cases, and Analysis.* Cambridge: Cambridge University Press.

Martinez, I. 2000. *El aceso a la justicia ambiental en Argentina, Brazil, Chile, Colombia, Mexico y Venezuela.* Mexico City: Programa de las Naciones Unidas para el Medio Ambiente.

–. 2001. "El acceso a la justicia ambiental en America Latina durante la decada de los Noventa: Reformas y desarollos." In *Environmental Law in Developing Countries: Selected Issues,* edited by N. Islam, I Martinez, I. Mgbeoji, and W. Xi, 27-66. Gland, Switzerland: International Union for Conservation of Nature.

Martins da Cruz, B. 2007. "The Constitutional Right to an Ecologically Balanced Environment in Portugal." In Larmusea 2007, 44-57.

Matanza-Riachuelo Watershed Authority. 2011. Comprehensive Environmental Restoration Plan: Update. Buenos Aires: ACUMAR. See www.acumar.gov.ar.

May, J.R. 2006. "Constituting Fundamental Environmental Rights Worldwide." *Pace Environmental Law Review* 23: 113-82.

May, J.R., and E. Daly. 2009. "Violating Fundamental Environmental Rights Worldwide." *Oregon Review of International Law* 11: 365-439.

Mayer, A.L. 2008. "Strengths and Weaknesses of Common Sustainability Indices for Multidimensional Systems." *Environment International* 34, 2: 277-91.

Mba, H.C., S.N. Uchegbu, C.A. Udeh, and L.N. Muoghalu, eds. 2004. *Management of Environmental Problems and Hazards in Nigeria.* Aldershot, UK: Ashcroft.

McAllister, L.K. 2005. "Public Prosecutors and Environmental Protection in Brazil." In *Environmental Issues in Latin America and the Caribbean,* edited by A. Romero and S. West, 207-29. New York: Springer.

–. 2008. *Making Law Matter: Environmental Protection and Legal Institutions in Brazil.* Stanford, CA: Stanford University Press.

–. 2009. "On Environmental Enforcement and Compliance. A Reply to Professor Crawford's Review of Making Law Matter: Environmental Protection and Legal Institutions in Brazil." *George Washington International Law Review* 40: 649-85.

McCallion, K.F., and H.R. Sharma. 2000. "Environmental Justice without Borders: The Need for an International Court of the Environment to Protect Fundamental Rights." *George Washington Journal of International Law and Economics* 32, 3: 351-65.

McCann, M. 1996. "Causal versus Constitutive Explanations (or, on the Difficulty of Being So Positive)." *Law and Social Inquiry* 21, 2: 457-82.

McCrudden, C. 2000. "Common Law of Human Rights? Transnational Judicial Conversations on Constitutional Rights." *Oxford Journal of Legal Studies* 20: 499-532.

McHugh, J.T. 2002. *Comparative Constitutional Traditions.* New York: Peter Lang.

McInerney-Lankford, S. 2009. "Climate Change and Human Rights: An Introduction to Legal Issues." *Harvard Environmental Law Review* 33, 2: 431-38.

McMichael, A.J., D.H. Campbell-Lendrum, C.F. Corvalán, K.L. Ebi, A.K. Githeko, J.D. Scheraga, and A. Woodward, eds. 2003. *Climate Change and Human Health: Risks and Responses.* Geneva: World Health Organization.

Mechlem, K. 2006. "Helping Make Rights a Reality: Support to the Judiciary in Implementing Mozambique's New Natural Resource Laws." In Greiber 2006, 3-7.

Medarova, K., and A. Antypas. 2006. "Implementation of the Aarhus Convention in Bulgaria: Limping towards Effectiveness." *Environmental Liability* 14, 1: 13-22.

Mehta, M.C. 1997. "Making the Law Work for the Environment." *Asia Pacific Journal of Environmental Law* 2, 4: 349-59.

–. 2006. "The Accountability Principle: Legal Solutions to Break Corruption's Impact on India's Environment." *Journal of Environmental Law and Litigation* 21: 141-56.

Mejia, H.M. 2009. "La tutela ambiental en el derecho salvadoreno." *Medio ambiente and derecho* 19. http://huespedes.cica.es/aliens/gimadus/19/04_henry_alexander_mejia.html.

Mendelson, S.E., and J.K. Glenn, eds. 2002. *The Power and Limits of NGOs: A Critical Look at Building Democracy in Eastern Europe and Eurasia.* New York: Columbia University Press.

Merrills, J.G. 2007. "Environmental Rights." In *The Oxford Handbook of International Environmental Law*, edited by D. Bodansky, J. Brunnee, and E. Hey, 663-80. Oxford: Oxford University Press.

Merryman, J.H. 1985. *The Civil Law Tradition: An Introduction to the Legal Systems of Western Europe and Latin America.* 2nd ed. Stanford, CA: Stanford University Press.

Mesa Suarez, R. 2006. "Judicial Enforcement as an Effective Citizen's Tool against Government Non-Compliance: The Case of La Oroya." *IUCN Environmental Law Programme Newsletter* 6-9.

Mestad, O. 2002. "Rights to Public Participation in Norwegian Mining, Energy, and Resource Development." In Zillman, Lucas, and Pring 2002, 383-400.

Michaels, D. 2008. *Doubt Is Their Product: How Industry's Assault on Science Threatens Your Health.* Oxford: Oxford University Press.

Mickwitz, P. 2006. *Environmental Policy Evaluation: Concepts and Practice.* Vaajakoski, Finland: Finnish Society of Sciences and Letters.

Milieu Ltd. 2007a. *Measures on Access to Justice in Environmental Matters: Country Report for the Czech Republic.* Prepared for the European Commission, DG Environment. Brussels: Milieu Ltd.

–. 2007b. *Measures on Access to Justice in Environmental Matters: Country Report for France.* Report prepared for the European Commission. Brussels: Milieu Ltd.

–. 2007c. *Measures on Access to Environmental Justice in Environmental Matters: Country Report for the Netherlands.* Report prepared for the European Commission. Brussels: Milieu Ltd.

–. 2007d. *Measures on Access to Justice in Environmental Matters: Country Report for Slovenia.* Report prepared for the European Commission. Brussels: Milieu Ltd.

–. 2007e. *Measures on Access to Justice in Environmental Matters: Country Report for Spain.* Report prepared for the European Commission. Brussels: Milieu Ltd.

–. 2007f. *Summary Report on the Inventory of EU Member States Measures on Access to Justice in Environmental Matters.* Report prepared for the European Commission. Brussels: Milieu Ltd.

Millennium Ecosystem Assessment. 2005. *Ecosystems and Human Wellbeing: Synthesis.* Washington, DC: Island Press.

Miller, C. 1998. *Environmental Rights: Critical Perspectives.* London: Routledge.

Millett, R.L., J.S. Holmes, and O.J. Perez. 2009. *Latin American Democracy: Emerging Reality or Endangered Species?* New York: Routledge.

Mischenko, V.L. 2001. "Public Participation in Environmentally Sound Decision-Making." In *The Role of Environmental NGOs: Russian Challenges, American Lessons; Proceedings of a Workshop,* 179-90. Washington, DC: National Academy Press.

Mischenko, V.L., and E. Rosenthal. 1999. "Citizen Environmental Enforcement in Russia: The First Successful Nationwide Case." In *Proceedings of the Fifth International Conference on Environmental Compliance and Enforcement,* 419-21. Washington, DC: INECE.

–. 2002. "Conflicts over Transnational Oil and Gas Development off Sakhalin Island in the Russian Far East: A David and Goliath Tale." In *Human Rights and the*

Environment: Conflicts and Norms in a Globalizing World, edited by L. Zarsky, 96-121. London: Earthscan.

Mitchell, R.B. 2003. "International Environmental Agreements: A Survey of Their Features, Form, and Effects." *Annual Review of Environment and Resources* 28: 429-61.

Mohamed Salih, M.A. 1999. "Introduction: Environmental Planning, Policies, and Politics in Eastern and Southern Africa." In *Environmental Planning, Policies, and Politics in Eastern and Southern Africa,* edited by M.A. Mohamed Salih and S. Tedla, 1-17. London: Macmillan.

Monahan, P.J. 2006. *Constitutional Law.* 3rd ed. Toronto: Irwin Law.

Montenegro, A.A. 1995. "Constitutional Design and Economic Performance." *Constitutional Political Economy* 6, 2: 161-69.

Moran, D.D., M. Wackernagel, J.A. Kitzes, S.H. Goldfinger, and A. Boutaud. 2008. "Measuring Sustainable Development – Nation by Nation." *Ecological Economics* 64, 3: 470-74.

Morris, C. 1964. "The Rights and Duties of Beasts and Trees: A Law Teacher's Essay for Landscape Architects." *Journal of Legal Education* 17, 2: 185-92.

Morse, S., and E.D.G. Fraser. 2005. "Making 'Dirty' Nations Look Clean? The Nation State and the Problem of Selecting and Weighting Indices as Tools for Measuring Progress towards Sustainability." *Geoforum* 36: 625-40.

Moseley, W.G. 2004. "Whither African Environment and Development." In *African Environment and Development: Rhetoric, Programs, Realities,* edited by W.G. Moseley and B.I Logan, 229-40. Aldershot, UK: Ashgate.

Mowery, L.A. 2002. "Earth Rights, Human Rights: Can International Environmental Human Rights Affect Corporate Accountability?" *Fordham Environmental Law Journal* 13, 2: 343-73.

Mubangizi, J.C. 2006. "The Constitutional Protection of Socio-Economic Rights in Selected African Countries: A Comparative Evaluation." *African Journal of Legal Studies* 2, 1: 1-19.

–. 2007. *Prospects and Challenges in the Protection and Enforcement of Socio-economic Rights.* Paper presented at the 7th World Congress of the International Association of Constitutional Law, Athens, 11-15 June 2007.

Mulyono, B.H. 2006. "Obstacles and Strategy of Environmental Law Enforcement in Indonesia." In Greiber 2006, 43-49.

Mushkat, R. 2004. *International Environmental Law and Asian Values.* Vancouver: UBC Press.

–. 2009. "Contextualizing Environmental Human Rights: A Relativist Perspective." *Pace Environmental Law Review* 26, 1: 119-77.

Mwafongo, W.M.K., and M.L.M. Kapila. 1999. "Environmental Management in Malawi: Lessons from Failure." In *Environmental Planning, Policies, and Politics in Eastern and Southern Africa,* edited by M.A. Mohamed Salih and S. Tedla, 59-79. London: Macmillan.

Myers, R.A., and B. Worm. 2003. "Rapid Worldwide Depletion of Predatory Fish Communities." *Nature* 423: 280-83.

Nanda, V.P., and G. Pring. 2003. *International Environmental Law and Policy for the 21st Century*. Ardsley, NY: Transnational Publishers.

Narain, U., and R.G. Bell. 2006. *Who Changed Delhi's Air? The Roles of the Court and the Executive in Environmental Policymaking*. Discussion Paper 05-48. Washington, DC: Resources for the Future.

Narain, U., and A. Krupnick. 2007. *The Impact of Delhi's CNG Program on Air Quality*. Washington, DC: Resources for the Future.

Nash, R.F. 1989. *The Rights of Nature: A History of Environmental Ethics*. Madison: University of Wisconsin Press.

Nedelsky, J. 2008. "Reconceiving Rights and Constitutionalism." *Journal of Human Rights* 7: 139-73.

Nelken, D. 1995. "Disclosing/Invoking Legal Culture: An Introduction." *Social and Legal Studies* 4, 4: 435-52.

Nergelius, J. 2006. "The Republic of Finland: Introductory Note." In Wolfrum and Grote 2011.

Nespor, S. 2005. "Italy." In de Sadeleer, Roller, and Dross 2005, 85-96.

Ness, B., E. Urbel-Piirsalu, S. Anderberg, and L. Olsson. 2007. "Categorising Tools for Sustainability Assessment." *Ecological Economics* 60: 498-508.

Neuray, J-F., and M. Pallemaerts. 2008. "L'environnement et le developpement durable dans le constitution belge." *Amenagement-Environnement* Special: 131-66.

New Economics Foundation. 2009. *The Happy Planet Index 2.0: Why Good Lives Don't Have to Cost the Earth*. http://www.happyplanetindex.org/public-data/files/happy-planet-index-2-0.pdf.

Nickel, J.W. 1993. "The Human Right to a Safe Environment: Philosophical Perspectives on Its Scope and Justification." *Yale Journal of International Law* 18, 1: 281-95.

Nikolopolous, T., and M. Haidarlis. 2005. "La constitution, la jurisprudence et la protection de l'environnement en Grece." *Revue juridique de l'environement* Special: 63-72.

Nimushakavi, V. 2006. *Constitutional Policy and Environmental Jurisprudence in India*. New Delhi: Macmillan India.

Nwobike, J.C. 2005. "The African Commission on Human and Peoples' Rights and the Demystification of Second and Third Generation Rights under the African Charter: *Social and Economic Rights Action Center (SERAC) and the Center for Economic and Social Rights (CESR) v. Nigeria*." *African Journal of Legal Studies* 1, 2: 129-46.

Obasanjo, O. 2006. *Niger Delta Human Development Report*. Abuja, Nigeria: UN Development Programme.

Ojeda-Mestre, R. 2007. "Environmental Justice in Mexico: Hopes and Disappointments." *Environmental Policy and Law* 37, 2-3: 142-57.

Okidi, C.O. 2007. "How Constitutional Entrenchment Could Mitigate Conflicts and Poverty in Resource-Rich African Countries." *Environmental Policy and Law* 37, 2/3: 158-69.

Okoth-Ogendo, H.W.O. 1993. "Constitutions without Constitutionalism: An African Political Paradox." In Greenberg, Katz, Oliviero, and Wheatley 1993, 65-82.

Oldfield, J.D. 2005. *Russian Nature: Exploring the Environmental Consequences of Societal Change*. Aldershot, UK: Ashcroft.

Olowu, D. 2006. "Human Rights and the Avoidance of Domestic Implementation: The Phenomenon of Non-Justiciable Constitutional Guarantees." *Saskatchewan Law Review* 69: 39-78.

Orakhelashvili, A. 2006. *Peremptory Norms in International Law.* Oxford: Oxford University Press.

Organisation for Economic Co-operation and Development. 2000. *Environmental Performance Reviews: Greece.* Paris: OECD.

–. 2001. *Environmental Performance Reviews: Portugal.* Paris: OECD.

–. 2002. *Environmental Performance Review of the Slovak Republic.* Paris: OECD.

–. 2003. *Environmental Indicators: Development, Measurement and Use.* Paris: OECD.

–. 2004. *Environmental Performance Reviews: Spain.* Paris: OECD.

–. 2005a. *Environmental Performance Reviews: Chile.* Paris: OECD.

–. 2005b. *Environmental Performance Reviews: France.* Paris: OECD.

–. 2005c. *Environmental Performance Reviews: Mexico.* Paris: OECD.

–. 2006. *Environmental Data Compendium.* Paris: OECD.

–. 2007a. *Environmental Data Compendium 2007.* Paris: OECD.

–. 2007b. *Environmental Performance Reviews: Belgium.* Paris: OECD.

–. 2007c. *Environmental Performance Reviews: Denmark.* Paris: OECD.

–. 2007d. *Policies for a Better Environment: Progress in Eastern Europe, Caucasus, and Central Asia.* Paris: OECD.

–. 2008a. *Environmental Performance Reviews: Hungary.* Paris: OECD.

–. 2008b. *Environmental Performance Reviews: Turkey.* Paris: OECD.

–. 2009. *Environmental Performance Reviews: Finland.* Paris: OECD.

Organization of the Islamic Conference. 1990. *Cairo Declaration on Human Rights in Islam.* UN Doc. A/45/421-S/21797, 200; A/CONF.157/PC/35; A/CONF.157/PC/62/Add. 18, 2. 5 August 1990.

Oxfam International. 2008. *Climate Wrongs and Human Rights: Putting People at the Heart of Climate Change Policy.* Oxford: Oxfam.

Pacific Environment. 2007. "Siberia Pacific Pipeline: Another Important Victory." http://www.pacificenvironment.org/article.php?id=2421.

Padhy, S. 2008. *Greening Law: A Socio-Legal Analysis of Environmental Human Rights in India.* Doctoral dissertation, University of Southern California.

Pallangyo, D.M. 2007. "Environmental Law in Tanzania: How Far Have We Come?" *Law, Environment and Development Journal* 3, 1: 26-39.

Pallemaerts, M. 1994. "International Environmental Law from Stockholm to Rio: Back to the Future?" In *Greening International Law,* edited by P. Sands, 1-19. London: Earthscan.

–. 2002. "The Human Right to the Environment as a Substantive Right." In Dejeant-Pons and Pallemaerts 2002, 11-21.

–. 2003. "International Law and Sustainable Development: Any Progress in Johannesburg?" *Review of European Community and International Environmental Law* 12, 1: 1-11.

Palmer, A., and C.A.R. Robb. 2005. "International Environmental Law in National Courts." *International Environmental Law Reports* 4.

Panjwani, R. 2008. "Evolution of Wildlife Laws in India." In *Wildlife Law: A Global Perspective,* edited by R. Panjwani, 93-132. Chicago: American Bar Association.

Papadopoulou, O.M. 2006. "Le droit a un environnement sain: L'approache du conseil d'État hellenique dans les contentieux de l'excès de pouvoir." *Annuaire international des droits de l'homme* 1: 505-29.

Parliamentary Assembly of the Council of Europe. 2010. *Reply to Recommendation 1885: Drafting an Additional Protocol to the European Convention on Human Rights Concerning the Right to a Healthy Environment.* Doc. No. 12298, 16 June 2010.

Passos de Freitas, V. 2003. "The Importance of Environmental Judicial Decisions: The Brazilian Experience." In Di Paola 2003, 59-64.

Patel, T. 2011. "France Vote Outlaws 'Fracking' for Natural Gas, Oil Extraction," *Bloomberg News*, July 1, 2011. http://www.bloomberg.com/news/2011-07-01/france-vote-outlaws-fracking-shale-for-natural-gas-oil-extraction.html.

Pathak, R.S. 1992. "The Human Rights System as a Conceptual Framework for Environmental Law." In Weiss 1992, 205-43.

Patz, J., D. Campbell-Lendrum, T. Holloway, and J.A. Foley. 2005. "Impact of Regional Climate Change on Human Health." *Nature* 438: 310-17.

Pearce, F. 2009. "The Biologist Who Broke the Berlin Wall." *New Scientist*, 203, 2716: 46-47.

Pedersen, O.W. 2008. "European Environmental Human Rights and Environmental Rights: A Long Time Coming?" *Georgetown International Environmental Law Review* 2, 11: 73-111.

Pendergrass, J. 2006. "A Review of Global Initiatives Conducted by the Environmental Law Institute." In Greiber 2006, 9-11.

Percival, R. 2009. "The Globalization of Environmental Law." *Pace Environmental Law Review* 26, 2: 451-64.

Perez Perdomo, R. 2005. "Judicialization and Regime Transformation: The Venezuelan Supreme Court." In Sieder, Schjolden, and Angell 2005b, 131-60.

Perry, M.J. 1982. *The Constitution, the Courts, and Human Rights.* New Haven, CT: Yale University Press.

Persson, T., and G. Tabellini. 2003. *The Economic Effects of Constitutions.* Boston: MIT Press.

Peterson, D.J. 1993. *Troubled Lands: The Legacy of Soviet Environmental Destruction.* Boulder, CO: Westview Press.

Pevato, P.M. 1999. "A Right to Environment in International Law: Current Status and Future Outlook." *Review of European Community and International Environmental Law* 8, 3: 309-21.

Pickvance, C. 2003. *Local Environmental Regulation in Post-Socialism: A Hungarian Case Study.* Aldershot, UK: Ashgate.

Picolotti, R. 2005. "The Right to Safe Drinking Water as a Human Right." *Housing and ESC Rights Quarterly* 2, 1: 1-5.

Picolotti, R., and M.-C. Cordonnier-Segger. 2005. "Enforcing Sustainable Development through the Inter-American Court System." In *Sustainable Justice: Reconciling Economic, Social and Environmental Law*, edited by M.-C. Cordonnier-Segger and Judge C.G. Weeramantry, 513-48. Leiden, Netherlands: Martinus Nijhoff.

Plesser, W., and P. Luiki. 1996. "Environmental Law of Austria." In *Comparative Environmental Law and Regulation*, edited by N.A. Robinson, Binder 1, Release 96-1, 1-30. Dobbs Ferry, NY: Oceana Publications.

Poland. 2008. *National Implementation Report Submitted by Poland.* [Aarhus Convention] UN Doc. ECE/MP.PP/IR/2008/POL. 7 May 2008.

Pompe, S. 2005. *The Indonesian Supreme Court: A Study of Institutional Collapse.* Ithaca, NY: Cornell University Press.

Popovic, N. 1995-96. "In Pursuit of Environmental Human Rights: Commentary on the Draft Declaration of Principles on Human Rights and the Environment." *Columbia Human Rights Law Review* 27: 487-603.

Pound, R. 1917. "The Limits of Effective Legal Action." *International Journal of Ethics* 27: 150-67.

Powell, L. 2002. "Western and Russian Environmental NGOs: A Greener Russia?" In Mendelson and Glenn 2002, 125-51.

Prieur, M. 2008. "La charte de l'environnement: Droit dur ou gadget politique?" *Pouvoirs* 127, 4: 49-65.

—. 2011. "Urgently Acknowledging the Principle of Non-Regression in Environmental Rights." *IUCN Academy of Environmental Law E-Journal* 1: 26-40.

Programa de las Naciones Unidas para el Medio Ambiente. 2000. *El aceso a la justicia ambiental en America Latina.* Mexico City: PNUMA.

Prüss-Üstün, A., and C. Corvalán. 2006. *Preventing Disease through Healthy Environments: Towards an Estimate of the Environmental Burden of Disease.* Geneva: World Health Organization.

Puechavy, M. 2006. "La legislation francaise." *Annuaire international des droits de l'homme* 1: 413-26.

Pureza, J.M., C. Frade, and C.S. Dias. 1997. *Tribunais, naturaleza, y sociedade: O direito do ambiente em Portugal.* Lisbon: Center for Social Studies.

Puvimanasinghe, S. 2004. "Public Interest Litigation, Human Rights, and the Environment in the Experience of Sri Lanka." In *International Law and Sustainable Development: Principles and Practice,* edited by N. Schrijver and F. Weiss, 653-76. Leiden, Netherlands: Martinus Nijhoff.

Ramcharan, B.G. 2005. *Judicial Protection of Economic, Social, and Cultural Rights: Cases and Materials.* Boston: Martinus Nijhoff.

Ramesh, J. 2010. "The Two Cultures Revisited: The Environment-Development Debate in India." *Economic and Political Weekly* 45, 42: 13-16.

Ratnawati, R.V. 2008. "Compliance and Enforcement Priorities and Successes in Indonesia." Presentation at 2008 AECEN Regional Forum in Bali, Indonesia.

Ravindra, K., E. Wauters, S. Tyagi, S. Mor, and R. Van Grieken. 2006. "Assessment of Air Quality after the Implementation of Compressed Natural Gas (CNG) as Fuel in Public Transport in Delhi." *Indian Environmental Monitoring and Assessment* 115, 1: 405-17.

Raz, J. 1979. *The Authority of Law: Essays on Law and Morality.* Oxford: Oxford University Press.

—. 1986. *The Morality of Freedom.* Oxford: Clarendon Press.

Razzaque, J. 2004. *Public Interest Environmental Litigation in India, Pakistan, and Bangladesh.* The Hague: Kluwer Law International.

Redgwell, C. 1996. "Life, the Universe and Everything: A Critique of Anthropocentric Rights." In Boyle and Anderson 1996, 71-87.

Rees, W.E. 2002. "An Ecological Economics Perspective on Sustainability and Prospects for Ending Poverty." *Population and Environment* 24: 15-46.

Regional Environmental Center. 2007. *Striving for Sustainability: A Regional Assessment of the Environmental Civil Society Organizations in the Western Balkans.* Szentendre, Hungary: REC.

–. 2009. *A Decade's Difference: The Regional Environmental Reconstruction Programme for South Eastern Europe.* Szentendre, Hungary: REC.

–. n.d. *Assessment of Access to Justice in Montenegro* (Conclusions). Szentendre, Hungary: REC.

Rehbinder, E. 2009. "Germany." In Kotze and Paterson 2009a, 123-50.

Reis, J.P., and M. de Andrade Neves. 2002. "Portugal." In Ebbesson 2002, 399-420.

Rekosh, E. 2008. "Constructing Public Interest Law: Transnational Collaboration and Exchange in Central and Eastern Europe." *UCLA Journal of International Law and Foreign Affairs* 13, 1: 55-96.

Repetto, R.S. 2003. "Opening Words." In Di Paola 2003, 15-17.

Revkin, A.C. 2008. "Ecuador Constitution Grants Rights to Nature." *New York Times* 30 September.

Richardson, B.J. 2004. "Is East Asia Industrializing Too Quickly? Environmental Regulation in Its Special Economic Zones." *UCLA Pacific Basin Law Journal* 22: 150-244.

Risse, T., S.C. Copp, and K. Sikkink, eds. 1999. *The Power of Human Rights: International Norms and Domestic Change.* Cambridge: Cambridge University Press.

Roberts, A.E. 2001. "Traditional and Modern Approaches to Customary International Law: A Reconciliation." *American Journal of International Law* 95, 4: 757-91.

Roberts, J.T., and N.D. Thanos. 2003. *Trouble in Paradise: Globalization and Environmental Crises in Latin America.* New York: Routledge.

Robertson, A.H., and J.G. Merrills. 1989. *Human Rights in the World: An Introduction to the Study of the International Protection of Human Rights.* 3rd ed. New York: Manchester University Press.

Robinson, N. 2003. "Challenges Confronting the Development of a Second Generation of Environmental Laws." In *Towards a Second Generation in Environmental Laws in the Asian and Pacific Region,* edited by L. Lin-Heng and M.S.Z. Manguiat, 27-32. Gland, Switzerland: IUCN.

–. 2009. "United States of America." In Kotze and Paterson 2009a, 181-208.

Rockström, J., W. Steffen, K. Noone, A. Persson, F.S. Chapin III, E.F. Lambin, T.M. Lenton, et al. 2009. "A Safe Operating Space for Humanity." *Nature* 461: 472-45.

Rodriguez-Rivera, L. 2001. "Is the Human Right to Environment Recognized under International Law? It Depends on the Source." *Colorado Journal of International Environmental Law and Policy* 12, 1: 1-45.

Rogge, M.J. 2001. "Human Rights, Human Development, and the Right to a Healthy Environment: An Analytical Framework." *Canadian Journal of Development Studies* 22, 1: 33-50.

Rojas, G.A., and A. Iza. 2009. *Derecho ambiental en Centroamerica.* Vols. 1 and 2. Gland, Switzerland: IUCN.

Rosenberg, G. 1991. *The Hollow Hope: Can Courts Bring About Social Change?* Chicago: University of Chicago Press.

Rosencranz, A., E. Boenig, and B. Dutta. 2007. "The Godavarman Case: The Indian Supreme Court's Breach of Constitutional Boundaries in Managing India's Forests." *Environmental Law Reporter* 37: 10032-42.

Rosencranz, A., and M. Jackson. 2003. "The Delhi Pollution Case: The Supreme Court of India and the Limits of Judicial Power." *Columbia Journal of Environmental Law* 28: 223-54.

Rosencranz, A., and S. Lele. 2008. "Supreme Court and India's Forests." *Economic and Political Weekly* 43, 5: 11-14.

Ruhl, J.B. 1997. "An Environmental Rights Amendment: Good Message, Bad Idea." *Natural Resources and Environment* 11, 3: 46-49.

–. 1999. "The Metrics of Constitutional Amendments: And Why Proposed Constitutional Amendments Don't Add Up." *Notre Dame Law Review* 74, 2: 245-82.

Ruiz Mendoza, B.J., and J.H. Martinez Torres. 2003. "El derecho a un medio ambiente sano en una perspectiva Latinoamericana." In *El derecho humano a un medio ambiente sano: Sexto certamen de ensayo sobre derechos humanos*, 11-39. Toluca, Mexico: Commission of Human Rights of the State of Mexico.

Sabsay, D.A. 2003. "Constitution and Environment in Relation to Sustainable Development." In Di Paola 2003, 33-43.

–. n.d. *Citizen Advocacy and Government Reform Achieved through Work for the Environment in Argentina*. Buenos Aires: Foundation for the Environment and Natural Resources (FARN).

Sachs, A. 2007. "Enforcement of Social and Economic Rights." *American University International Law Review* 22: 673-708.

Sahu, G. 2008. "Implications of Indian Supreme Court Innovations for Environmental Jurisprudence." *Law, Environment, and Development Journal* 4, 1: 1-19.

Salazar, R. 2004. "Environmental Law of Costa Rica: Development and Enforcement." In *Biodiversity Conservation in Costa Rica: Learning the Lessons in a Seasonal Dry Forest*, edited by G.W. Frankie, A. Mata, and S.B. Vinson, 281-88. Berkeley: University of California Press.

Salvo, M.N. 1997. "Constitutional Law and Sustainable Development in Central Europe: Are We There Yet?" *South Carolina Environmental Law Journal* 5, 2: 141-56.

Sandel, M.J. 1982. *Liberalism and the Limits of Justice*. Cambridge: Cambridge University Press.

Sands, P. 1996. "Human Rights, Environment, and the Lopez-Ostra Case: Content and Consequences." *European Human Rights Law Review* 6: 608-11.

–. 2003. *Principles of International Environmental Law*. 2nd ed. Cambridge: Cambridge University Press.

Sarat, A., and T.R. Kearns, eds. 1993. *Law in Everyday Life*. Ann Arbor: University of Michigan Press.

Sarlet, I., and T. Fensterseifer. 2009. "Brazil." In Kotze and Paterson 2009a, 249-68.

Sax, J. 1971. *Defending the Environment: A Strategy for Citizen Action*. New York: Knopf.

Saxe, D. 1990. *Environmental Offences: Corporate Responsibility and Executive Liability*. Aurora, ON: Canada Law Book.

Schaffrin, D., and M. Mehling. 2007. "Public Interest Litigation in Environmental Matters: A German Perspective." *Environmental Law Network International Review* 2: 13-19.

Schall, C. 2008. "Public Interest Litigation Concerning Environmental Matters before Human Rights Courts: A Promising Future Concept?" *Journal of Environmental Law* 20, 3: 417-53.

Scheffer, M., S. Carpenter, J. Foley, C. Folke, and B. Walker. 2001. "Catastrophic Shifts in Ecosystems." *Nature* 413: 591-96.

Scheingold, S. 1974. *The Politics of Rights: Lawyers, Public Policy, and Political Change.* New Haven, CT: Yale University Press.

–. 1989. "Constitutional Rights and Social Change: Civil Rights in Perspective." In *Judging the Constitution: Critical Essays on Judicial Law-Making,* edited by M.W. McCann and G.L. Houseman, 73-91. Glenview, IL: Scott, Foresman.

Schrage, W., K. Bull, and A. Karadjova. 2008. "Environmental Legal Instruments in the UNECE Region." *Yearbook of International Environmental Law 2007* 18: 3-31.

Schrijver, N.J., and F. Weiss. 1995. *Report of the Expert Group on Identification of Principles of International Law for Sustainable Development.* London: International Law Association.

Schwartz, H. 1992. "In Defence of Aiming High: Why Economic and Social Rights Belong in the New Constitutions of Post-Communist Europe." *Eastern European Constitutional Review* 1, 3: 25-28.

Schwartz, K.Z.S. 2006. *Nature and National Identity after Communism: Globalizing the Ethnoscape.* Pittsburgh: University of Pittsburgh Press.

Scott, I.K. 2000. "The Inter-American System of Human Rights: An Effective Means of Environmental Protection?" *Virginia Environmental Law Journal* 19: 197-237.

Scrieciu, S.S., and L.C. Stringer. 2008. "The Transformation of Post-Communist Societies in Central and Eastern Europe and the Former Soviet Union: An Economic and Ecological Sustainability Perspective." *European Environment* 18: 168-85.

Segal, S.H. 2004. "Environmental Regulation of Nanotechnology: Avoiding Big Mistakes for Small Machines." *Nanotechnology Law and Business* 1: 290-304.

Serafin, K.J. 1991. "Bridging the Gap: Forty Years of Communist Indifference and the New Environmental Realities in Poland." *Dickinson Journal of International Law* 10: 159-88.

Shaheed, A. 2009. "Climate Justice." *World Conservation* 39, 2: 13.

Shapiro, M. 2004. "Judicial Review in Developed Democracies." In Gloppen, Gargarella, and Sklaar 2004, 7-26.

Sharma, C. 2007. "Human Rights and Environmental Wrongs: Integrating the Right to Environment and Developmental Justice in the Indian Constitution." In *Human Rights, Justice, and Constitutional Empowerment,* edited by C.R. Kumar and K. Chockalingam, 310-34. New Delhi: Oxford University Press.

Sharma, R. 2005. "Judicial Environmental Activism: Lessons from India." *International Environmental Law Newsletter* (American Bar Association Section of Energy, Environment and Natural Resources) 7, 2: 8-13.

–. 2008. "Green Courts in India: Strengthening Environmental Governance." *Law, Environment and Development Journal* 4, 1: 50-71.

Sharom, A. 2002. "Malaysian Environmental Law: Ten Years after Rio." *Singapore Journal of International and Comparative Law* 6: 855-90.

Shaw, M.N. 2003. *International Law.* 5th ed. Cambridge: Cambridge University Press.

Shelton, D. 1991. "Human Rights, Environmental Rights and the Right to Environment." *Stanford Journal of International Law* 28: 103-38.

–. 1993. "What Happened in Rio to Environmental Rights?" *Yearbook of International Environmental Law 1992* 3: 75-93.

–. 2001. "Environmental Rights." In *Peoples' Rights,* edited by P. Alston, 185-258. Oxford: Oxford University Press.

–. 2004a. "Human Rights and the Environment." *Yearbook of International Environmental Law 2002* 13: 199-206.

–. 2004b. "The Links between International Human Rights Guarantees and Environmental Protection." Unpublished paper, University of Chicago. On file with author.

–. 2006. "Human Rights and the Environment: What Specific Rights Have Been Recognized?" *Denver Journal of International Law and Policy* 35, 1: 129-71.

–. 2008. *Regional Protection of Human Rights.* New York: Oxford University Press.

–. 2009. *Human Rights and the Environment: Past, Present, and Future Linkages and the Value of a Declaration.* Paper prepared for UNEP High Level Meeting on the New Future of Human Rights and the Environment, Nairobi, 30 November to 1 December.

Shemshuchenko, Y. 1995. "Human Rights in the Field of Environmental Protection in the Draft of the New Constitution of the Ukraine." In *Environmental Rights: Law, Litigation and Access to Justice,* edited by S. Deimann and B. Dyssli, 33-40. London: Cameron May.

Shue, H. 1996. *Basic Rights: Subsistence, Affluence, and US Foreign Policy.* 2nd ed. Princeton, NJ: Princeton University Press.

Sieder, R., L. Schjolden, and A. Angell. 2005a. "Introduction." In Sieder, Schjolden, and Angell 2005b, 1-20.

Sieder, R., L. Schjolden, and A. Angell, eds. 2005b. *The Judicialization of Politics in Latin America.* New York: Palgrave Macmillan.

Sikkink, K. 2005. "The Transnational Dimension of the Judicialization of Politics in Latin America." In Sieder, Schjolden, and Angell 2005b, 263-92.

Simon Fraser University Sustainable Planning Research Group, School of Resource and Environmental Management. 2005. *Canada's Environmental Record.* Vancouver: Simon Fraser University.

Simpson, J., M. Jaccard, and N. Rivers. 2007. *Hot Air: Meeting Canada's Climate Change Challenge.* Toronto: McClelland and Stewart.

Singh, N. 1997. "The Right to Environment and Sustainable Development as a Principle of International Law." In *La droit a la qualite de l'environnement: Un droit endevenir, un droit a definir* (Proceedings of the Fifth International Conference on Constitutional Law), edited by N. Duple, 199-223. Montreal: Amérique.

Sioutis, G. 2006. "Protection de l'environnement et protection de la propriete dans la jurisprudence du Conseil d'Etat hellenique." *Annuaire international des droits de l'homme* 1: 495-529.

Sioutis, G.P., and G. Gerapetritis. 2002. "Greece." In Ebbesson 2002, 261-78.

Slaughter, A.-M. 1994. "A Typology of Transjudicial Communication." *University of Richmond Law Review* 29, 1: 99-137.

–. 2000. "Judicial Globalization." *Virginia Journal of International Law* 40, 4: 1103-24.

–. 2003. "A Global Community of Courts." *Harvard International Law Journal* 44, 1: 191-219.

Slovenia. 2008. *National Implementation Report, Aarhus Convention.* ECE/MP.PP/IR/2008/ SVN. 4 June 2008.

Smith, R.K.M. 2003. *Textbook on International Human Rights.* Oxford: Oxford University Press.

Smorenburg-van Middelkoop, L. 2004. "European Environmental Principles in Dutch Case Law." In Macrory 2004, 131-58.

Smulovitz, C. 2005. "Petitioning and Creating Rights: Judicialization in Argentina." In Sieder, Schjolden, and Angell 2005b, 161-86.

Snajdr, E. 2008. *Nature Protests: The End of Ecology in Slovakia.* Seattle: University of Washington Press.

Sobrevivencia and Amigas de la Tierra Paraguay. 2006. "Right to a Healthy Environment: Environmental Crisis Aggravated by Carelessness, Negligence and Breach of Environmental Laws." In *Human Rights – 2006 – Paraguay.* Asunción: Sobrevivencia.

Sohn, L.B. 1973. "The Stockholm Declaration on the Human Environment." *Harvard International Law Journal* 14, 3: 423-515.

Soveroski, M. 2007. "Environment Rights versus Environmental Wrongs: Forum over Substance?" *Review of European Community and International Environmental Law* 16, 3: 261-73.

Spindler, Z.A., and X. De Vanssay. 2002. "Constitutions and Economic Freedom: An International Comparison." *South African Journal of Economics* 70, 6: 1135-46.

Staddon, C., and B. Cellarius. 2002. "Paradoxes of Conservation and Development in Post-Socialist Bulgaria: Recent Controversies." *European Environment* 12: 105-16.

Stec, S. 1998. "Ecological Rights Advancing the Rule of Law in Eastern Europe." *Environmental Law and Litigation* 13: 275-358.

–, ed. 2003a. *Handbook on Access to Justice under the Aarhus Convention.* Szentendre, Hungary: Regional Environmental Center for Central and Eastern Europe.

–. 2003b. "Russia Case 3: The Shrinking Park." In Stec 2003a, 181-83.

–. 2005. "Aarhus Environmental Rights in Eastern Europe." In *The Yearbook of European Environmental Law,* vol. 5, edited by T.F.M. Etty and H. Somsen, 1-22. Oxford: Oxford University Press.

–. 2009. "Environmental Justice through Courts in Countries in Economic Transition." In *Environmental Law and Justice in Context,* edited by J. Ebbesson and P. Okowa, 158-75. Cambridge: Cambridge University Press.

Stec, S., A. Antypas, and T. Steger. 2006. "Transition and Governance: The Case of Post-Communist States." In *Multilevel Governance of Global Environment,* edited by G. Winter, 358-84. Cambridge: Cambridge University Press.

Steiner, H.J., P. Alston, and R. Goodman. 2008. *International Human Rights in Context: Law, Politics, Morals.* 3rd ed. Oxford: Oxford University Press.

Stephens, T. 2009. *International Courts and Environmental Protection.* Cambridge: Cambridge University Press.

Stevenson, C.P. 1983. "A New Perspective on Environmental Rights after the Charter." *Osgoode Hall Law Journal* 21, 3: 390-421.

Stoehglener, G., and M. Narodoslawsky. 2008. "Implementing Ecological Footprinting in Decision-Making Processes." *Land Use Policy* 25, 3: 421-31.

Stone, C.D. 1972. "Should Trees Have Standing? Toward Legal Rights for Natural Objects." *Southern California Law Review* 45, 2: 450-501.

Stotzky, I.P. 2004. "Lessons Learned and the Way Forward." In Gloppen, Gargarella, and Sklaar 2004, 198-202.

Strauss, D.A. 1996. "Common Law Constitutional Interpretation." *University of Chicago Law Review* 63, 3: 877-935.

Subedi, S. 1999. "Are the Principles of Human Rights 'Western' Ideas? An Analysis of the Claim of the 'Asian' Concept of Human Rights from the Perspective of Hinduism." *California Western International Law Journal* 30: 45-70.

–. 2007. "Access to Environmental Justice in a Politically Unstable Environment." In Harding 2007a, 157-76.

Sunstein, C. 1990. *After the Rights Revolution: Reconceiving the Regulatory State.* Cambridge, MA: Harvard University Press.

–. 1993. "Against Positive Rights." *East European Constitutional Review* 2: 35-38.

–. 1994. "On Property and Constitutionalism." In *Constitutionalism, Identity, Difference, and Legitimacy: Theoretical Perspectives,* edited by M. Rosenfeld, 383-412. Durham, NC: Duke University Press.

–. 1999. "Standing for Animals." Public Law and Legal Theory Working Paper No. 06. Chicago: University of Chicago Law School.

–. 2001. *Designing Democracy: What Institutions Do.* Oxford: Oxford University Press.

Swaigen, J., and R.E. Woods. 1981. "A Substantive Right to Environmental Quality." In *Environmental Rights in Canada,* edited by J. Swaigen, 195-241. Toronto: Butterworth.

Szekely, A. 1997. "Compliance with Environmental Treaties: The Empirical Evidence – A Commentary on the Softening of International Environmental Law." *Proceedings of the American Society of International Law* 91: 234-41.

Szuniewicz-Wenzel, M. 2008. "Regional Report: Baltic States." *Yearbook of International Environmental Law 2007* 18: 420-29.

Taillant, J.D. 2003. "Environmental Advocacy and the Inter-American Human Rights System." In *Linking Human Rights and the Environment,* edited by R. Picolotti and J.D. Taillant, 118-61. Tucson: University of Arizona Press.

Takahashi, K. 2002. "Why Do We Study Constitutional Laws of Foreign Countries, and How?" In *Defining the Field of Comparative Constitutional Law,* edited by V.C. Jackson and M. Tushnet, 35-59. Westport, CT: Praeger Publishers.

Tamanaha, B.Z. 2004. *On the Rule of Law: History, Politics, Theory.* Cambridge: Cambridge University Press.

Tan, A.K.-J. 2004. "Environmental Laws and Institutions in Southeast Asia: A Review of Recent Developments." *Singapore Yearbook of International Law* 8: 177-92.

Tarr, G.A., R.F. Williams, and J. Marko, eds. 2004. *Federalism, Subnational Constitutions, and Minority Rights.* Westport, CT: Greenwood.

Tate, C.N. 1995. "Why the Expansion of Judicial Power?" In Tate and Vallinder 1995a, 27-42.

Tate, C.N., and T. Vallinder, eds. 1995a. *The Global Expansion of Judicial Power.* New York: New York University Press.

—. 1995b. "Judicialization and the Future of Politics and Policy." In Tate and Vallinder 1995a, 515-27.

Taylor, P. 1998a. *An Ecological Approach to International Law: Responding to Challenges of Climate Change.* London: Routledge.

—. 1998b. "From Environmental to Ecological Human Rights: A New Dynamic in International Law?" *Georgetown International Environmental Law Review* 10, 2: 309-97.

The Energy and Resources Institute. 2006. *Looking Back to Change Track: GREEN India 2047.* Delhi: TERI.

Thomas, C., A. Cameron, R. Green, M. Bakkenes, L.J. Beaumont, Y.C. Collingham, B.F.N. Erasmus, et al. 2004. "Extinction Risk from Climate Change." *Nature* 427: 145-48.

Thompson, B.H., Jr. 2006. "The Environment and Natural Resources." In *State Constitutions for the Twenty-First Century: The Agenda of State Constitutional Reform,* edited by G.A. Tarr and R.F. Williams, 307-39. Albany, NY: State University of New York Press.

Thorme, M. 1991. "Establishing Environment as a Human Right." *Denver Journal of International Law and Policy* 19, 2: 301-42.

Tickle, A., and I. Welsh. 1998. "Environmental Politics, Civil Society, and Post-Communism." In *Environment and Society in Eastern Europe,* edited by A. Tickle and I. Welsh, 156-85. Essex: Longman.

Tilleman, W.A. 1995. "Public Participation in the Environmental Impact Assessment Process: A Comparative Study of Impact Assessment in Canada, the United States, and the European Community." *Columbia Journal of Transnational Law* 33, 2: 337-439.

Toebes, B.C.A. 1999. *The Right to Health as a Human Right in International Law.* Oxford: Intersentia.

Tookey, D.L. 1999. "Southeast Asian Environmentalism at Its Crossroads: Learning Lessons from Thailand's Eclectic Approach to Environmental Law and Policy." *Georgetown International Environmental Law Review* 11, 2: 307-62.

Torras, M., and J.K. Boyce. 1998. "Income, Inequality, and Pollution: A Reassessment of the Environmental Kuznets Curve." *Ecological Economics* 25: 147-60.

Tribe, L.H. 1974. "Ways Not to Think about Plastic Trees: New Foundations for Environmental Law." *Yale Law Journal* 83: 1315-48.

Trilsch, M. 2009. "European Committee of Social Rights: The Right to a Healthy Environment." *International Journal of Constitutional Law* 7, 3: 529-38.

Tucker, J.C. 2000. "Constitutional Codification of an Environmental Ethic." *Florida Law Review* 52: 299-326.

Turner, S.J. 2009. *A Substantive Environmental Right: An Examination of the Legal Obligations of Decision-Makers towards the Environment.* New York: Kluwer Law.

Tushnet, M. 2002. "State Action, Social Welfare Rights, and the Judicial Role: Some Comparative Observations." *Chicago Journal of International Law* 3, 2: 435-53.

Twinomugisha, B.K. 2007. "Some Reflections on Judicial Protection of the Right to a Clean and Healthy Environment in Uganda." *Law, Environment, and Development Journal* 3, 3: 244-58.

UN Committee on Economic, Social and Cultural Rights. 1990. *General Comment No. 3: The Nature of States Parties Obligations.* UN Doc. E/1991/23. 14 December 1990.

–. 1998. *General Comment No. 9: The Domestic Application of the Covenant.* UN Doc. E/C.12/1998/24. 3 December 1998.

–. 2000. *General Comment No. 14: Substantive Issues Arising in the Implementation of the International Covenant on Economic, Social and Cultural Rights: The Right to the Highest Attainable Standard of Health.* UN Doc. E/C.12/2000/4. 11 August 2000.

UN Development Programme. 2008. *Human Development Report 2007/08, Fighting Climate Change: Human Solidarity in a Divided World.* New York: UNDP.

UN Economic Commission for Europe, Committee on Environmental Policy. 2003. *Environmental Performance Reviews: Georgia.* Environmental Performance Reviews Series No. 18. New York: United Nations.

–. 2004. *Environmental Performance Reviews: Azerbaijan.* Environmental Performance Reviews Series No. 19. New York: United Nations.

–. 2005. *Environmental Performance Reviews: Moldova, Second Review.* Environmental Performance Reviews Series No. 23. New York: United Nations.

–. 2006. *Environmental Performance Reviews: Belarus, Second Review.* Environmental Performance Reviews Series No. 22. New York: United Nations.

–. 2007a. *Environmental Performance Reviews: Montenegro, Second Review.* Environmental Performance Reviews Series No. 25. New York: United Nations.

–. 2007b. *Environmental Performance Reviews: Serbia, Second Review.* Environmental Performance Reviews Series No. 26. New York: United Nations.

–. 2007c. *Environmental Performance Reviews: Ukraine, Second Review.* Environmental Performance Reviews Series No. 24. New York: United Nations.

UN Economic Commission for Latin America and the Caribbean. 2002. *The Sustainability of Development in Latin America and the Caribbean: Challenges and Opportunities.* Santiago, Chile: United Nations.

UN Educational, Scientific and Cultural Organization and the UN High Commissioner for Human Rights. 1999. *Bizkaia Declaration on the Right to Environment.* Issued at the International Seminar of Experts on the Right to the Environment. UN Doc. 30C/INF.11. 24 September 1999.

UN Environment Programme. 2010. *The Economics of Ecosystems and Biodiversity: Mainstreaming the Economics of Nature: Synthesis Report.* Nairobi: UNEP.

UN Food and Agriculture Organization. 2006. "Justiciability of the Right to Food." In *The Right to Food Guidelines: Information Papers and Case Studies,* 71-95. Rome: FAO.

–. n.d. Right to Food Project website. http://www.fao.org/righttofood/portal_en.htm.

UN High Commissioner for Human Rights. 2002. *Handbook on National Human Rights Plans of Action.* New York: United Nations.

UN High Commissioner for Human Rights and UN Environment Programme. 2002. *Meeting of Experts on Human Rights and the Environment, Final Text* (16 January 2002). http://www2.ohchr.org/english/issues/environment/environ/conclusions.htm.

UN Population Fund. 2002. *People, Poverty, and Possibilities: Making Development Work for the Poor.* New York: UNPF.

US Centers for Disease Control. 2005. *National Report on Human Exposure to Environmental Chemicals.* Atlanta, GA: CDC.

US Department of State. 2009. *Report on International Religious Freedom – Maldives.* Washington, DC: Department of State.

US National Research Council. 2001. *Abrupt Climate Change: Inevitable Surprises.* Washington, DC: National Academy of Sciences.

Vaarmari, K. 2009. "Selected Issues of Application of the Aarhus Convention in Estonia." In Justice and Environment 2009, 26-32.

Vallinder, T. 1995. "Where the Courts Go Marching in." In Tate and Vallinder 1995a, 13-26.

van den Bergh, J.C.J.M., and H. Verbruggen. 1999. Spatial Sustainability, Trade and Indicators: An Evaluation of the 'Ecological Footprint.'" *Ecological Economics* 29: 61-72.

van Kooten, G.C., and E.H. Bulte. 2000. "The Ecological Footprint: Useful Science or Politics?" *Ecological Economics* 32: 385-89.

van Rijswick, M., and J. Robbe. 2007. "Does a Constitutional Right to Environmental Protection and Improvement Guarantee Environmental Protection and Improvement?" In Larmusea 2007, 30-37.

van Tatenhove, J.P.M., and H.J.M. Goverde. 2002. "Strategies in Environmental Policy: A Historical Institutional Perspective." In *Greening Society: The Paradigm Shift in Dutch Environmental Politics,* edited by P.P.J. Driessen and P. Glasbergen, 47-65. Dordrecht, Netherlands: Kluwer Academic.

Vasconcelos, L., and I. Baptista. 2002. "The Role of Environmental Activism in Society." In *Environmental Activism in Society,* edited by L. Vasconcelos and I. Baptista, 110-25. Lisbon: LUSO-American Development Foundation.

Veinla, H., and K. Relve. 2005. "The Aarhus Convention in Estonia." *European Environmental Law Review* (December): 326-31.

Velasco, P.B., Jr. 2009. *Manila Bay: A Daunting Challenge in Environmental Rehabilitation and Restoration.* Paper presented at Forum on Environmental Justice: Upholding the Right to a Balanced and Healthful Ecology, Supreme Court of the Philippines, 16-17 April 2009.

Venetoulis, J., and J. Talberth. 2008. "Refining the Ecological Footprint." *Environment, Development and Sustainability* 10: 441-69.

Verschuuren, J.M. 1993. "The Constitutional Right to Protection of the Environment in the Netherlands." *Austrian Journal for Public and International Law* 46, 1: 67-77.

–. 2005. "The Netherlands." In de Sadeleer, Roller, and Dross 2005, 97-117.

–. 2009. "The Netherlands." In Kotze and Paterson 2009a, 55-84.

Viana Ferreira, E.A. 2003. "State, Environment and Pertinent Process: Of the Duties Assumed and of the Rights to Securing Effective Compliance." In Di Paola 2003, 149-59.

Vieira, S.C. 2008. "Country Report: Brazil." *Yearbook of International Environmental Law 2007* 18: 395-402.

Viljoen, F., and L. Louw. 2007. "State Compliance with the Recommendations of the African Commission on Human and Peoples' Rights, 1994-2004." *American Journal of International Law* 101, 1: 1-34.

Vinogradov, S.V. 2004. "Russian Federation: Country/Region Reports." *Yearbook of International Environmental Law 2002* 13: 585-95.

Vogel, D. 1993. "Representing Diffuse Interests in Environmental Policy-Making." In *Do Institutions Matter? Government Capabilities in the United States and Abroad,* edited by R.K. Weaver and B.A. Rockman, 237-71. Washington, DC: Brookings Institution.

Wackernagel, M. 2009. "Methodological Advancements in Footprint Analysis." *Ecological Economics* 68, 7: 1925-27.

Wackernagel, M., and W.E. Rees. 1996. *Our Ecological Footprint: Reducing Human Impact on the Earth.* Gabriola Island, BC: New Society Publishers.

Wackernagel, M., N.B.Schulz, D. Deumling, A.C. Linares, M. Jenkins, V. Kapos, C. Monfreda, et al. 2002. "Tracking the Ecological Overshoot of the Human Economy." *Proceedings of the National Academy of Sciences USA* 99, 14: 9266-71.

Walcacer, F.C. 2002. "Brazil and Environmental Law." *Florida Journal of International Law* 15: 54-58.

Waldron, J. 1993. "A Rights-Based Critique of Constitutional Rights." *Oxford Journal of Legal Studies* 13: 18-51.

–. 1999. *Law and Disagreement.* Oxford: Oxford University Press.

–. 2006. "The Core of the Case against Judicial Review." *Yale Law Journal* 115: 1346-1406.

Walker, S. 1998. *The Rights Revolution: Rights and Community in Modern America.* New York: Oxford University Press.

Walsh, J.R. 2007. "Argentina's Constitution and General Environmental Law as the Framework for Comprehensive Land Use Regulation." In Chalifour, Kameri-Mbote, Lye, and Nolon 2007, 503-25.

Watson, A. 1993. *Legal Transplants: An Approach to Comparative Law.* 2nd ed. Athens, GA: University of Georgia Press.

Weaver, R.K., and B.A. Rockman. 1993. "Institutional Reform and Constitutional Design." In *Do Institutions Matter? Government Capabilities in the United States and Abroad,* edited by R.K. Weaver and B.A. Rockman, 462-81. Washington, DC: Brookings Institution.

Weil, P. 1983. "Towards Relative Normativity in International Law." *American Journal of International Law* 77, 3: 413-42.

Weinthal, E., and P. Jones Luong. 2002. "Environmental NGOs in Kazakhstan: Democratic Goals and Non-democratic Outcomes." In Mendelson and Glenn 2002, 152-76.

Weiss, E.B. 1989. *In Fairness to Future Generations: International Law, Common Patrimony, and Intergenerational Equity.* Tokyo: UN University Press.

–, ed. 1992. *Environmental Change and International Law: New Challenges and Dimensions.* Tokyo: UN University Press.

Weissbrodt, D., and C. de la Vega. 2007. *International Human Rights Law: An Introduction.* Philadelphia: University of Pennsylvania Press.

West, J.M., and D.K. Yoon. 1992. "The Constitutional Court of the Republic of Korea: Transforming the Jurisprudence of the Vortex." *American Journal of Comparative Law* 40, 1: 73-119.

Wiener, J.B. 2001. "Something Borrowed for Something Blue: Legal Transplants and the Evolution of Global Environmental Law." *Ecology Law Quarterly* 27, 4: 1295-371.

Wigle, D.T. 2003. *Child Health and the Environment.* Oxford: Oxford University Press.

Wiles, E. 2006. "Aspirational Principles or Enforceable Rights: The Future for Socio-Economic Rights in National Law." *American University International Law Review* 22, 1: 35-64.

Wilfling, P. 2009. "Slovakia: Convention against Public Participation?" *Participate* 24: 1-2.

Wilson, B.M. 2005. "Changing Dynamics: The Political Impact of Costa Rica's Constitutional Court." In Sieder, Schjolden, and Angell 2005b, 47-66.

–. 2007. "Individual Rights through a Constitutional Court: The Example of Gays in Costa Rica." *International Journal of Constitutional Law* 5, 2: 242-57.

–. 2009. "Rights Revolutions in Unlikely Places: The Cases of Colombia and Costa Rica." *Journal of Politics in Latin America* 1, 2: 59-85.

Wilson, B.M., and J.C. Rodriguez Cordero. 2006. "Legal Opportunity Structures and Social Movements: The Effects of Constitutional Change on Costa Rican Politics." *Comparative Political Studies* 39, 3: 325-51.

Wilson, E.O. 1992. *The Diversity of Life.* Cambridge, MA: Harvard University Press.

Wilson, J., P. Tyedmers, and R. Pelot. 2007. "Contrasting and Comparing Sustainable Development Indicator Metrics." *Ecological Indicators* 7, 2: 299-314.

Wirth, D.A. 1994-95. "The Rio Declaration on Environment and Development: Two Steps Forward and One Back, or Vice Versa." *Georgia Law Review* 29, 3: 599-652.

Wolfe, K. 2003. "Greening the International Human Rights Sphere? Environmental Rights and the Draft Declaration of Principles on Human Rights and the Environment." *Appeal: Review of Current Law and Law Reform* 9: 45-58.

Wolfrum, R. and R. Grote. 2005. "The French Republic: Introductory Notes." In Wolfrum and Grote 2011.

–. 2008. "The Republic of Mongolia: Introductory Note." In Wolfrum and Grote 2011.

–, eds. 2011. *Constitutions of the Countries of the World.* G.H. Flanz, ed. emeritus. New York: Oceana Law.

Wood, M.C. 2009a. "Advancing the Sovereign Trust of Government to Safeguard the Environment for Present and Future Generations (Part I): Ecological Realism and the Need for a Paradigm Shift." *Environmental Law* 39: 43-89.

–. 2009b. "Advancing the Sovereign Trust of Government to Safeguard the Environment for Present and Future Generations (Part II): Instilling a Fiduciary Obligation in Governance." *Environmental Law* 39: 91-139.

World Bank. 2005. *For a Breath of Fresh Air: Ten Years of Progress and Challenges in Urban Air Quality Management in India 1993-2002.* New Delhi: Environment and Social Development Unit, South Asia Region, World Bank.

–. 2009. *Project Appraisal Document on a Proposed Adaptable Loan Program in the Amount of US$840 Million to the Argentine Republic for the Matanza-Riachuelo Basin Sustainable Development Project, Phase 1.* Report No. 48443-AR. Washington, DC: World Bank.

World Commission on Environment and Development (Brundtland Commission). 1987. *Our Common Future.* Oxford: Oxford University Press.

World Health Organization. 1989. *European Charter on Environment and Health.* Excerpts in Dejeant-Pons and Pallemaerts 2002, 271-72.

World Wildlife Fund, Zoological Society of London, and Global Footprint Network. 2010. *Living Planet Report 2010.* London: WWF.

Worm, B., E.B. Barbier, N. Beaumont, J.E. Duffy, C. Folke, B.S. Halpern, J.B.C. Jackson, et al. 2006. "Impact of Biodiversity Loss on Ocean Ecosystem Services." *Science* 314: 787-90.

Yamin, A.E., and O. Parra-Vera. 2009."How Do Courts Set Health Policy? The Case of the Colombian Constitutional Court." *PLoS Med* 6(2) e1000032.

Yang, T., and R.V. Percival. 2009. "The Emergence of Global Environmental Law." *Ecology Law Quarterly* 36: 615-64.

Yepes, R.U. 2006. "The Enforcement of Social Rights by the Colombian Constitutional Court." In Gargarella, Domingo, and Roux 2006, 127-51.

York, R., E.A. Rosa, and T. Dietz. 2003. "Footprints on the Earth: The Environmental Consequences of Modernity." *American Sociological Review* 68, 2: 279-300.

Young, O.R. 1999. "Regime Effectiveness: Taking Stock." In *The Effectiveness of International Environmental Regimes,* edited by O.R. Young, 249-79. Cambridge MA: MIT Press.

Zaharchenko, T.R., and G. Goldenman. 2004. "Accountability in Governance: The Challenge of Implementing the Aarhus Convention in Eastern Europe and Central Asia." *International Environmental Agreements: Politics, Law, and Economics* 4, 3: 229-51.

Zakane, V. 2008. "Problematique de l'efectivite du droit de l'environnement en Afrique: L'exemple du Burkina Faso." In *Aspects contemporains du droit de l'environnement en Afrique de l'ouest et centrale,* edited by L. Granier, 13-34. Gland, Switzerland: IUCN.

Zalasiewicz, J., M. Williams, A. Smith, T.L. Barry, A.L. Coe, P.R. Brown, P. Benchley, et al. 2008. "Are We Now Living in the Anthropocene?" *GSA Today* (Geological Society of America) 18, 2: 4-8.

Zillman, D.N., A.R. Lucas, and G. Pring, eds. 2002. *Human Rights in Natural Resource Development: Public Participation in the Sustainable Development of Mining and Energy Resources.* Oxford: Oxford University Press.

Zimbabwe Lawyers for Human Rights and National Constitutional Assembly. 2009. *Economic, Social, and Cultural Rights in Zimbabwe: Options for Constitutional Reform.* Cambridge, MA: Harvard Law School International Human Rights Clinic.

Zito, A., M. d'Orsogna, and C.F. Giordano. 2002. "Italy." In Ebbesson 2002, 313-45.

LEGISLATION

A comprehensive database of environmental laws for all UN nations is available on the FAOLEX website. http://faolex.fao.org/.

WESTERN EUROPE

Andorra
Decree on access to environmental information relating to waste management (2008).

Belgium
Law on the public access to environmental information (5 August 2006).

Finland
Environmental Protection Act, Law No. 86/2000.

France
Environmental Code (2000).

Greece
Law No. 1650/86 on the protection for the environment, as amended by *Law No. 3010/2002.*
Law No. 3422/2005 of 12 December 2005, ratifying *Aarhus Convention.*

The Netherlands
Environmental Management Act (2004 version, published in 2002 and amended).

Norway
Environment Information Act No. 31 of 2003 relative to the right to information regarding the environment and the right to participate in decision-making processes affecting the environment.
Pollution Control Act of 13 March 1981, No.6, most recently amended by Act of 20 June 2003, No. 45.

Portugal
Environmental NGOs Law, Law No. 35/98.
Framework Law on the Environment, Law No. 11/87.
Popular Action Law, Law No. 83/95.

Spain
Environmental Responsibility Law, Law No. 26/2007.
Law 27/2006 on Access to Information, Public Participation and Access to Justice in Environmental Matters.
Law on Natural Heritage and Biodiversity, Law No. 42/2007.

EASTERN EUROPE

Albania
Law No. 8934 on Environmental Protection (9 May 2002).

Armenia
Law No. ZR-21 of 1995 on Expertise of Environmental Impact.
Law on Ecological Education of the Population (20 November 2001).
Law on Provision of Sanitary-Epidemiological Security of the Population (29 December 1998).

Belarus
Law on Protection of the Environment, No. 1982-XII of November 26, 1992.
Law on Public Associations (amended in 1999).

Bulgaria
Law of Preservation of Environment, SG 91/25 (September 2002).

Croatia
Environmental Protection Act, Class: 011-01/07-01/122, Reg. No. 71-05-03/1-07-2, 10 October 2007.

Czech Republic
Act on Environment, No. 17/1992.

Georgia
Law of 1996 on Environmental Protection.

Hungary
Environmental Protection Act (1995).

Latvia
Environmental Protection Law (2006).

Macedonia
Act on Environment and Nature Protection and Promotion (1996).
Law on Ambient Air Quality (2004).

Moldova
Law on environmental protection (1993).

Montenegro
Law on Administrative Fees (Official Gazette of Montenegro, No. 55/03, 81/05, 2/06).
Law on Environment (2008) (Official Gazette of Montenegro, No. 48/08).
Law on Non-Governmental Organizations (Official Gazette, Republic of Montenegro, No. 27/1999).

Poland
Act on making information on environment and its protection available (2008).
Environmental Protection Law (2001).

Romania
Government Emergency Ordinance No. 243/2000 on atmospheric protection (approved by Law No. 655/2001).
Law on the Protection of the Environment, Law No. 137/1995.

Russia
Federal Law No. 7-FZ on environmental protection (2002).

Serbia
Environmental Protection Law (2004).

Slovakia
Act 454/2007 amending the Nature and Landscape Conservation Act (No. 543/2002).
Environmental Protection Act (No.17/1992).

Slovenia
Environmental Protection Act 2004, No. 41/04.

Ukraine
Law No. 1264-XII on environmental protection (25 June 1995).

ASIA

Azerbaijan
Law on Access to Environmental Information (2002).
Law on Environmental Protection (8 June 1999).
Law on Environmental Safety (1999).
Law on Protection of Air (2001, No. 109).
Law on Sanitary-Epidemiological Services (1992).

India
National Green Tribunal Act of 2010 (No. 19 of 2010, 2 June 2010).

Indonesia
Environmental Management Act (No. 23 of 1997).

Iran
Environmental Protection Law (1974).

Iraq
Law No. 3 of 1997 on protection and improving the environment.

Kazakhstan
Environmental Code, Law No. 212-Z (9 January 2007).

Kyrgyzstan
Law No. 53 on environmental protection (1999).

Maldives
Environmental Protection and Preservation Act of Maldives, Law No. 4/93.

Mongolia
Environmental Protection Law of Mongolia (1995).

Nepal
Environmental Protection Act 1997 (No. 24 of 1997).
Environmental Protection Regulations 1997.

Philippines
Clean Air Act of 1999, R.A. No. 8749 (23 June 1999).
Clean Water Act, R.A. No. 9275 (22 March 2004).
Climate Change Act of 2009, R.A. No. 9729 (27 July 2009).
Ecological Solid Waste Management Act, R.A. No. 9003 (26 January 2001).
Executive Order No. 446, *Mandating the Phase-Out of Leaded Gasoline as One of the Means of Solving Air Pollution* (26 September 1997).
Local Government Code (1991), R.A. No. 7160.
National Environmental Awareness and Education Act of 2008, R.A. No. 9512 (12 December 2008).
Rules of Procedure for Environmental Cases (2010). *Resolution A.M. No. 09-6-8-SC,* Supreme Court of the Philippines.

South Korea
  Air Quality Conservation Act (1990).
  Environmental Education Promotion Act (2008).
  Framework Act on Environmental Policy (1990, as amended).
  Toxic Chemicals Control Act (1991).
  Water Quality and Ecosystem Conservation Act (1990).

Sri Lanka
  National Environmental (Air, Fuel and Vehicle Importation Standards) Regulations No. 01
    of 2003. Gazette Extraordinary No. 1295/11, dated 30 June 2003 with an oper-
    ational date of 1 July 2003.

Thailand
  National Health Act, B.E. 2550 (2007).

Turkey
  Law No. 5491 Amending the Environmental Law No. 2872 (2006).

Turkmenistan
  Law No. 600-XII on Environmental Protection (12 November 1991).

AFRICA

Angola
  General Environmental Law, Law No. 5 (1998).

Benin
  Decree 2001-094 Establishing Drinking Water Quality Standards for Benin (20 February
    2001).
  Decree 2001-110 Establishing Air Quality Standards for Benin (4 April 2001).
  Decree 2001-235 Establishing Environmental Impact Study Regulations for Benin (12 July
    2001).
  Decree 2005-437 Organizing Environmental Inspections for Benin (22 July 2005).
  Framework Law on the Environment, Law No. 98-030 (1999).

Burkina Faso
  Environmental Code for Burkina Faso (1997), Law No. 005/97/ADP. See also Act No.
    002/2001/AN Act *Guidance Law on Water Management*.

Burundi
  Code on the Environment, Law No. 1/010 (30 June 2000).

Cameroon
  Law No. 96-12 Concerning Law on Environmental Management (5 August 1996).

Cape Verde
  Act No. 86/IV/93 of 26 June 1993 Defining Environmental Policy.

Chad
  Law No. 014/PR/98 Act Defining the General Principles of Environmental Protection.

Comoros
Framework law relating to the environment, Law No. 94-018 (22 June 1994).

Congo-Brazzaville
Law on the Protection of the Environment, Law No. 003/91.

Congo, Democratic Republic of the
Ordinance No. 75-231 Determining the Functions of the Department of Environment, Nature Conservation and Tourism and Supplementing Ordinance No. 69-147 of 1 August 1969.

Cote d'Ivoire
Framework Law No. 96-766 on the Environmental Code (1996).

Egypt
Law No. 4 of 1994 on Environment.

Ethiopia
Environmental Impact Assessment Proclamation (No. 299 of 2002).
Environmental Protection Organs Establishment Proclamation (No. 295 of 2002).

Gabon
Loi n° 16/93 relative à la protection de l'environnement.

Guinea
Ordonnance n° 045\\PRG\\87 portant Code sur la protection et la mise en valeur de l'environnement (1987).

Kenya
Environmental Management and Co-ordination Act, 1999 (No. 8 of 1999).

Malawi
Environment Management Act (No. 23 of 1996).

Mali
Law No. 01-020 Relating to Pollution and Nuisance.

Mauritania
Law No. 2000-045 Concerning the Framework Environmental Law (26 July 2000).

Mozambique
Environment Act, Law No. 20/97 (1997).

Niger
Framework Law on Environmental Management, Law 98-56 (1998).

Rwanda
Organic Law No. 04/2005 Laying Down Rules to Protect, Preserve and Promote the Environment in Rwanda.

São Tomé and Príncipe

Basic Law of the Environment, Law No. 10/1999.

Senegal

Code on the Environment, Law No. 2001-01.

Seychelles

Environmental Protection Act, Act 9 of 1994, Chapter 71.

South Africa

Local Government Municipal Structures Act, Act No. 117 of 1998.
Local Government Municipal Systems Act, Act No. 32 of 2000.
National Environmental Management: Air Quality Act, 2004, Act No. 39 of 2004.
National Environmental Management Act, 1998, Act No. 107 of 1998.
National Environmental Management of Biodiversity Act, 2004, No. 10 of 2004.
National Water Act, Act No. 36 of 1998.
Promotion of Access to Information Act 2000.
Promotion of Administrative Justice Act 2000.

Sudan

Environmental Protection Act of 2001.

Tanzania

Environmental Management Act, Cap. 191 of Laws of Tanzania, rev. ed. 2002.

Togo

Framework Law on the Environment, Law 2008-005.

Uganda

National Environment Act, 1995 (Statute No. 4 of 1995), Ch. 153.
National Environmental (Control of Smoking in Public Places) Regulations, Statutory Instrument No.12/04.

LATIN AMERICA

Argentina

Environmental Impact Assessment Law, Rio Negro Law No. 3266 (16 December 1998).
General Law on the Environment, Law No. 25.675 (B.O. 28 November 2002).
Law on the Matanza-Riachuelo Watershed, Law No. 26.168 (B.O. 15 November 2006).
Minimum Standard Law Regarding Industrial Waste, Law No. 25.612 (B.O. 29 July 2002).
Minimum Standard Law Regarding Management and Elimination of PCBs, Law No. 25.670 (B.O. 19 November 2002).
System of Free Public Access to Environmental Information, Law No. 25.831 (B.O. 26 November 2003).
Water Law, Law No. 25.688 (B.O. 3 January 2003).

Bolivia
  Law on the Environment, (1992) Law No. 1333 of April 1992.
  Law of the Rights of Mother Earth, (2010) Law No. 71 of December 2010.

Brazil
  Environmental Crimes Act, Law 9,605/1998.
  National Environmental Education Policy Act, Law 9,795 of 1999.
  National Environmental Policy Law, Law 6,938/1981.
  Public Civil Action Law, Federal Law 7,347 of 24 July 1985.

Chile
  General Environment Framework Law (1994), No. 19.300. Amended by Law No. 20.173
    (2007).

Colombia
  Law No. 99 of 1993.

Costa Rica
  Law on Biodiversity, Law No. 7.788 of 23 April 1998.
  Organic Law on the Environment, Law 7554 of 4 October 1995.

Dominican Republic
  General Law on Environment and Natural Resources (2000), No. 64-00.

Ecuador
  Decree 1040 of 22 April 2008, outlining participation mechanisms of the *Law on
    Environmental Management*.
  Law on Environmental Management (1999), No. 99-37.

El Salvador
  Environmental Law 1988, Decree No. 233.

Honduras
  Environmental Protection Act (55 June 1996).
  General Environmental Law (1993), Decree No. 104/93.

Mexico
  Amparo Law, Congress of the United Mexican States, Official Journal of the Federation,
    10 January 1936.
  General Law on Ecological Equilibrium and Environmental Protection, 1 March 1988.

Nicaragua
  General Law of Environment and Natural Resources (1996), Law No. 217.

Panama
  General Law on Environment (1998), Law No. 41.

Paraguay
  Sanctioning Crimes against the Environment (2 May 1996), Law 716/96.

Peru

Code for Environment and Natural Resources (7 September 1990), Legislative Decree 613.

General Law on the Environment (15 October 2005), Law No. 28611.

Framework Law for the Creation of Private Investment (13 November 1991), Legislative Decree 757.

Uruguay

Law of Environmental Protection (28 November 2000), Law No. 17,283.

Venezuela

Organic Law on the Environment, 2006.

INTERNATIONAL INSTRUMENTS

Aarhus Convention on Access to Information, Public Participation in Decision Making and Access to Justice in Environmental Matters, 1999, 38 ILM 515.

Additional Protocol to the American Convention on Human Rights in the Area of Economic, Social, and Cultural Rights, 17 November 1988, 28 ILM 156.

African (Banjul) Charter on Human and Peoples' Rights, 1982, 21 ILM 58 (adopted 27 June 1981; entered into force 21 October 1986).

American Convention on Human Rights, OAS Treaty Series No. 36 (entered into force 18 July 1978).

American Declaration of the Rights and Duties of Man (1948), reprinted in *Basic Documents Pertaining to Human Rights in the Inter-American System*, OEA/Ser.L.V/II.82/Doc.6, rev.1 (1992).

Arab Charter on Human Rights (22 May 2004) (entered into force 15 March 2008; reprinted in *International Human Rights Report* 12 [2005]: 893).

Asian Human Rights Charter, reproduced in Shelton 2008.

Ban Amendment to the Basel Convention on the Control of Transboundary Movements of Hazardous Wastes and their Disposal (22 September 1995). http://basel.int/ratif/ban-alpha.htm.

Cartagena Protocol on Biosafety to the Convention on Biological Diversity (2000), 39 ILM 1027.

Charter of the Association of Southeast Asian Nations (2007) (entered into force 15 December 2008). http://www.unhcr.org/refworld/.

Convention on the Elimination of All Forms of Discrimination against Women, 1979, 19 ILM 33.

Convention on the Rights of the Child, 1989, 28 ILM 1448 (adopted 20 November 1989; entered into force 2 September 1990).

Hague Declaration on the Environment, 11 March 1989, 28 ILM 1308.

International Covenant on Civil and Political Rights, 16 December 1966, 6 ILM 368 (adopted in 1966; entered into force in 1976).

International Covenant on Economic, Social and Cultural Rights, 16 December 1966, 6 ILM 360 (adopted in 1966; entered into force in 1976).

Kyoto Protocol to the United Nations Framework Convention on Climate Change, 1997, 37 ILM 22.

Optional Protocol to the International Covenant on Economic, Social and Cultural Rights, UNGAOR, 10 December 2008, UN Doc.A/63/435, opened for signature 24 September 2009.

Optional Protocol to the International Covenant on Civil and Political Rights, GA Res. 2200A(XXI), UNGAOR, 1976, Supp. No. 16, UN Doc. A/6316, entered into force 23 March 1976.

Protocol to the African Charter on Human and Peoples' Rights on the Rights of Women in Africa, 2003, OAU Doc. CAB/LEG/66.6, entered into force 25 November 2005.

Rio Declaration on Environment and Development, UN Conference on Environment and Development, 13 June 1992, UN Doc. A/CONF.151/5/Rev.1 (1992), 31 ILM 874.

Rotterdam Convention on the Prior Informed Consent Procedure for Certain Hazardous Chemicals and Pesticides in International Trade (1999), 38 ILM 1.

Stockholm Convention on Persistent Organic Pollutants, 2001, 40 ILM 532.

Stockholm Declaration (Declaration of the United Nations Conference on the Human Environment), 1972, UN Doc. A/Conf.48/14/Rev.1.

UN Charter, 26 June 1945, 59 Stat. 1031.

UN Convention on Transboundary Air Pollution, 1979, 18 ILM 1442.

UN Framework Convention on Climate Change, 1992, 31 ILM 849.

UN General Assembly. 1968. GA Res. 2398, UNGAOR, Supp. No. 18, Doc. A/L553 and Add. 1-4.

–. 1986. *Setting International Standards in the Field of Human Rights,* GA Res. 41/120, UNGAOR, 97th Plenary Meeting, 4 December 1986.

–. 1990. *Need to Ensure a Healthy Environment for the Well-Being of Individuals,* GA Res. 45/94, UNGAOR, 68th Plenary Meeting, UN Doc. A/45/749, 14 December 1990.

–. 2000. GA Res. 55/107, UNGAOR, 55th Sess., UN Doc. A/Res/55/107, 3(k).

UN Human Rights Commission. 1991. *Human Rights and the Environment,* Res. 1991/44, E/CN.4/RES/1991/44.

–. 2001. *Promotion of a Democratic and Equitable International Order.* Res. 2001/65, E/CN.4/RES/2001/65.

–. 2003. *Effects of Structural Adjustment Policies and Foreign Debt on the Full Enjoyment of All Human Rights, Particularly Economic, Social and Cultural Rights,* Res. 2003/21, E/CN.4/2003/L.11/Add. 3.

–. 2005. *Human Rights Resolution 2005/57: Promotion of a Democratic and Equitable International Order,* Res. 2005/57, E/CN.4/2005/L.73.

Universal Declaration of Human Rights, GA Res. 217A(III), UNGAOR, 3d Sess., Supp. No. 13, UN Doc. A/810 (1948).

Universal Declaration of the Rights of Mother Earth (2010). Draft published 22 April 2010 at the World People's Conference on Climate Change and the Rights of Mother Earth, Cochabamba, Bolivia.

Vienna Convention for the Protection of the Ozone Layer, 1985, 26 ILM 1529.

Vienna Declaration on Human Rights and Programme of Action, 25 June 1993, UN Doc. A/CONF.157/24 (Part I).

COURT DECISIONS

Note: Entries preceded by (*) refer to the websites of national courts where decisions can often be accessed.

WESTERN EUROPE

Andorra
* Constitutional Court, http://www.tribunalconstitucional.ad
  Association for the Protection of Animals, Plants and the Environment, Causa 96-6-RE. No. 102-1996. Recurs d'empara. 7 September 1996. Constitutional Court.
  Causa 2003-1-CC, No. 43-2003. 13 March 2003. Constitutional Court.

Belgium
* Constitutional Court, http://www.const-court.be/
* Council of State, www.raadvst-consetat.be
  Commune Woluwe-Saint-Pierre and Others, Council of State No. 126669, 19 December 2003.
  Constitutional Court, no. 135/2006, 14 September 2006, B.10.
  Constitutional Court, no. 137/2006, 14 September 2006, B.7.1.
  Constitutional Court, no. 145/2006, 28 September 2006, B.5.1.
  Cornelis and Others, Council of State No. 149312, 22 September 2005.
  De Becker and Others, Council of State No. 145.837, 13 June 2005.
  Inter-Environnement Wallonie v. Walloon Government, Constitutional Court 11/2005, 19 June 2005; 83/2005, 27 April 2005.
  Jacobs v. Flemish Region (1999), Council of State No. 80.018, 29 April 1999.
  Judgment No. 36/98, 1 April 1998, Court of Arbitration.
  N.V. Hazegras v. Flemish Government, Constitutional Court No. 41/95, 6 June 1995.
  SA Mobistar, Council of State No. 118.214, 10 April 2003.
  Van Doren and Others, Council of State No. 144320, 11 May 2005.
  Venter, Council of State No. 82.130, 20 August 1999.

Finland
* Supreme Court and Supreme Administrative Court, http://www.finlex.fi/fi

France
* Constitutional Council, http://www.conseil-constitutionnel.fr/cde
* Council of State, http://www.conseil-etat.fr/cde
* Court of Cassation, http://www.courdecassation.fr/
  L'Association France Nature Environnement, Conseil d'État, No. 306242.
  Commune d'Annecy, Conseil d'État, No. 297931.
  Conseil d'État, No. 295918, 9 February 2007.
  Decision No. 2008-564 DC – 19 June 2008, *Law on Genetically Modified Organisms,* Constitutional Council.
  Groupement des Agriculteurs Biologistes et Biodynamistes de Maine-et-Loire, Conseil d'État, No. 253696.

Greece
* Council of State, http://www.ste.gr/councilofstate/index_gr.jsp
* Supreme Court of Civil and Penal Law (also known as the Court of Cassation), http://www.areiospagos.gr/en/INDEX.htm
    Council of State decisions 2034/78, 1362/81, 2196/82, 695/1986, 2281/92, 2844/1993, 1784/1993, 6500/1995, 2818/97, 4503/1997, 772/98, 1675/99, 3478/2000, 613/2002, and 1468/2004.
    First Instance Court of Athens, Injunction Order 4531/2004.
    First Instance Court of Piraeus 187/2004, NoV 52, 1251.
    Hellenic Ornithological Society, et al. v. Minister of National Economy and Tourism (1994) 4 International Environmental Law Reports 227 (Council of State 2759/1994, 2760/1994).
    Hellenic Society for Protection of Environment & Cultural Heritage, et al. v. Minister for the Enviroment (1995) 4 International Environmental Law Reports 237 (Council of State 3955/1995).

Italy
* Constitutional Court, http://www.cortecostituzionale.it
    Decision 127/1990, Constitutional Court.
    Decision 210/1987, 22 May 1987, Constitutional Court.

The Netherlands
* Administration of Justice, http://www.rechtspraak.nl/
* Council of State, http://www.raadvanstate.nl/
    Council of State, 31 January 1991, *Kort geding* (Interim measures) 1991-181.
    Council of State, 22 April 1991, *Administratieve beslissingen* (Administrative decisions) 1991-592.
    Council of State, 29 May 1992, *Milieu en Recht* 1992, page 477.
    Council of State, 18 July 1991, *Administratieve beslissingen* (Administrative decisions) 1991-591.
    Supreme Court, 14 April 1989, *Milieu en Recht* 1989, page 258.

Norway
* Supreme Court of Norway, http://www.domstol.no/

Portugal
* Constitutional Court, http://www.tribunalconstitucional.pt/
    Coruche Stork Nests case, Judicial Court of First Instance, Coruche, 23 February 1990. No. 278/89.
    Maia Petrol Pump case, Supreme Court of Justice, 2 July 1996. No. 483/96.
    Nisa Swallow Nests case, Supreme Court of Justice, 27 June 2000. No. 413/00.
    Povoa de Lanhoso Landfill case I, Supreme Court of Justice, 23 September 1998. No. 200/98.
    Povoa de Lanhoso Landfill case II, Judicial Court of Second Instance, Oporto, 12 June 2001. No. 422/00.

Spain

* Constitutional Court, http://www.tribunalconstitucional.es/
* Supreme Court, http://www.poderjudicial.es/

Constitutional Court decisions include Sentencia 247/2007, 12 December 2007; Sentencia 179/2006, 13 June 2006; Auto 351/2005, 27 September 2005; Sentencia 173/2005, 23 June 2005; Sentencia 194/2004, 4 November 2004; Sentencia 195/2003; Decision 199/1996, 3 December 1996; Decision 102/1995, 26 June 1995.

Supreme Court decisions include STS 4076/2008; STS 274/2008; STS 5364/2007; STS 8509/2007 (26/11/2007); and STS 5964/2006.

United Kingdom

R. *(on the application of Limbuela) v. Secretary of State for the Home Department* [2006] 1 AC 396 (HL).

EASTERN EUROPE

Albania

* Constitutional Court, http://www.gjk.gov.al/

Armenia

* Constitutional Court, http://www.concourt.am/

Association of Investigative Journalists v. Ministry of Environment (2003), Central and Nork-Marash First Instance Court.

Belarus

* Constitutional Court, http://www.ncpi.gov.by/constsud/eng/

Bulgaria

* Constitutional Court Decision, http://www.constcourt.bg/
* Supreme Administrative Court, http://www.sac.government.bg/

Decision No. 10 of 10 July 1995, CC No. 8/95.
Decision No. 3 of 13 April 2006, CC No. 4/2006.

Croatia

* Constitutional Court, http://www.usud.hr/

Decision U-III/69/2002.
Decision U-II/4833/2005.

Czech Republic

* Supreme Administrative Court, http://www.nssoud.cz/
* Constitutional Court, http://www.usoud.cz/clanek/interneten/

Decision of the Constitutional Court (ÚS 282/97).
Hnuti Duha v. Sumava National Park Authority, Decision No. U-I-30/95-26 (1996).
Supreme Administrative Court: 1 As 39/2006-55; 2 As 59/2005-136; 3 As 38/2007-81; 5 As 19/2006-59; 2 As 12/2006-111.

Estonia

Administrative Court of Tallinn (3 June 2002) No. 3-35/2002.
Administrative Court of Tallinn (5 June 2002) No. 3-693/2002.
Administrative Court of Tallinn (19 January 2004) No. 3-205/2004.
Administrative Court of Tartu (14 May 2004) No. 3-96/2004.
Circuit Court of Tallinn (15 December 2004) No. 2-3/140/2004.

Georgia

* Constitutional Court, http://www.constcourt.ge/
* Supreme Court of Georgia, http://www.supremecourt.ge/

Hungary

* Constitutional Court, www.mkab.hu/en/enmain.htm
Judgment 11/2005. (IV. 5.) AB Decision.
Judgment 996/G/1990.
Judgment 28/1994, V.20 AB, p. 1919.
Judgment 48/1997. (X. 6.) AB Decision.
Judgment 1/2004, Uniformity Decision.

Latvia

* Constitutional Court, http://www.satv.tiesa.gov.lv/?lang=2/
Judgment of 5 December 2001 in the case No. 2001-07-0103.
Judgment of 14 February 2003 in the case No. 2002-14-04.
Judgment of 8 February 2007 in the case No. 2006-09-03.
Judgment of 21 December 2007 in the case No. 2007-12-03.
Judgment of 17 January 2008 in the case No. 2007-11-03.

Macedonia

* Constitutional Court, http://www.ustavensud.mk/domino/WEBSUD.nsf
No. 152/2004 (20/04/2005).
No. 176/2004 (05/04/2005).
No. 192/2004 (02/03/2005).
No. 197/2004 (13/04/2005).

Moldova

* Constitutional Court, http://www.constcourt.md/

Montenegro

* Constitutional Court, http://www.ustavnisudcg.co.me/

Poland

* Constitutional Tribunal, http://www.trybunal.gov.pl/eng/index.htm

Romania

* Constitutional Court, http://www.ccr.ro/default.aspx?lang=EN
Asociatia Aurarilor Alburnus Maior in Rosia Montana v. Alba Local Council (5199/2004)
(Decision No. 349/CA/2005, Alba Tribunal, Commercial and Administrative
Section, 12 October 2005).

Asociatia Aurarilor Alburnus Maior in Rosia Montana v. Inspectoratul de Protectie a Mediului Alba (4052/2005) (Decision No. 279/CA/2005, Alba Tribunal, Commercial and Administrative Section, 6 September 2005).

Asociatia Aurarilor Alburnus Maior in Rosia Montana v. Inspectoratul de Protectie a Mediului Alba (5057/2005) (Decision No. 363/CA/2005, Alba Tribunal, Commercial and Administrative Section, 26 October 2005).

Asociatia Aurarilor Alburnus Maior in Rosia Montana v. Inspectoratul de Protectie a Mediului Alba (5132/2005) (Decision No. 14/CA/2006, Alba Tribunal, Commercial and Administrative Section, 17 January 2006).

Decision 1112 of 12 June 1997, Supreme Court of Justice.

Decision 148 of 16 April 2003, Constitutional Court of Romania.

Russia

* Supreme Court, http://www.supcourt.ru/
* Constitutional Court, http://www.ksrf.ru/

Ledyayeva v. Russia, Vologda Regional Court, 11 February 2002.

No. 8, 31 October 1995, Supreme Court of the Russian Federation.

T.V. Zlotnikova, K.E. Lebedeva et al. v. Russian Federation, 1998, Supreme Court of the Russian Federation, No. GPKI 97-249, Ruling of 17 February 1998.

Serbia

* Constitutional Court, http://www.ustavni.sud.rs/

Slovakia

* Constitutional Court, http://www.concourt.sk/

Finding of the Constitutional Court of the Slovak Republic Ref. No. II. ÚS 58/01 of 31 October 2001 (No. 45/01).

Slovenia

* Constitutional Court, http://www.us-rs.si/

Case No. U-I-254/99.

Case No. U-I-113/00.

Case No. U-I-80-04, Official Gazette RS, No. 109/2005, Doc. No. AN02813, 24 November 2005.

Case No. U-I-386/06, Official Gazette RS, No. 32/2008, Doc. No. US28039, 13 March 2008.

Decision No. U-I-30/95. Official Gazette RS, No. 3/96, Doc. No. AN01045, 21 December 1995.

National Association of Ecologists (1996), Decision No. U-I-30/95-26, 1/15-1996.

Pavel Ocepek, Breg pri Komendi (1999), Up-344/96, 04/01/1999.

Ukraine

* Constitutional Court, http://www.ccu.gov.ua/

ASIA

Azerbaijan
* Supreme Court. http://www.supremecourt.gov.az/
* Constitutional Court. http://www.constcourt.gov.az/

Bangladesh
  Dr. M. Farooque v. Bangladesh (1997) 49 Dhaka Law Reports 1 (Chowdhury J.)

East Timor
* Supreme Court of Justice, http://www.timor-leste.gov.tl/

India
* Supreme Court of India and several High Courts, http://judis.nic.in/
  Animal and Environment Legal Defence Fund v. Union of India 1997 (3) SCC 549.
  AP Pollution Control Board v. M.V. Nayudu AIR 1999 SC 812, 2001 (2) SCC 62, 2001
    (9) SCC 605.
  Aruna Rodrigues v. Union of India, WP. No. 260 of 2005, Order dated 22/09/2006.
  Deepak Nitrite Ltd. v. State of Gujarat (2004) 6 SCC 402.
  Essar Oil Ltd. v. Halar Utkarsh Samiti and Others (2004) 2 SCC 392.
  Indian Council for Enviro-Legal Action v. Union of India (1996) 3 SCC 247.
  Jagannath v. Union of India AIR 1997 SC 811.
  Karnataka Industrial Areas Development Board v. Sri C. Kenchappa and Others (2006) 6
    SCC 371.
  L.K. Koolwal v. State of Rajasthan AIR 1988 Raj 2.
  M.C. Mehta v. Kamal Nath AIR 2000 SC 1997; 2002 SCC 653.
  M.C. Mehta v. Kamal Nath 1997 (1) SCC 388.
  M.C. Mehta v. Union of India 2004 (12) SC 118.
  M.C. Mehta v. Union of India 2002(4) SCC 356.
  M.C. Mehta v. Union of India 2000 (9) SCC 411.
  M.C. Mehta v. Union of India 1998 (8) SCC 206.
  M.C. Mehta v. Union of India AIR 1997 SC 735.
  M.C. Mehta v. Union of India (1997) 2 SCC 411
  M.C. Mehta v. Union of India (1997) 11 SCC 312.
  M.C. Mehta v. Union of India (1997) 11 SCC 327.
  M.C. Mehta v. Union of India 1996 8 SCC 462.
  M.C. Mehta v. Union of India AIR 1992 SC 382.
  M.C. Mehta v. Union of India 1991 2 SCC 353.
  M.C. Mehta v. Union of India AIR 1988 SC 1031.
  M.C. Mehta v. Union of India AIR 1988 SC 1037.
  M.C. Mehta v. Union of India AIR 1988 SC 1115.
  M.C. Mehta v. Union of India AIR 1987 SC 1086.
  Milk Producers Association, Orissa v. State of Orissa and Others 2006 AIR 3508.
  Murli S. Deora v. Union of India (2001) 8 SCC 765.
  N.D. Jayal and Others v. Union of India and Others (2004) 9 SCC 362.
  Narmada Bachao Andolan v. Union of India AIR 1999 SC 3345.

P.N. Kumar v. Municipal Corp. of Delhi (1987) 4 SCC 609.

Ramasubramnayam v. Member Secretary, Chennai Metropolitan DA AIR 2002 Madras 125.

Ramgopal Estates v. State of Tamil Nadu [2007] INTNHC 786 (2 March 2007). W.P. No.17195 of 1998.

Research Foundation for Science Technology and Natural Resources Policy v. Union of India (2005) 13 SCC 186.

Rural Litigation and Entitlement Kendra v. Uttar Pradesh AIR 1985 SC 652; AIR 1987 SC 359.

State of Himachal Pradesh v. Ganesh Wood Products 1995 3 SCC 363.

Subhash Kumar v. State of Bihar AIR 1991 SC 420.

T. Damodar Rao v. Municipal Corp. of Hyderabad AIR 1987 AP 171.

T.N. Godavaraman Thirumulpad v. Union of India and Others 2007 (3) SCALE 430.

T.N. Godavarman Thirumulpad v. Union of India and Others AIR 1999 SC 43; (1998) 6 SCC 190; (1998) 9 SCC 632; 2000 (7) SCALE 380.

Tarun Bharat Sangh, Alwar v. Union of India AIR 1992 SC 514.

Th. Majra Singh v. Indian Oil Corporation AIR 1999 J&K 81 (HC).

UP Pollution Board v. Mohan Meakins Ltd. 2000 (3) SCC 745.

Vellore Citizens Welfare Forum v. Union of India AIR 1996 SC 2715.

Virender Gaur v. State of Haryana 1995 (2) SCC 577.

Indonesia

* Constitutional Court, http://www.mahkamahkonstitusi.go.id/

Judicial Review of the Law No. 7 of 2004 on Water Resources, Constitutional Court of the Republic of Indonesia, Judgment of 13 July 2005, No. 058-059-060-063/PUU-II/2004.

Mandalawangi Landslide Class Action Case (Civil Litigation). No.49/PDT.G/2003/PN. District Court Bandung, 4 September, 2003.

WALHI v. PT Inti Indorayon Utama, 1989, Jakarta District Court, 14 August 1989.

Iran

* Supreme Court, http://www.dadiran.ir/

Iraq

* Supreme Federal Court, http://www.iraqja.iq/

Israel

Adam, Teva ve'Din (Human Being, Nature, and Law) v. Prime Minister of Israel et al. (2004) No. 4128/02, 16 March 2004, Supreme Court.

Malaysia

Ketua Pengarah Jabatan Alam Sekitar and Anor v. Kajing Tubek and Ors [1997] 3 MLJ 23.

Malaysian Vermicelli Manufacturers (Melaka) Sdn Bhd v. PP [2001] 7 CLJ.

Pihak Berkuasa Negeri Sabah v. Sugumar Balakrishnan and Anor [2002] 3 MLJ 72.

Tan Tek Seng v. Suruhanjaya Perkhidmatan Pendidikan [1996] 1 MLJ 261.

Mongolia

* Constitutional Court, http://www.conscourt.gov.mn/

Nepal
* Supreme Court, http://www.supremecourt.gov.np/
    K.B. Shrestha v. HMG, Department of Transportation and Others, Writ No. 3109 (1999)
        Supreme Court of Nepal.
    Prakash Mani Sharma v. His Majesty's Government Cabinet Secretariat and Others, WP
        2237/1990, Supreme Court of Nepal.
    Suray Prasad Sharma Dhungel v. Godavari Marble Industries and Others (1995), WP
        35/1991, Supreme Court of Nepal.

Pakistan
    Anjum Irfan v. LDA, PLD 2002 Lahore 555.
    Dr. Zahir Ansari v. Karachi Development Authority, PLD 2000 Karachi 168.
    Environment Pollution in Balochistan, HR case No. 31-K/92(Q), PLD 1994 SC 102.
    *General Secretary West Pakistan Salt Miners Labour Union v. Director Industries and Mineral
        Development* (1994) SCMR 2061 (SC).
    Human Rights Case No. 20-K/92.
    *Muhammad Yousuf and Others v. Province of the Punjab through Secretary, Local Government
        and Others*, 2003 CLC 576 (Lahore HC).
    Shehla Zia v. WAPDA (1994) PLD 693 (SC).
    Shehri v. the Province of Sindh 2001 YLR 1139.
    Sheri-CBE Human Rights Case 6-K/93, Supreme Court.
    Syed Mansoor Ali Shah v. Government of the Punjab and Others, Writ Petition No.
        11148/1997.

Philippines
* Supreme Court, http://sc.judiciary.gov.ph/
* Other courts, http://www.lawphil.net/
    Alfredo Tano and others v. Hon. Gov. Salvador P. Socrates and others (1997) PHSC 1472,
        Supreme Court of the Philippines.
    A.L. Momongan v. R.B. Omipon, No. MTJ-93-874, 14 March 1995, Supreme Court,
        Third Division.
    *C and M Timber Corporation v. A.C. Alcala, Secretary of the Department of Environment
        and Natural Resources* (1997) GR. No. 111088, 13 June 1997.
    *Concerned Residents of Manila Bay et al. v. Metropolitan Manila Development Authority,
        Department of Environment and Natural Resources and Others* (2008) G.R. Nos.
        171947-48, Supreme Court.
    H.M. Henares, Jr. et al. v. Land Transportation Franchising and Regulatory Board et al.,
        G.R. No. 158290, 23 October 2006, Supreme Court, Third Division.
    J.C. Reyes et al. v. Republic of the Philippines, G.R. No. 150862, 3 August 2006, Supreme
        Court.
    Laguna Lake Development Authority v. Court of Appeals, G.R. No. 110120, 16 March
        1994 (Supreme Court).
    Metropolitan Manila Development Authority et al. v. Concerned Residents of Manila Bay
        (2011) G.R. 171947-48, 15 February 2011 (S.C.).
    *Minors Oposa v. Factoran, Jr., Secretary of the Department of the Environment and Natural
        Resources* [1993] 224 SCRA 792, 33 ILM 173 (1994).

South Korea
* Constitutional Court, http://english.ccourt.go.kr/
* Supreme Court, http://eng.scourt.go.kr/eng/main/Main.work
  Busan High Court 1995 RA 4.
  Busan University Case, Supreme Court, 1995 DA 23378.
  Cheongju District Court 1997 KAHAP 613 (26 February 1998).
  Constitutional Complaint against Article 21 of the Urban Planning Act 89 Hun-Ma 214
    [1998] KRCC 2 (24 December 1998).
  Excessive Audits Case 2001 Hun-Ma754 [2003] KRCC 17 (18 December 2003).
  Naewonsa Temple, Mitaam and the Friends of Salamanders v. Korea Rail Network Authority
    (2006) Supreme Court Decisions in 2004MA1148 and 2004MA1149, 2 June 2006.
  Revocation of a Corrective Order et al. (2006) Du330 [2006] KRSC 6 (26 March 2006)
    Supreme Court, Full Bench Decision.
  Saemangeum Case (2006) 2006 DU 330 (Supreme Court).
  Seoul Civil District Court 1994 KAHAP 6253.

Sri Lanka
  Bulankulama et al. v. The Secretary, Minister of Industrial Development et al. 2000. S.C.
    Application No. 884/99 (F.R.) Supreme Court of Sri Lanka.
  Lalanath de Silva v. Minister of Forestry and Environment (1998) Fundamental Rights
    Application 569/98, Supreme Court of Sri Lanka.

Thailand
* Supreme Administrative Court, http://www.admincourt.go.th/amc_eng/login_eng.
  aspx
* Constitutional Court, http://www.constitutionalcourt.or.th/english/

Turkey
* Constitutional Court, http://www.anayasa.gov.tr/
* Supreme Court, http://www.yargitay.gov.tr/
  S. Ozay v. Ministry of the Environment and Eurogold, Ref. No 1996/5477; Ruling No.
    1997/2312, Supreme Administrative Court, 4 Int'l Envt'l L. Rep. 452.

AFRICA

Angola
* Constitutional Court, http://www.tribunalconstitucional.ao

Benin
* Constitutional Court, http://www.cour-constitutionnelle-benin.org/

Burkina Faso
* Constitutional Court, http://www.conseil-constitutionnel.gov.bf/

Burundi
* Constitutional Court, no website available

Cameroon
* Supreme Court, http://www.coursupreme.cm/

Cape Verde
* Supreme Court of Justice, http://www.stj.cv/

Central African Republic
* No website available

Chad
* Supreme Court, http://www.primature-tchad.org/index.php?option=com_content&view=article&id=16&Itemid=20

Comoros
* Constitutional Court, no website available

Congo-Brazzaville
* No website available

Congo, Democratic Republic of the
* No website available

Cote d'Ivoire
* Constitutional Court, http://www.gouv.ci/conconst.php#

Egypt
* Supreme Constitutional Court, no website available

Ethiopia
* Federal Supreme Court, no website available

Gabon
* Constitutional Court, no website available

Guinea
* Supreme Court, no website available

Kenya
  P.K. Waweru v. Republic of Kenya (2006) High Court of Kenya, Misc. Civil Application No. 118 of 2004, 2 March 2006. KLR (Environment and Land) 1 (2006) 677.
  Rodeers Muema Nzioka and Others v. Tiomin Kenya Limited (2001) HCCC No. 97 of 2001
  Wangari Maathai v. Kenya Times Media Trust (1989) Civil Case No. 5403, High Court of Kenya.

Malawi
* Supreme Court of Appeal and High Court, no website available. See Malawi Legal Information Institute for selected judgments, http://www.malawilii.org.
  Kamuzu (Administrator of Deceased Estate) v. Attorney General (Civil Case No. 1839 (A) of 1997) [2004] MWHC 3 (11 January 2004) Malawi High Court.

Maldives
* Supreme Court, no website available

Mali
* Constitutional Court, no website available

Mozambique
* Constitutional Council, no website available

Niger
* Constitutional Court, http://juriniger.lexum.umontreal.ca/juriniger/index.do

Nigeria
  Gani Fawehinmi v. Abacha (1996) 9 N.W.L.R. (pt. 475) 710.
  Jonah Gbemre v. Shell Petroleum Development Company Nigerian Limited and Others,
    Federal High Court of Nigeria, Benin Division, Judgment of 14 November 2005,
    Suit No: FHC/B/CS/53/05.
  Oronto Douglas v. Shell Petroleum Development Company (1999) 2 Nigerian Weekly Law
    Reports, Pt. 591.

Rwanda
* Supreme Court, http://www.supremecourt.gov.rw/

São Tomé and Príncipe
* Constitutional Court, no website available

Senegal
* Constitutional Council, http://www.gouv.sn/spip.php?article480

Seychelles
  R. v. Marengo, Azemia, Antat, et al. (2004) 18 May 2004, Supreme Court of Seychelles,
    Perera J.

South Africa
* Constitutional Court, http://www.constitutionalcourt.org.za/
  Cases from other South African courts available through http://www.saflii.org/
  Biowatch Trust v. Registrar, Genetic Resources et al. 2009. Case CCT 80/08 [2009] ZACC
    14, 3 June 2009.
  BP South Africa v. MEC for Agriculture, Conservation and Land Affairs [2004] 5 SA 124
    WLD.
  Chief Pule Shadrack VII Bareki NO and Another v. Gencor Limited and Others (2005)
    ZAGPHC 109, High Court of South Africa, 19 October 2005.
  Director, Mineral Development, Gauteng Region and Another v. Save the Vaal Environment
    and Others (1999) ZASCA 9, Supreme Court of Appeal of South Africa.
  Earthlife Africa (Cape Town) v. Director General Department of Environmental Affairs and
    Tourism and Another (2005) ZAWCHC 7; 2005 (3) SA 156 (C) High Court of South
    Africa.

Fuel Retailers Association of South Africa v. Director-General: Environmental Management, Department of Agriculture, Conservation and Environment, Mpumalanga Province, et al. (2007) 6 S.A.L.R. 4 (CC).

Government of the Republic of South Africa and Others v. Grootboom and Others (2000) 11 BCLR 1169 (CC).

Harmony Gold Mining Company Limited v. Regional Director Free State Department of Water Affairs and Forestry and Another (269/05) [2006] ZASCA 66; [2006] SCA 65 (RSA) (29 May 2006) Supreme Court of Appeal of South Africa.

Khabisi NO and Another v. Aquarella Investment 83 (Pty) Ltd and Others (9114/2007) [2007] ZAGPHC 116; 2008 (4) SA 195 (T); [2007] 4 All SA 1439 (T) (22 June 2007).

Lindiwe Mazibuko et al. v. The City of Johannesburg et al., (2010) 3 BCLR 239, (CC).

Minister of Health v. Woodcarb (Pty) Ltd and Another, High Court of South Africa, Natal Division, 1996 (3) SA 155.

Pretoria City Council v. Walker 1998 (2) SA 363 (CC).

State v. Acheson 1991 2 SA 805 (Nm).

Wildlife and Environment Society of South Africa v. MEC for Economic Affairs, Environment and Tourism, Eastern Cape Provincial Government and Others (2005) ZAECHC 14, High Court of South Africa.

Sudan
* Constitutional Court, no website available

Tanzania
Festo Balegele et al. v. Dar es Salaam City Council (1991) Civil Appeal No. 90 of 1991 (High Court).

Joseph Kessy et al. v. Dar es Salaam City Council Civil C. No. 299 of 1998, High Court of Tanzania, *IELR* 4: 445-49.

Togo
* Constitutional Court, no website available

Uganda
* Judiciary of the Republic of Uganda, http://www.judicature.go.ug/
* Case law at website of Uganda Legal Information Institute, http://www.ulii.org

Advocates Coalition for Development and Environment v. Attorney General (2004) High Court of Uganda at Kampala. Misc. Cause No. 0100 of 2004.

B.G. Thaddeus v. Mukwano Industries Misc. App. No. 909 of 2000, arising from Civil Suit No. 466 of 2000. High Court.

British American Tobacco Ltd. v. the Environmental Action Network, High Court Civil Application No. 27/2003.

Grace Sentongo v. Yakubu Taganza, Magistrates Court Nakawa, Uganda, Misc App. No. 8 of 2003, arising from Civil Suit No. 16 of 2003.

Greenwatch v. Attorney General and National Environmental Management Authority, Miscellaneous Application 139 of 2001.

Greenwatch v. Attorney General and National Environmental Management Authority, Miscellaneous Application 140 of 2002.

Greenwatch v. Uganda Wildlife Authority and the Attorney General (2004) High Court of Uganda at Kampala. Misc. Application No. 92 of 2004 (arising from Misc. Cause No. 15 of 2004).

National Association of Professional Environmentalists v. AES Nile Power Ltd. (1999) Miscellaneous Cause 268 of 1999. Ruling delivered 23 April 1999. High Court.

Nyakana, A.G. v. National Environmental Management Authority et al. (2009) Constitutional Petition No. 03/05, decided 9 November 2009. Constitutional Court.

The Environmental Action Network Ltd. v. Joseph Eryau, National Environmental Management Authority and the Attorney General (Civil Application No.98/05) [2008] UGCA 15 (20 February 2008).

The Environmental Action Network v. Attorney General and National Environmental Management Authority, Miscellaneous Application 13 of 2001.

Uganda Electricity Transmission Co. Ltd. v. De Samaline Ltd. Miscellaneous Cause No. 181 of 2004. High Court.

LATIN AMERICA AND THE CARIBBEAN

Argentina

* Supreme Court of Justice, http://www.csjn.gov.ar/

Beatriz Silvia Mendoza and others v. National Government and Others, 20 June 2006, Supreme Court.

Beatriz Silvia Mendoza and Others v. National Government and Others in regards to damages suffered (Damages stemming from contamination of the Matanza-Riachuelo River), 2008, M. 1569, 8 July 2008.

Margarita v. Copetro, ruling of 10 May 1993, Cámara Civil y Comercial de La Plata.

Maria del Carmen Cosimi, v. Direccion Provincial de Energia de Corrientes (Accion de Amparo), 05 October 2005, Cámara Civil y Comercial de la Ciudad de Corrientes – Sala IV, Expte. No 2.575, Rodríguez C., A.; Casco J., J.

Bolivia

* Constitutional Court, http://www.tribunalconstitucional.gob.bo/
* Supreme Court of Justice, http://suprema.poderjudicial.gob.bo/

Manuel Zurita Sanchez et al. v. Justino Orellana Carballo, Presidente de la Asociacion de Augua Potable de la Comunidad Muyurina Wasa Kjochi (2010) Decision 1106/2010R, 27 August 2010 (Constitutional Court).

Brazil

* Supreme Court of Justice, http://www.stj.jus.br/SCON/

SCJ Appeal No. 575.998 (Minas Gerais), 16 November 2004.

SCJ Appeal No. 70011759842 (Rio Grande do Sul), 1 December 2005.

SCJ Appeal No. 70012091278 (Rio Grande do Sul), 25 January 2006.

Chile

* Constitutional Court, http://www.tribunalconstitucional.cl/

Comunidad de Chañaral v. CODELCO, 1988, Division El Salvador, Sentencia de la Corte de Apelaciones de Copiapo, afirmado por la Corte Suprema por via de apelacion. File No. 2.052, 23/06/88.

Municipalidad de Calbuco v. Empresa de Servicios Sanitarios de Los Lagos, No. 3535-2007.

Colombia
* Constitutional Court, http://www.corteconstitucional.gov.co/
Antonio Mauricio Monroy Cespedes, Constitutional Court, Sala de Revision de Tutelas, T92/93, 19 February 1993.
Decision C-519, 21 November 1994 (Constitutional Court).
Decision T-411, 17 June 1992 (Constitutional Court).
Fundepúblico v. La Compania Maritima de Transporte Croatia Line y Comar S.A., Tradenet S.A y otros. Expediente No. 076 (Tribunal Superior del Distrito Judicial de Santa Marta, Sala Civil, 22 de Julio, 1994).
Fundepúblico v. Mayor of Bugalagrande and Others (1992) Constitutional Court, Decision T-415-92, 17 June 1992, Expediente No. T-101.
Victor Ramon Castrillon Vega y otros v. La Federacion Nacional de Algonoderos y CORPOCESAR, Expediente No. 4577 (Corte Suprema de Justicia, Sala de Casacion Civil y Agraria, 19 de Noviembre 1997).

Costa Rica
* Constitutional Chamber of the Supreme Court (Sala IV), http://www.poder-judicial. go.cr/salaconstitucional/
A. *Cederstav and Others v. National Technical Secretary for the Environment, Municipality of Santa Cruz and Others*, 2008. Exp. 05-002756-0007-CO, Res. No. 2008007549, 30 April 2008, Constitutional Chamber of the Supreme Court of Costa Rica.
Asociación Interamericana para la Defensa del Ambiente (AIDA) y otros Recurso de Amparo (2009). Constitutional Court.
Caribbean Conservation Corporation et al. v. Costa Rica (Executive Decree No. 14535-A, enacted 26 May 1983), Expediente 98-003684-0007-CO. Decision 01250-99.
Carlos Roberto García Chacón. Constitutional Chamber of the Supreme Court, Vote No. 3705, 30 July 1993.
Expediente 01-011865-0007-CO, Resolución 2002-2486. Constitutional Chamber of the Supreme Court of Costa Rica.
M.M. Levy y Asociacion Ecologista Limonense v. Ministerio del Ambiente y Energia, Decision 2001-13295, Expediente 00-007280-0007-CO, 21/12/2001.
Presidente de la sociedad MARLENE S.A. v. Municipalidad de Tibás Marlene, Decision 6918/94, November 1994. Constitutional Chamber of the Supreme Court of Costa Rica.
Sala Constitucional No. 18442 de las 18:00 hrs. del 11 de diciembre 2008. 744. Municipalidad de San José. Constitutional Chamber of the Supreme Court of Costa Rica.
Sala Constitucional No. 02154 de las 09:49 hrs. del 16 de febrero, 2007. Municipalidad de Aserrí.
Sala Constitucional de Costa Rica, resolución no. 2004-01923 del 25 de febrero del 2004.
Sala Constitucional de Costa Rica, resolución no. 2003-04654, 27 May 2003.

Sala Constitucional, resolución no. 2002-2486, 8 de marzo del 2002, considerando IV.

Vote No. 2812 de 20 de abril de 1999, Constitutional Chamber of the Supreme Court of Costa Rica.

Vote No. 5393 of 1995, Constitutional Chamber of the Supreme Court of Costa Rica.

Dominican Republic

* Supreme Court of Justice, http://www.suprema.gov.do/

Appeal by Deputy Attorney for the Defense of the Environment and Natural Resources against sentence rendered by Criminal Chamber of the Court of Appeal in San Cristobal, 27 November 2008. Supreme Court of Justice, Judgment of 6 May 2009.

Judgment No. 024-2009 of the Tax and Administrative Law Court in Case No. 030-09-00209, 19 June 2009.

Ecuador

* Constitutional Court, http://www.corteconstitucional.gov.ec/

Arco Iris v. Ecuador Mineral Institute, No. 224-90 (Constitutional Court), Resolution No. 054-93-CP (12 March 1993).

Baba Dam Case, Third Chamber, Constitutional Court, 12 December 2008, Case No. 1212-2007-RA (Acción de Amparo Constitucional).

Confederation of Indigenous Nations v National Assembly et al. Decision No. 001-10-SIN-CC, 18 March 2010 (Constitutional Court).

Fundacion Natura v. Petro Ecuador (1998) No. 221-98-RA (Constitutional Court), upholding *Fundacion Natura v. Petro Ecuador*, Case 1314 (11th Civil Court).

Maria Aguinda et al. v. Chevron Corporation (2011) Provincial Court of Justice of Sucumbios, First Chamber, 14 February 2011.

R.F. Wheeler and E.G. Huddle v. Attorney General of the State of Loja (2011) Judgment No. 11121-2011-0010, 30 March 2011, Loja Provincial Court of Justice.

El Salvador

* Supreme Court of Justice, Constitutional Chamber, http://www.jurisprudencia.gob.sv/

No. 242-2001. Sala de lo Constitucional de la Corte Suprema de Justicia: San Salvador, 26 de Junio 2003.

Guatemala

Concesiones otorgadas por el Ministerio de Energía y minas a Empresas Petroleras. Resolución en Conciencia del Procurador de los Derechos Humanos de Guatemala en Materia Ambiental. Exp. 002-98/D.S. 10.10.98. *Acción de inconstitucionalidad total. Promovido contra el congreso de la República* Corte de Constitucionalidad. Decision 575/98. 23.2.99.

Fundación Defensores de la Naturaleza v. Particular. Cited in Bruch, Coker and VanArsdale 2007, 75.

Honduras

* Centro Electrónico de Documentación e Información Judicial, http://www.poderjudicial.gob.hn/ejes/institucional/organizacion/dependencias/cedij

Jamaica
* Supreme Court, http://www.sc.gov.jm/Judgments/judgments.htm
  Northern Jamaica Conservation Association et al. v. Natural Resources Conservation Authority et al. (2006). Judgment HCV 3002 of 2005, Supreme Court.

Mexico
* Supreme Court of Justice, http://www.scjn.gob.mx/2010/Paginas/PrincipalV2010.aspx

Nicaragua
* Supreme Court of Justice, http://www.web.poderjudicial.gob.ni/buscador/

Panama
* Supreme Court of Justice, http://www.organojudicial.gob.pa/
  La Sala Tercera de lo Contencioso Administrativo y Laboral de la Corte Suprema de Justicia, 30 de Junio, 2009.
  La Sala Tercera de la Corte Suprema de Justicia, 9 de Julio 2009.
  Luis González et al. v. General Directorate of Health of Veraguas (Panama S. Ct., Plenary Ch., reversed on appeal 24 February 2010), Jud. Rptr. (February 2010), pp. 30-40.

Paraguay
* Supreme Court of Justice, Constitutional Chamber, http://www.pj.gov.py/
  Agreement and Sentence No. 426, 8 July 1999. Agreement and Sentence No. 98, 5 April 1999.
  Agreement and Sentence No. 78, 19 August 2003, Court of Appeal de Asuncion.
  Federacion de Asociacion Organizacion de Afectados por La Represa y Acyreta de Itapua y Misiones – Fedayin S/ Amparo Constitucional (2008) No. 1037, 24 December 2008. Supreme Court of Justice.
  Interlocutory Order No. 21 of 20 March 2003, Court of Appeals, San Juan Bautista, Misiones.
  Pedro Viudes v. Ley No. 816/96 (Adopting Measures to Protect Natural Resources), 1997. Exp. No. 728. Accion de Inconstitucionalidad. Corte Suprema de Justicia, Sala Constitucional.

Peru
* Constitutional Court, http://www.tc.gob.pe/search/search.pl
  Asociacion de Propietarios del Sector Imperial del Asentamiento Humano Pamplona Alta v. Comision de Formalizacion de la Propiedad Informal (Expediente No. 03448-2005-PA/TC).
  Colegio de Abogados del Santa (2001) Exp. No. 0018-2001-AI/TC.
  Jose Clemente y Arqueno Garay, Exp. No. 6777-2008-PA/TC Huanuco Resolution of the Constitutional Court, Lima, 22 June 2009.
  Pablo Miguel Fabián Martínez and Others v. Minister of Health and Director General of Environmental Health (2006), Second Chamber of the Constitutional Court, Exp. No. 2002-2006-PC/TC.
  Proterra v. Metropolitan Municipality of Lima (Expediente No. 2682-2005-PA/TC) Constitutional Court.

Sandro Chavez Vasquez and Channels Lopez v. Provincial Municipal Council of Pisco (2004) Exp. No. 0021-2003-AI/TC.

Sociedad Peruana de Derecho Ambiental v. Direccion Regional Del Ministerio de Pesqueria (1993) Exp. No. 1058-92, Dictamen Fiscal No. 1476-92, 17 February 1993 (Supreme Court of Justice).

Sociedad Peruana de Derecho Ambiental v. Ministerio de Energía y Minas (Habeas Data), Expediente No. 1658-95, Dictamen Fiscal No. 122-96. Sala de Derecho Constitucional y Social, 19 June 1996.

Venezuela

* Supreme Court of Justice, http://www.tsj.gov.ve/

NORTH AMERICA

Canada

Ontario v. Canadian Pacific Ltd. [1995] 2 SCR 1031.

R. v. Hydro-Quebec [1997] 3 SCR 213.

United States

Marbury v. Madison 5 US 137 (1803).

Rhodes et al. v. E.I. Du Pont (2009) Civil Action No. 6:06-cv-00530, US District Court, Southern District, West Virginia, Decision of 28 September 2009, Goodwin, C.J.

Sierra Club v. Morton, 405 US 727 (1972).

INTERNATIONAL

African Commission on Human and Peoples' Rights

* Decisions available at http://www.achpr.org

Centre for Minority Rights Development on behalf of Endorois Community v. Kenya (2010), Communication 276/2003.

Social and Economic Rights Action Centre (SERAC) and the Centre for Economic and Social Rights (CESR) v. Nigeria (2001), Communication No. 155/96.

European Committee of Social Rights

Marangopoulos Foundation for Human Rights v. Greece, Complaint No. 30/2005 (6 December 2006).

European Court of Human Rights

* All European Court decisions and judgments can be found at http://www.echr.coe. int/ECHR/EN/Header/Case-Law/HUDOC/HUDOC+database/.

Alatulkkila and Others v. Finland, Appl. No. 33538/96, 28 July 2005.

Atanasov v. Bulgaria, No. 12853/03, 11 April 2011.

Bladet Tromso and Stensaas v. Norway, No. 21980/93, 20 May 1999.

Branduse v. Romania, No. 6586/03, 7 April 2009.

Fadeyeva v. Russia, No. 55723/00, 9 June 2005.

Fägerskiöld v. Sweden, No. 37664/04, 26 February 2008.

Giacomelli v. Italy, No. 59909/00, 2 November 2006.

Grimkovskaya v. Ukraine, No. 38182/03, 21 July 2011.

Guerra et al. v. Italy, Grand Chamber, 19 February 1998. 3 *IELR* 260. Also 26 EHRR 357.

Hatton and Others v. United Kingdom, No. 36022/97, Grand Chamber, 8 July 2003.

Kyrtatos v. Greece, No. 41666/98, 22 May 2003.

Ledyayeva, Dobrokhotova, Zolotareva et Romashina v. Russia, Nos. 53157/99, 53247/99, 53695/00 and 56850/00, 26 October 2006.

Lopez Ostra v. Spain, Judgment of 9 December 1994 (1994) 20 EHRR 277.

Moreno Gomez v. Spain, No. 4143/02, 16 November 2004.

Okyay et al. v. Turkey, No. 36220/97, 12 July 2005.

Oneryildiz v. Turkey, No. 48939/99, Grand Chamber, 30 November 2004.

Pine Valley Development Ltd. et al. v. Ireland, No. 12742/87, 29 November 1991.

Taskin and Others v. Turkey, No. 46117/99, 10 November 2004.

Tatar and Tatar v. Romania, No. 67021/01, 27 January 2009.

Tebieti Mühafize Cemiyyeti and Israfilov v. Azerbaijan, No. 37083/03, 10 May 2010.

Vides Aizsardzibas Klubs v. Latvia, No. 57829/00, 27 May 2004.

Zander v. Sweden, No. 14282/88, 25 November 1993.

Zeleni Balkani v. Bulgaria, No. 63778/00, 12 April 2007.

Inter-American Commission on Human Rights

* Reports and other documents available at http://www.cidh.org/

Association of Lhaka Honhat Aboriginal Communities (Nuestra Tierra/Our Land) v. Argentina, Precautionary Measures Request, IACHR (2000) No.P12.094.

Case of Yanomani Indians, Case 7615 (Brazil), IACHR, OEA/Ser.L/V/II.66 doc. 10 rev. 1 at 6 (1985), available at 3 IELR 841.

Community of La Oroya v. Peru, Petition 1473-06, *Admissibility Report 76/09,* 5 August 2009.

Community of La Oroya v. Peru, Petition 1473-06, *Precautionary measures* (2007).

Community of San Mateo de Huanchor and its members v. Peru, Case 504/03, Report No. 69/04, IACHR, OEA/Ser.L/V/II.122 Doc. 5 rev. 1 (2004).

–. *Kichwa Peoples of the Sarayaku Indigenous Community v. Ecuador,* IACHR Report No. 64/05, Petition No. 167/03, 2004.

Maya Indigenous Communities of the Toledo District (Belize Maya), Case 12.053, IACHR Report 40/04 (2004) (Belize).

Maya People of the Sipacapa and San Miguel Ixtahuacán Municipalities v. Guatemala (2010), Precautionary Measures 260-07, 20 May 2010.

Inter-American Court of Human Rights

* Decisions and other documents available at http://www.corteidh.or.cr/

Case of the Sarayaku Indigenous Community v. Ecuador 2004. Order regarding Provisional Measures, 6 July 2004.

Case of the Yakye Axa Indigenous Community v. Paraguay (2005). Judgment of 17 June 2005.

Caso de la Comunidad Mayagna (Sumo) Awas Tingni ("Awas Tingni"), Ser. C, No. 79 ¶ 151 (Nicaragua) (2001).

Sawhoyamaxa Indigenous Community of the Enxet People v. Paraguay (2006) Case 0322/2001. Judgment of 29 March 2006. Related compliance order issued by the Inter-American Court in 2007.

Twelve Saramaka Clans v. Suriname (2007), No. 12,338. Judgment of 28 November 2007.

International Court of Justice

Gabčíkovo-Nagymaros Project (Hungary v. Slovakia), [1997] ICJ Rep. 7, reprinted in 37 ILM 168.

Legality of the Threat or Use of Nuclear Weapons, Advisory Opinion, [1996] ICJ Rep. 226.

United Nations Human Rights Committee

Ms. Susila Malani Dahanayake and 41 Other Sri Lankan Citizens v. Sri Lanka, Communication No. 1331/2004, 14 September 2006, UN Doc. CCPR/C/87/D/1331/2004 (2006).

E.H.P. v. Canada, Communication No. 67/1980, 27 October 1982, UN Doc. CCPR/C/ OP 1 (1984).

Index

Lesley Erickson
Westward Bound: Sex, Violence, the Law, and the Making of a Settler Society (2011)

Elaine Craig
Troubling Sex: Toward a Legal Theory of Sexual Integrity (2011)

Laura DeVries
Conflict in Caledonia: Aboriginal Land Rights and the Rule of Law (2011)

Jocelyn Downie and Jennifer J. Llewellyn (eds.)
Being Relational: Reflections on Relational Theory and Health Law (2011)

Grace Li Xiu Woo
Ghost Dancing with Colonialism: Decolonization and Indigenous Rights at the Supreme Court of Canada (2011)

Fiona Kelly
Transforming Law's Family: The Legal Recognition of Planned Lesbian Motherhood (2011)

Colleen Bell
The Freedom of Security: Governing Canada in the Age of Counter-Terrorism (2011)

Andrew S. Thompson
In Defence of Principles: NGOs and Human Rights in Canada (2010)

Aaron Doyle and Dawn Moore (eds.)
Critical Criminology in Canada: New Voices, New Directions (2010)

Joanna R. Quinn
The Politics of Acknowledgement: Truth Commissions in Uganda and Haiti (2010)

Patrick James
Constitutional Politics in Canada after the Charter: Liberalism, Communitarianism, and Systemism (2010)

Louis A. Knafla and Haijo Westra (eds.)
Aboriginal Title and Indigenous Peoples: Canada, Australia, and New Zealand (2010)

Janet Mosher and Joan Brockman (eds.)
Constructing Crime: Contemporary Processes of Criminalization (2010)

Stephen Clarkson and Stepan Wood
A Perilous Imbalance: The Globalization of Canadian Law and Governance (2009)

Amanda Glasbeek
Feminized Justice: The Toronto Women's Court, 1913-34 (2009)

Kim Brooks (ed.)
Justice Bertha Wilson: One Woman's Difference (2009)

Wayne V. McIntosh and Cynthia L. Cates
Multi-Party Litigation: The Strategic Context (2009)

Renisa Mawani
Colonial Proximities: Crossracial Encounters and Juridical Truths in British Columbia, 1871-1921 (2009)

James B. Kelly and Christopher P. Manfredi (eds.)
Contested Constitutionalism: Reflections on the Canadian Charter of Rights and Freedoms (2009)

Catherine Bell and Robert K. Paterson (eds.)
Protection of First Nations Cultural Heritage: Laws, Policy, and Reform (2008)

Hamar Foster, Benjamin L. Berger, and A.R. Buck (eds.)
The Grand Experiment: Law and Legal Culture in British Settler Societies (2008)

Richard J. Moon (ed.)
Law and Religious Pluralism in Canada (2008)

Catherine Bell and Val Napoleon (eds.)
First Nations Cultural Heritage and Law: Case Studies, Voices, and Perspectives (2008)

Douglas C. Harris
Landing Native Fisheries: Indian Reserves and Fishing Rights in British Columbia, 1849-1925 (2008)

Peggy J. Blair
Lament for a First Nation: The Williams Treaties of Southern Ontario (2008)

Lori G. Beaman
Defining Harm: Religious Freedom and the Limits of the Law (2007)

Stephen Tierney (ed.)
Multiculturalism and the Canadian Constitution (2007)

Julie Macfarlane
The New Lawyer: How Settlement Is Transforming the Practice of Law (2007)

Kimberley White
Negotiating Responsibility: Law, Murder, and States of Mind (2007)

Dawn Moore
Criminal Artefacts: Governing Drugs and Users (2007)

Hamar Foster, Heather Raven, and Jeremy Webber (eds.)
Let Right Be Done: Aboriginal Title, the Calder Case, and the Future of Indigenous Rights (2007)

Dorothy E. Chunn, Susan B. Boyd, and Hester Lessard (eds.)
Reaction and Resistance: Feminism, Law, and Social Change (2007)

Margot Young, Susan B. Boyd, Gwen Brodsky, and Shelagh Day (eds.)
Poverty: Rights, Social Citizenship, and Legal Activism (2007)

Rosanna L. Langer
Defining Rights and Wrongs: Bureaucracy, Human Rights, and Public Accountability (2007)

C.L. Ostberg and Matthew E. Wetstein
Attitudinal Decision Making in the Supreme Court of Canada (2007)

Chris Clarkson
Domestic Reforms: Political Visions and Family Regulation in British Columbia, 1862-1940 (2007)

Jean McKenzie Leiper
Bar Codes: Women in the Legal Profession (2006)

Gerald Baier
Courts and Federalism: Judicial Doctrine in the United States, Australia, and Canada (2006)

Avigail Eisenberg (ed.)
Diversity and Equality: The Changing Framework of Freedom in Canada (2006)

Randy K. Lippert
Sanctuary, Sovereignty, Sacrifice: Canadian Sanctuary Incidents, Power, and Law (2005)

James B. Kelly
Governing with the Charter: Legislative and Judicial Activism and Framers' Intent (2005)

Dianne Pothier and Richard Devlin (eds.)
Critical Disability Theory: Essays in Philosophy, Politics, Policy, and Law (2005)

Susan G. Drummond
Mapping Marriage Law in Spanish Gitano Communities (2005)

Louis A. Knafla and Jonathan Swainger (eds.)
Laws and Societies in the Canadian Prairie West, 1670-1940 (2005)

Ikechi Mgbeoji
Global Biopiracy: Patents, Plants, and Indigenous Knowledge (2005)

Florian Sauvageau, David Schneiderman, and David Taras,
with Ruth Klinkhammer and Pierre Trudel
The Last Word: Media Coverage of the Supreme Court of Canada (2005)

Gerald Kernerman
Multicultural Nationalism: Civilizing Difference, Constituting Community (2005)

Pamela A. Jordan
Defending Rights in Russia: Lawyers, the State, and Legal Reform in the Post-Soviet Era (2005)

Anna Pratt
Securing Borders: Detention and Deportation in Canada (2005)

Kirsten Johnson Kramar
Unwilling Mothers, Unwanted Babies: Infanticide in Canada (2005)

W.A. Bogart
Good Government? Good Citizens? Courts, Politics, and Markets in a Changing Canada (2005)

Catherine Dauvergne
Humanitarianism, Identity, and Nation: Migration Laws in Canada and Australia (2005)

Michael Lee Ross
First Nations Sacred Sites in Canada's Courts (2005)

Andrew Woolford
Between Justice and Certainty: Treaty Making in British Columbia (2005)

John McLaren, Andrew Buck, and Nancy Wright (eds.)
Despotic Dominion: Property Rights in British Settler Societies (2004)

Georges Campeau
From UI to EI: Waging War on the Welfare State (2004)

Alvin J. Esau
The Courts and the Colonies: The Litigation of Hutterite Church Disputes (2004)

Christopher N. Kendall
Gay Male Pornography: An Issue of Sex Discrimination (2004)

Roy B. Flemming
Tournament of Appeals: Granting Judicial Review in Canada (2004)

Constance Backhouse and Nancy L. Backhouse
The Heiress vs the Establishment: Mrs. Campbell's Campaign for Legal Justice (2004)

Christopher P. Manfredi
Feminist Activism in the Supreme Court: Legal Mobilization and the Women's Legal Education and Action Fund (2004)

Annalise Acorn
Compulsory Compassion: A Critique of Restorative Justice (2004)

Jonathan Swainger and Constance Backhouse (eds.)
People and Place: Historical Influences on Legal Culture (2003)

Jim Phillips and Rosemary Gartner
Murdering Holiness: The Trials of Franz Creffield and George Mitchell (2003)

David R. Boyd
Unnatural Law: Rethinking Canadian Environmental Law and Policy (2003)

Ikechi Mgbeoji
Collective Insecurity: The Liberian Crisis, Unilateralism, and Global Order (2003)

Rebecca Johnson
Taxing Choices: The Intersection of Class, Gender, Parenthood, and the Law (2002)

John McLaren, Robert Menzies, and Dorothy E. Chunn (eds.)
Regulating Lives: Historical Essays on the State, Society, the Individual, and the Law (2002)

Joan Brockman
Gender in the Legal Profession: Fitting or Breaking the Mould (2001)